BLACK SCIENCE

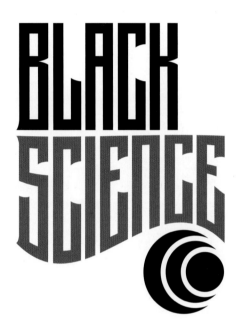

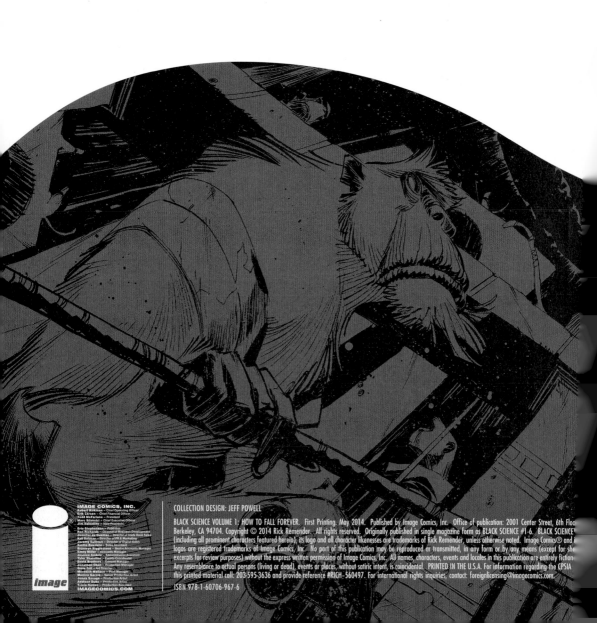

IMAGE COMICS, INC.
Robert Kirkman – Chief Operating Officer
Erik Larsen – Chief Financial Officer
Todd McFarlane – President
Marc Silvestri – Chief Executive Officer
Jim Valentino – Vice-President

Eric Stephenson – Publisher
Ron Richards – Director of Business Development
Jennifer de Guzman – Director of Trade Book Sales
Kat Salazar – Director of PR & Marketing
Jeremy Sullivan – Director of Digital Sales
Emilio Bautista – Sales Assistant
Branwyn Bigglestone – Senior Accounts Manager
Emily Miller – Accounts Manager
Jessica Ambriz – Administrative Assistant
Tyler Shainline – Events Coordinator
David Brothers – Content Manager
Jonathan Chan – Production Manager
Drew Gill – Art Director
Meredith Wallace – Print Manager
Monica Garcia – Senior Production Artist
Jenna Savage – Production Artist
Addison Duke – Production Artist
Tricia Ramos – Production Assistant
IMAGECOMICS.COM

COLLECTION DESIGN: JEFF POWELL

BLACK SCIENCE VOLUME 1: HOW TO FALL FOREVER. First Printing. May 2014. Published by Image Comics, Inc. Office of publication: 2001 Center Street, 6th Floor, Berkeley, CA 94704. Copyright © 2014 Rick Remender. All rights reserved. Originally published in single magazine form as BLACK SCIENCE #1-6. BLACK SCIENCE™ (including all prominent characters featured herein), its logo and all character likenesses are trademarks of Rick Remender, unless otherwise noted. Image Comics® and its logos are registered trademarks of Image Comics, Inc. No part of this publication may be reproduced or transmitted, in any form or by any means (except for short excerpts for review purposes) without the express written permission of Image Comics, Inc. All names, characters, events and locales in this publication are entirely fiction. Any resemblance to actual persons (living or dead), events or places, without satiric intent, is coincidental. PRINTED IN THE U.S.A. For information regarding the CPSIA on this printed material call: 203-595-3636 and provide reference #RICH-560497. For international rights inquiries, contact: foreignlicensing@imagecomics.com.
ISBN 978-1-60706-967-6

RICK REMENDER
WRITER

MATTEO SCALERA
ARTIST

DEAN WHITE
PAINTED ART

RUS WOOTON
LETTERING + LOGO DESIGN

SEBASTIAN GIRNER
EDITOR

BLACK SCIENCE CREATED BY
RICK REMENDER & MATTEO SCALERA

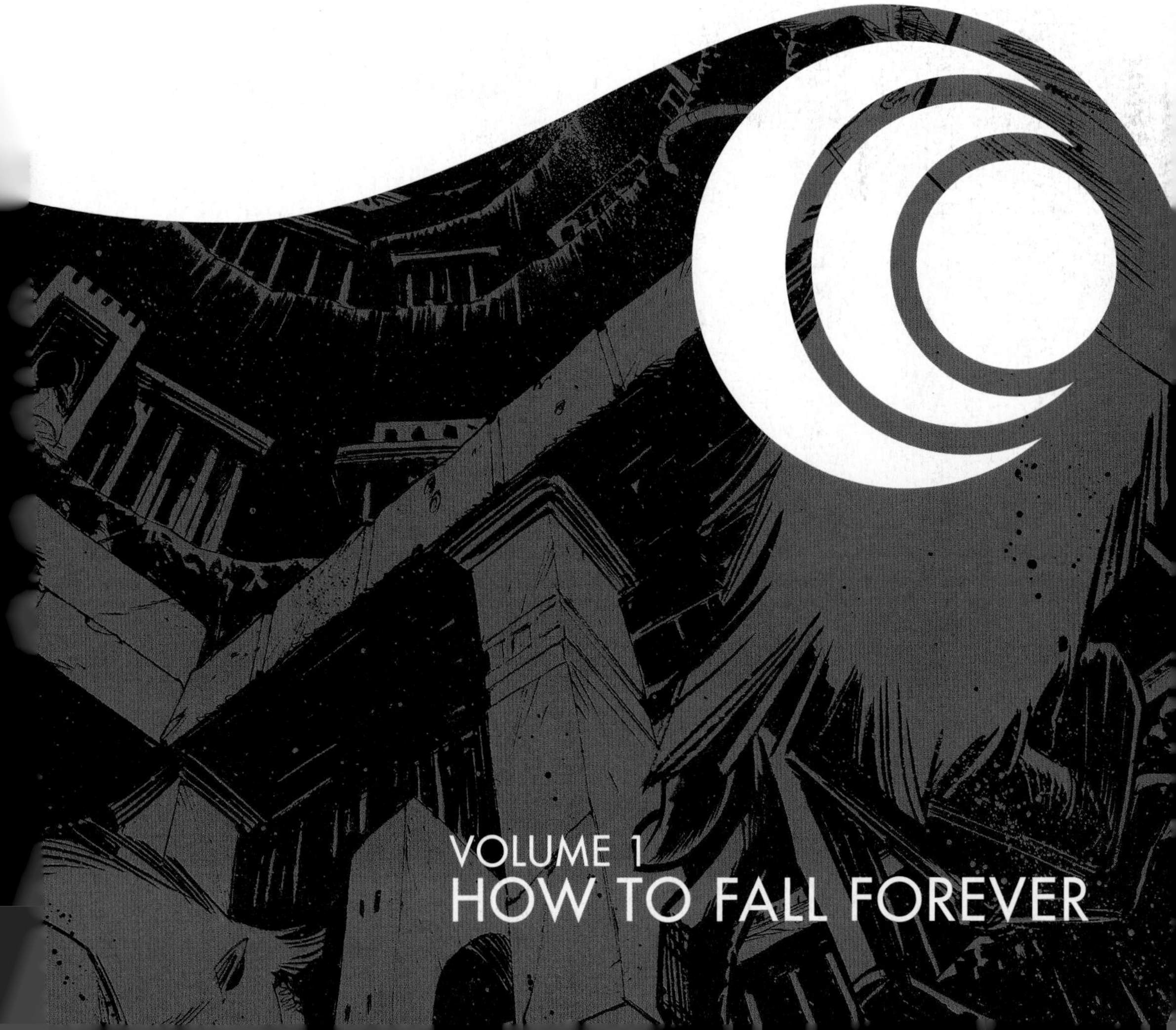

VOLUME 1
HOW TO FALL FOREVER

I'M NOT SURE THAT I R
BECAME AWARE OF RIC

If memory serves me correctly, it may have been his graphic novels *Sea of Red* and *Night Mary*, the latter of which I liked so much I've always wanted to adapt it into a film. Yes, I think that was it. His name stuck in my head from there and so I was looking out for Rick's work as it appeared. I recall his work on *Punisher* caught my eye – when the creation of "Franken-Castle" brought the ire of comics' mainstream readers down upon him (that is until he turned Frank back to normal) at which time the fans baying for his blood died down, and grudgingly came to admit how good the series had been.

But it was with Rick's unique space fantasy, *Fear Agent*, that I truly fell in love with the guy's work. Heath Hudson the Fear Agent and his world of the future was a unique combination of science fiction plotted as only Rick could conceive with its maddeningly original subversion of a classic – like something created during the Golden Age of Sci Fi and then turned on its head so at the same time it seemed entirely fresh and new. Sometimes fresh and funny, something dark and sad, and a series unlike anything before it. One that should be on every serious comic readers' shelf.

Other wonderful stories also came from his work (still ongoing) at Marvel, with my favorite being the *Uncanny X-Force* which in my opinion ranks up there as one of the greatest Marvel runs of all time. (Although I have to say I also have great affection for his run in *Secret Avengers*, which he did with his partner in crime on *Black Science*, Matteo Scalera.)

Bottom line, if Rick is consistent in anything, apart from obviously being a great writer, it's that his work is fantastically unconventional, constantly subverting and playing with the norms of the genre and turning our expectations on its head. Oh, and he tends to kill a lot of characters.

I think it's now with Black Science that we see Rick drawing from his old work — not, I stress, in a self-referential or derivative way, but rather, more combining

MEMBER WHEN I FIRST I REMENDER'S WRITING.

the essence and feeling of his prior comics into something entirely unique. We see the unorthodox narrative, turning plots on their head and sending the readers in directions they could never expect – and combining this with a new science fiction tapestry very unlike that of *Fear Agent* but equally as bizarre and excellent. Throw in the pure fun of a superhero comic (while never actually having superheroes in it) and you'll have something of what I love about the book you hold, Black Science – which, I should add, is so unique that I don't think you'll agree with me, in my conclusion. I think any five, ten, a hundred of you would each get other different things from this series, with all the many different, amazing creative choices made by Rick and Matteo in it, page-by-panel-by-page.

And of course, I should also make mention of Matteo's art. His line work is gorgeous and somewhat of the European school of comic art (which with Matteo being Italian would make sense obviously), with it reminding me in places of geniuses Alberto Breccia and Sergio Toppi in that Matteo's line-work and use of blacks are so deft and intelligently placed but with an added explosive stylized flair all of his own. Add to that color that adds gasoline to the fire of the art's visual spectacle, instead of detracting from Matteo's detailed line work, and you have a comic that's as beautiful to look at as it is, but exciting and thought-provoking to read.

Suffice to say *Black Science* is one of my current favorite comics. If you've read the story already as issues then have fun reliving the excitement of this saga as it unfolds. If this is your first encounter with Grant McKay and his family, you're in for a treat.

Expect the unexpected.

James Robinson
San Francisco, 2014

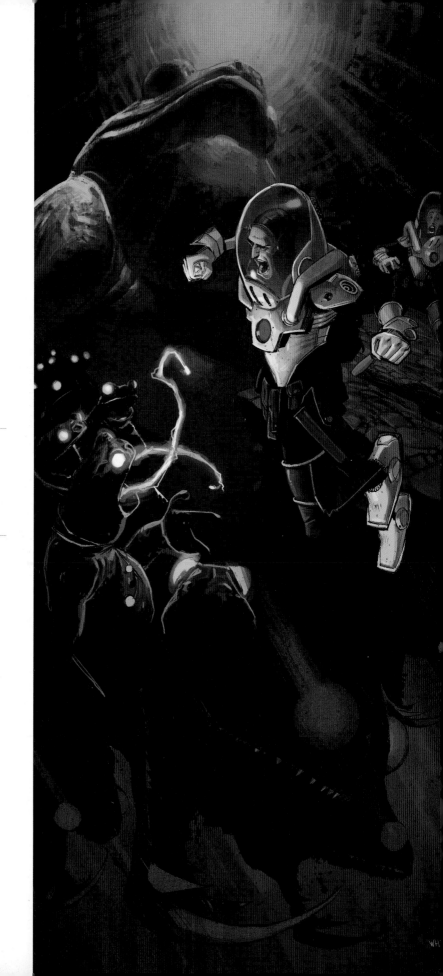

1

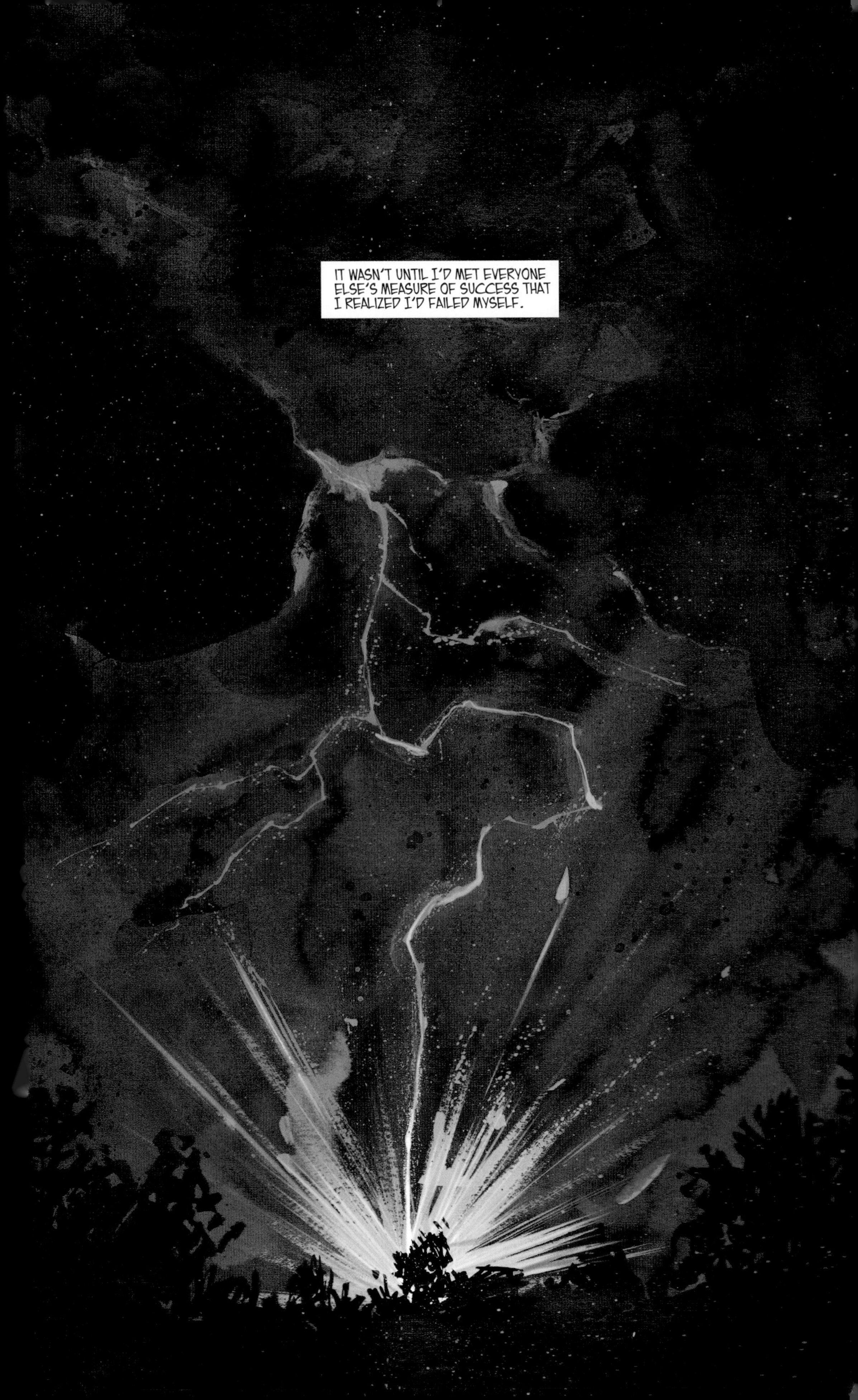
IT WASN'T UNTIL I'D MET EVERYONE ELSE'S MEASURE OF SUCCESS THAT I REALIZED I'D FAILED MYSELF.

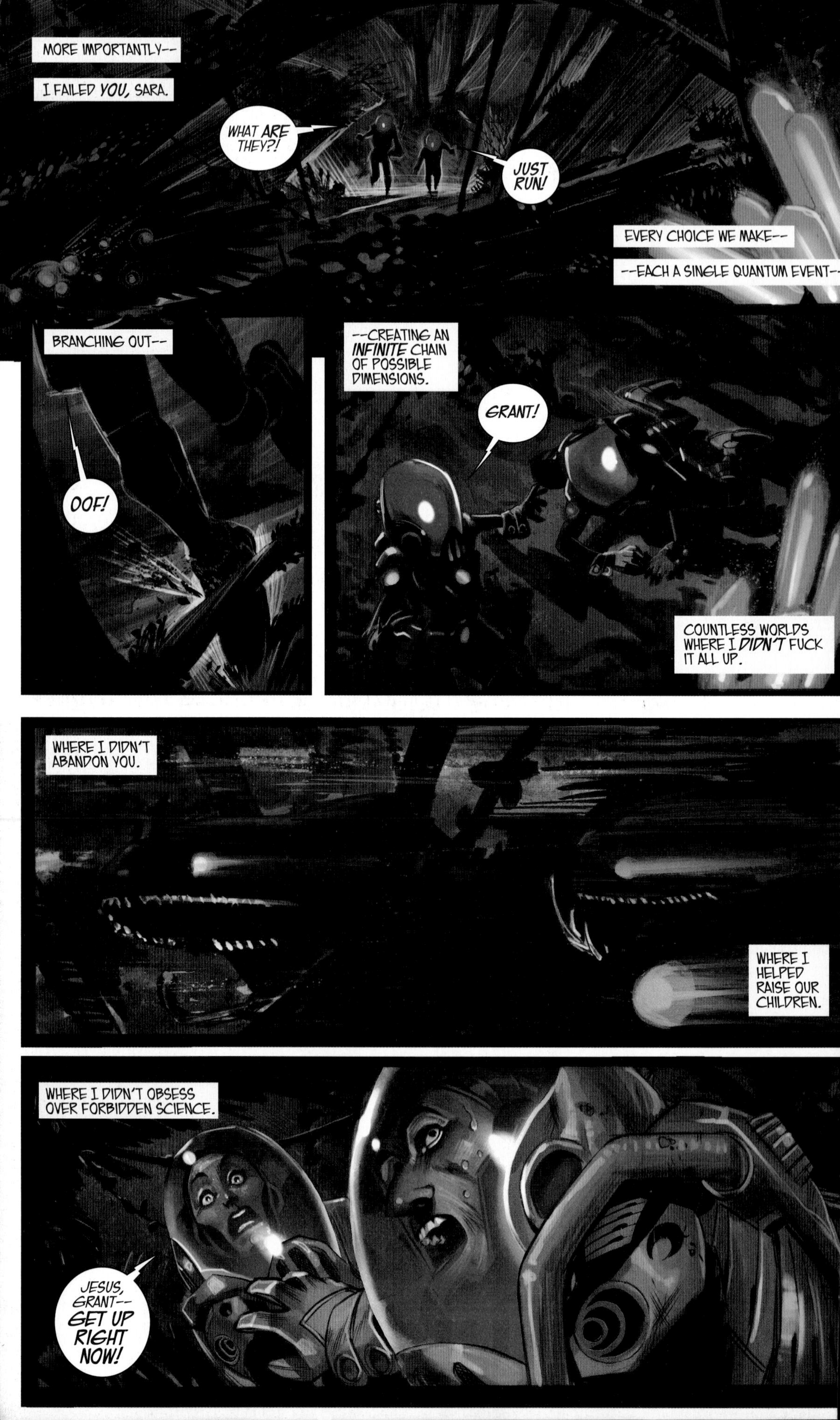
MORE IMPORTANTLY--
I FAILED YOU, SARA.
WHAT ARE THEY?!
JUST RUN!
EVERY CHOICE WE MAKE--
--EACH A SINGLE QUANTUM EVENT--
BRANCHING OUT--
OOF!
--CREATING AN INFINITE CHAIN OF POSSIBLE DIMENSIONS.
GRANT!
COUNTLESS WORLDS WHERE I DIDN'T FUCK IT ALL UP.
WHERE I DIDN'T ABANDON YOU.
WHERE I HELPED RAISE OUR CHILDREN.
WHERE I DIDN'T OBSESS OVER FORBIDDEN SCIENCE.
JESUS, GRANT-- GET UP RIGHT NOW!

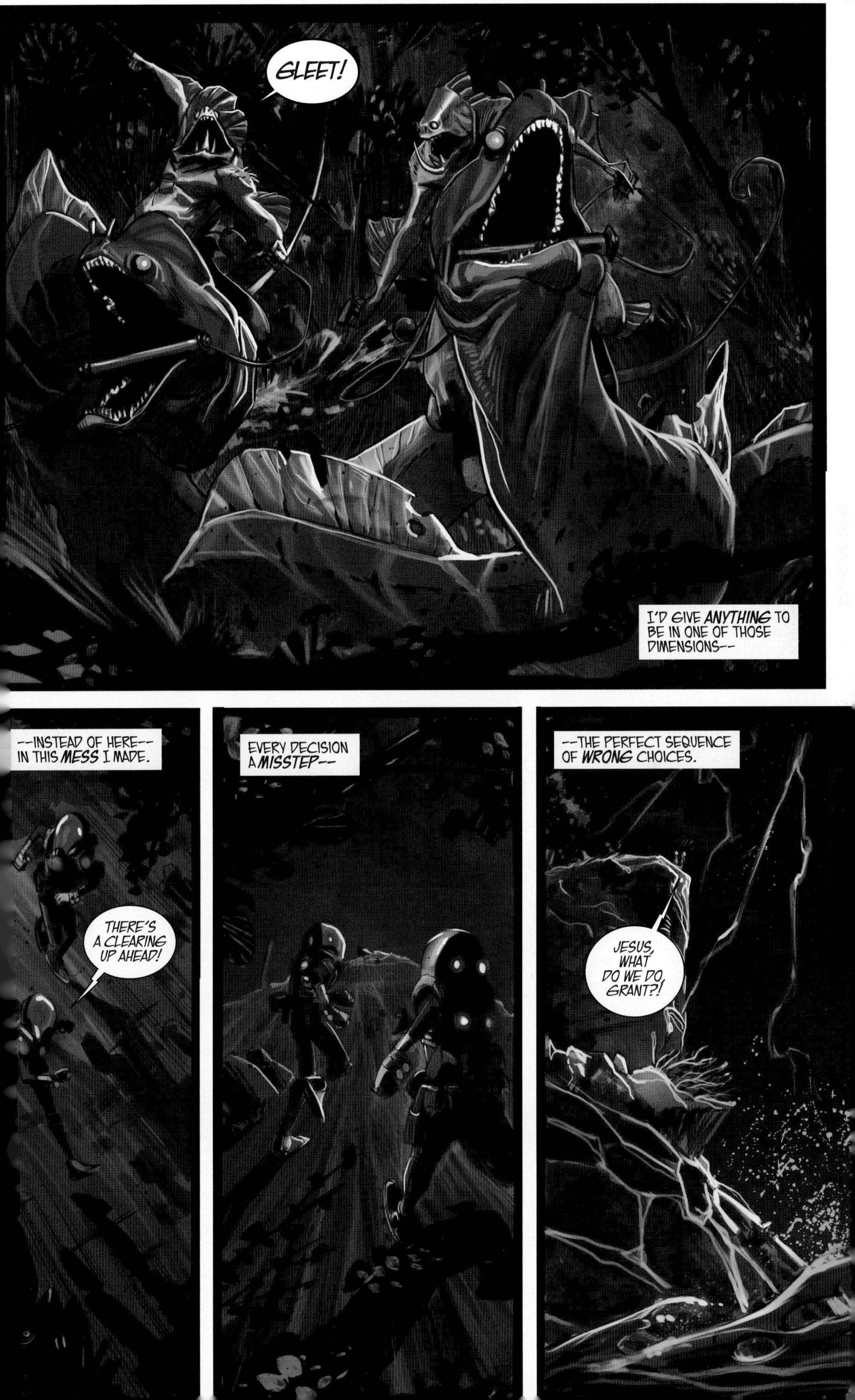
GLEET!
I'D GIVE ANYTHING TO BE IN ONE OF THOSE DIMENSIONS--
--INSTEAD OF HERE-- IN THIS MESS I MADE.
THERE'S A CLEARING UP AHEAD!
EVERY DECISION A MISSTEP--
--THE PERFECT SEQUENCE OF WRONG CHOICES.
JESUS, WHAT DO WE DO, GRANT?!

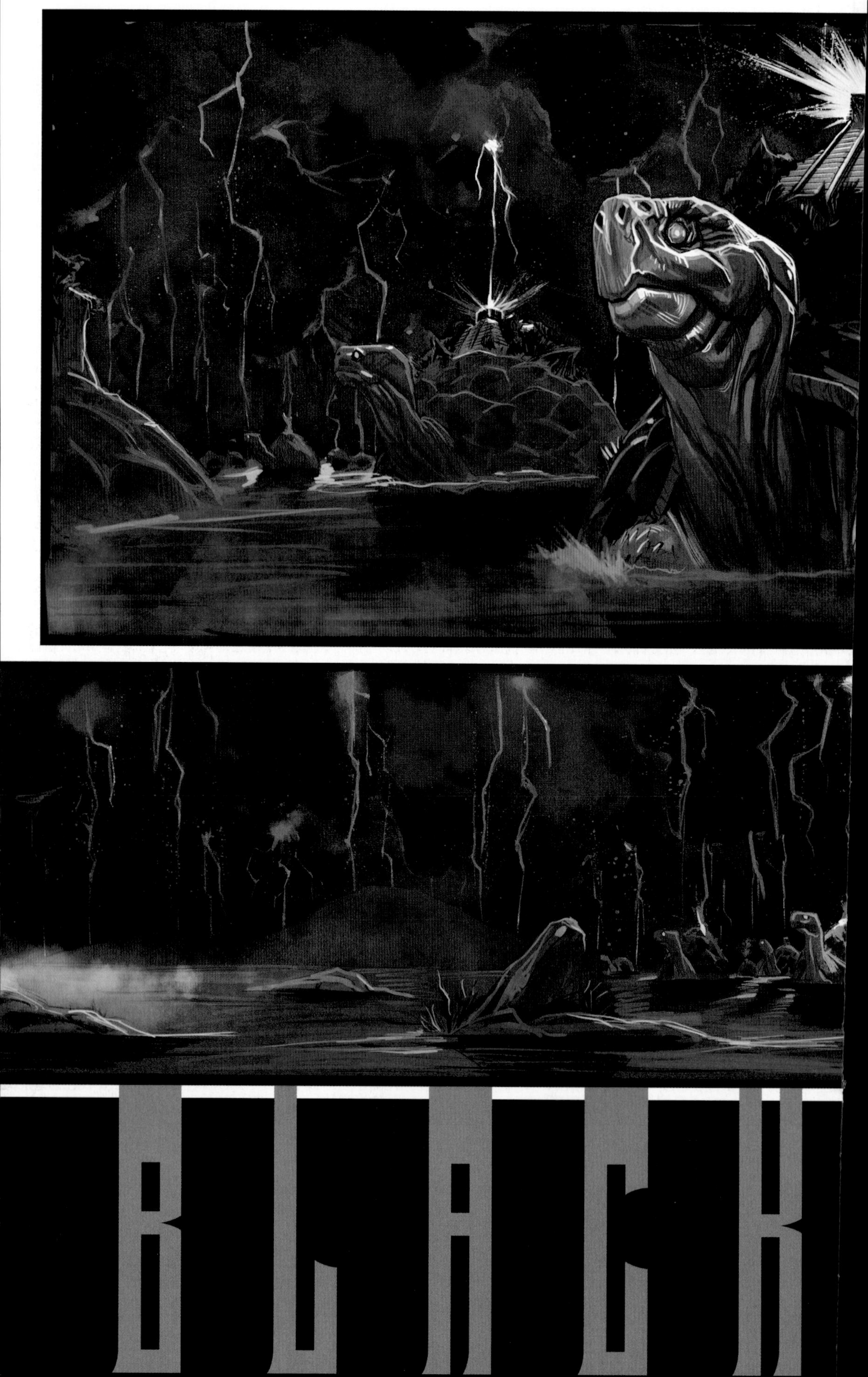
BLACK

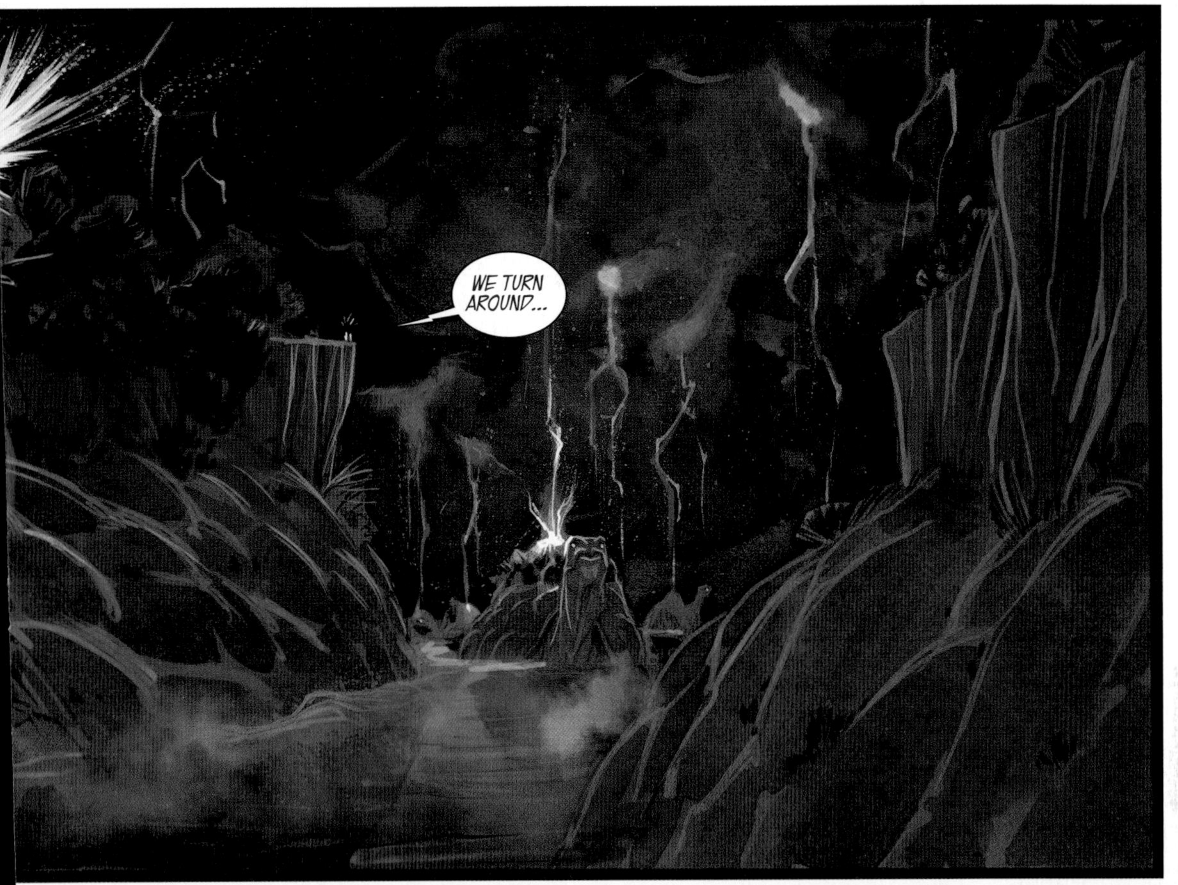
WE TURN AROUND...

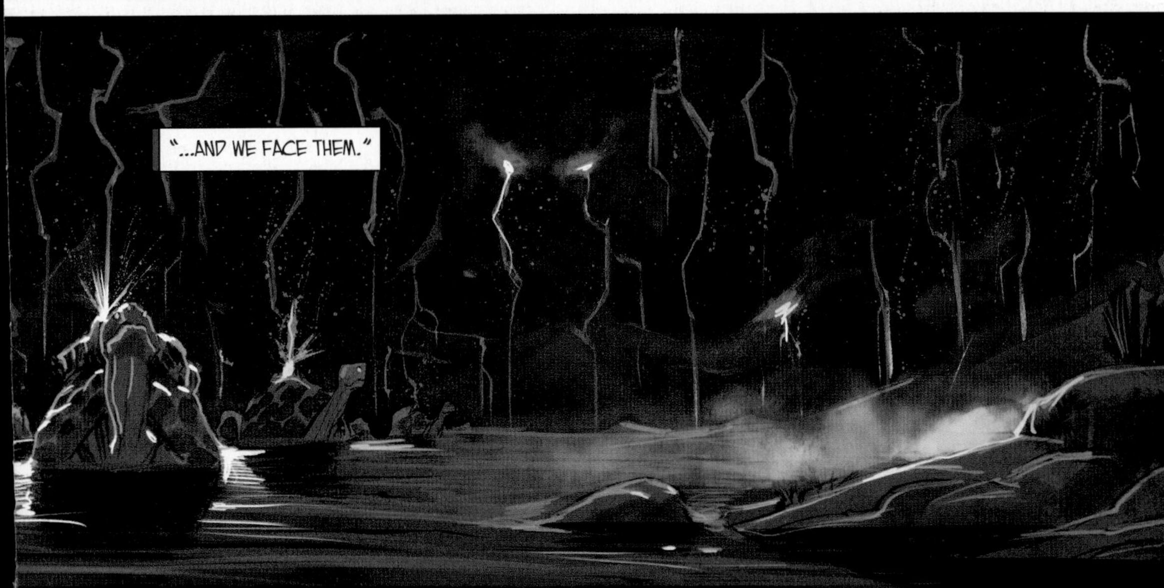
"...AND WE FACE THEM."

SCIENCE

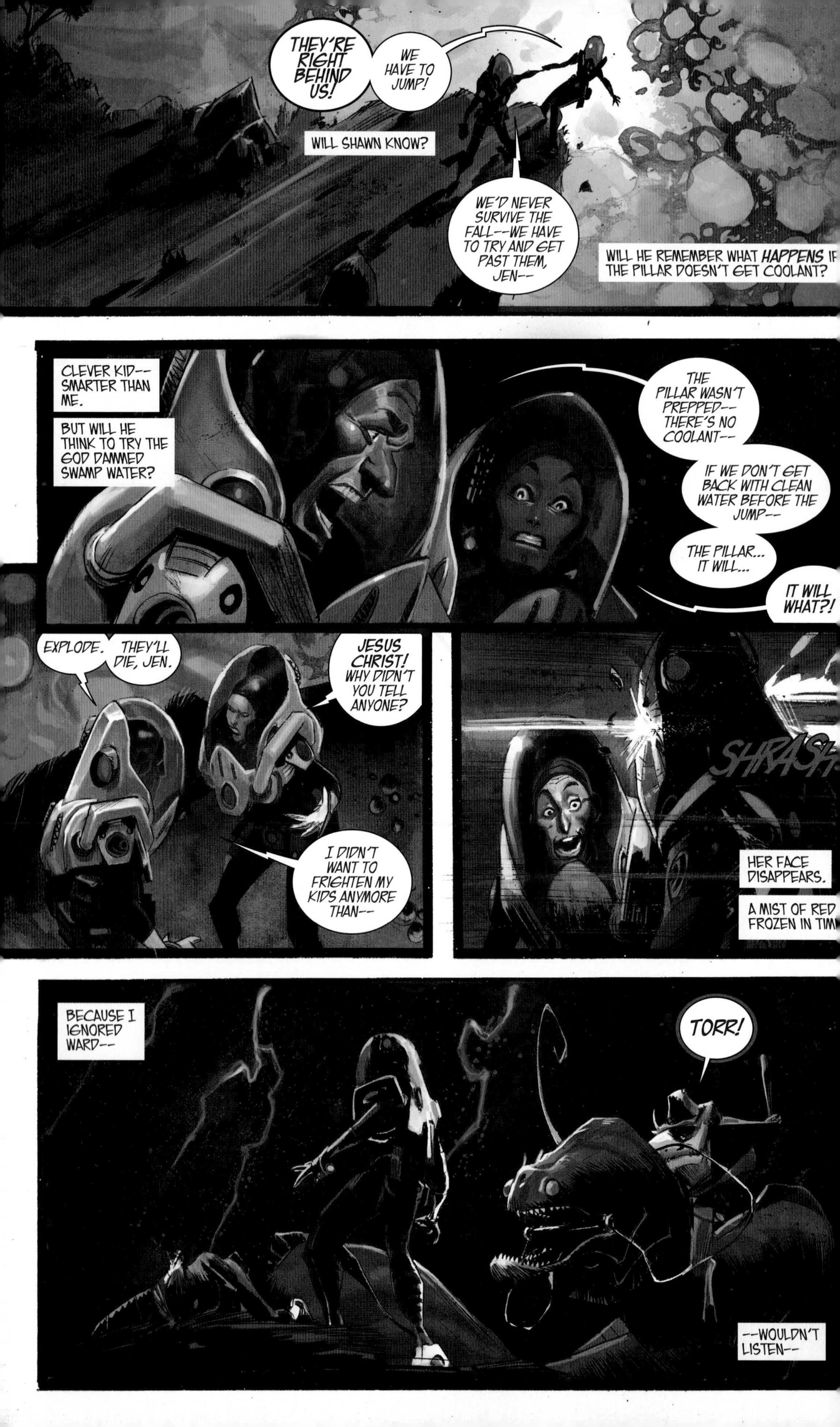
THEY'RE RIGHT BEHIND US!
WE HAVE TO JUMP!
WILL SHAWN KNOW?
WE'D NEVER SURVIVE THE FALL--WE HAVE TO TRY AND GET PAST THEM, JEN--
WILL HE REMEMBER WHAT HAPPENS IF THE PILLAR DOESN'T GET COOLANT?
CLEVER KID--SMARTER THAN ME.
BUT WILL HE THINK TO TRY THE GOD DAMMED SWAMP WATER?
THE PILLAR WASN'T PREPPED--THERE'S NO COOLANT--
IF WE DON'T GET BACK WITH CLEAN WATER BEFORE THE JUMP--
THE PILLAR... IT WILL...
IT WILL WHAT?!
EXPLODE.
THEY'LL DIE, JEN.
JESUS CHRIST! WHY DIDN'T YOU TELL ANYONE?
I DIDN'T WANT TO FRIGHTEN MY KIDS ANYMORE THAN--
SHRASH
HER FACE DISAPPEARS.
A MIST OF RED FROZEN IN TIM
BECAUSE I IGNORED WARD--
TORR!
--WOULDN'T LISTEN--

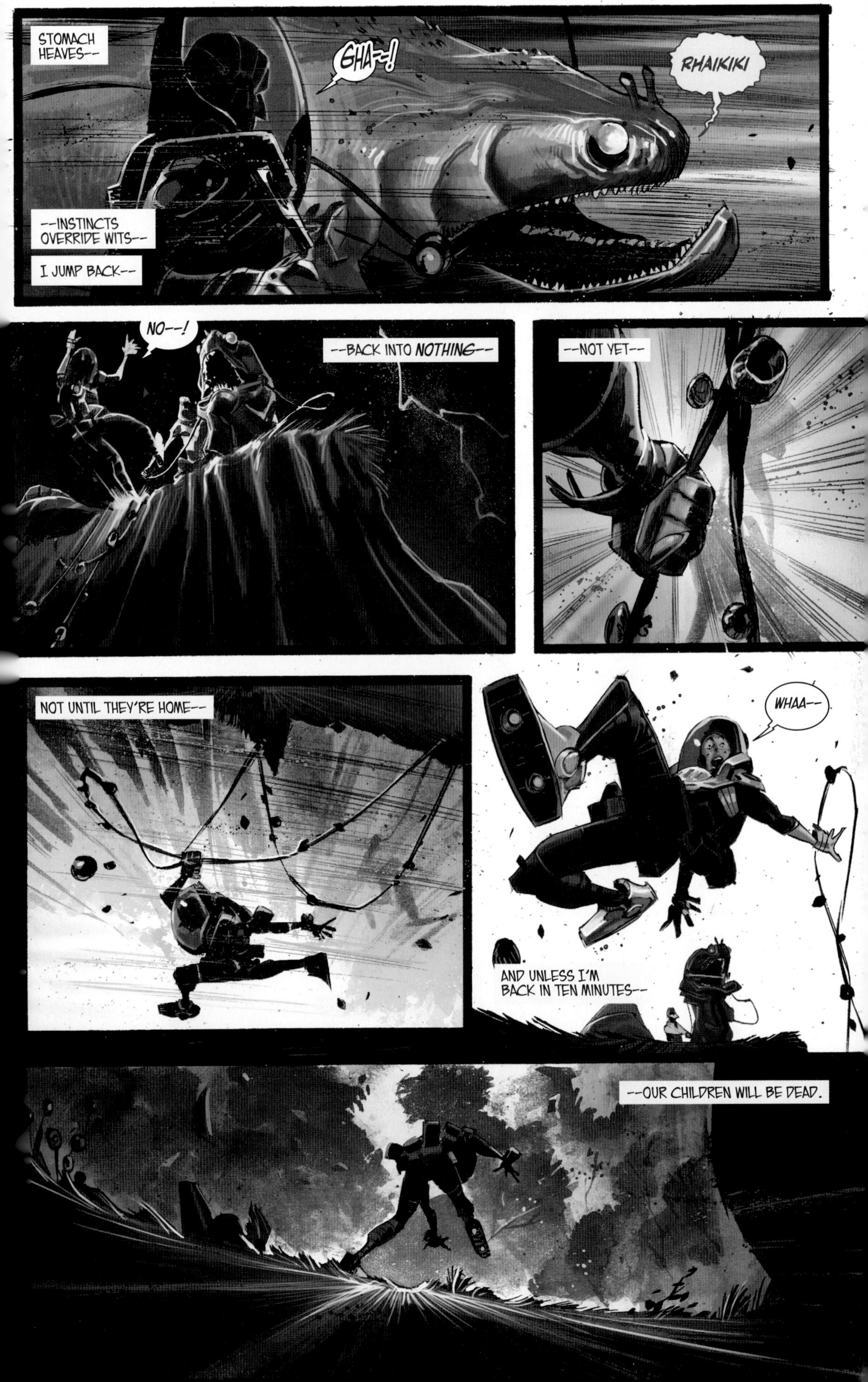
STOMACH HEAVES--
GHA--!
RHAIKIKI
--INSTINCTS OVERRIDE WITS--
I JUMP BACK--
NO--!
--BACK INTO *NOTHING*--
--NOT YET--
NOT UNTIL THEY'RE HOME--
WHAA--
AND UNLESS I'M BACK IN TEN MINUTES--
--OUR CHILDREN WILL BE DEAD.

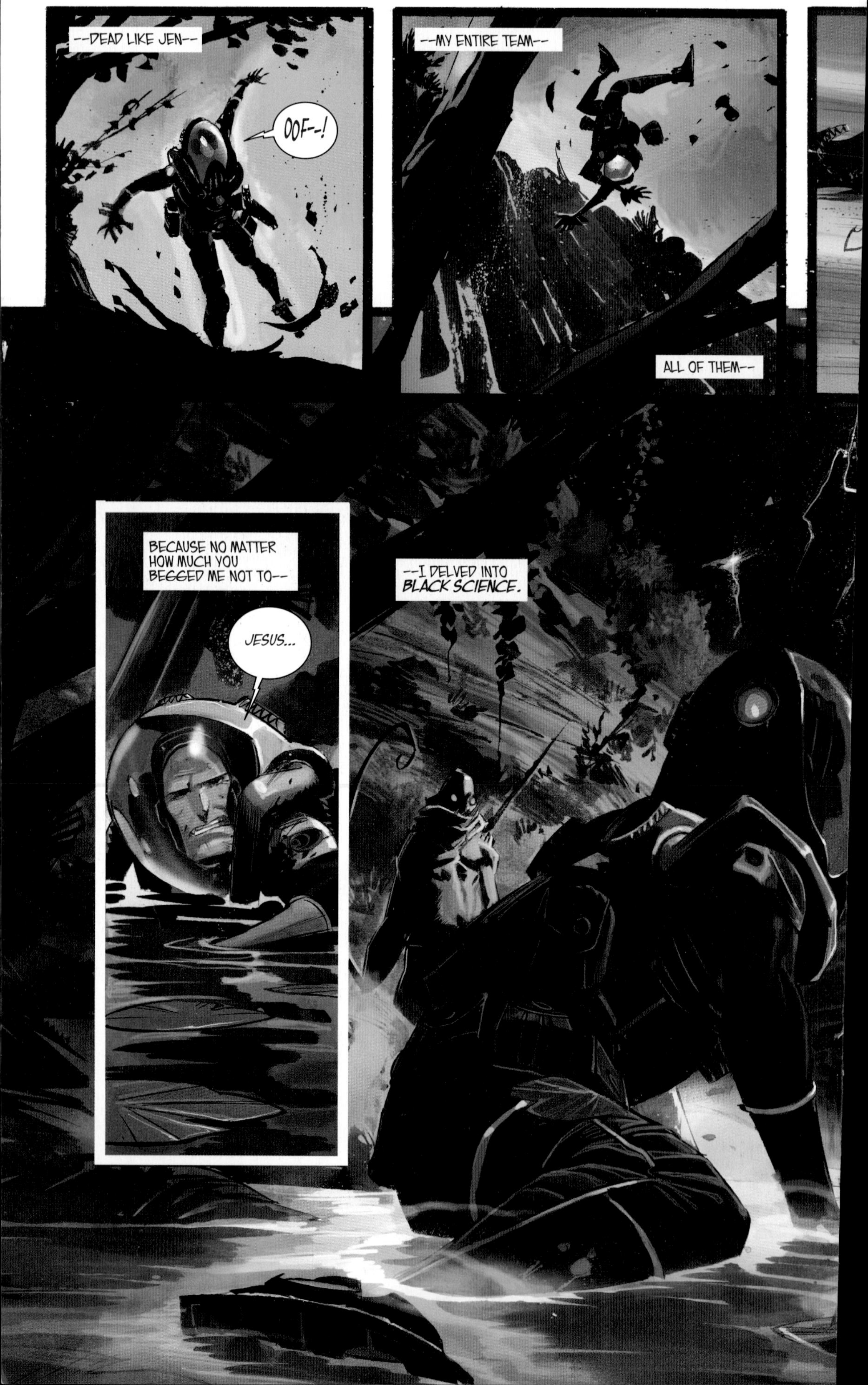
--DEAD LIKE JEN--
OOF--!
--MY ENTIRE TEAM--
ALL OF THEM--
BECAUSE NO MATTER HOW MUCH YOU BEGGED ME NOT TO--
JESUS...
--I DELVED INTO BLACK SCIENCE.

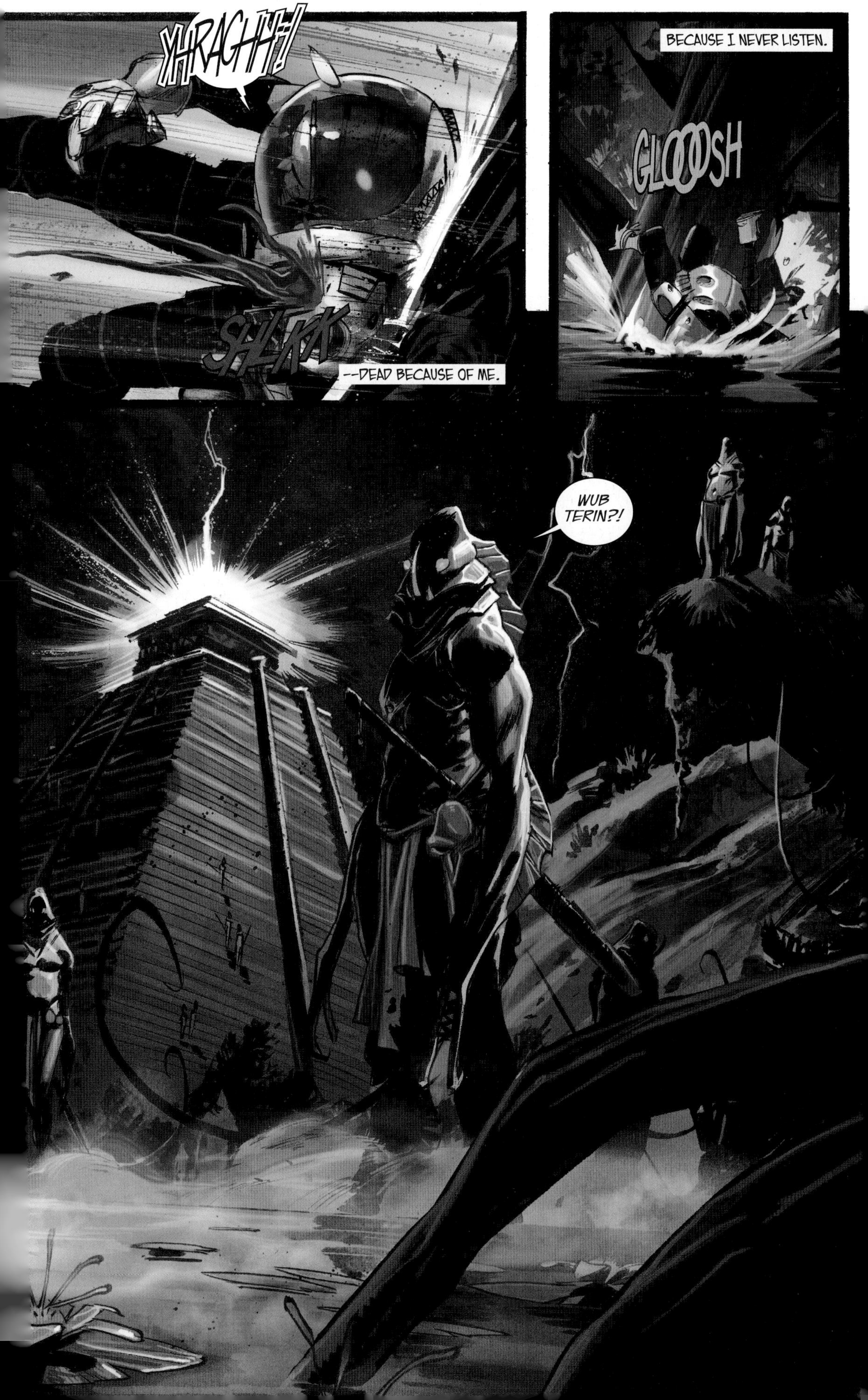
YHRAGHH!
SHLKK
--DEAD BECAUSE OF ME.
BECAUSE I NEVER LISTEN.
GLOOOSH
WUB TERIN?!

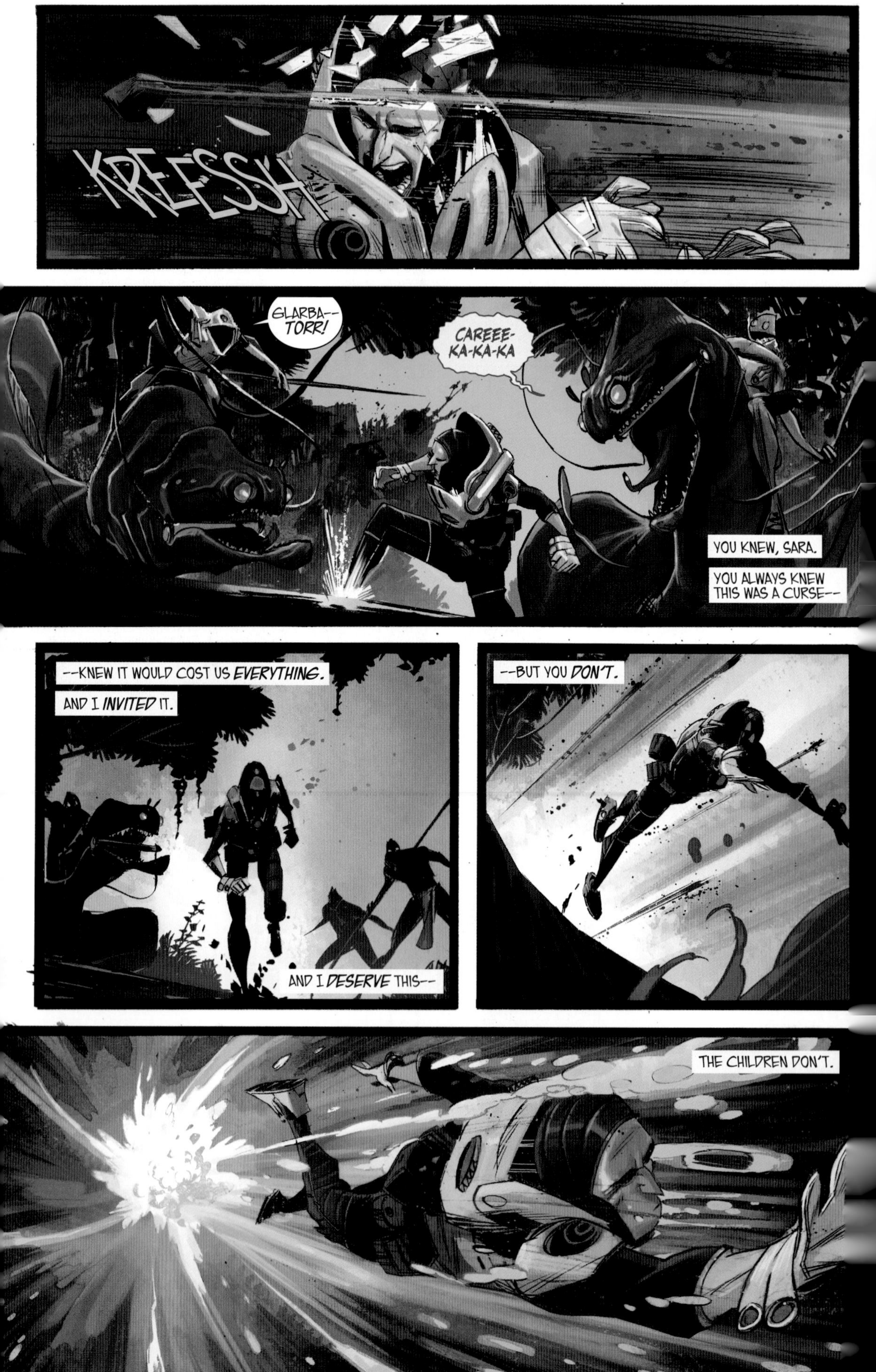
KRESSH
GLARBA--TORR!
CAREEE-KA-KA-KA
YOU KNEW, SARA.
YOU ALWAYS KNEW THIS WAS A CURSE--
--KNEW IT WOULD COST US EVERYTHING.
AND I INVITED IT.
AND I DESERVE THIS--
--BUT YOU DON'T.
THE CHILDREN DON'T.

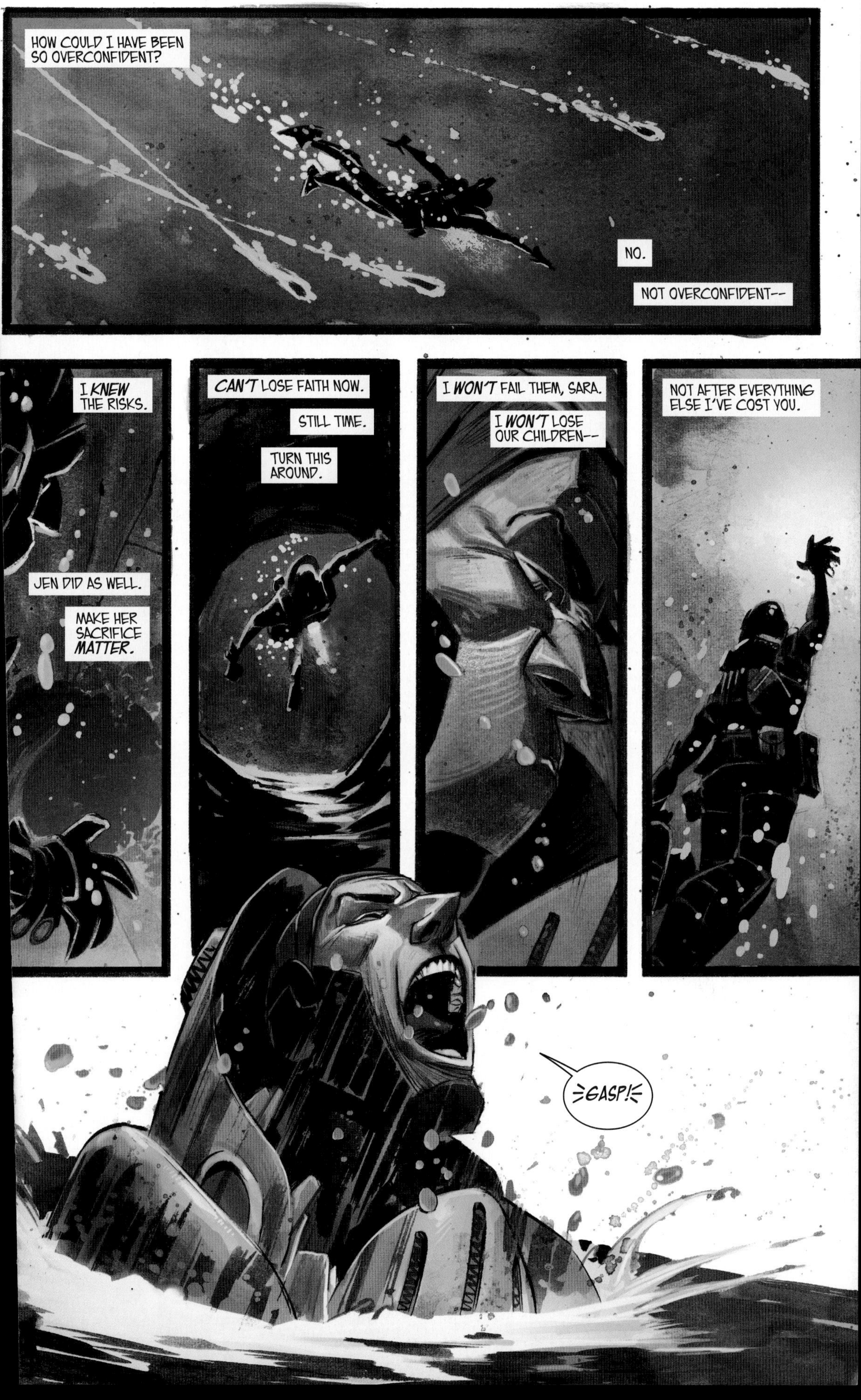

HOW COULD I HAVE BEEN SO OVERCONFIDENT?
NO.
NOT OVERCONFIDENT--
I *KNEW* THE RISKS.
JEN DID AS WELL.
MAKE HER SACRIFICE *MATTER*.
CAN'T LOSE FAITH NOW.
STILL TIME.
TURN THIS AROUND.
I *WON'T* FAIL THEM, SARA.
I *WON'T* LOSE OUR CHILDREN--
NOT AFTER EVERYTHING ELSE I'VE COST YOU.
GASP!

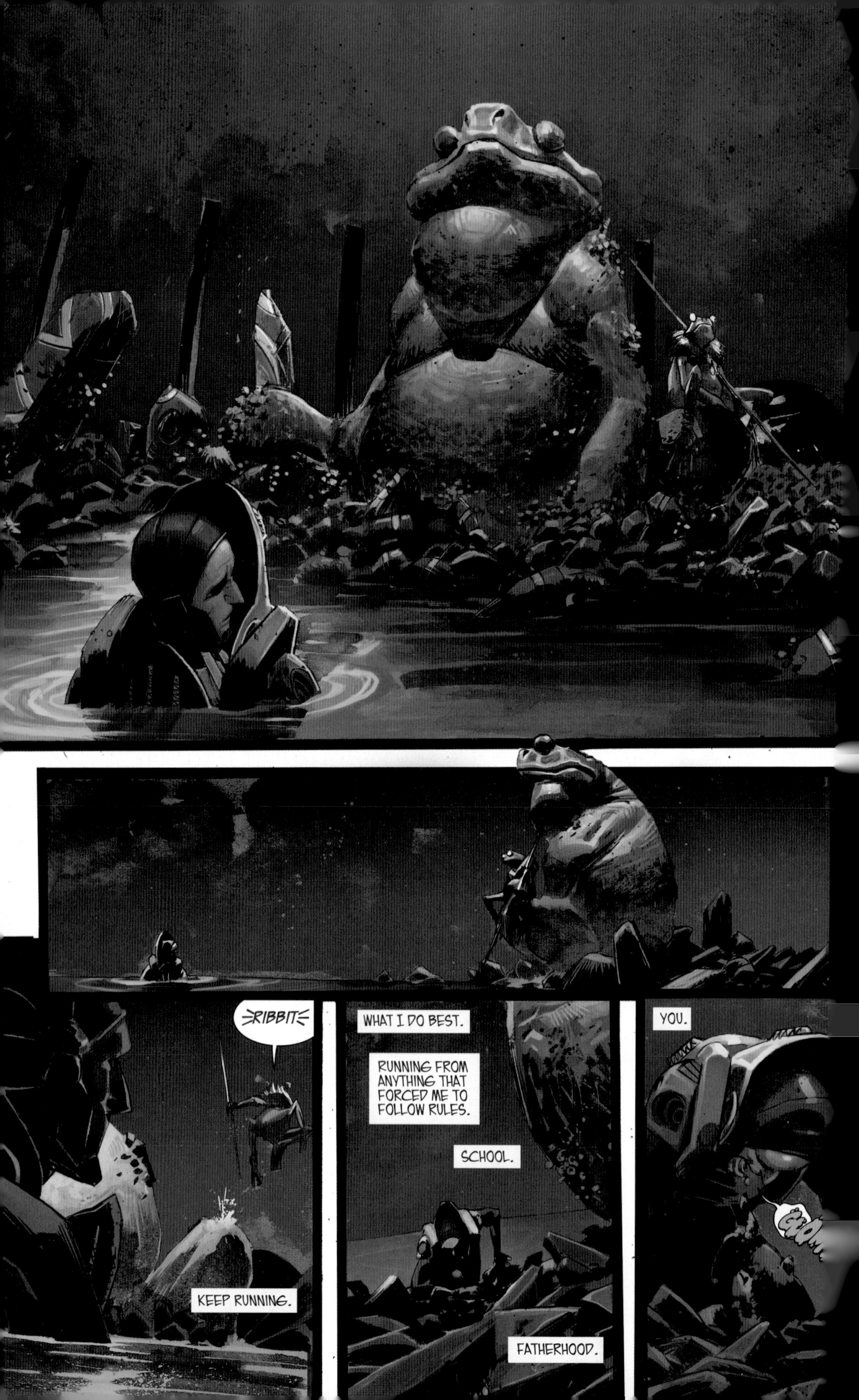
RIBBIT
KEEP RUNNING.
WHAT I DO BEST.
RUNNING FROM ANYTHING THAT FORCED ME TO FOLLOW RULES.
SCHOOL.
FATHERHOOD.
YOU.

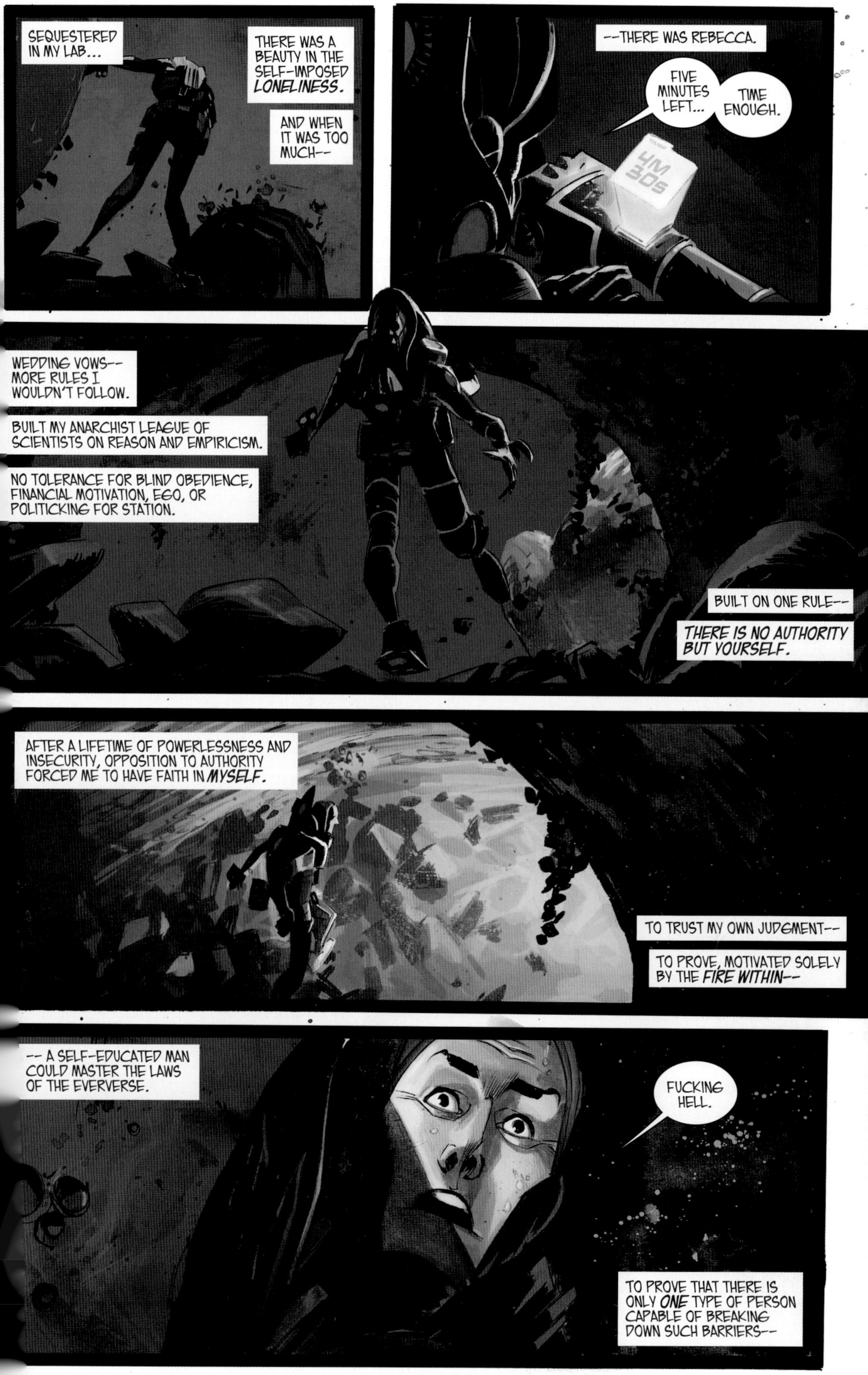
SEQUESTERED IN MY LAB...
THERE WAS A BEAUTY IN THE SELF-IMPOSED LONELINESS.
AND WHEN IT WAS TOO MUCH--
--THERE WAS REBECCA.
FIVE MINUTES LEFT...
TIME ENOUGH.
4M 30s
WEDDING VOWS--MORE RULES I WOULDN'T FOLLOW.
BUILT MY ANARCHIST LEAGUE OF SCIENTISTS ON REASON AND EMPIRICISM.
NO TOLERANCE FOR BLIND OBEDIENCE, FINANCIAL MOTIVATION, EGO, OR POLITICKING FOR STATION.
BUILT ON ONE RULE--
THERE IS NO AUTHORITY BUT YOURSELF.
AFTER A LIFETIME OF POWERLESSNESS AND INSECURITY, OPPOSITION TO AUTHORITY FORCED ME TO HAVE FAITH IN MYSELF.
TO TRUST MY OWN JUDGEMENT--
TO PROVE, MOTIVATED SOLELY BY THE FIRE WITHIN--
-- A SELF-EDUCATED MAN COULD MASTER THE LAWS OF THE EVERVERSE.
FUCKING HELL.
TO PROVE THAT THERE IS ONLY ONE TYPE OF PERSON CAPABLE OF BREAKING DOWN SUCH BARRIERS--

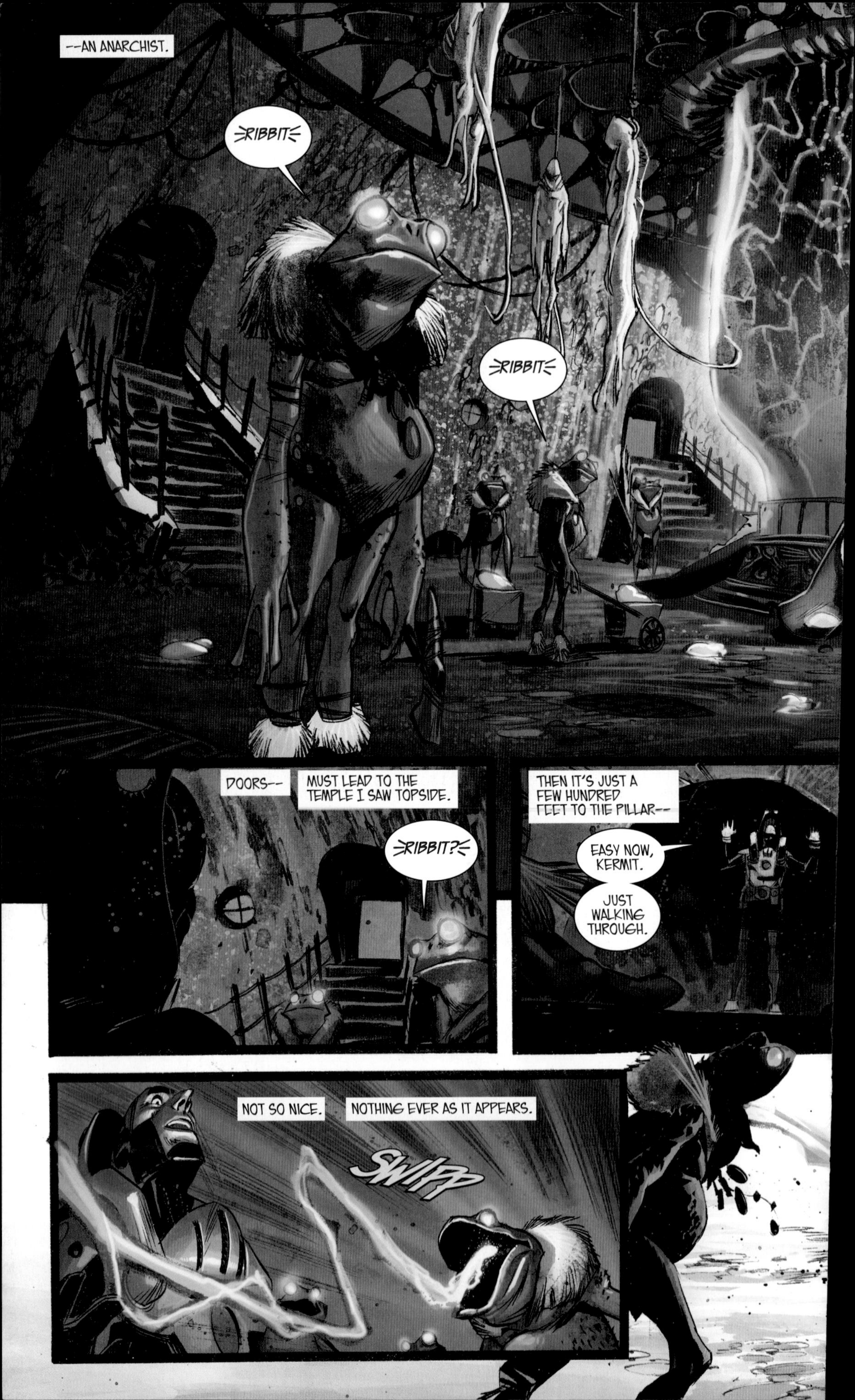

--AN ANARCHIST.
RIBBIT
RIBBIT
DOORS--
MUST LEAD TO THE TEMPLE I SAW TOPSIDE.
RIBBIT?
THEN IT'S JUST A FEW HUNDRED FEET TO THE PILLAR--
EASY NOW, KERMIT.
JUST WALKING THROUGH.
NOT SO NICE.
NOTHING EVER AS IT APPEARS.
SWIPP

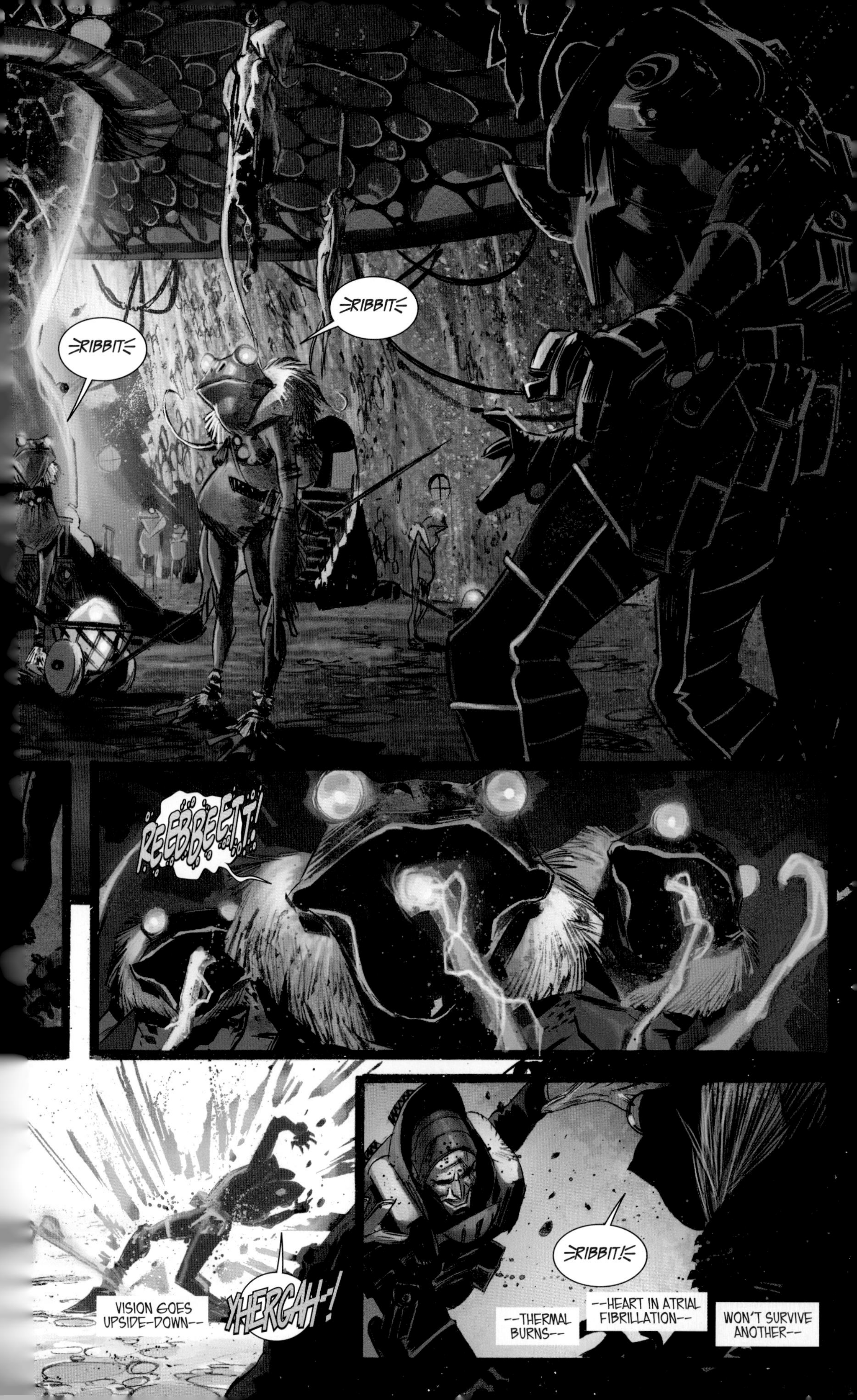
RIBBIT
RIBBIT
REEBBEETT!
VISION GOES UPSIDE-DOWN--
YHERGAH-!
RIBBIT!
--THERMAL BURNS--
--HEART IN ATRIAL FIBRILLATION--
WON'T SURVIVE ANOTHER--

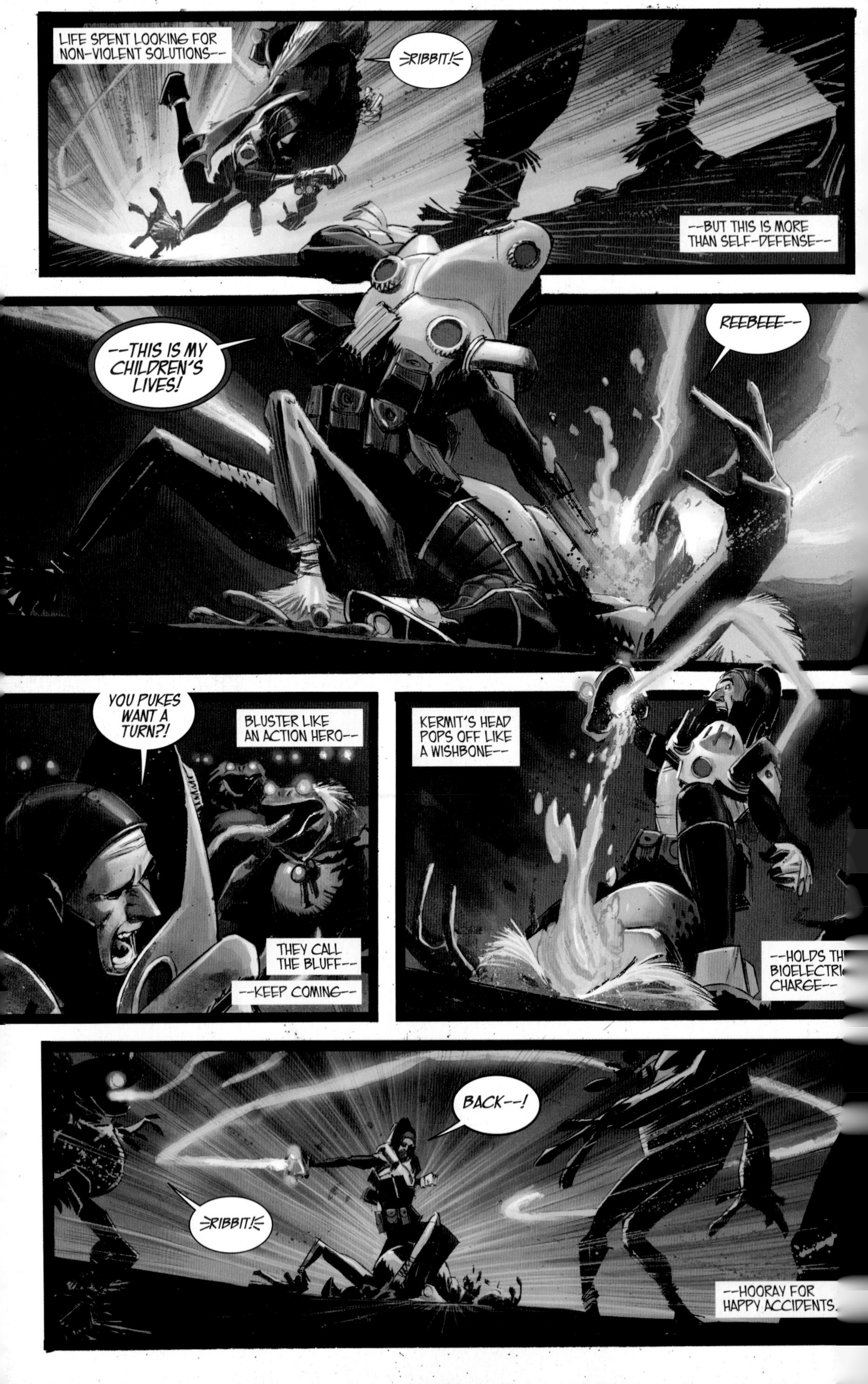
LIFE SPENT LOOKING FOR NON-VIOLENT SOLUTIONS--
RIBBIT!
--BUT THIS IS MORE THAN SELF-DEFENSE--
--THIS IS MY CHILDREN'S LIVES!
REEBEEE--
YOU PUKES WANT A TURN?!
BLUSTER LIKE AN ACTION HERO--
THEY CALL THE BLUFF--
--KEEP COMING--
KERMIT'S HEAD POPS OFF LIKE A WISHBONE--
--HOLDS TH BIOELECTRI CHARGE--
BACK--!
RIBBIT!
--HOORAY FOR HAPPY ACCIDENTS.

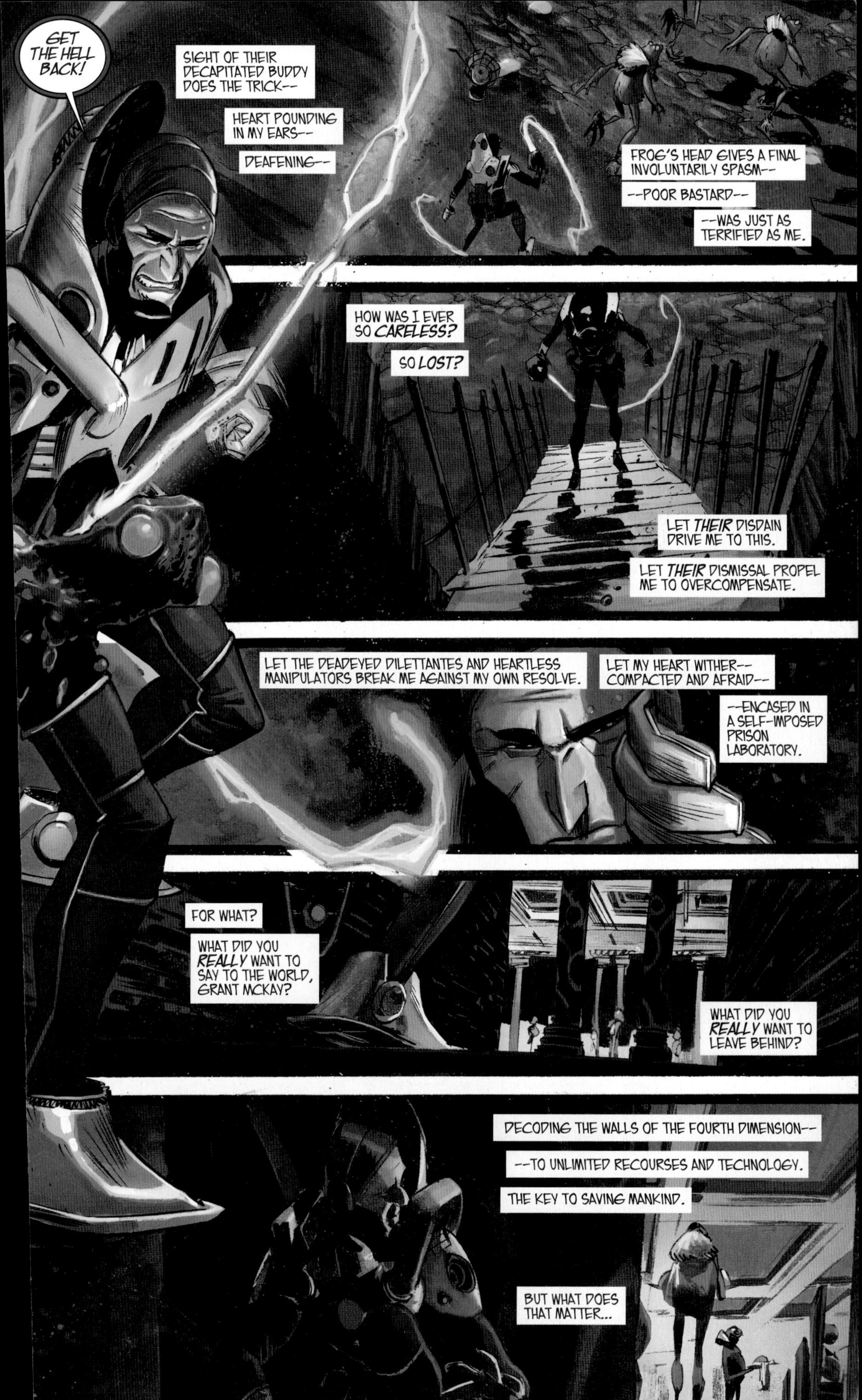
GET THE HELL BACK!
SIGHT OF THEIR DECAPITATED BUDDY DOES THE TRICK--
HEART POUNDING IN MY EARS--
DEAFENING--
FROG'S HEAD GIVES A FINAL INVOLUNTARILY SPASM--
--POOR BASTARD--
--WAS JUST AS TERRIFIED AS ME.
HOW WAS I EVER SO CARELESS?
SO LOST?
LET THEIR DISDAIN DRIVE ME TO THIS.
LET THEIR DISMISSAL PROPEL ME TO OVERCOMPENSATE.
LET THE DEADEYED DILETTANTES AND HEARTLESS MANIPULATORS BREAK ME AGAINST MY OWN RESOLVE.
LET MY HEART WITHER-- COMPACTED AND AFRAID--
--ENCASED IN A SELF-IMPOSED PRISON LABORATORY.
FOR WHAT?
WHAT DID YOU REALLY WANT TO SAY TO THE WORLD, GRANT MCKAY?
WHAT DID YOU REALLY WANT TO LEAVE BEHIND?
DECODING THE WALLS OF THE FOURTH DIMENSION--
--TO UNLIMITED RECOURSES AND TECHNOLOGY.
THE KEY TO SAVING MANKIND.
BUT WHAT DOES THAT MATTER...

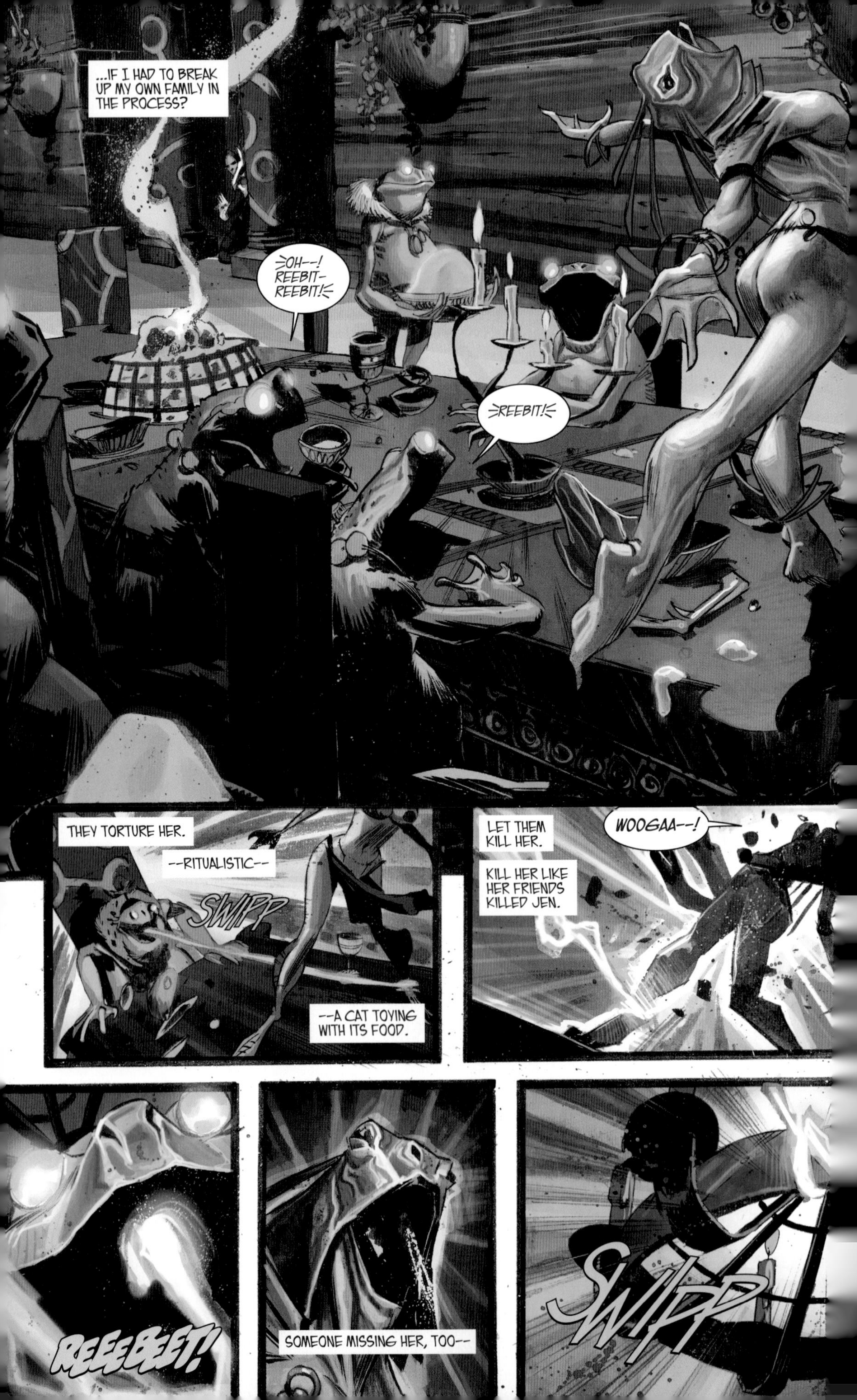
...IF I HAD TO BREAK UP MY OWN FAMILY IN THE PROCESS?
OH--! REEBIT-REEBIT!
REEBIT!
THEY TORTURE HER.
--RITUALISTIC--
SWIPP
--A CAT TOYING WITH ITS FOOD.
LET THEM KILL HER.
KILL HER LIKE HER FRIENDS KILLED JEN.
WOOGAA--!
REEEBEET!
SOMEONE MISSING HER, TOO--
SWIPP

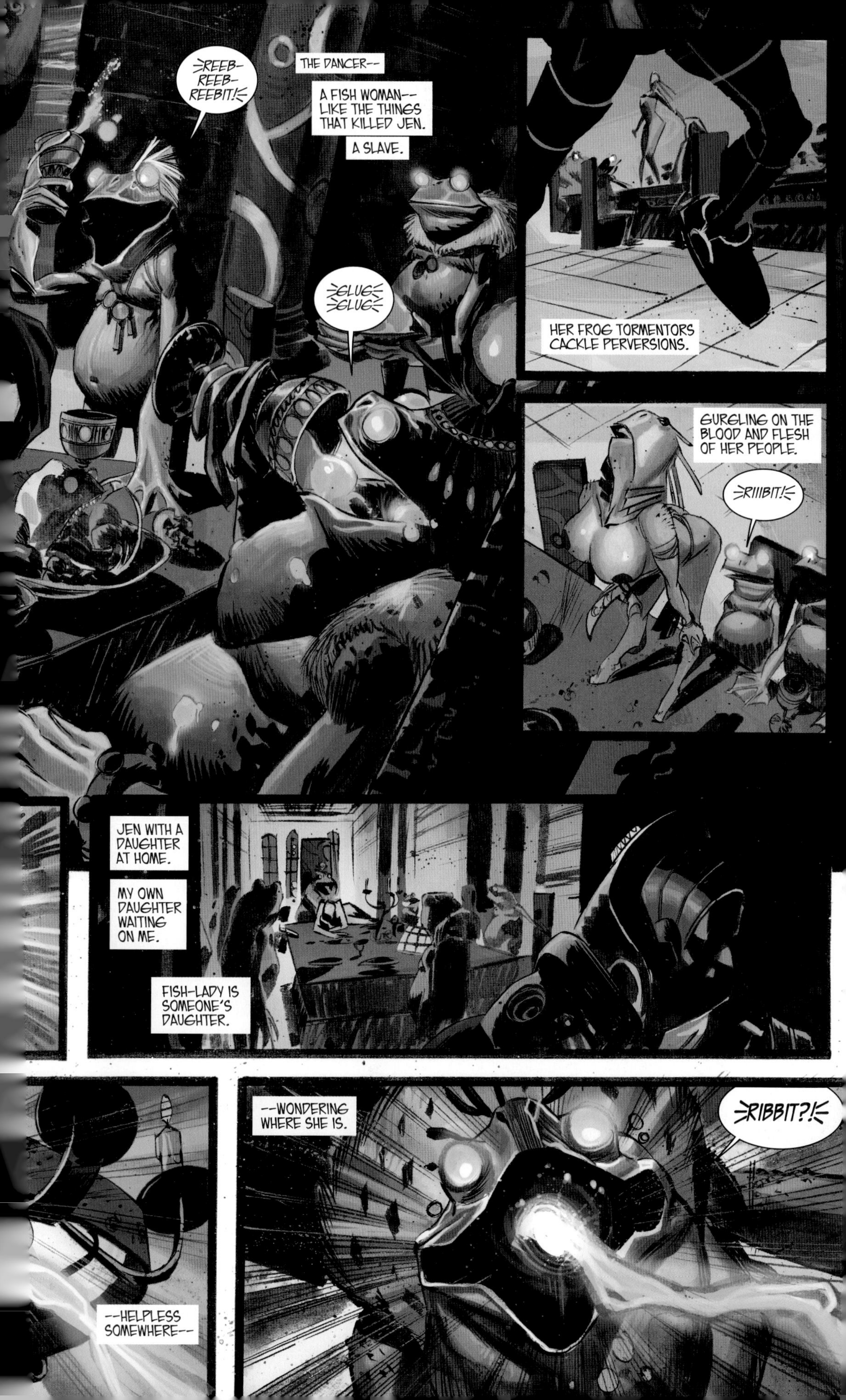

=REEB-REEB-REEBIT!=
THE DANCER--
A FISH WOMAN--LIKE THE THINGS THAT KILLED JEN.
A SLAVE.
=GLUG=GLUG=
HER FROG TORMENTORS CACKLE PERVERSIONS.
GURGLING ON THE BLOOD AND FLESH OF HER PEOPLE.
=RIIIBIT!=
JEN WITH A DAUGHTER AT HOME.
MY OWN DAUGHTER WAITING ON ME.
FISH-LADY IS SOMEONE'S DAUGHTER.
--HELPLESS SOMEWHERE--
--WONDERING WHERE SHE IS.
=RIBBIT?!=

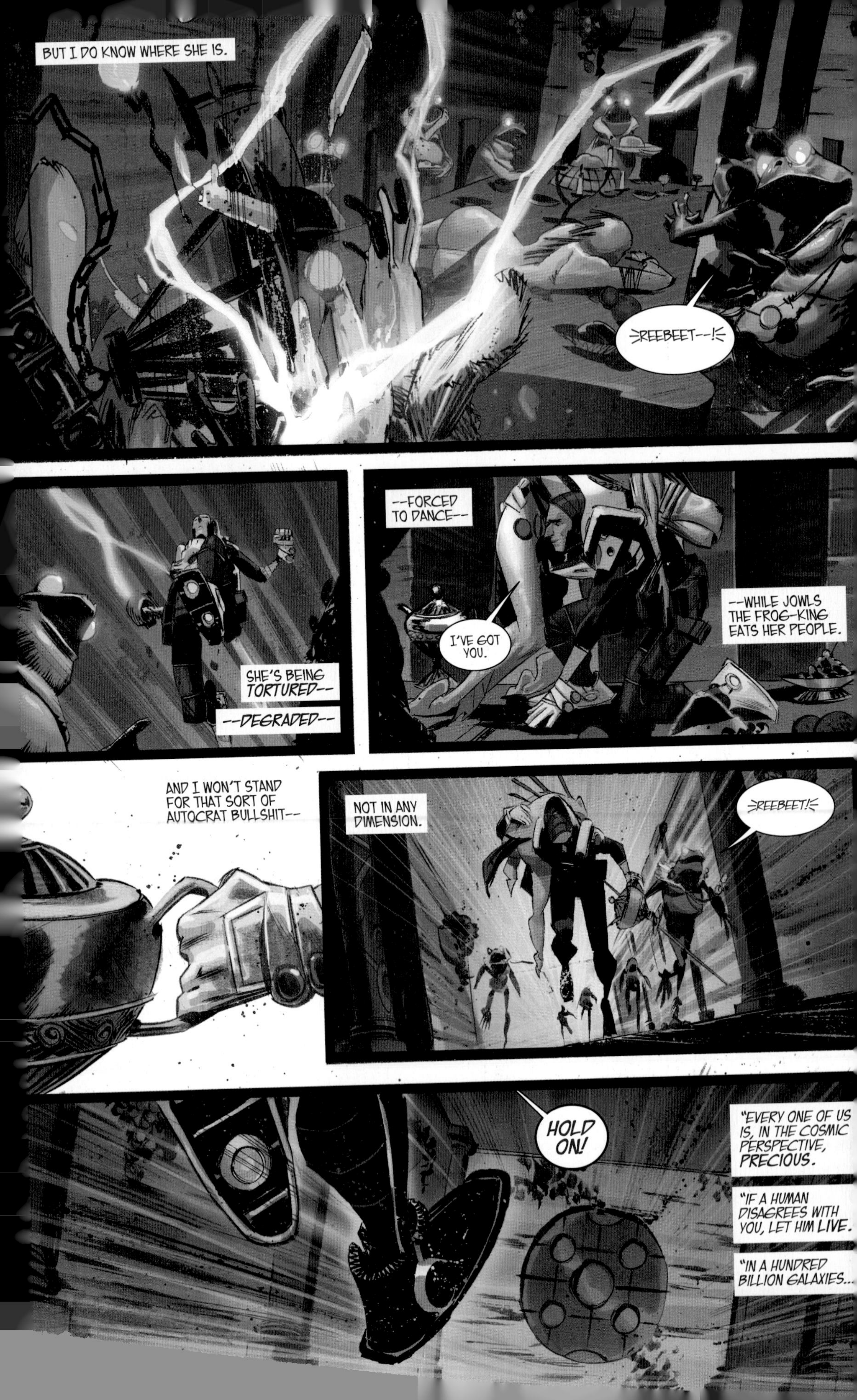

BUT I DO KNOW WHERE SHE IS.
REEBEET--!
SHE'S BEING TORTURED--
--DEGRADED--
--FORCED TO DANCE--
I'VE GOT YOU.
--WHILE JOWLS THE FROG-KING EATS HER PEOPLE.
AND I WON'T STAND FOR THAT SORT OF AUTOCRAT BULLSHIT--
NOT IN ANY DIMENSION.
REEBEET!
HOLD ON!
"EVERY ONE OF US IS, IN THE COSMIC PERSPECTIVE, PRECIOUS.
"IF A HUMAN DISAGREES WITH YOU, LET HIM LIVE.
"IN A HUNDRED BILLION GALAXIES...

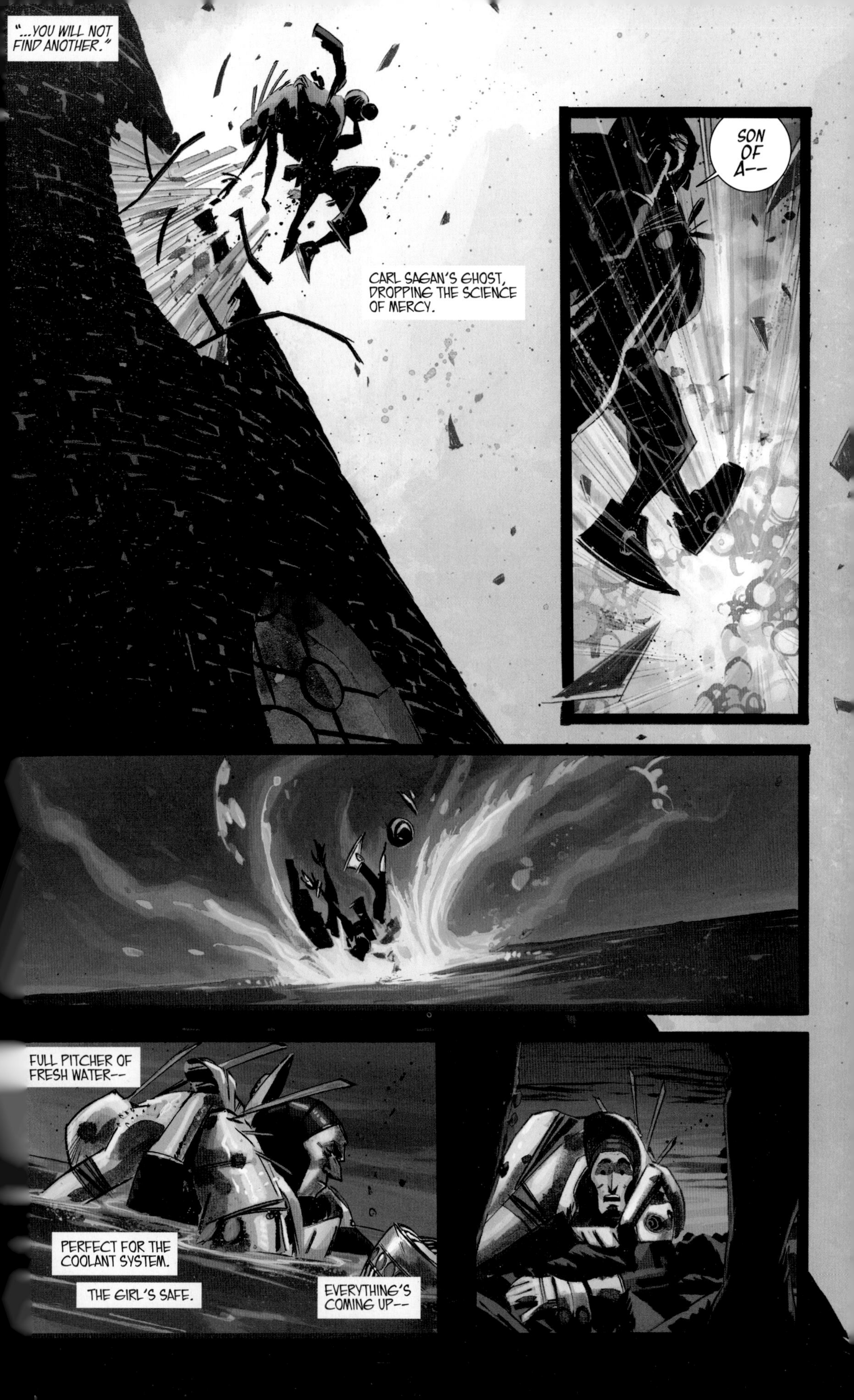
"...YOU WILL NOT FIND ANOTHER."
CARL SAGAN'S GHOST, DROPPING THE SCIENCE OF MERCY.
SON OF A--
FULL PITCHER OF FRESH WATER--
PERFECT FOR THE COOLANT SYSTEM.
THE GIRL'S SAFE.
EVERYTHING'S COMING UP--

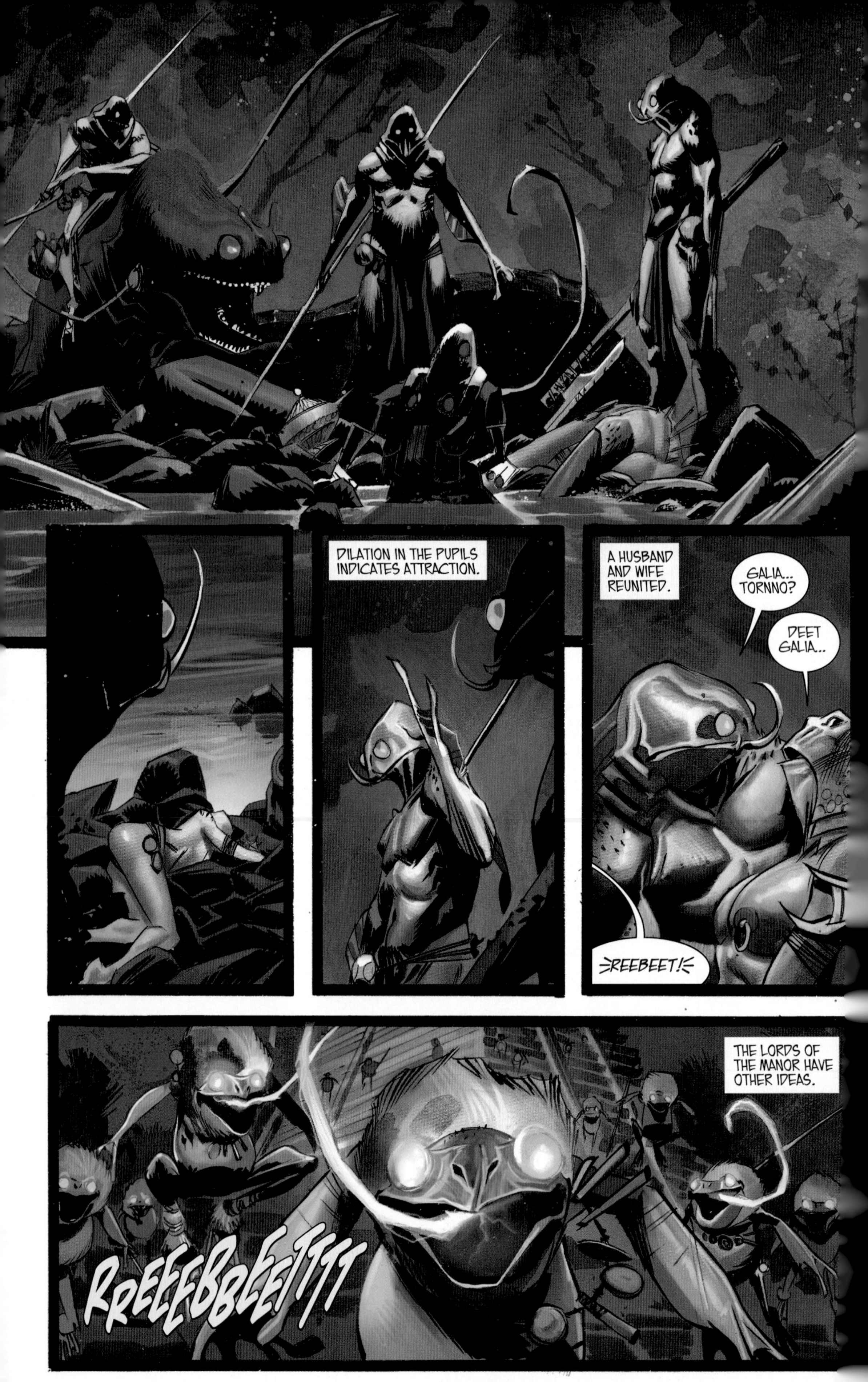
DILATION IN THE PUPILS INDICATES ATTRACTION.
A HUSBAND AND WIFE REUNITED.
GALIA... TORNNO?
DEET GALIA...
REEBEET!
THE LORDS OF THE MANOR HAVE OTHER IDEAS.
RREEEBBEETTTT

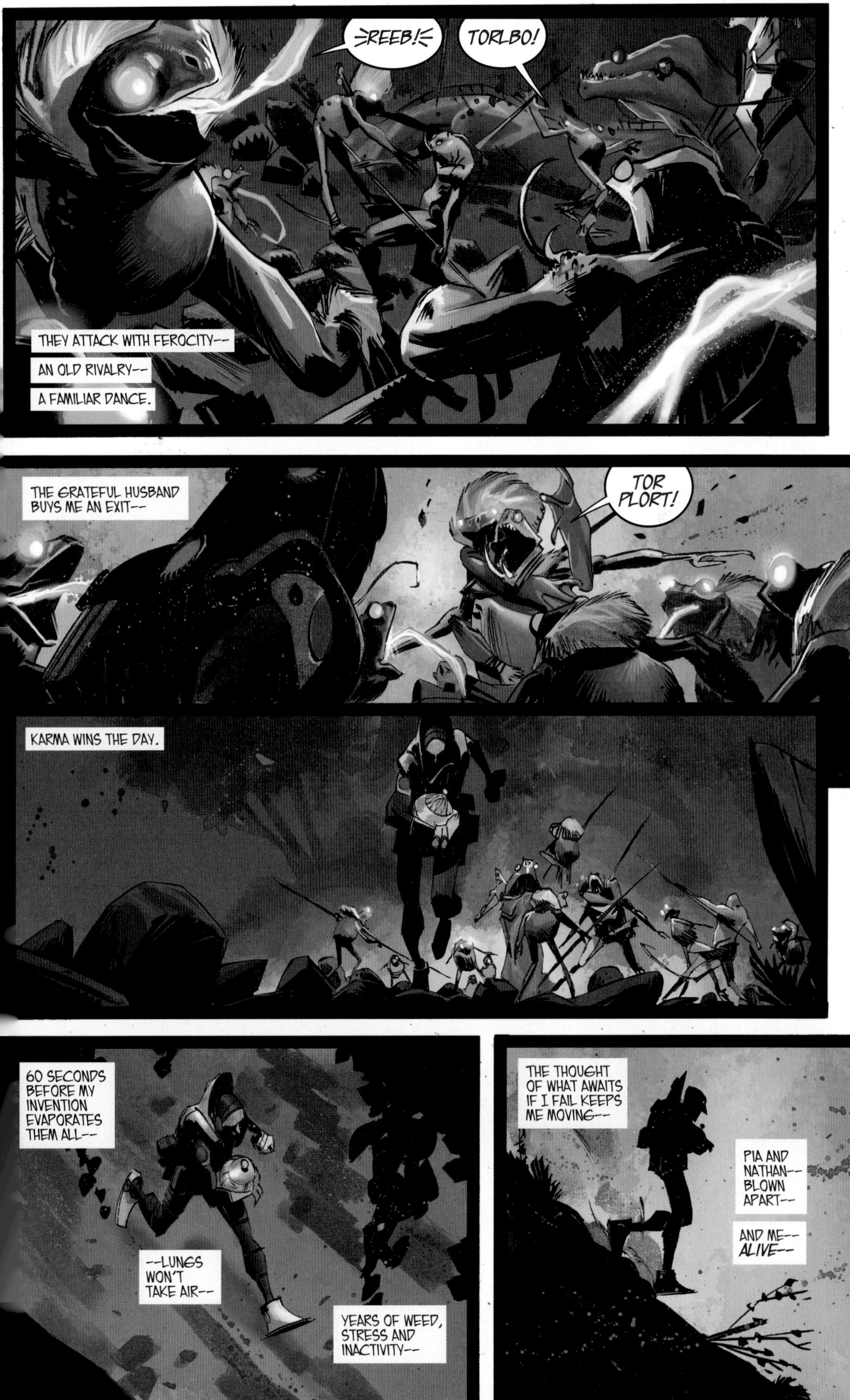

=REEB!=
TORLBO!
THEY ATTACK WITH FEROCITY--
AN OLD RIVALRY--
A FAMILIAR DANCE.
THE GRATEFUL HUSBAND BUYS ME AN EXIT--
TOR PLORT!
KARMA WINS THE DAY.
60 SECONDS BEFORE MY INVENTION EVAPORATES THEM ALL--
--LUNGS WON'T TAKE AIR--
YEARS OF WEED, STRESS AND INACTIVITY--
THE THOUGHT OF WHAT AWAITS IF I FAIL KEEPS ME MOVING--
PIA AND NATHAN-- BLOWN APART--
AND ME-- ALIVE--

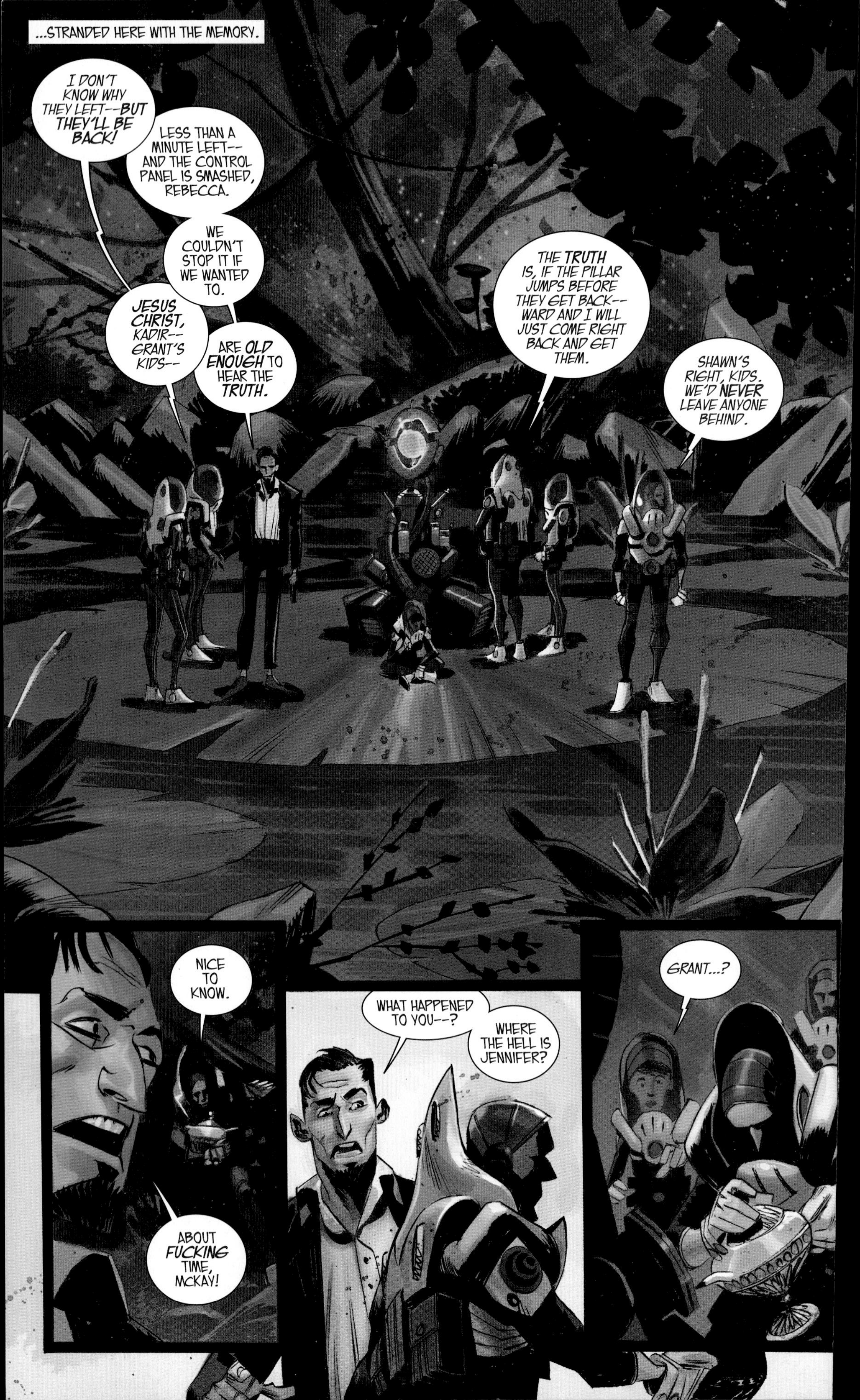
...STRANDED HERE WITH THE MEMORY.
I DON'T KNOW WHY THEY LEFT--BUT THEY'LL BE BACK!
LESS THAN A MINUTE LEFT-- AND THE CONTROL PANEL IS SMASHED, REBECCA.
WE COULDN'T STOP IT IF WE WANTED TO.
JESUS CHRIST, KADIR-- GRANT'S KIDS--
ARE OLD ENOUGH TO HEAR THE TRUTH.
THE TRUTH IS, IF THE PILLAR JUMPS BEFORE THEY GET BACK-- WARD AND I WILL JUST COME RIGHT BACK AND GET THEM.
SHAWN'S RIGHT, KIDS. WE'D NEVER LEAVE ANYONE BEHIND.
NICE TO KNOW.
ABOUT FUCKING TIME, MCKAY!
WHAT HAPPENED TO YOU--?
WHERE THE HELL IS JENNIFER?
GRANT...?

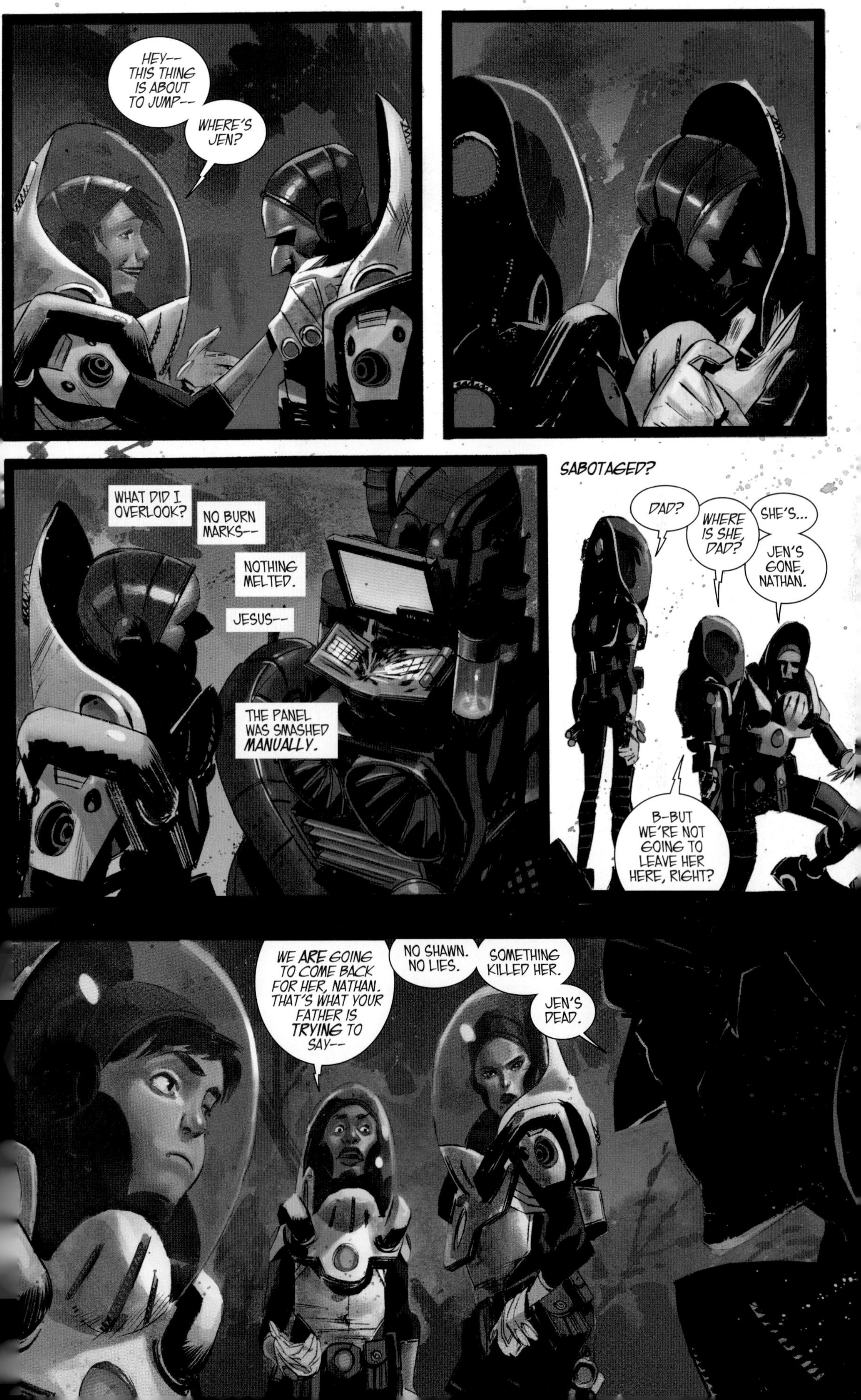
HEY-- THIS THING IS ABOUT TO JUMP--
WHERE'S JEN?
SABOTAGED?
WHAT DID I OVERLOOK?
NO BURN MARKS--
NOTHING MELTED.
JESUS--
THE PANEL WAS SMASHED MANUALLY.
DAD?
WHERE IS SHE, DAD?
SHE'S...
JEN'S GONE, NATHAN.
B-BUT WE'RE NOT GOING TO LEAVE HER HERE, RIGHT?
WE ARE GOING TO COME BACK FOR HER, NATHAN. THAT'S WHAT YOUR FATHER IS TRYING TO SAY--
NO SHAWN. NO LIES.
SOMETHING KILLED HER.
JEN'S DEAD.

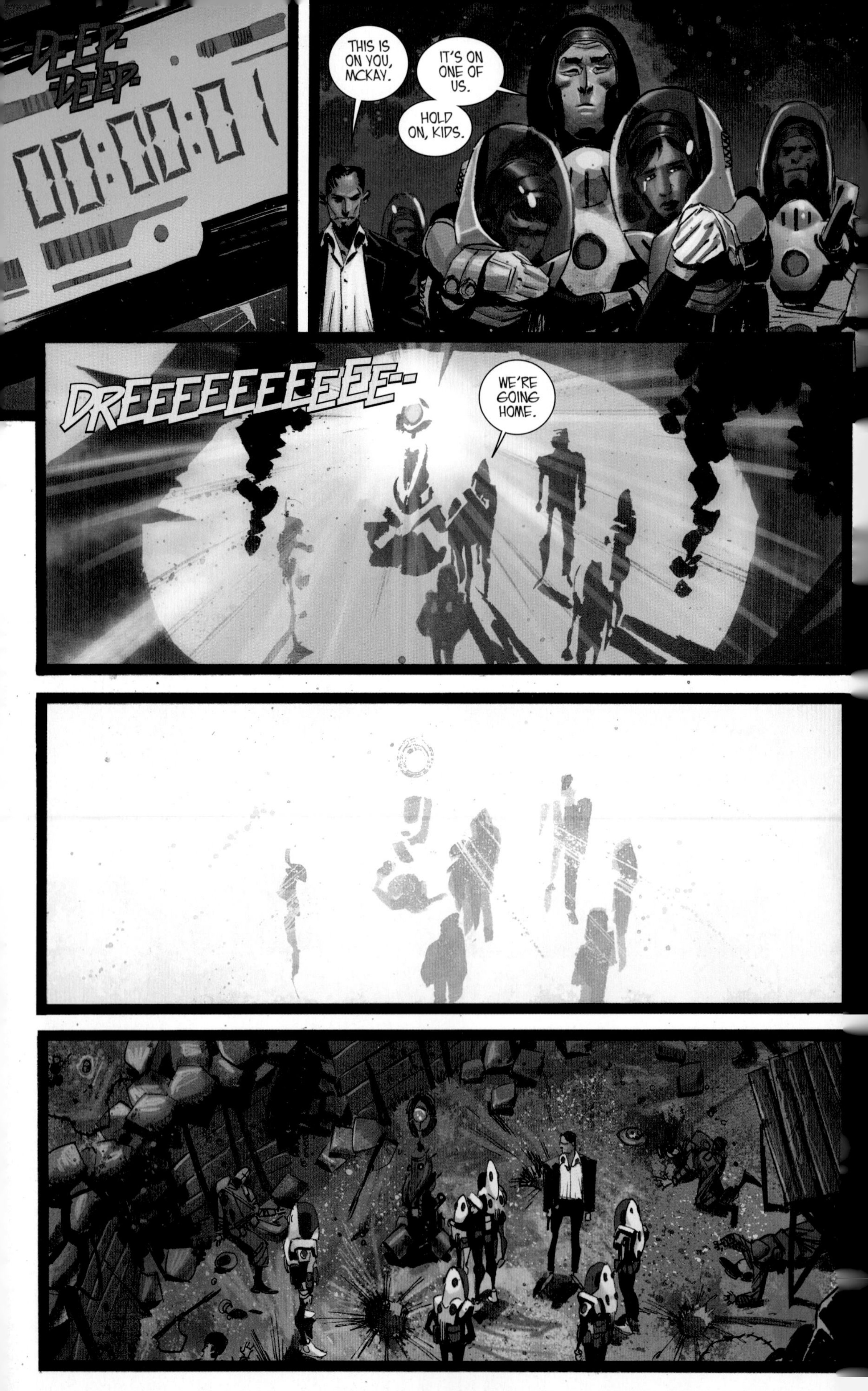
DEEP-DEEP-
00:00:01
THIS IS ON YOU, MCKAY.
IT'S ON ONE OF US.
HOLD ON, KIDS.
DREEEEEEEEEEEE--
WE'RE GOING HOME.

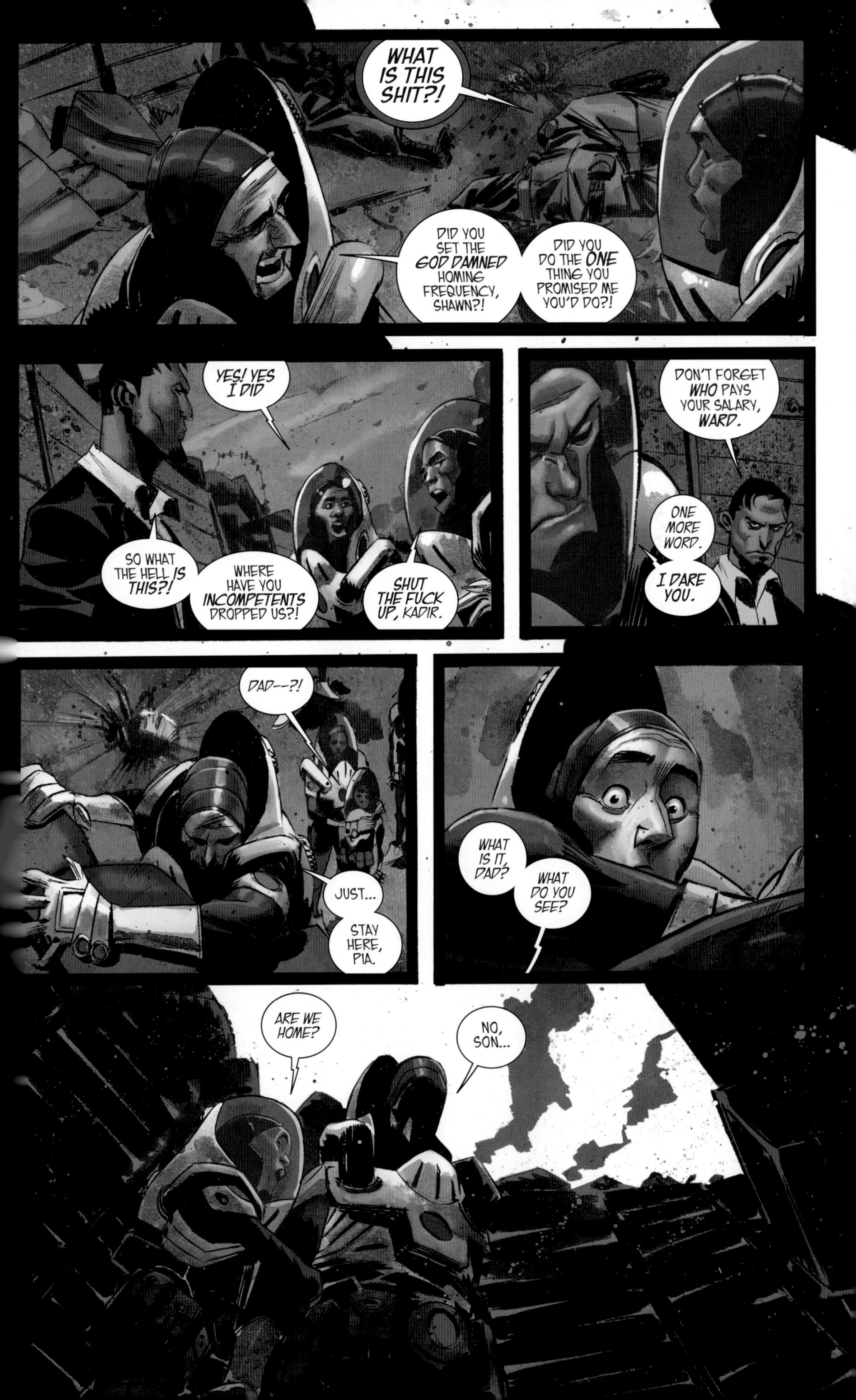
WHAT IS THIS SHIT?!
DID YOU SET THE GOD DAMNED HOMING FREQUENCY, SHAWN?!
DID YOU DO THE ONE THING YOU PROMISED ME YOU'D DO?!
YES! YES I DID
SO WHAT THE HELL IS THIS?!
WHERE HAVE YOU INCOMPETENTS DROPPED US?!
SHUT THE FUCK UP, KADIR.
DON'T FORGET WHO PAYS YOUR SALARY, WARD.
ONE MORE WORD.
I DARE YOU.
DAD--?!
JUST...
STAY HERE, PIA.
WHAT IS IT, DAD?
WHAT DO YOU SEE?
ARE WE HOME?
NO, SON...

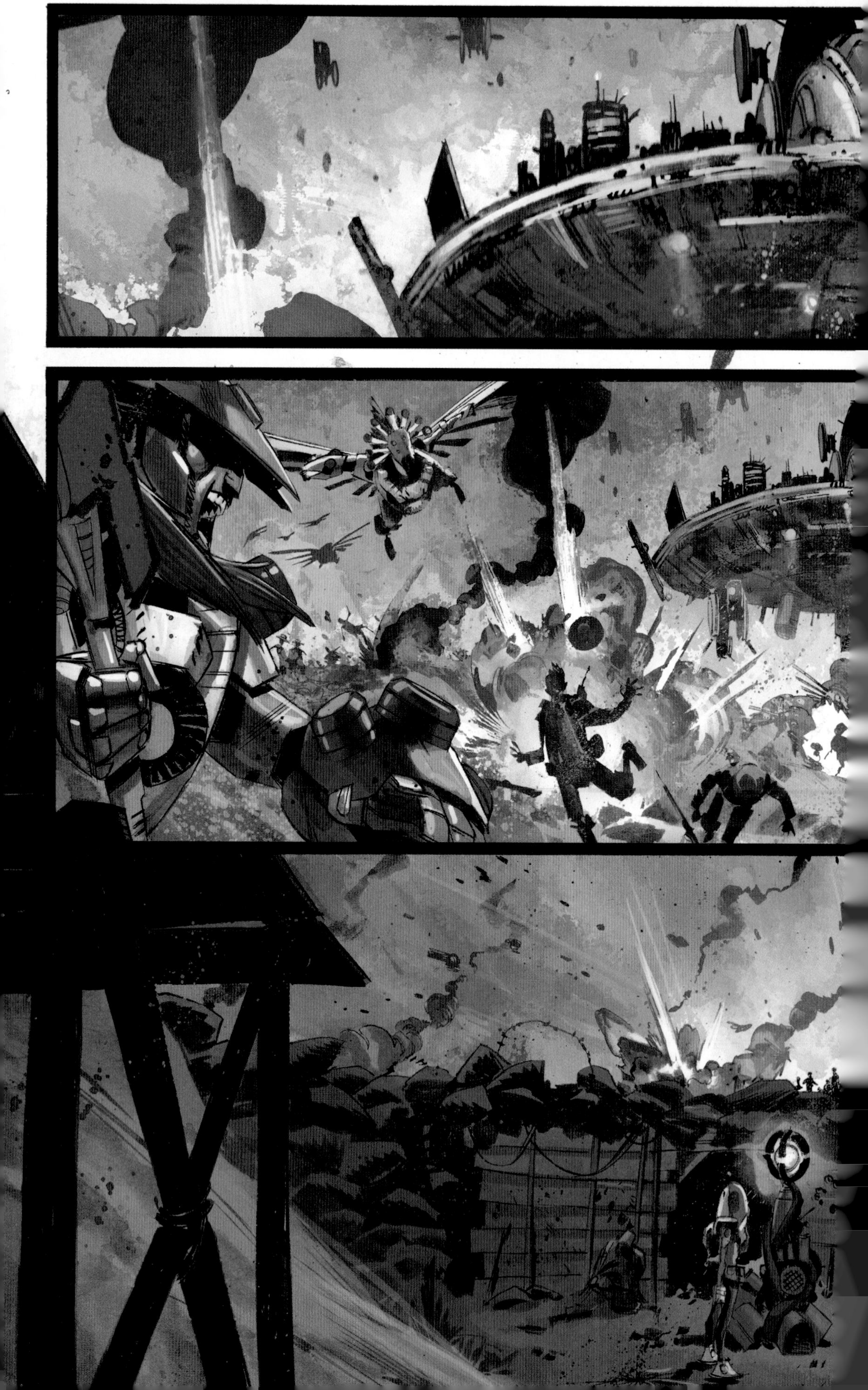

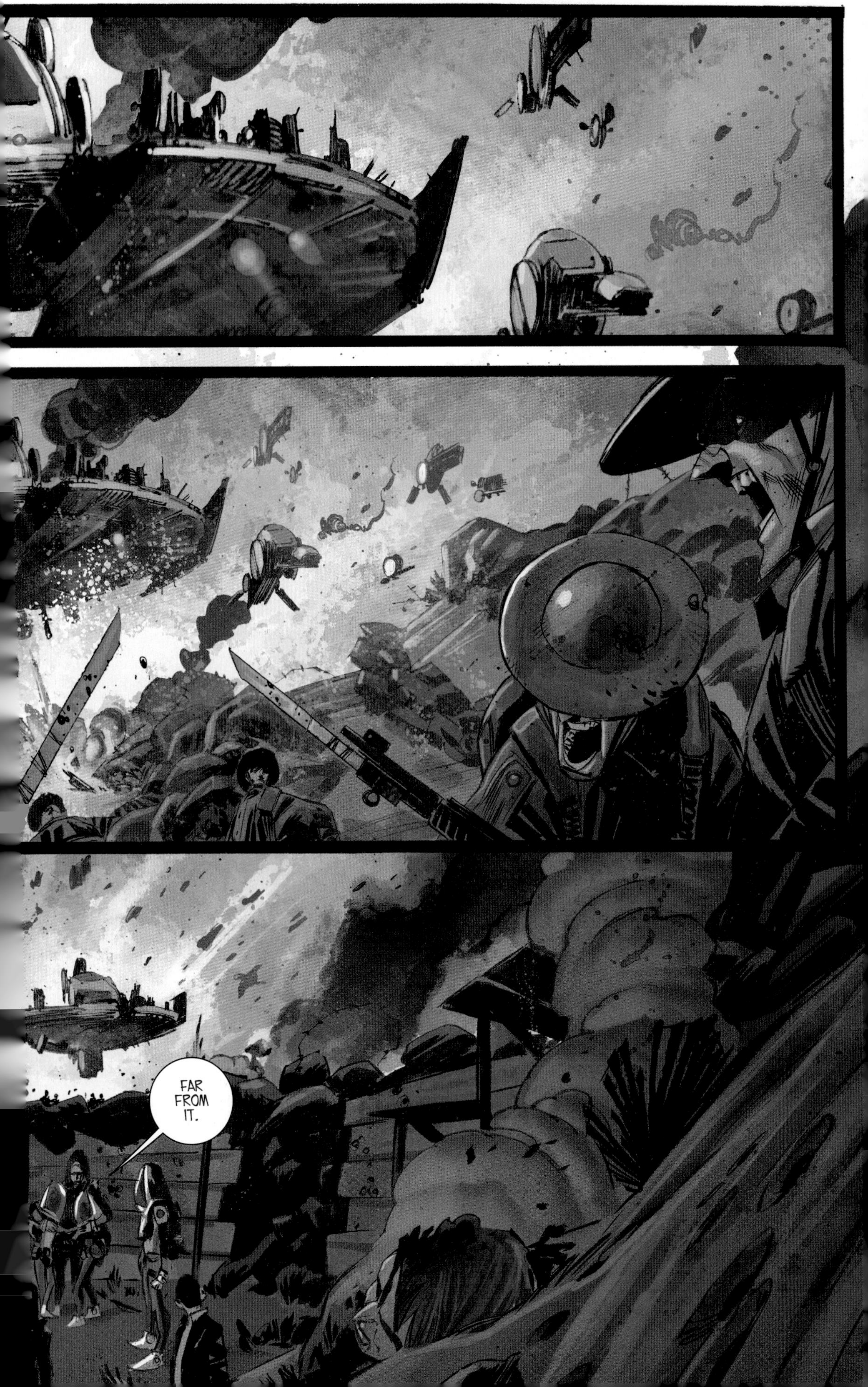
FAR FROM IT.

2

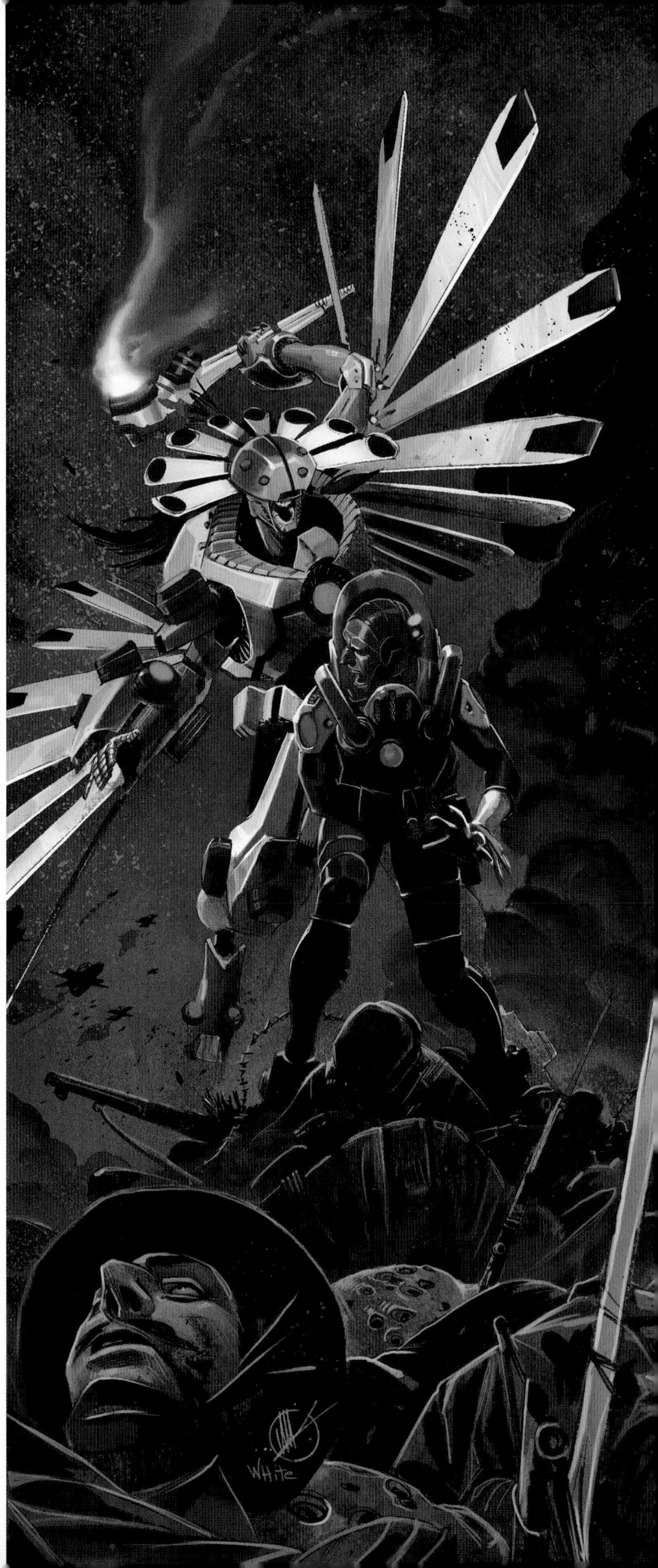
WHite

Idiom: From pillar to post.

a. From place to place, esp. aimlessly.

b. From one bad situation or predicament to another.

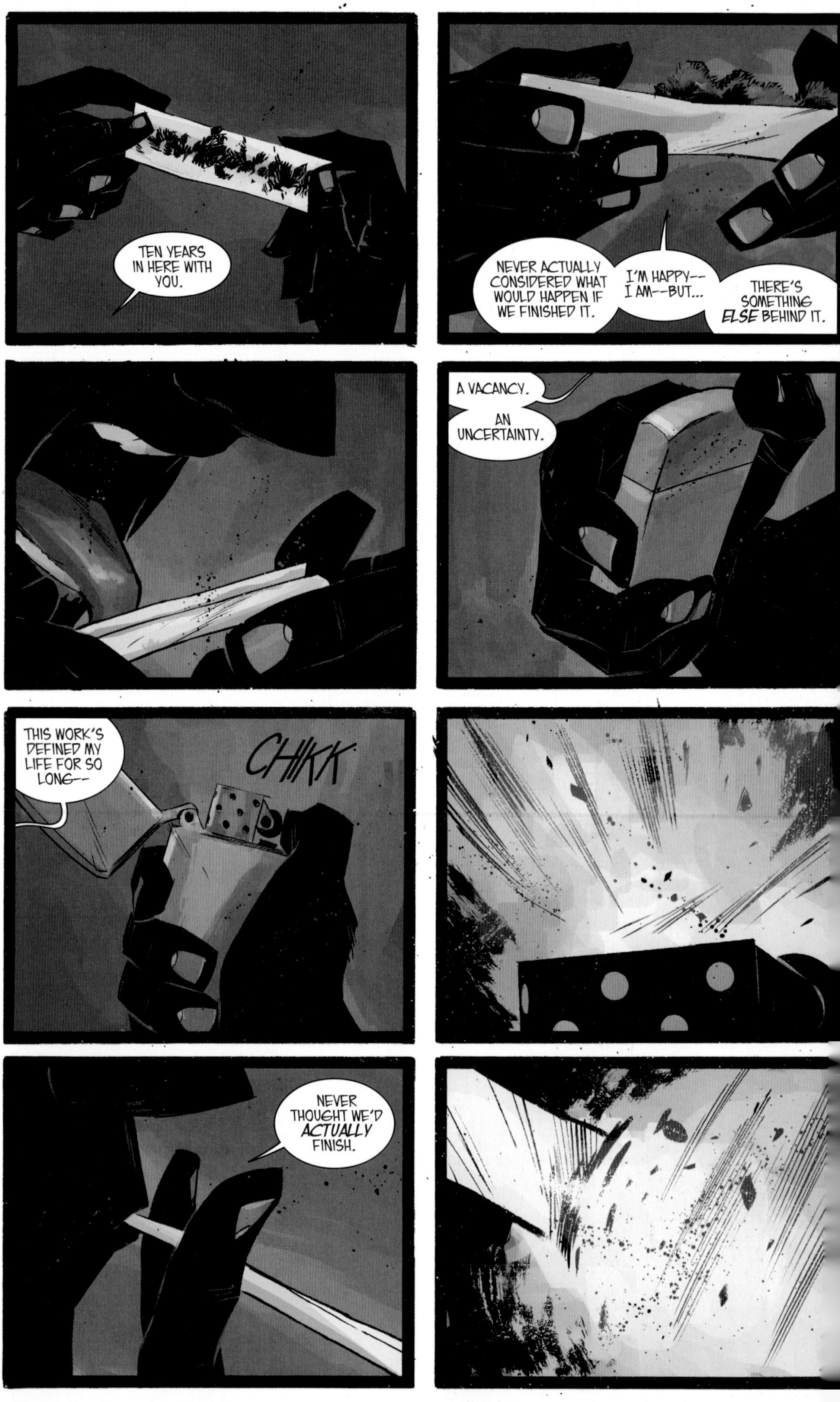
TEN YEARS IN HERE WITH YOU.
NEVER ACTUALLY CONSIDERED WHAT WOULD HAPPEN IF WE FINISHED IT.
I'M HAPPY-- I AM--BUT...
THERE'S SOMETHING ELSE BEHIND IT.
A VACANCY.
AN UNCERTAINTY.
THIS WORK'S DEFINED MY LIFE FOR SO LONG--
CHIKK
NEVER THOUGHT WE'D ACTUALLY FINISH.

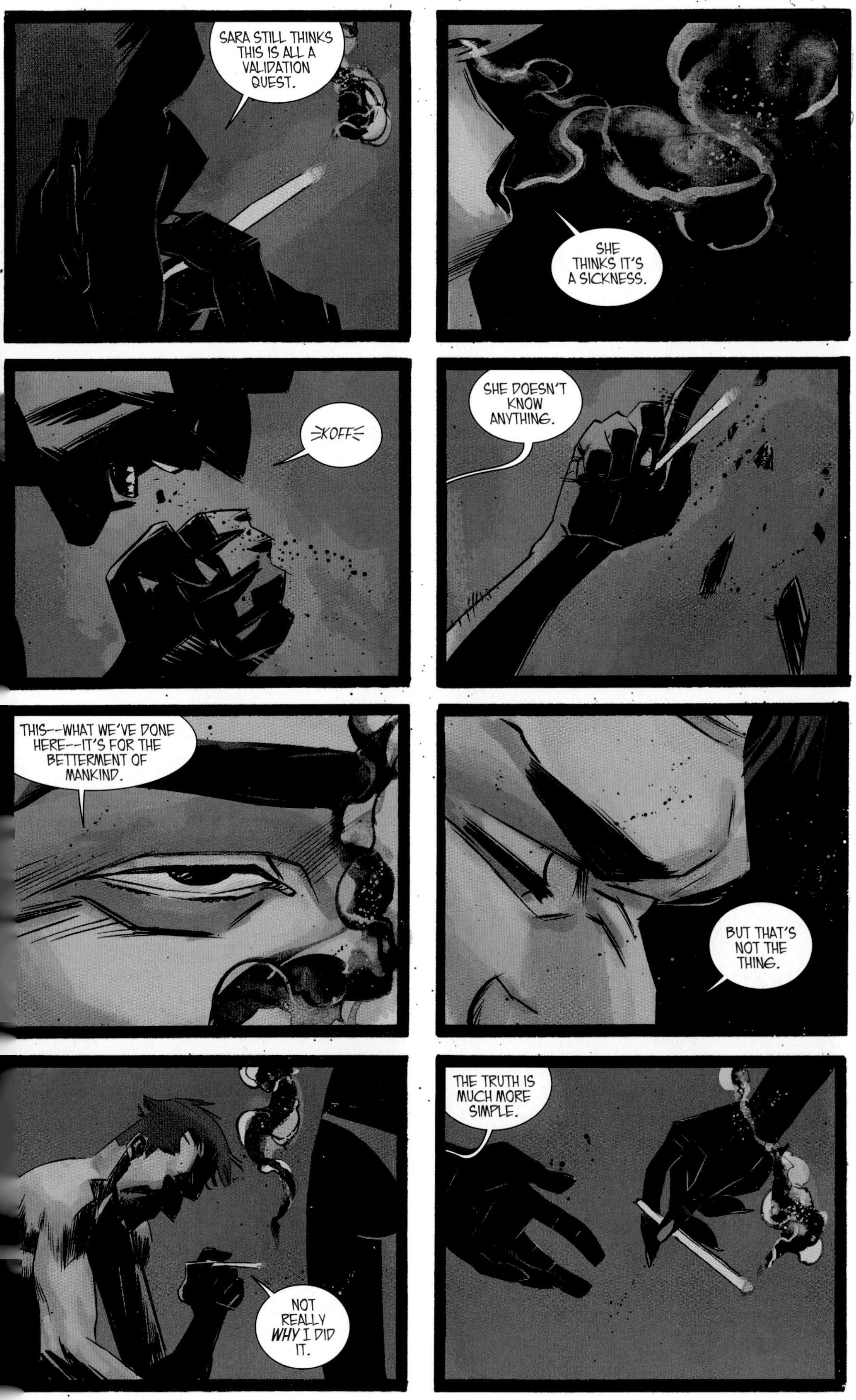
SARA STILL THINKS THIS IS ALL A VALIDATION QUEST.
SHE THINKS IT'S A SICKNESS.
KOFF
SHE DOESN'T KNOW ANYTHING.
THIS--WHAT WE'VE DONE HERE--IT'S FOR THE BETTERMENT OF MANKIND.
BUT THAT'S NOT THE THING.
NOT REALLY WHY I DID IT.
THE TRUTH IS MUCH MORE SIMPLE.

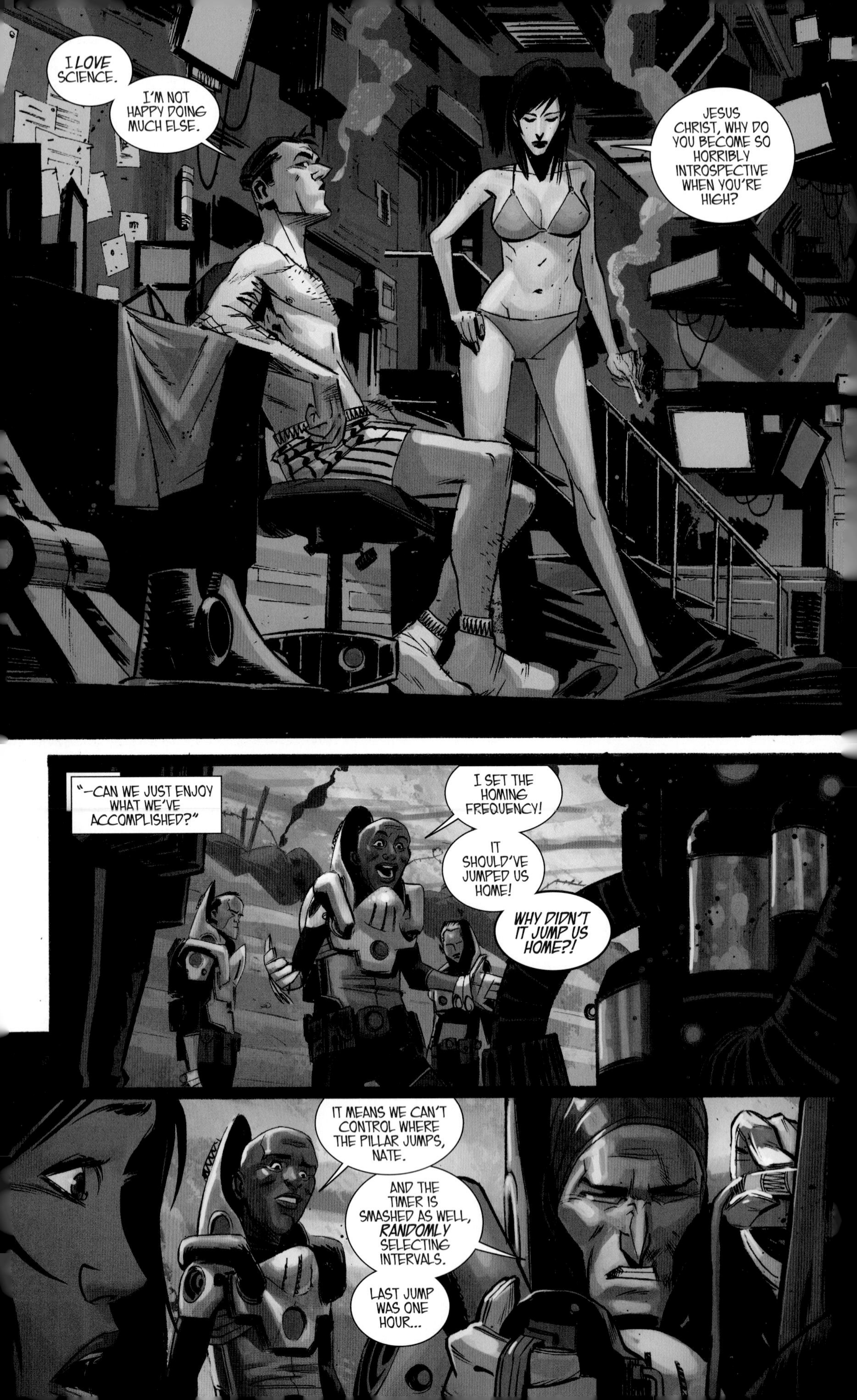
I LOVE SCIENCE.
I'M NOT HAPPY DOING MUCH ELSE.
JESUS CHRIST, WHY DO YOU BECOME SO HORRIBLY INTROSPECTIVE WHEN YOU'RE HIGH?
"--CAN WE JUST ENJOY WHAT WE'VE ACCOMPLISHED?"
I SET THE HOMING FREQUENCY!
IT SHOULD'VE JUMPED US HOME!
WHY DIDN'T IT JUMP US HOME?!
IT MEANS WE CAN'T CONTROL WHERE THE PILLAR JUMPS, NATE.
AND THE TIMER IS SMASHED AS WELL, RANDOMLY SELECTING INTERVALS.
LAST JUMP WAS ONE HOUR...

PLEASE-- JUST THIS ONCE--

BECAUSE SOME *GOD-DAMMED* THING SMASHED THE *HOMING BEACON.*

TOTALLY DESTROYED.

W-WHAT DOES THAT MEAN, DAD?

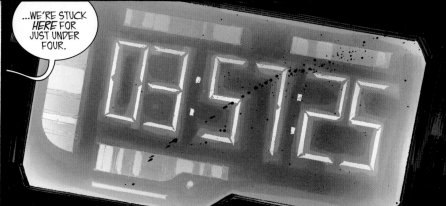

...WE'RE STUCK *HERE* FOR JUST UNDER FOUR.

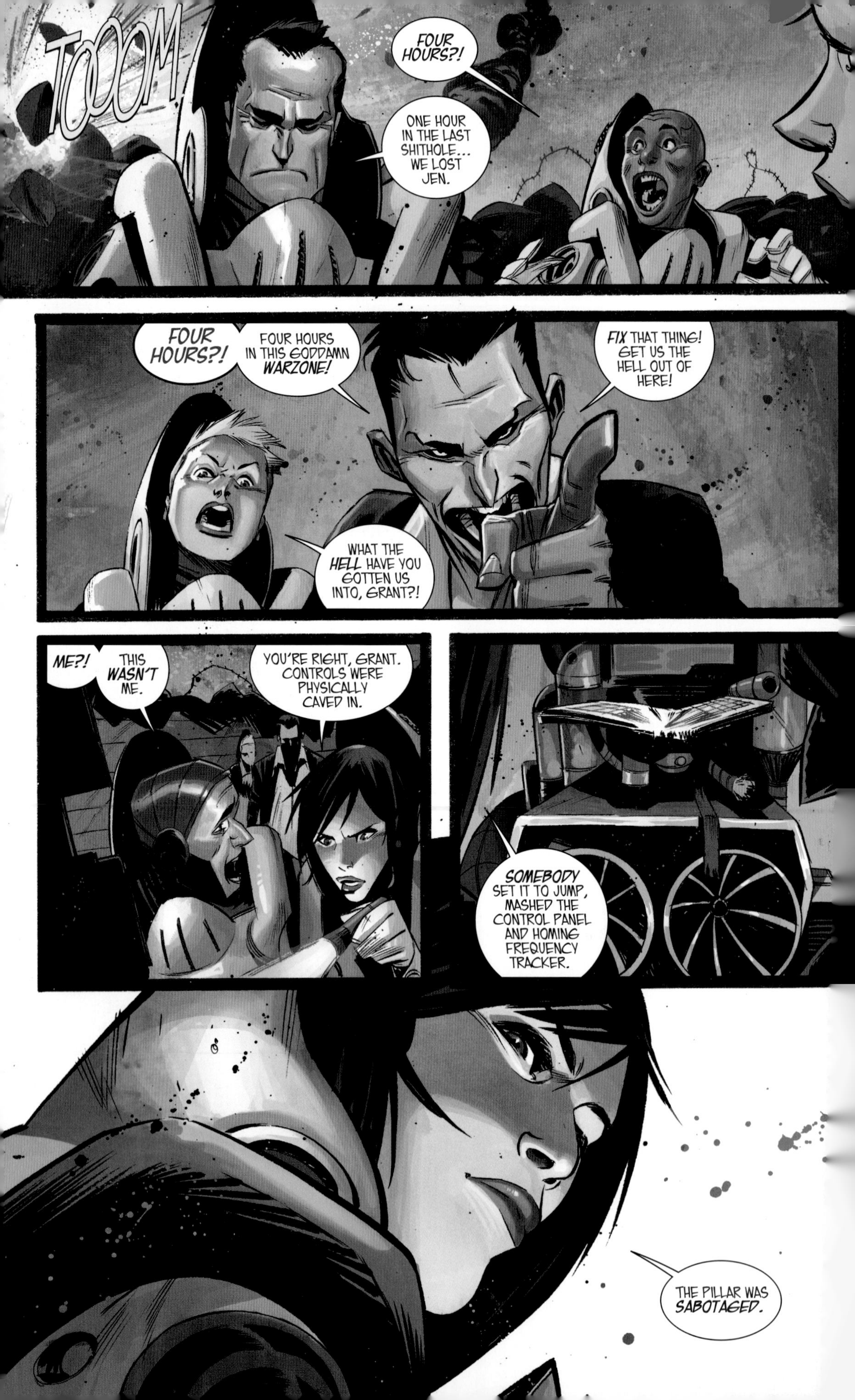
TOOOM
FOUR HOURS?!
ONE HOUR IN THE LAST SHITHOLE... WE LOST JEN.
FOUR HOURS?!
FOUR HOURS IN THIS GODDAMN WARZONE!
FIX THAT THING! GET US THE HELL OUT OF HERE!
WHAT THE HELL HAVE YOU GOTTEN US INTO, GRANT?!
ME?!
THIS WASN'T ME.
YOU'RE RIGHT, GRANT. CONTROLS WERE PHYSICALLY CAVED IN.
SOMEBODY SET IT TO JUMP, MASHED THE CONTROL PANEL AND HOMING FREQUENCY TRACKER.
THE PILLAR WAS SABOTAGED.

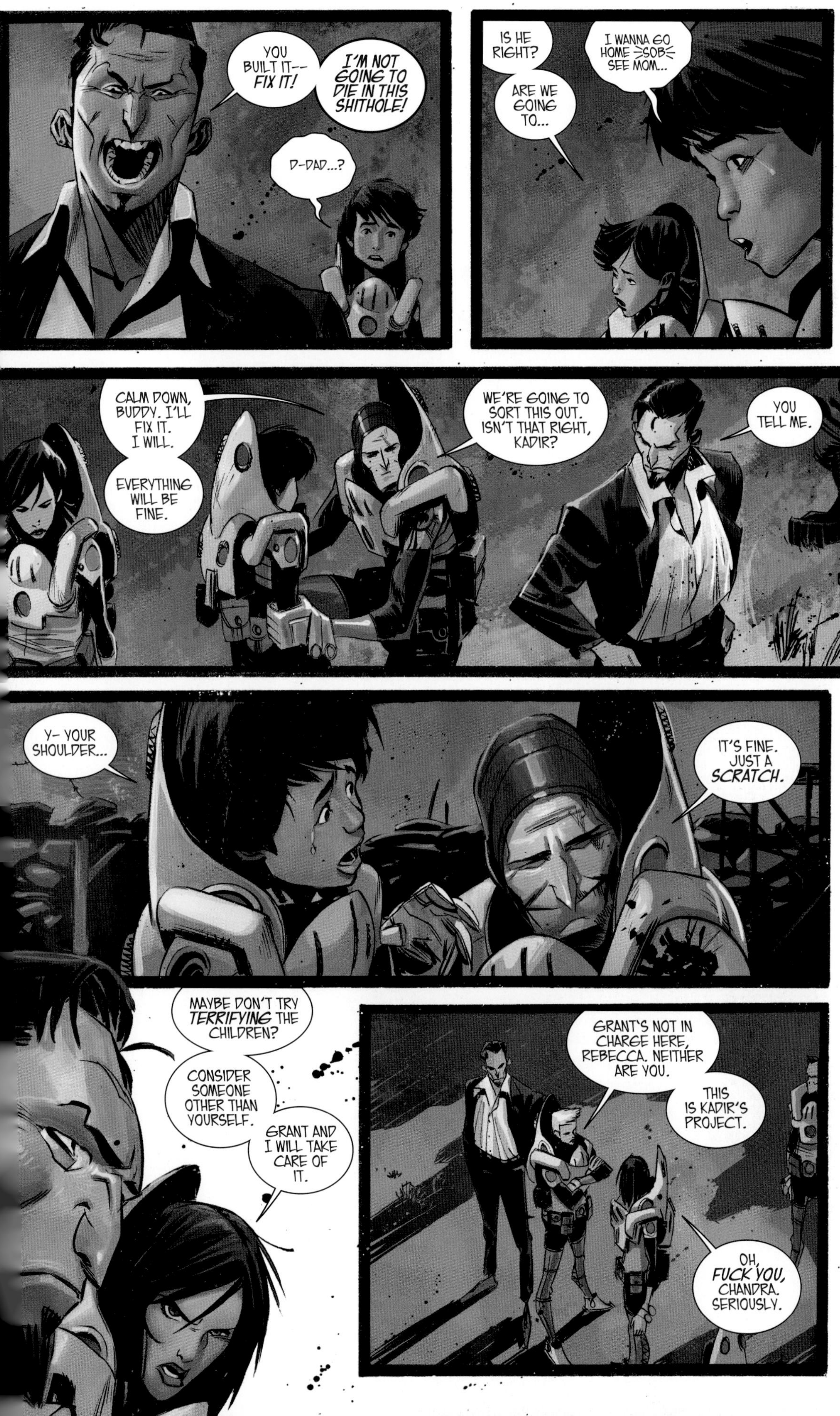
YOU BUILT IT-- FIX IT!
I'M NOT GOING TO DIE IN THIS SHITHOLE!
D-DAD...?
IS HE RIGHT?
ARE WE GOING TO...
I WANNA GO HOME ≥SOB≤ SEE MOM...
CALM DOWN, BUDDY. I'LL FIX IT. I WILL.
EVERYTHING WILL BE FINE.
WE'RE GOING TO SORT THIS OUT. ISN'T THAT RIGHT, KADIR?
YOU TELL ME.
Y- YOUR SHOULDER...
IT'S FINE. JUST A SCRATCH.
MAYBE DON'T TRY TERRIFYING THE CHILDREN?
CONSIDER SOMEONE OTHER THAN YOURSELF.
GRANT AND I WILL TAKE CARE OF IT.
GRANT'S NOT IN CHARGE HERE, REBECCA. NEITHER ARE YOU.
THIS IS KADIR'S PROJECT.
OH, FUCK YOU, CHANDRA. SERIOUSLY.

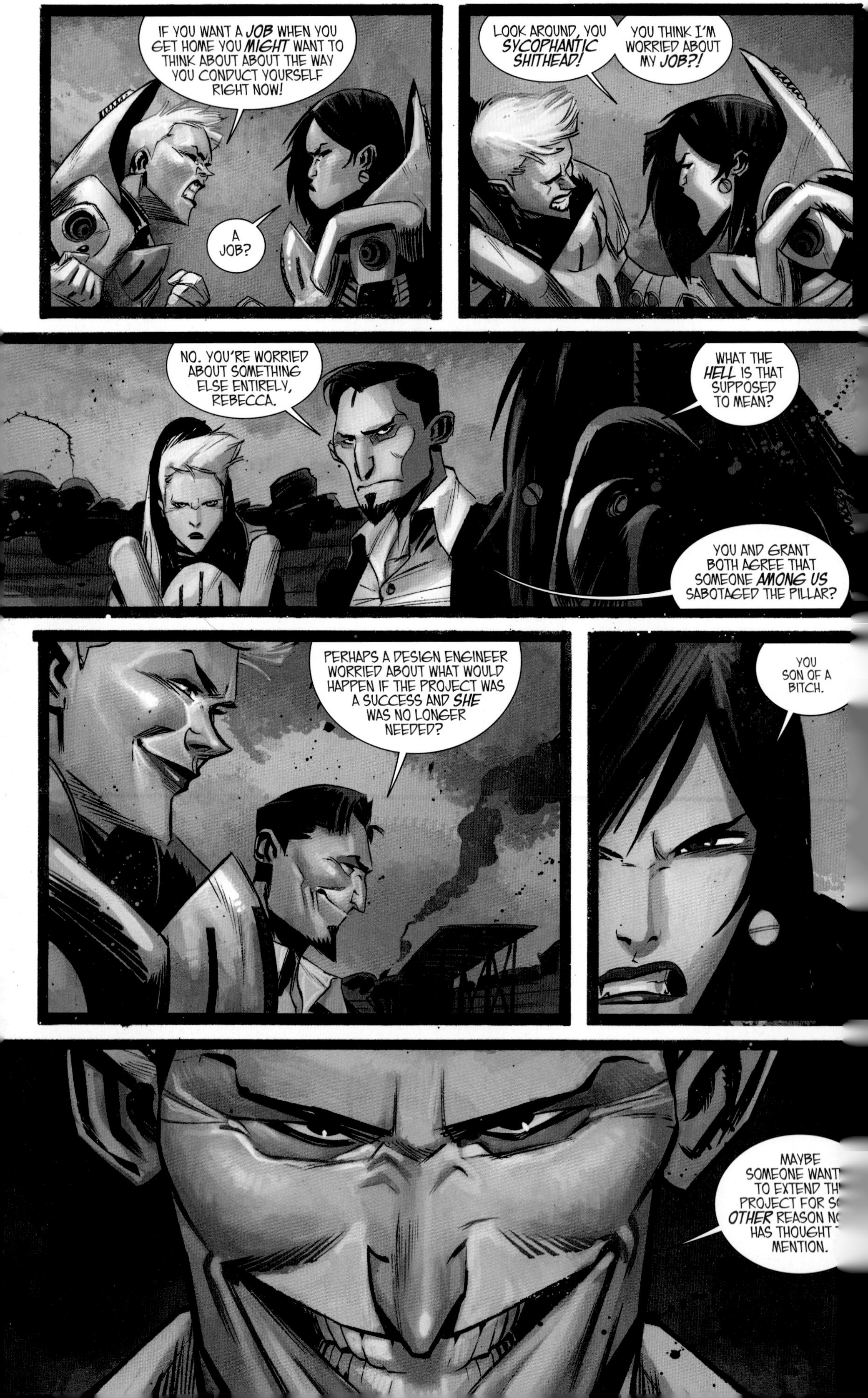

IF YOU WANT A JOB WHEN YOU GET HOME YOU MIGHT WANT TO THINK ABOUT ABOUT THE WAY YOU CONDUCT YOURSELF RIGHT NOW!
A JOB?
LOOK AROUND, YOU SYCOPHANTIC SHITHEAD!
YOU THINK I'M WORRIED ABOUT MY JOB?!
NO. YOU'RE WORRIED ABOUT SOMETHING ELSE ENTIRELY, REBECCA.
WHAT THE HELL IS THAT SUPPOSED TO MEAN?
YOU AND GRANT BOTH AGREE THAT SOMEONE AMONG US SABOTAGED THE PILLAR?
PERHAPS A DESIGN ENGINEER WORRIED ABOUT WHAT WOULD HAPPEN IF THE PROJECT WAS A SUCCESS AND SHE WAS NO LONGER NEEDED?
YOU SON OF A BITCH.
MAYBE SOMEONE WANT TO EXTEND TH PROJECT FOR SO OTHER REASON NO HAS THOUGHT MENTION.

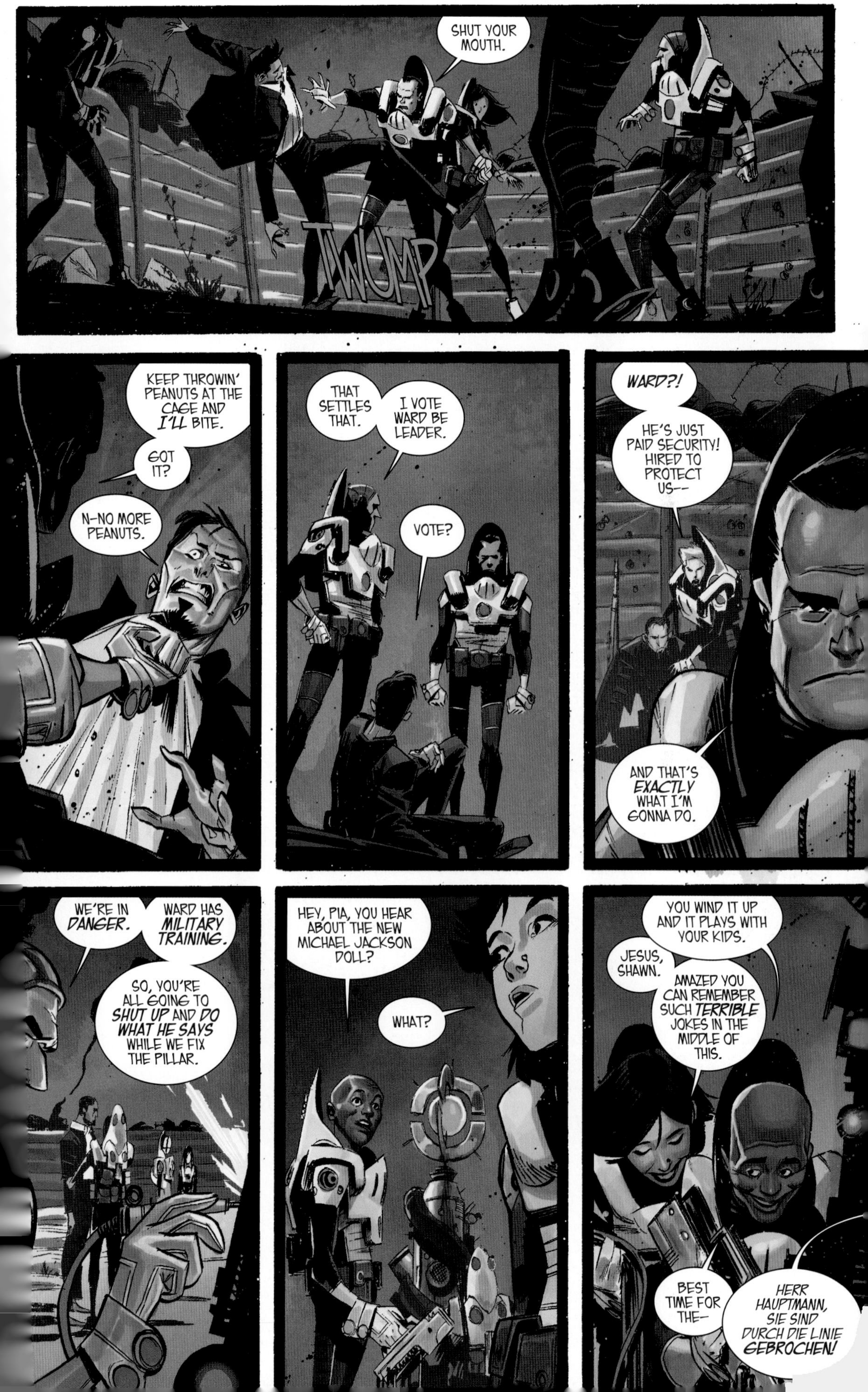
SHUT YOUR MOUTH.
TWUMP
KEEP THROWIN' PEANUTS AT THE CAGE AND I'LL BITE.
GOT IT?
N-NO MORE PEANUTS.
THAT SETTLES THAT.
I VOTE WARD BE LEADER.
VOTE?
WARD?!
HE'S JUST PAID SECURITY! HIRED TO PROTECT US--
AND THAT'S EXACTLY WHAT I'M GONNA DO.
WE'RE IN DANGER.
WARD HAS MILITARY TRAINING.
SO, YOU'RE ALL GOING TO SHUT UP AND DO WHAT HE SAYS WHILE WE FIX THE PILLAR.
HEY, PIA, YOU HEAR ABOUT THE NEW MICHAEL JACKSON DOLL?
WHAT?
YOU WIND IT UP AND IT PLAYS WITH YOUR KIDS.
JESUS, SHAWN.
AMAZED YOU CAN REMEMBER SUCH TERRIBLE JOKES IN THE MIDDLE OF THIS.
BEST TIME FOR THE-
HERR HAUPTMANN, SIE SIND DURCH DIE LINIE GEBROCHEN!

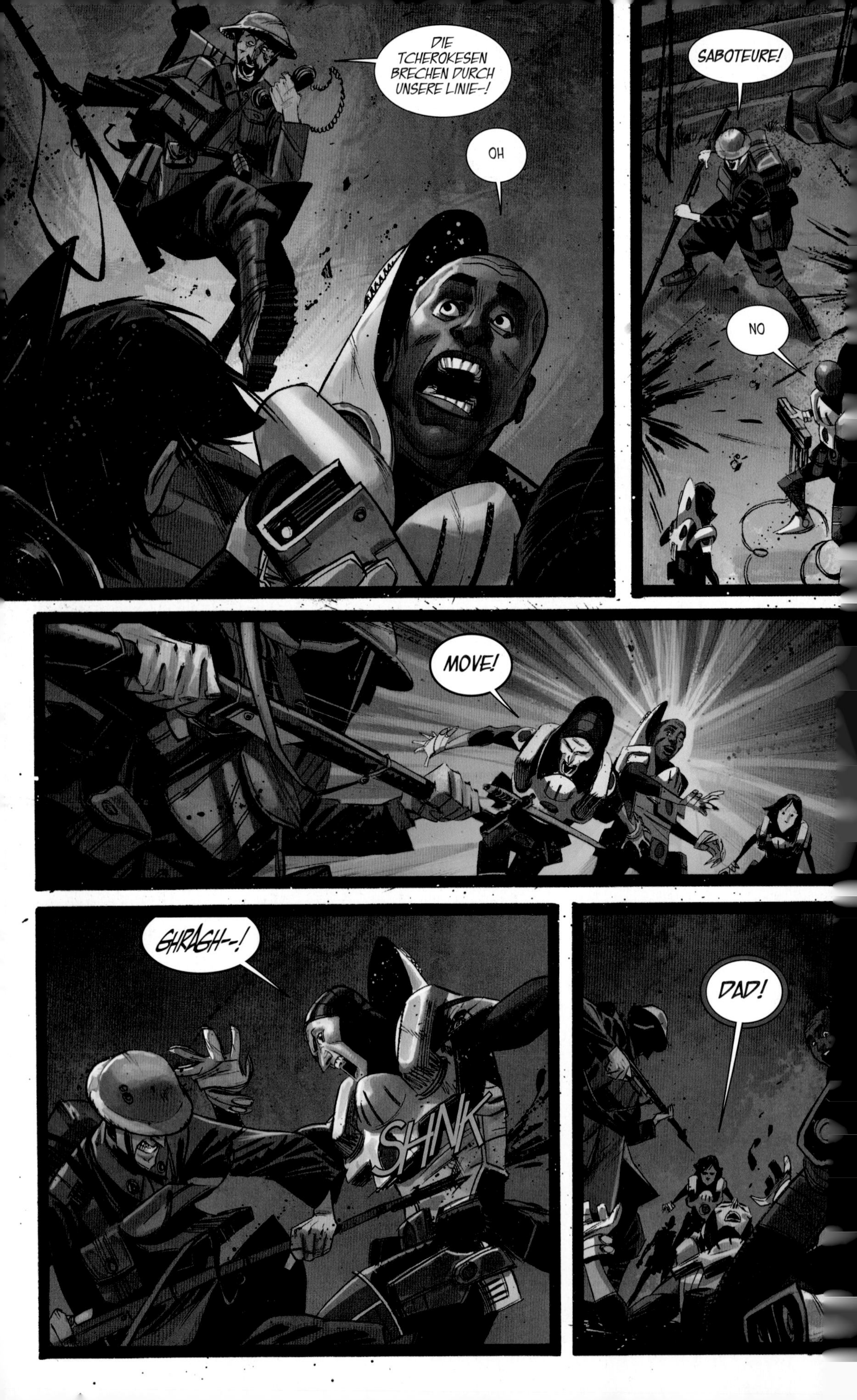
DIE TCHEROKESEN BRECHEN DURCH UNSERE LINIE-!
OH
SABOTEURE!
NO
MOVE!
GHRAGH--!
SHNK
DAD!

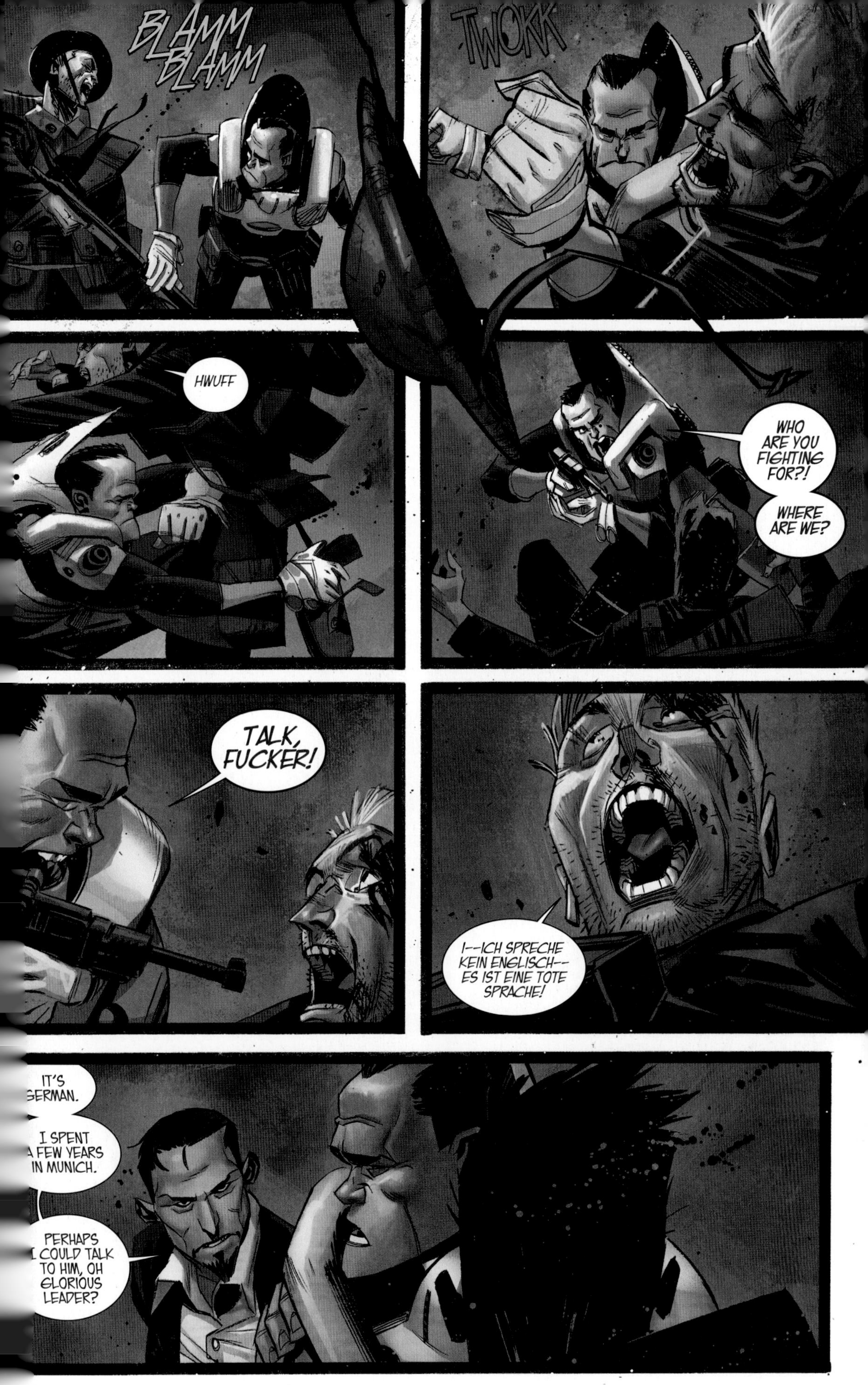
BLAMM BLAMM
TWOKK
HWUFF
WHO ARE YOU FIGHTING FOR?!
WHERE ARE WE?
TALK, FUCKER!
I--ICH SPRECHE KEIN ENGLISCH--ES IST EINE TOTE SPRACHE!
IT'S GERMAN.
I SPENT A FEW YEARS IN MUNICH.
PERHAPS I COULD TALK TO HIM, OH GLORIOUS LEADER?

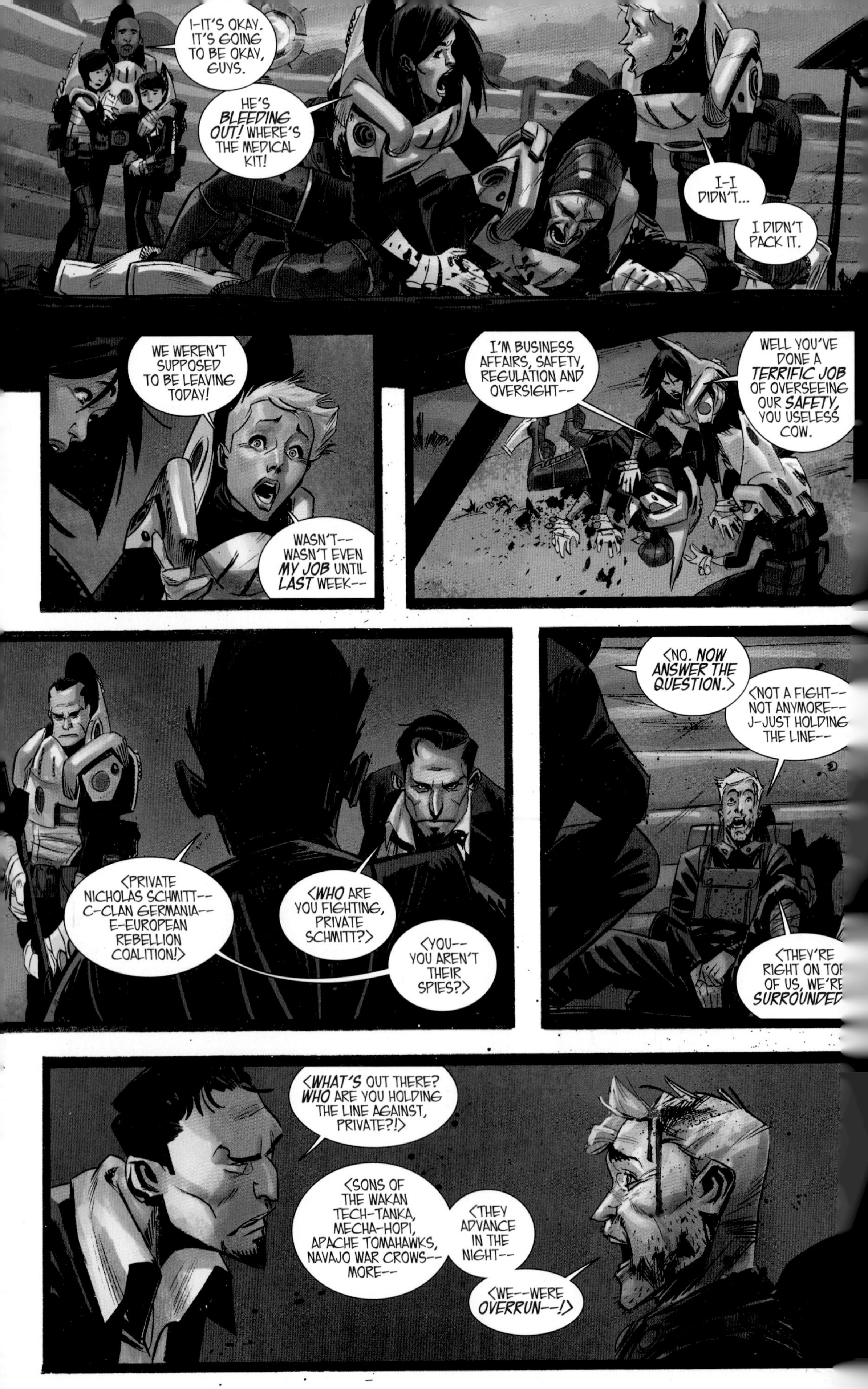
I-IT'S OKAY. IT'S GOING TO BE OKAY, GUYS.
HE'S BLEEDING OUT! WHERE'S THE MEDICAL KIT!
I-I DIDN'T...
I DIDN'T PACK IT.
WE WEREN'T SUPPOSED TO BE LEAVING TODAY!
WASN'T-- WASN'T EVEN MY JOB UNTIL LAST WEEK--
I'M BUSINESS AFFAIRS, SAFETY, REGULATION AND OVERSIGHT--
WELL YOU'VE DONE A TERRIFIC JOB OF OVERSEEING OUR SAFETY, YOU USELESS COW.
<PRIVATE NICHOLAS SCHMITT-- C-CLAN GERMANIA-- E-EUROPEAN REBELLION COALITION!>
<WHO ARE YOU FIGHTING, PRIVATE SCHMITT?>
<YOU-- YOU AREN'T THEIR SPIES?>
<NO. NOW ANSWER THE QUESTION.>
<NOT A FIGHT-- NOT ANYMORE-- J-JUST HOLDING THE LINE--
<THEY'RE RIGHT ON TOP OF US, WE'RE SURROUNDED
<WHAT'S OUT THERE? WHO ARE YOU HOLDING THE LINE AGAINST, PRIVATE?!>
<SONS OF THE WAKAN TECH-TANKA, MECHA-HOPI, APACHE TOMAHAWKS, NAVAJO WAR CROWS-- MORE--
<THEY ADVANCE IN THE NIGHT--
<WE--WERE OVERRUN--!>

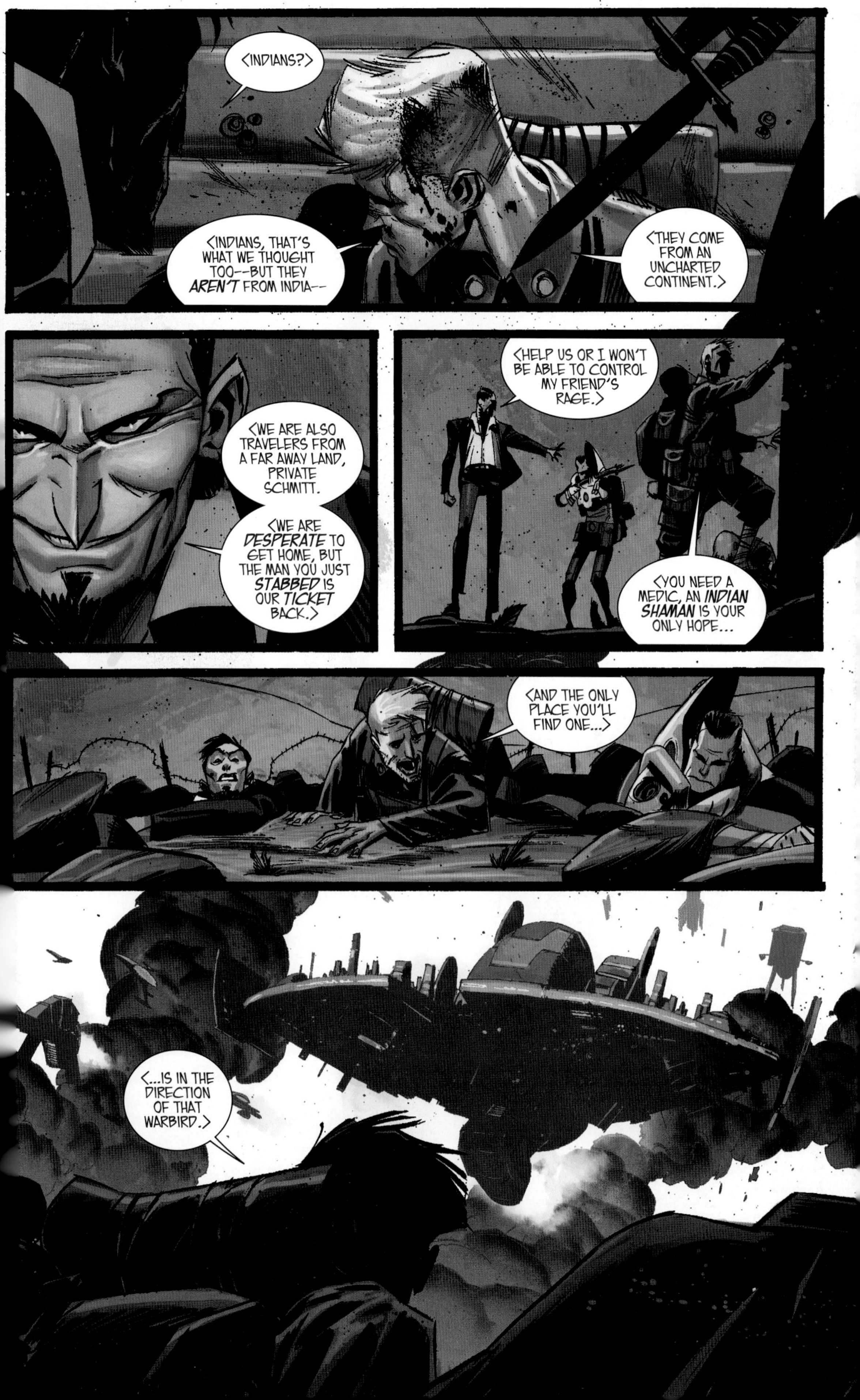
<INDIANS?>
<INDIANS, THAT'S WHAT WE THOUGHT TOO--BUT THEY AREN'T FROM INDIA--
<THEY COME FROM AN UNCHARTED CONTINENT.>
<WE ARE ALSO TRAVELERS FROM A FAR AWAY LAND, PRIVATE SCHMITT.
<WE ARE DESPERATE TO GET HOME, BUT THE MAN YOU JUST STABBED IS OUR TICKET BACK.>
<HELP US OR I WON'T BE ABLE TO CONTROL MY FRIEND'S RAGE.>
<YOU NEED A MEDIC, AN INDIAN SHAMAN IS YOUR ONLY HOPE...
<AND THE ONLY PLACE YOU'LL FIND ONE...>
<...IS IN THE DIRECTION OF THAT WARBIRD.>

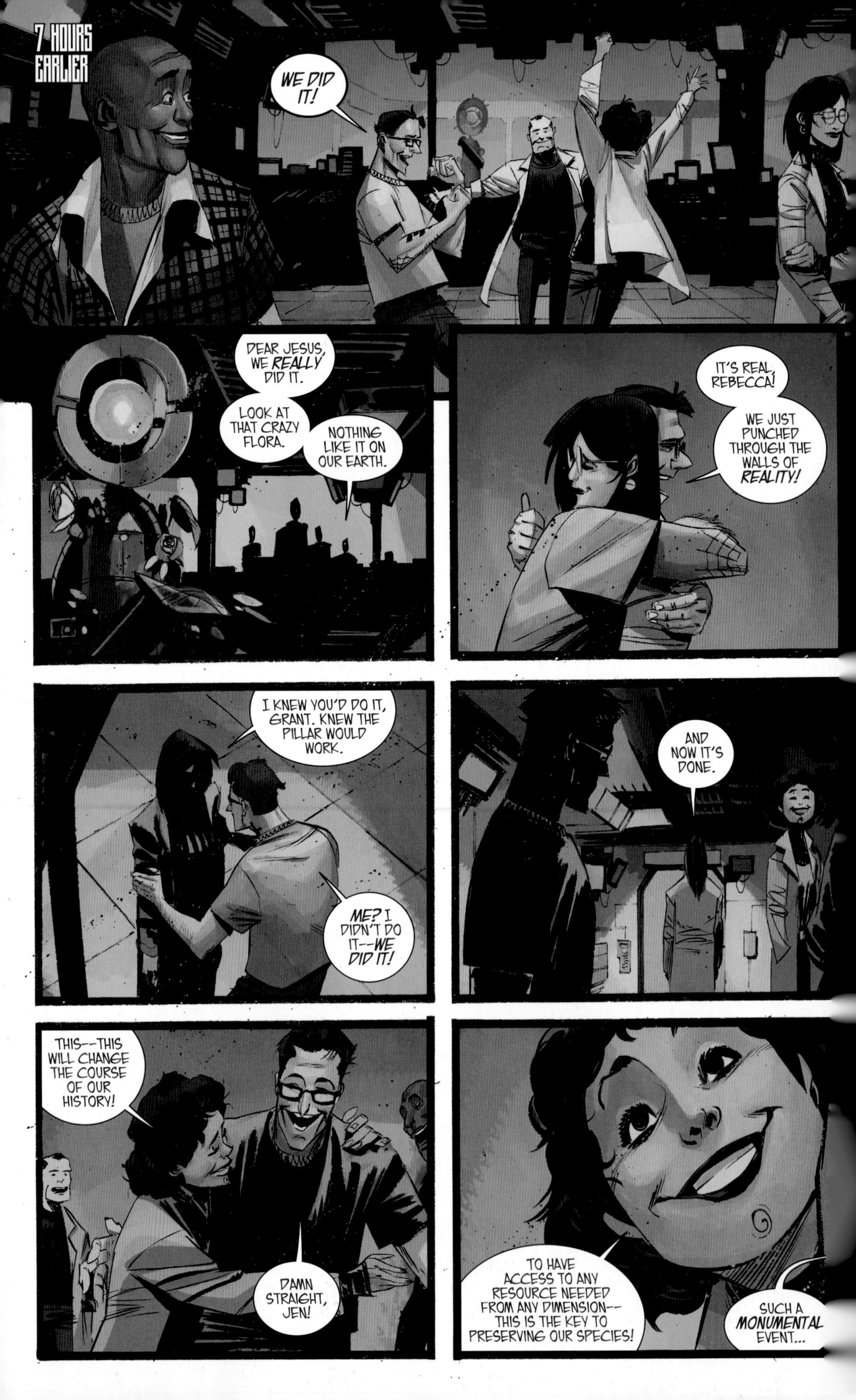

7 HOURS EARLIER
WE DID IT!
DEAR JESUS, WE REALLY DID IT.
LOOK AT THAT CRAZY FLORA.
NOTHING LIKE IT ON OUR EARTH.
IT'S REAL, REBECCA!
WE JUST PUNCHED THROUGH THE WALLS OF REALITY!
I KNEW YOU'D DO IT, GRANT. KNEW THE PILLAR WOULD WORK.
ME? I DIDN'T DO IT--WE DID IT!
AND NOW IT'S DONE.
THIS--THIS WILL CHANGE THE COURSE OF OUR HISTORY!
DAMN STRAIGHT, JEN!
TO HAVE ACCESS TO ANY RESOURCE NEEDED FROM ANY DIMENSION--THIS IS THE KEY TO PRESERVING OUR SPECIES!
SUCH A MONUMENTAL EVENT...

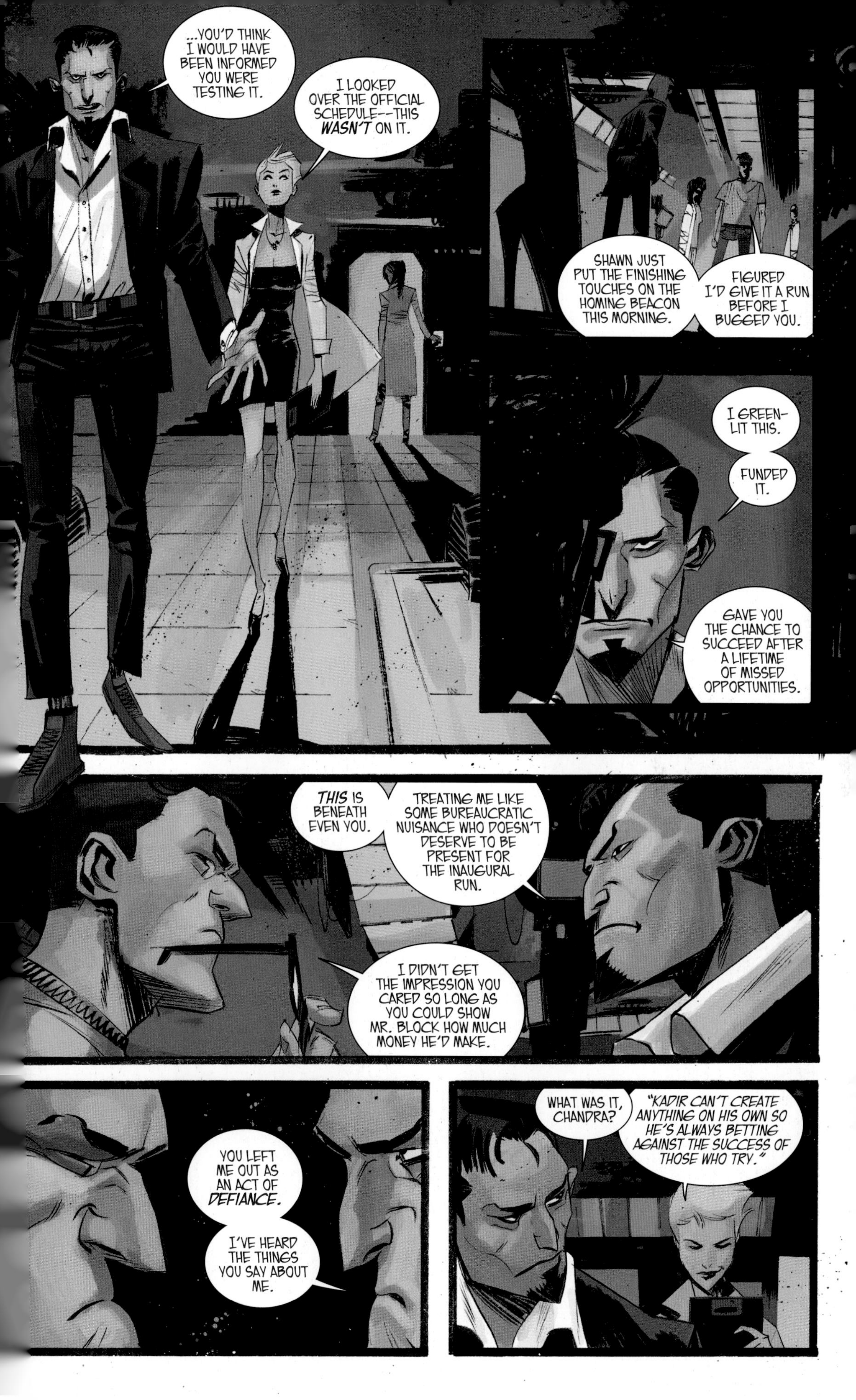
...YOU'D THINK I WOULD HAVE BEEN INFORMED YOU WERE TESTING IT.
I LOOKED OVER THE OFFICIAL SCHEDULE--THIS *WASN'T* ON IT.
SHAWN JUST PUT THE FINISHING TOUCHES ON THE HOMING BEACON THIS MORNING.
FIGURED I'D GIVE IT A RUN BEFORE I BUGGED YOU.
I GREEN-LIT THIS.
FUNDED IT.
GAVE YOU THE CHANCE TO SUCCEED AFTER A LIFETIME OF MISSED OPPORTUNITIES.
THIS IS BENEATH EVEN YOU.
TREATING ME LIKE SOME BUREAUCRATIC NUISANCE WHO DOESN'T DESERVE TO BE PRESENT FOR THE INAUGURAL RUN.
I DIDN'T GET THE IMPRESSION YOU CARED SO LONG AS YOU COULD SHOW MR. BLOCK HOW MUCH MONEY HE'D MAKE.
YOU LEFT ME OUT AS AN ACT OF *DEFIANCE*.
I'VE HEARD THE THINGS YOU SAY ABOUT ME.
WHAT WAS IT, CHANDRA?
"KADIR CAN'T CREATE ANYTHING ON HIS OWN SO HE'S ALWAYS BETTING AGAINST THE SUCCESS OF THOSE WHO TRY."

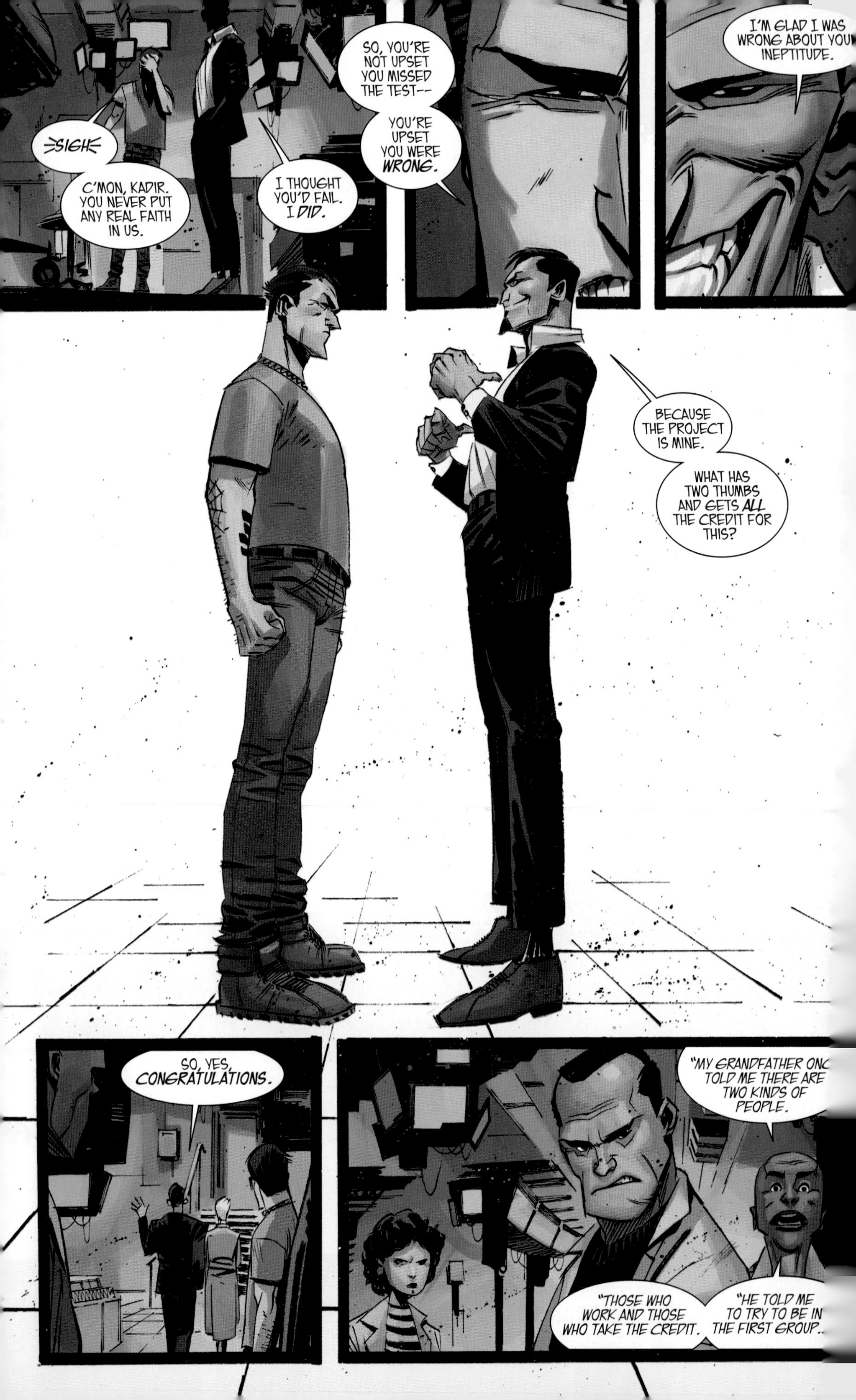
SIGH
C'MON, KADIR. YOU NEVER PUT ANY REAL FAITH IN US.
I THOUGHT YOU'D FAIL. I DID.
SO, YOU'RE NOT UPSET YOU MISSED THE TEST--
YOU'RE UPSET YOU WERE WRONG.
I'M GLAD I WAS WRONG ABOUT YOUR INEPTITUDE.
BECAUSE THE PROJECT IS MINE.
WHAT HAS TWO THUMBS AND GETS ALL THE CREDIT FOR THIS?
SO, YES, CONGRATULATIONS.
"MY GRANDFATHER ONC TOLD ME THERE ARE TWO KINDS OF PEOPLE.
"THOSE WHO WORK AND THOSE WHO TAKE THE CREDIT.
"HE TOLD ME TO TRY TO BE IN THE FIRST GROUP...

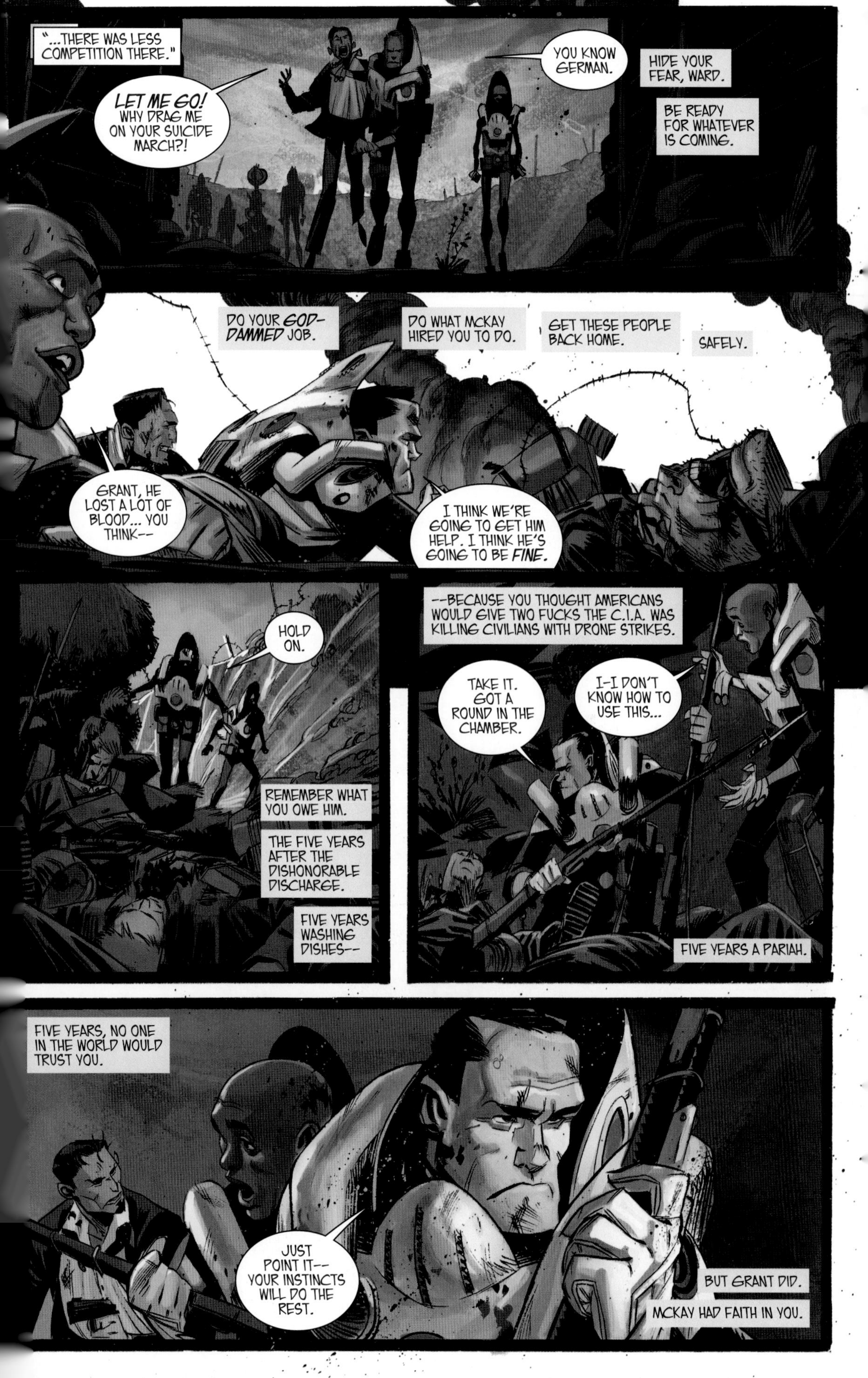
"...THERE WAS LESS COMPETITION THERE."
LET ME GO! WHY DRAG ME ON YOUR SUICIDE MARCH?!
YOU KNOW GERMAN.
HIDE YOUR FEAR, WARD.
BE READY FOR WHATEVER IS COMING.
DO YOUR GOD-DAMMED JOB.
DO WHAT MCKAY HIRED YOU TO DO.
GET THESE PEOPLE BACK HOME.
SAFELY.
GRANT, HE LOST A LOT OF BLOOD... YOU THINK--
I THINK WE'RE GOING TO GET HIM HELP. I THINK HE'S GOING TO BE FINE.
HOLD ON.
REMEMBER WHAT YOU OWE HIM.
THE FIVE YEARS AFTER THE DISHONORABLE DISCHARGE.
FIVE YEARS WASHING DISHES--
--BECAUSE YOU THOUGHT AMERICANS WOULD GIVE TWO FUCKS THE C.I.A. WAS KILLING CIVILIANS WITH DRONE STRIKES.
TAKE IT. GOT A ROUND IN THE CHAMBER.
I-I DON'T KNOW HOW TO USE THIS...
FIVE YEARS A PARIAH.
FIVE YEARS, NO ONE IN THE WORLD WOULD TRUST YOU.
JUST POINT IT-- YOUR INSTINCTS WILL DO THE REST.
BUT GRANT DID.
MCKAY HAD FAITH IN YOU.

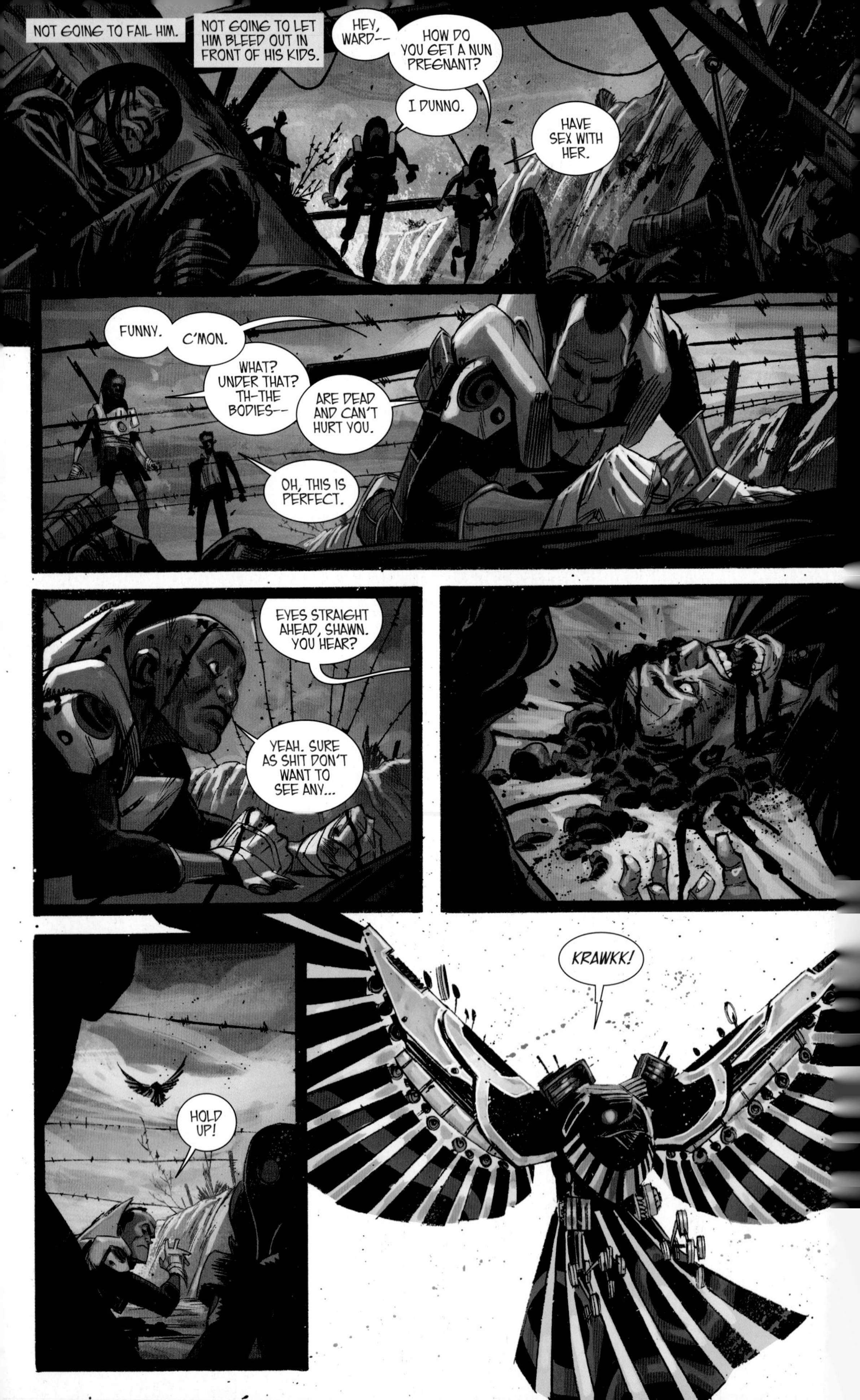
NOT GOING TO FAIL HIM.
NOT GOING TO LET HIM BLEED OUT IN FRONT OF HIS KIDS.
HEY, WARD--
HOW DO YOU GET A NUN PREGNANT?
I DUNNO.
HAVE SEX WITH HER.
FUNNY.
C'MON.
WHAT? UNDER THAT? TH-THE BODIES--
ARE DEAD AND CAN'T HURT YOU.
OH, THIS IS PERFECT.
EYES STRAIGHT AHEAD, SHAWN. YOU HEAR?
YEAH. SURE AS SHIT DON'T WANT TO SEE ANY...
HOLD UP!
KRAWKK!

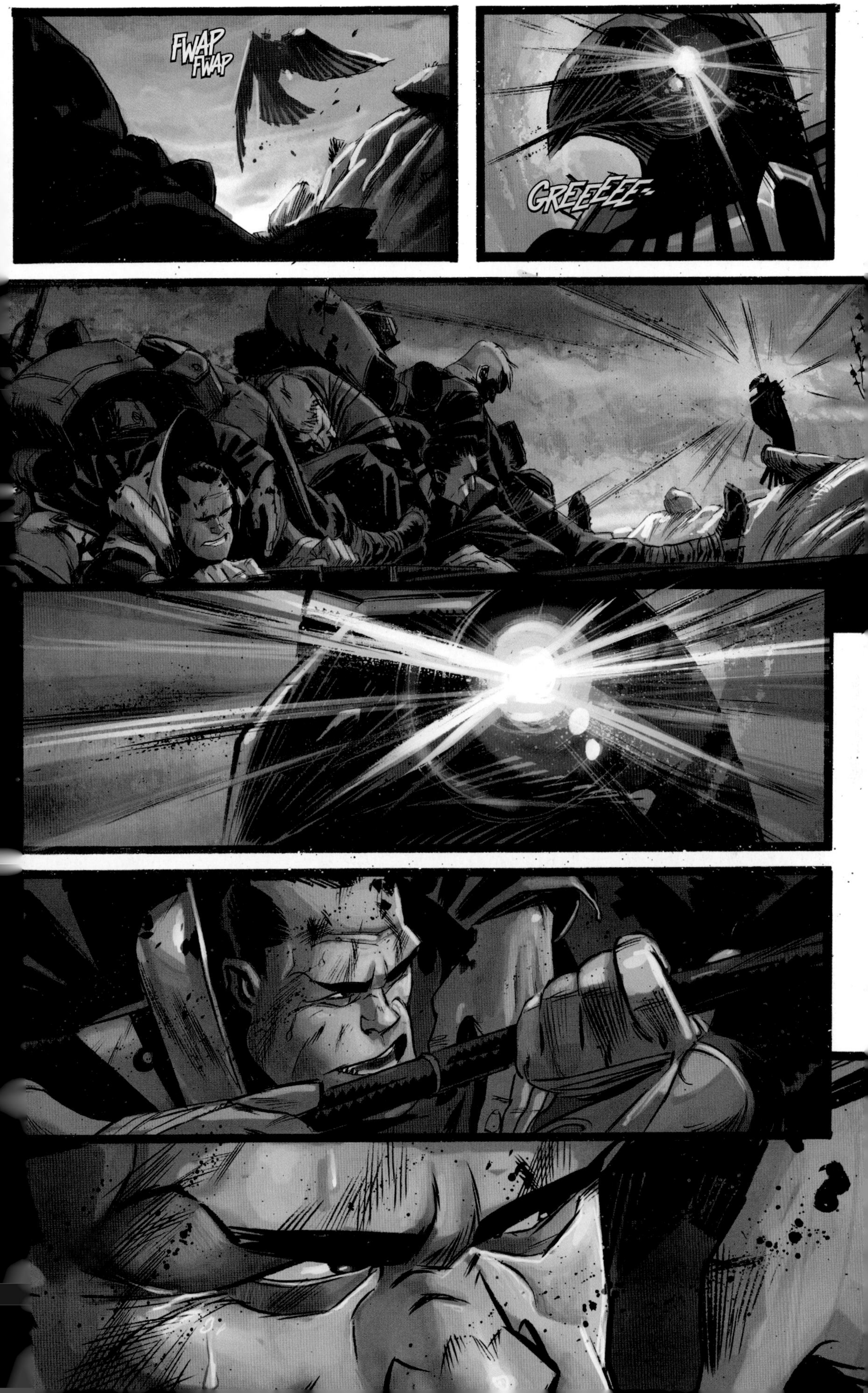
FWAP FWAP
GREEEEEE

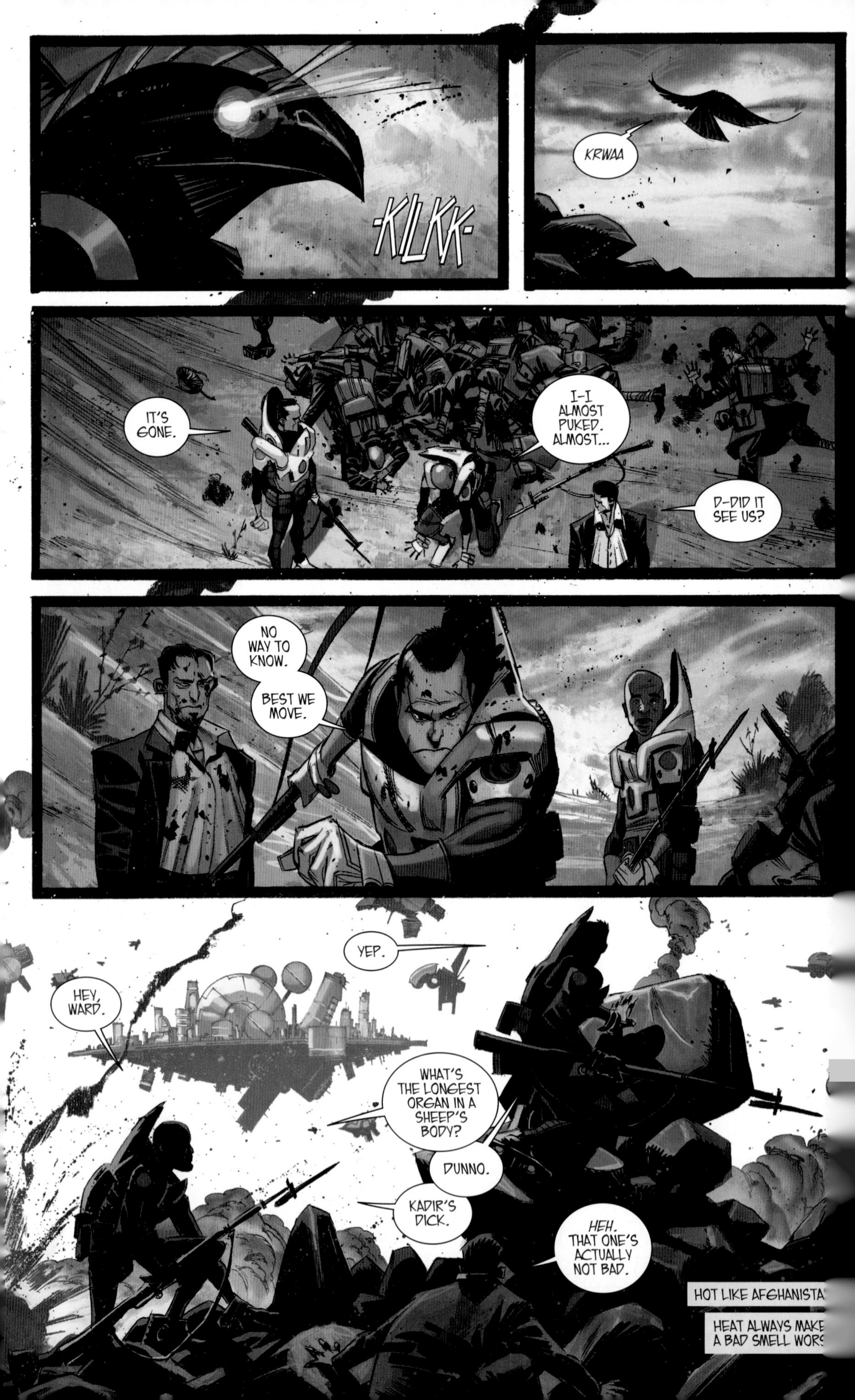
-KLKK-
KRWAA
IT'S GONE.
I-I ALMOST PUKED. ALMOST...
D-DID IT SEE US?
NO WAY TO KNOW.
BEST WE MOVE.
HEY, WARD.
YEP.
WHAT'S THE LONGEST ORGAN IN A SHEEP'S BODY?
DUNNO.
KADIR'S DICK.
HEH. THAT ONE'S ACTUALLY NOT BAD.
HOT LIKE AFGHANISTA
HEAT ALWAYS MAKE
A BAD SMELL WORS

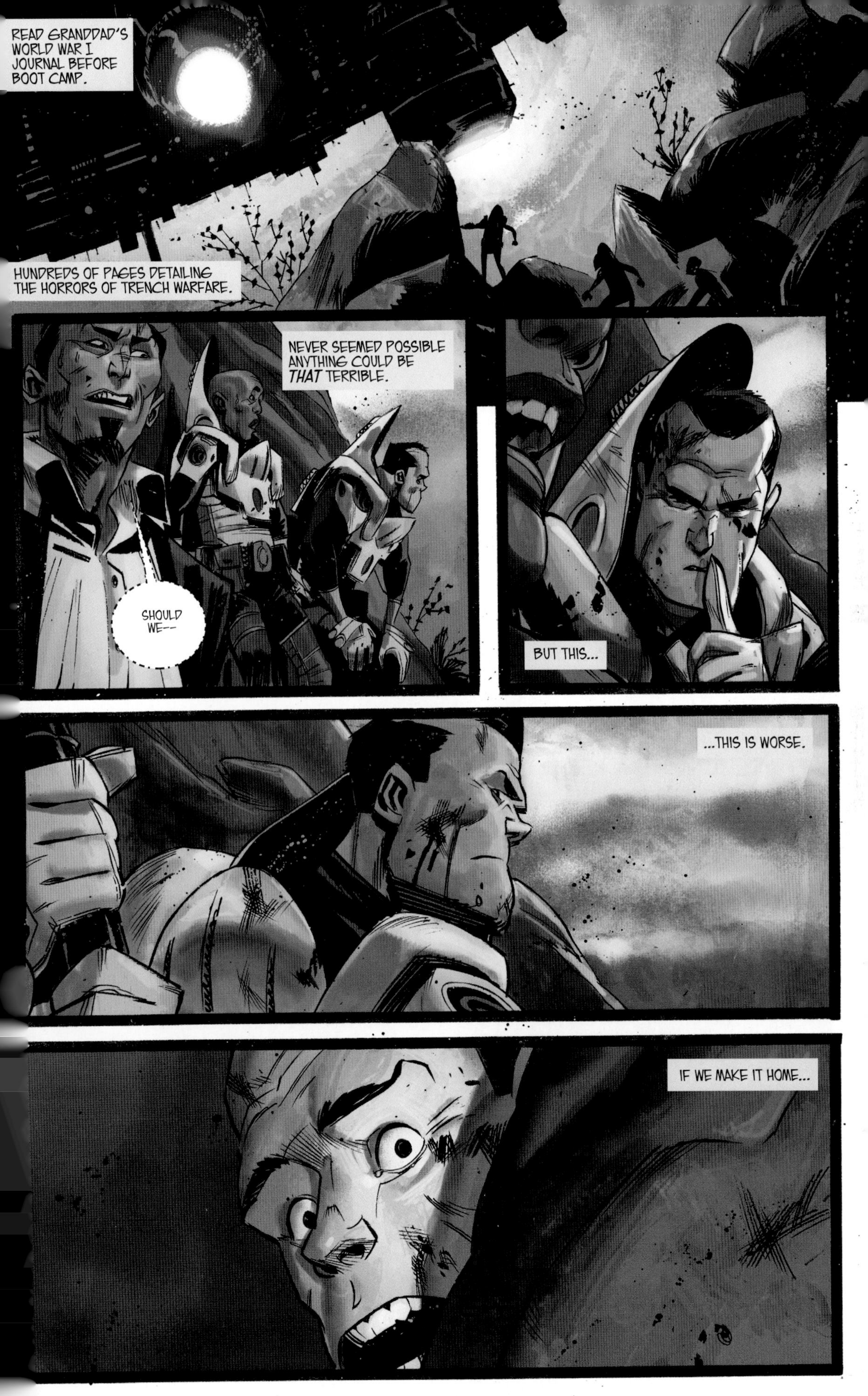
READ GRANDDAD'S WORLD WAR I JOURNAL BEFORE BOOT CAMP.
HUNDREDS OF PAGES DETAILING THE HORRORS OF TRENCH WARFARE.
NEVER SEEMED POSSIBLE ANYTHING COULD BE *THAT* TERRIBLE.
SHOULD WE--
BUT THIS...
...THIS IS WORSE.
IF WE MAKE IT HOME...

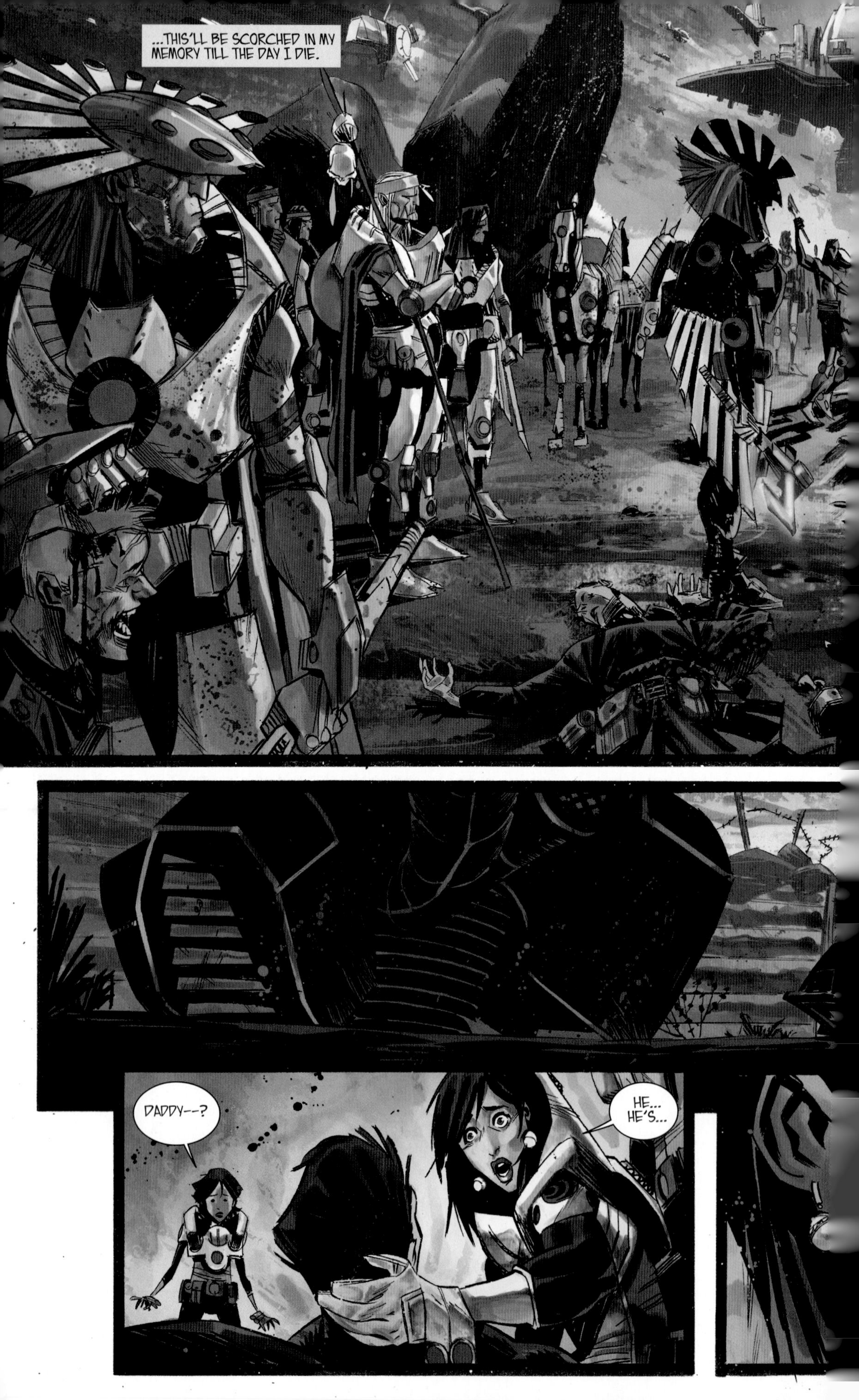
...THIS'LL BE SCORCHED IN MY MEMORY TILL THE DAY I DIE.
DADDY--?
HE... HE'S...

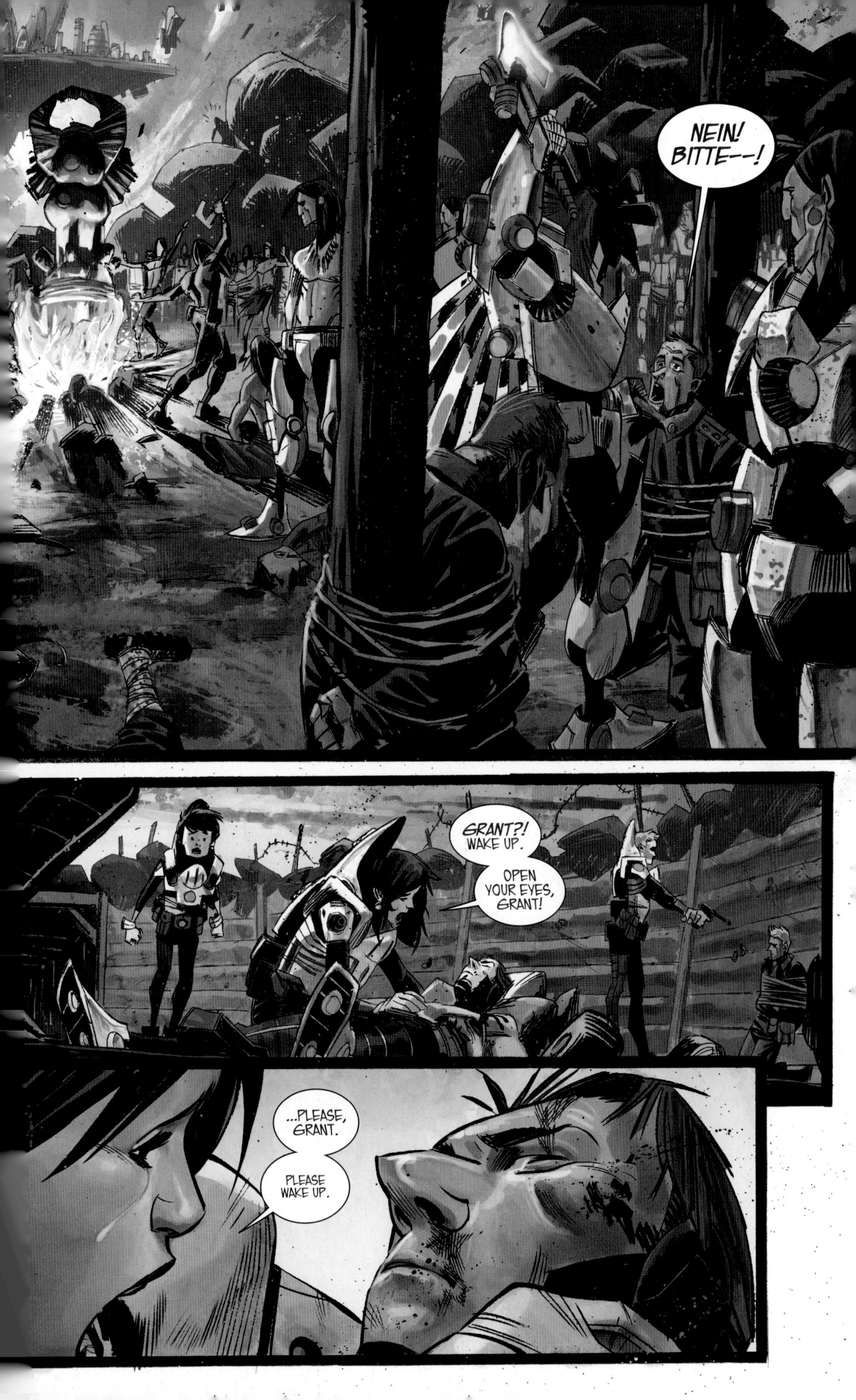
NEIN! BITTE--!
GRANT?! WAKE UP.
OPEN YOUR EYES, GRANT!
...PLEASE, GRANT.
PLEASE WAKE UP.

3

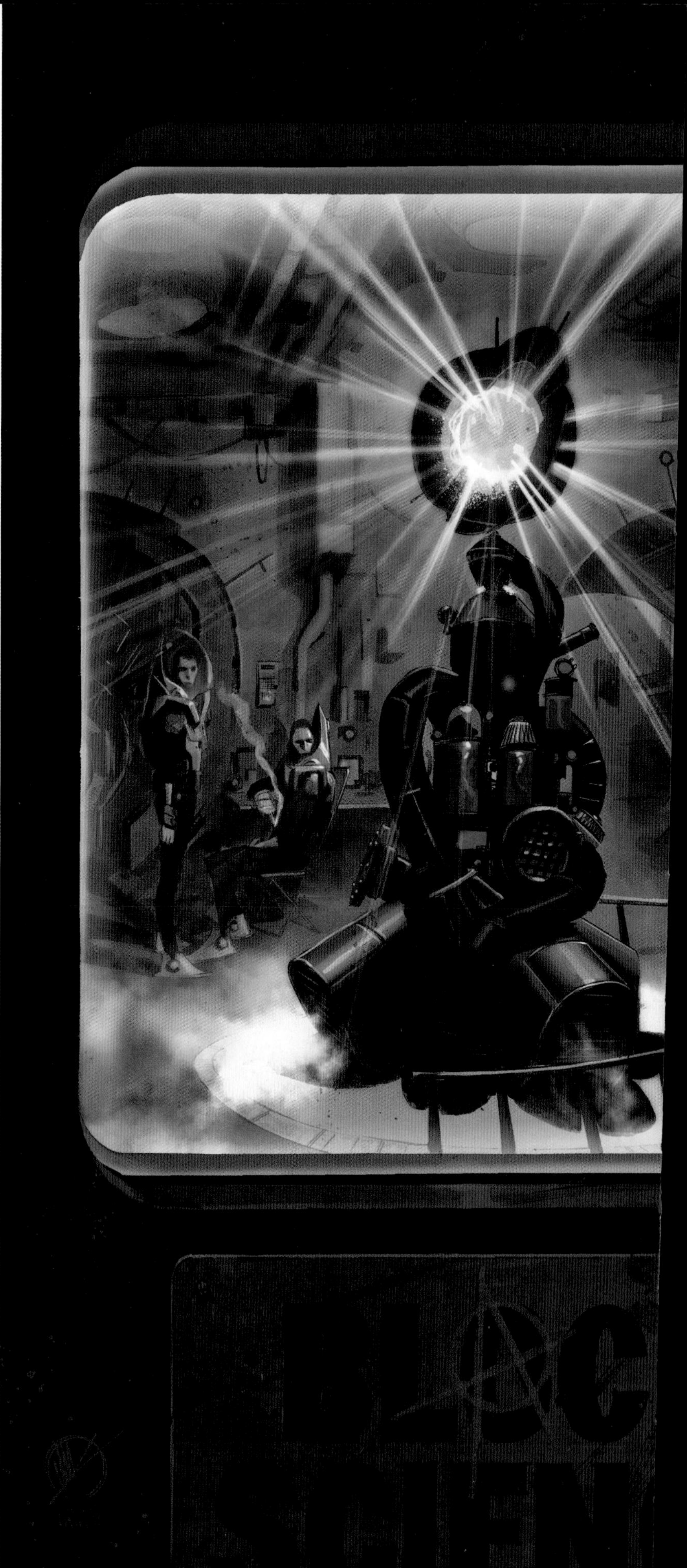

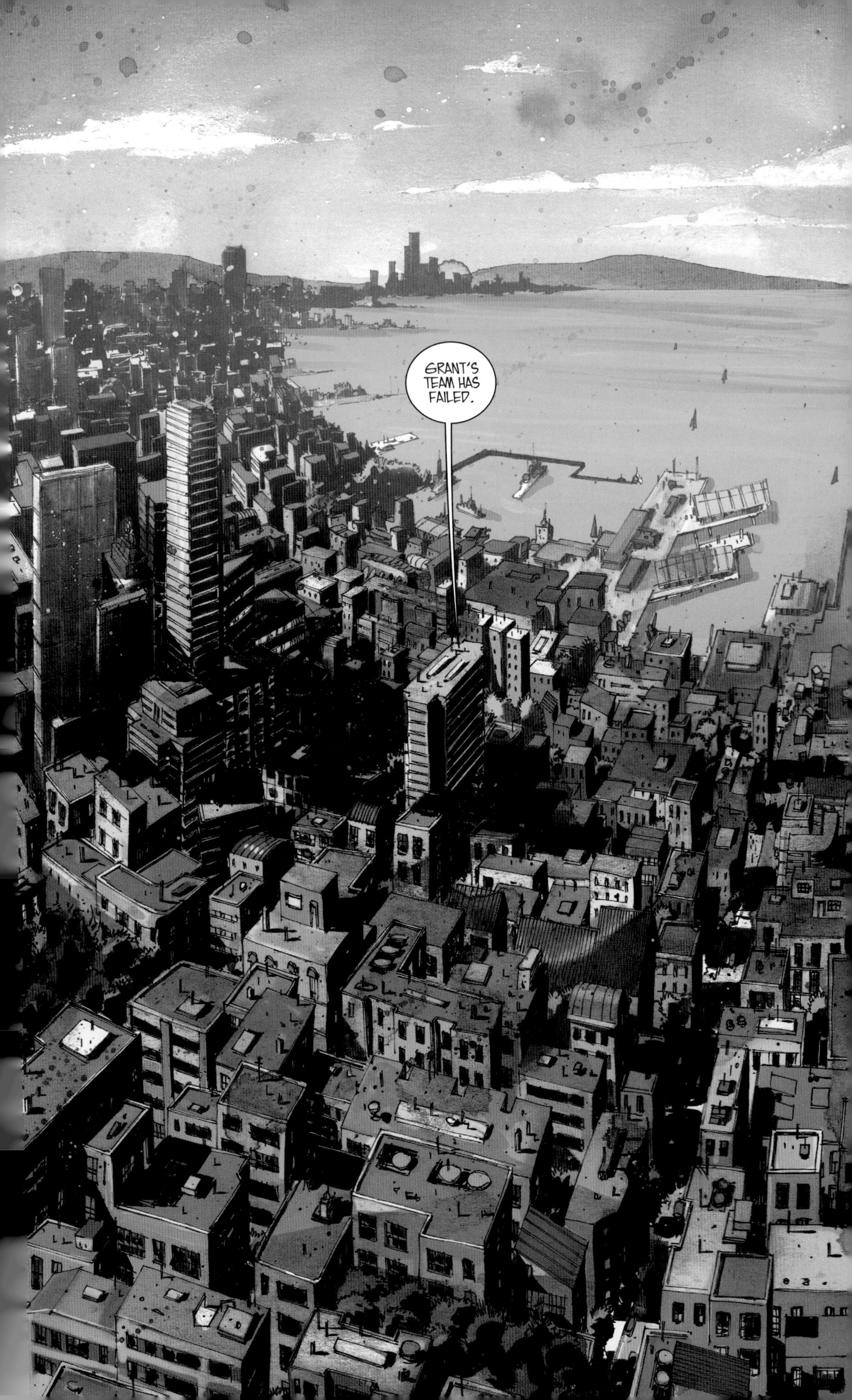
GRANT'S TEAM HAS FAILED.

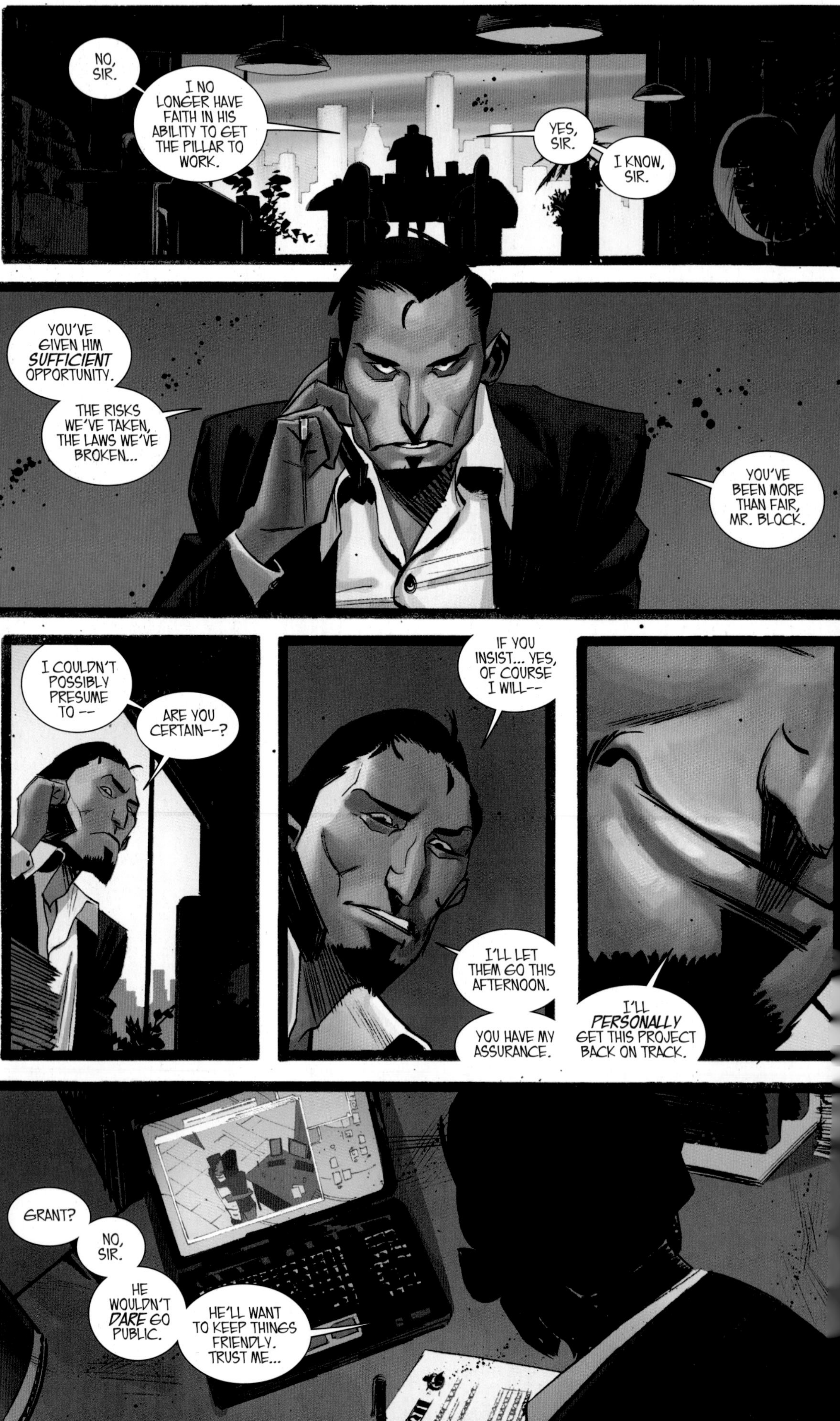
NO, SIR.
I NO LONGER HAVE FAITH IN HIS ABILITY TO GET THE PILLAR TO WORK.
YES, SIR.
I KNOW, SIR.
YOU'VE GIVEN HIM SUFFICIENT OPPORTUNITY.
THE RISKS WE'VE TAKEN, THE LAWS WE'VE BROKEN...
YOU'VE BEEN MORE THAN FAIR, MR. BLOCK.
I COULDN'T POSSIBLY PRESUME TO --
ARE YOU CERTAIN--?
IF YOU INSIST... YES, OF COURSE I WILL--
I'LL LET THEM GO THIS AFTERNOON.
YOU HAVE MY ASSURANCE.
I'LL PERSONALLY GET THIS PROJECT BACK ON TRACK.
GRANT?
NO, SIR.
HE WOULDN'T DARE GO PUBLIC.
HE'LL WANT TO KEEP THINGS FRIENDLY. TRUST ME...

"...I'VE GOT LEVERAGE ON MR. MCKAY."

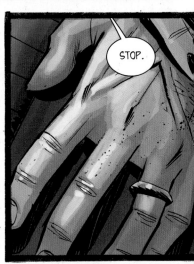

STOP.

YOUR WEDDING BAND IS A *REAL* MOOD KILLER.

IT'S JUST A PIECE OF METAL.

THAT YOU REFUSE TO TAKE OFF.

I HAVE TO KEEP UP APPEARANCES FOR MY--

DON'T.

DON'T YOU *DARE* BLAME IT ON YOUR KIDS.

JESUS.

YOU KNOW THE WORST PART OF THE LYING, AND SNEAKING, GRANT?

I THINK YOU LIKE IT.

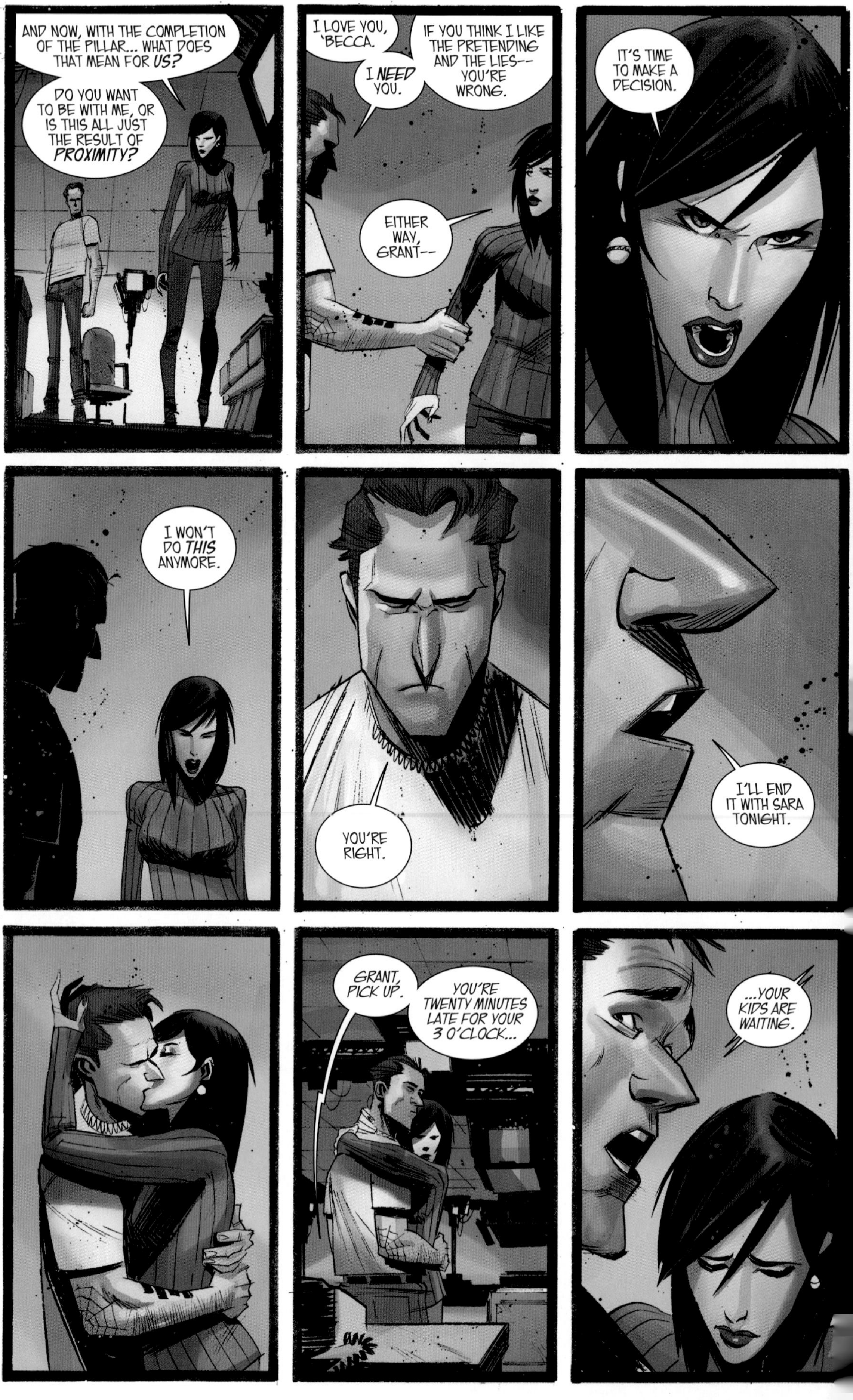
AND NOW, WITH THE COMPLETION OF THE PILLAR... WHAT DOES THAT MEAN FOR US?
DO YOU WANT TO BE WITH ME, OR IS THIS ALL JUST THE RESULT OF PROXIMITY?
I LOVE YOU, 'BECCA.
I NEED YOU.
IF YOU THINK I LIKE THE PRETENDING AND THE LIES-- YOU'RE WRONG.
EITHER WAY, GRANT--
IT'S TIME TO MAKE A DECISION.
I WON'T DO THIS ANYMORE.
YOU'RE RIGHT.
I'LL END IT WITH SARA TONIGHT.
GRANT, PICK UP.
YOU'RE TWENTY MINUTES LATE FOR YOUR 3 O'CLOCK...
...YOUR KIDS ARE WAITING.

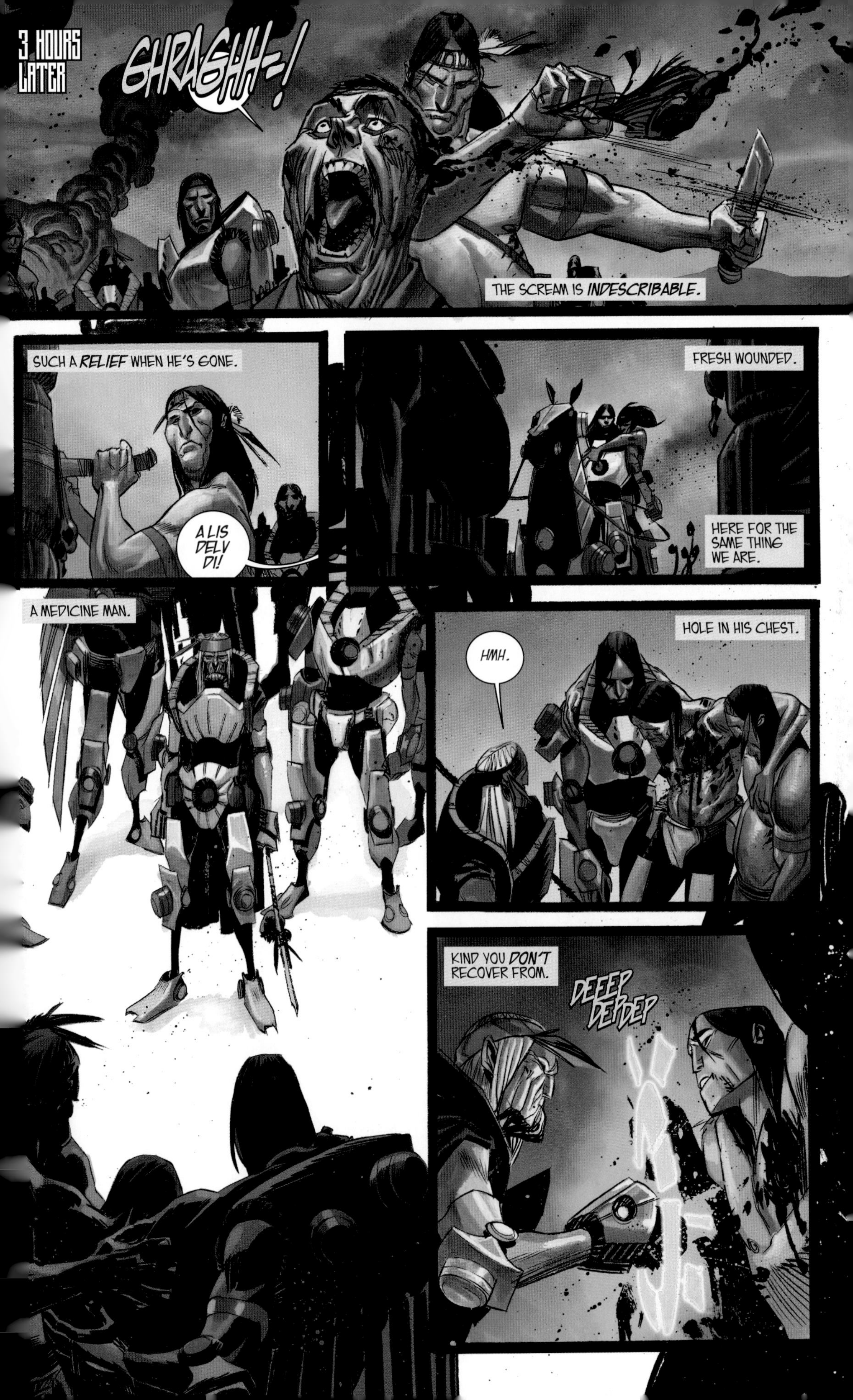
3 HOURS LATER
GHRAGHH-!
THE SCREAM IS INDESCRIBABLE.
SUCH A RELIEF WHEN HE'S GONE.
A LIS DELV DI!
FRESH WOUNDED.
HERE FOR THE SAME THING WE ARE.
A MEDICINE MAN.
HOLE IN HIS CHEST.
HMH.
KIND YOU DON'T RECOVER FROM.
DEEEP DEPDEP

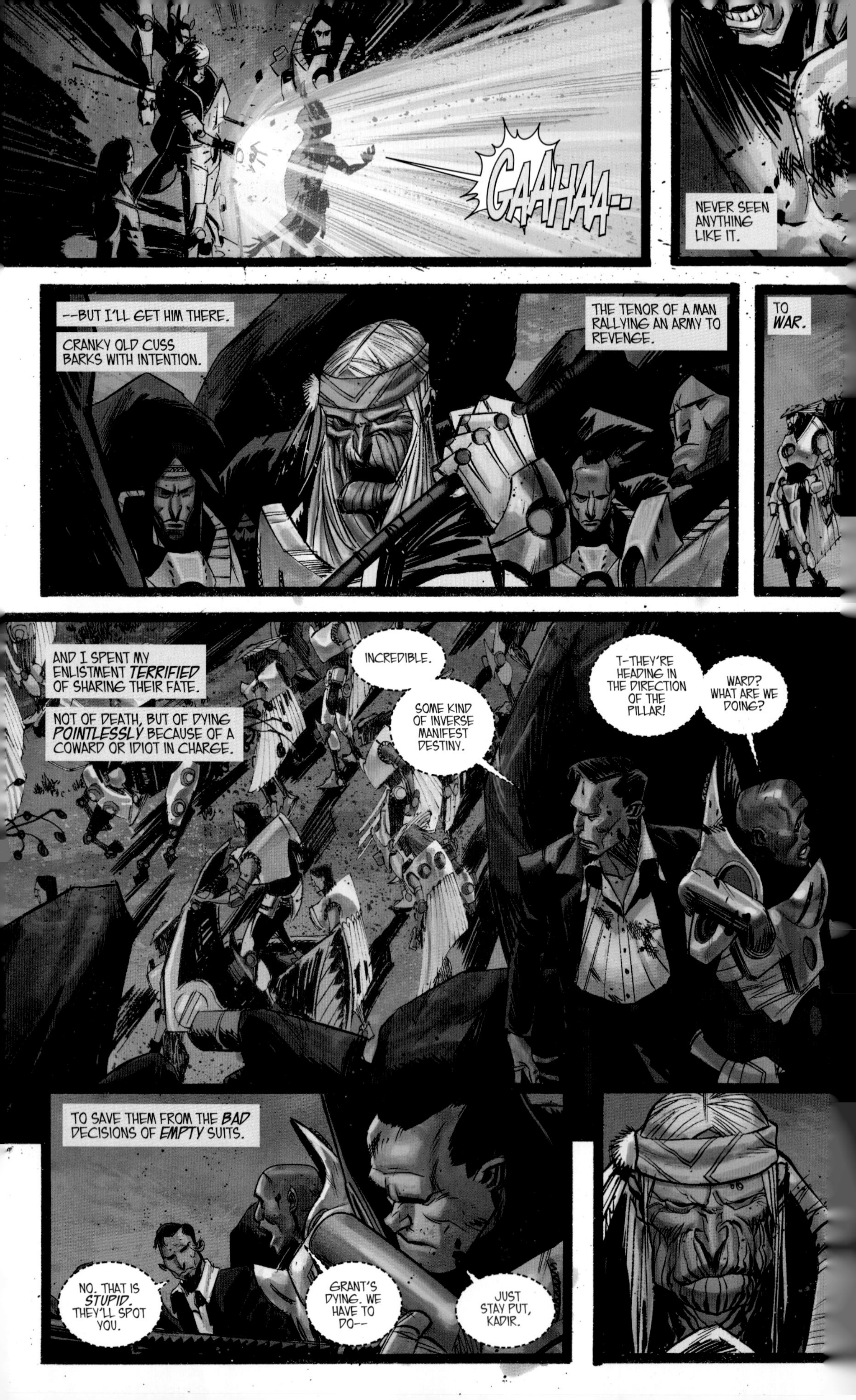
GAAHAA--
NEVER SEEN ANYTHING LIKE IT.
--BUT I'LL GET HIM THERE.
CRANKY OLD CUSS BARKS WITH INTENTION.
THE TENOR OF A MAN RALLYING AN ARMY TO REVENGE.
TO WAR.
AND I SPENT MY ENLISTMENT TERRIFIED OF SHARING THEIR FATE.
NOT OF DEATH, BUT OF DYING POINTLESSLY BECAUSE OF A COWARD OR IDIOT IN CHARGE.
INCREDIBLE.
SOME KIND OF INVERSE MANIFEST DESTINY.
T-THEY'RE HEADING IN THE DIRECTION OF THE PILLAR!
WARD? WHAT ARE WE DOING?
TO SAVE THEM FROM THE BAD DECISIONS OF EMPTY SUITS.
NO. THAT IS STUPID. THEY'LL SPOT YOU.
GRANT'S DYING. WE HAVE TO DO--
JUST STAY PUT, KADIR.

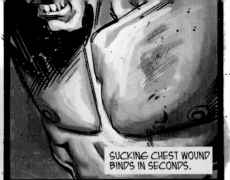

SUCKING CHEST WOUND BINDS IN SECONDS.

SHAMAN CAN SAVE GRANT.

MIGHT TAKE A GUN TO HIS HEAD TO CONVINCE HIM—

THREE GENERATIONS OF MY FAMILY ARE BURIED IN FIELDS LIKE THIS.

ALL BECAUSE OF THE *BAD* DECISIONS OF *INCOMPETENT* LEADERS.

GOTTA GRAB THAT SHAMAN.

THAT'S THE SHIT THAT KEEPS ME UP AT NIGHT.

WHY I DIDN'T TAKE THE PROMOTIONS.

TO KEEP MYSELF CLOSER TO THE BATTLEFIELD--CLOSER TO THE GRUNTS.

...KID HAS REAL HEART.

CAN SEE WHY GRANT LOVES HIM LIKE A SON.

NO REPORTS TO BE FILED OUT HERE.

BOY GENIUS FOLLOWS WITHOUT HESITATION...

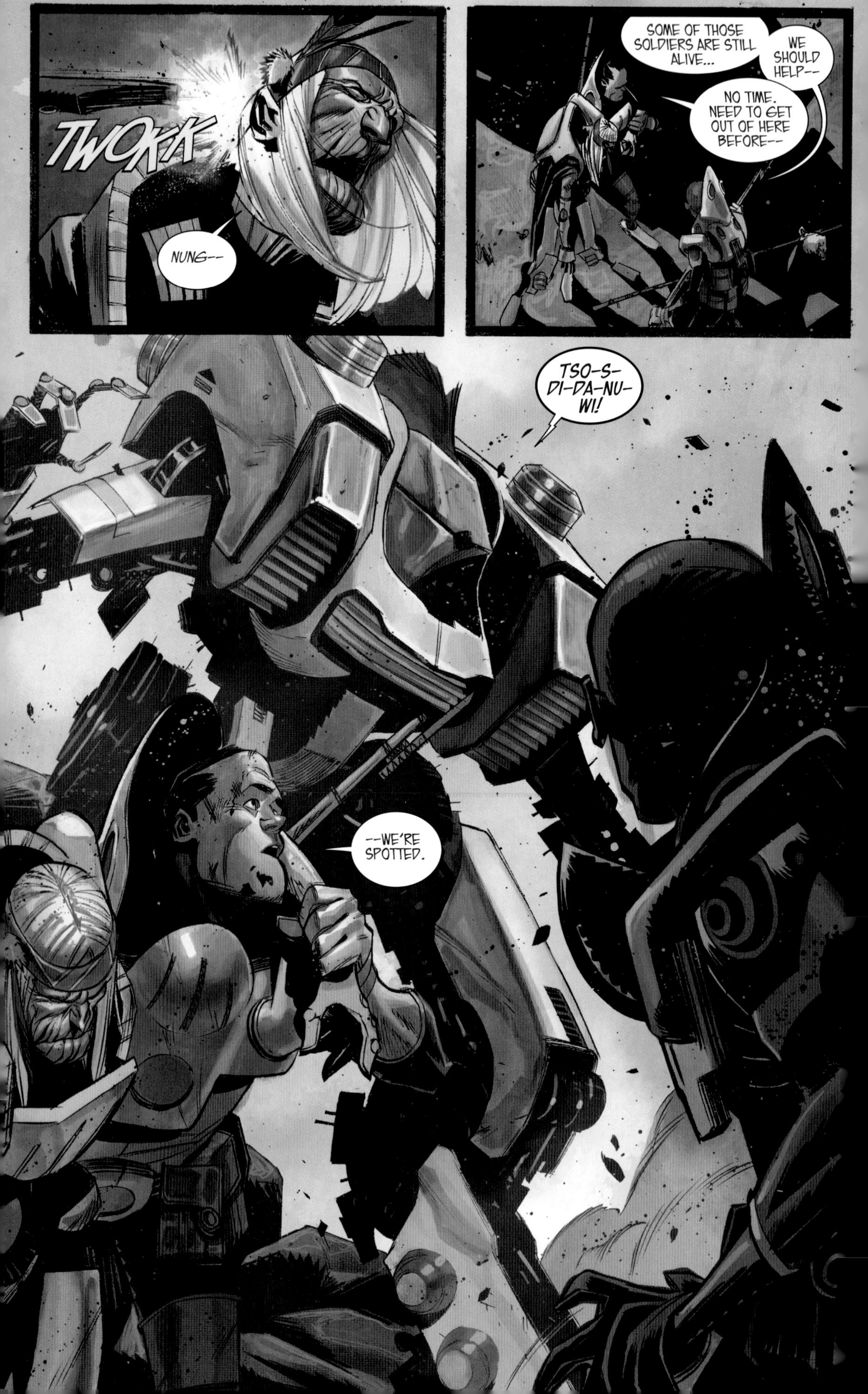
TWOKK
NUNG--
SOME OF THOSE SOLDIERS ARE STILL ALIVE...
WE SHOULD HELP--
NO TIME. NEED TO GET OUT OF HERE BEFORE--
TSO-S-DI-DA-NU-WI!
--WE'RE SPOTTED.

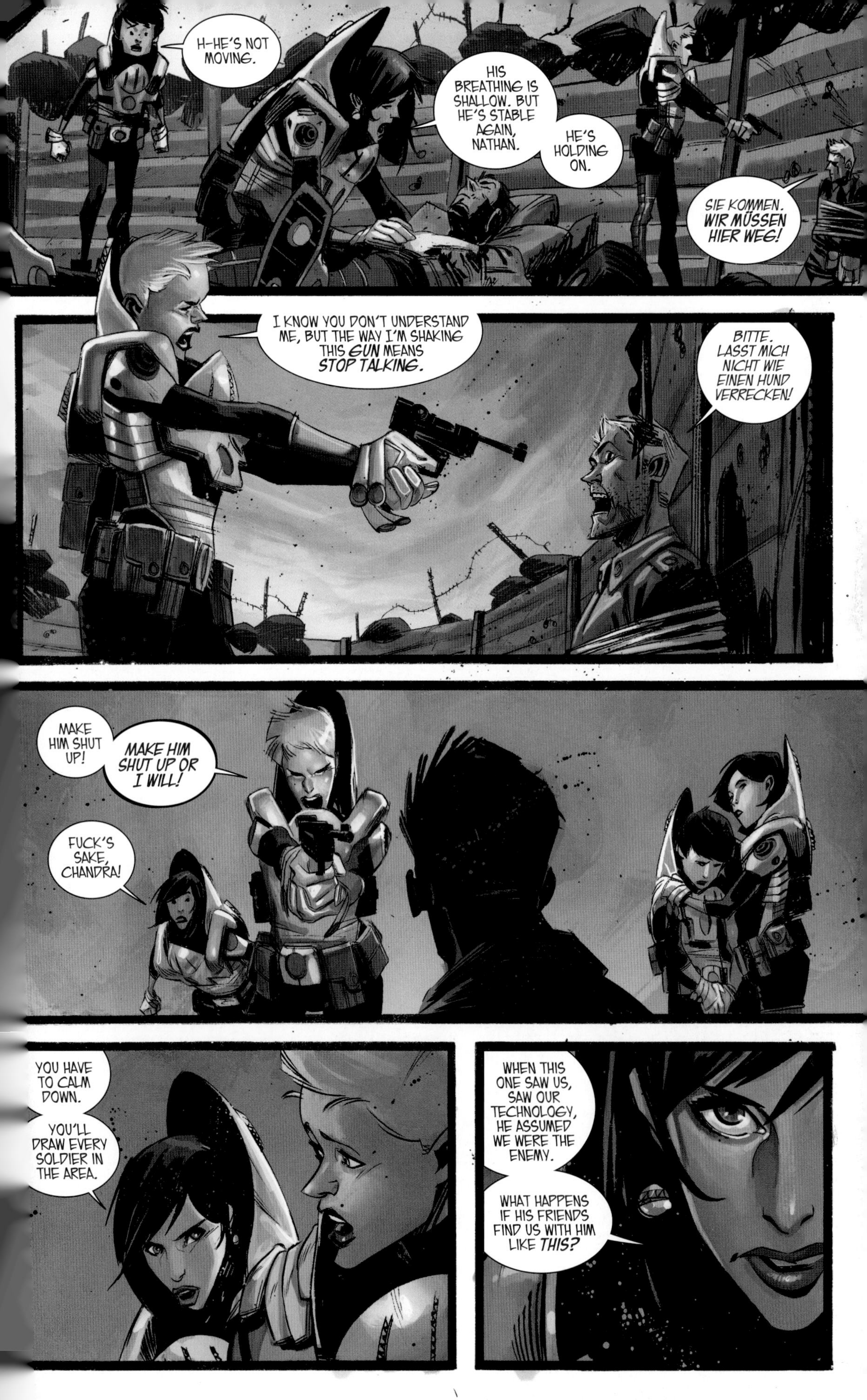
H-HE'S NOT MOVING.
HIS BREATHING IS SHALLOW. BUT HE'S STABLE AGAIN, NATHAN.
HE'S HOLDING ON.
SIE KOMMEN. WIR MÜSSEN HIER WEG!
I KNOW YOU DON'T UNDERSTAND ME, BUT THE WAY I'M SHAKING THIS GUN MEANS STOP TALKING.
BITTE. LASST MICH NICHT WIE EINEN HUND VERRECKEN!
MAKE HIM SHUT UP!
MAKE HIM SHUT UP OR I WILL!
FUCK'S SAKE, CHANDRA!
YOU HAVE TO CALM DOWN.
YOU'LL DRAW EVERY SOLDIER IN THE AREA.
WHEN THIS ONE SAW US, SAW OUR TECHNOLOGY, HE ASSUMED WE WERE THE ENEMY.
WHAT HAPPENS IF HIS FRIENDS FIND US WITH HIM LIKE THIS?

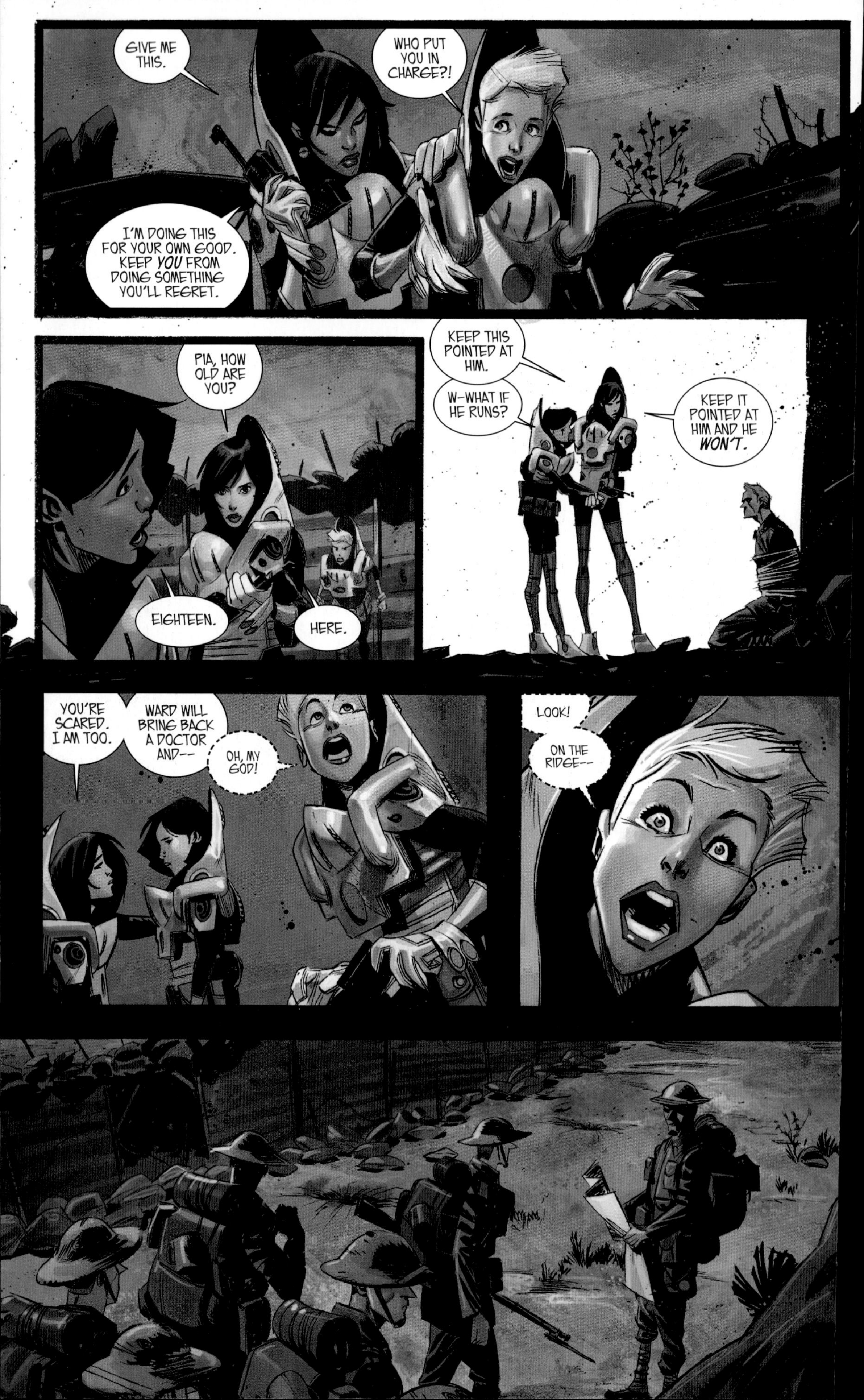
GIVE ME THIS.
WHO PUT YOU IN CHARGE?!
I'M DOING THIS FOR YOUR OWN GOOD. KEEP *YOU* FROM DOING SOMETHING YOU'LL REGRET.
PIA, HOW OLD ARE YOU?
EIGHTEEN.
HERE.
KEEP THIS POINTED AT HIM.
W-WHAT IF HE RUNS?
KEEP IT POINTED AT HIM AND HE *WON'T*.
YOU'RE SCARED. I AM TOO.
WARD WILL BRING BACK A DOCTOR AND--
OH, MY GOD!
LOOK!
ON THE RIDGE--

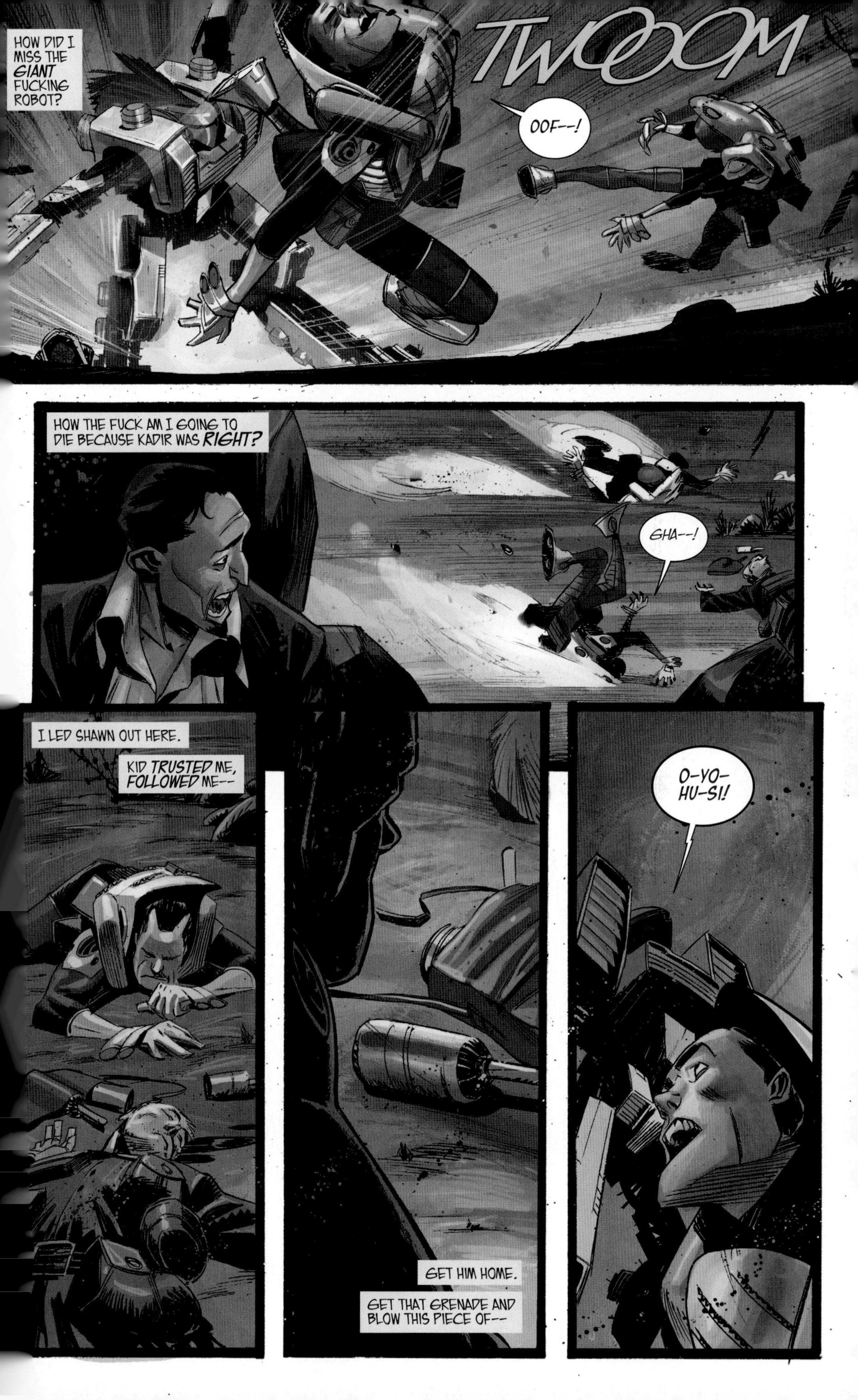

HOW DID I MISS THE GIANT FUCKING ROBOT?
TWOOOM
OOF--!
HOW THE FUCK AM I GOING TO DIE BECAUSE KADIR WAS RIGHT?
GHA--!
I LED SHAWN OUT HERE.
KID TRUSTED ME, FOLLOWED ME--
GET HIM HOME.
GET THAT GRENADE AND BLOW THIS PIECE OF--
O-YO-HU-SI!

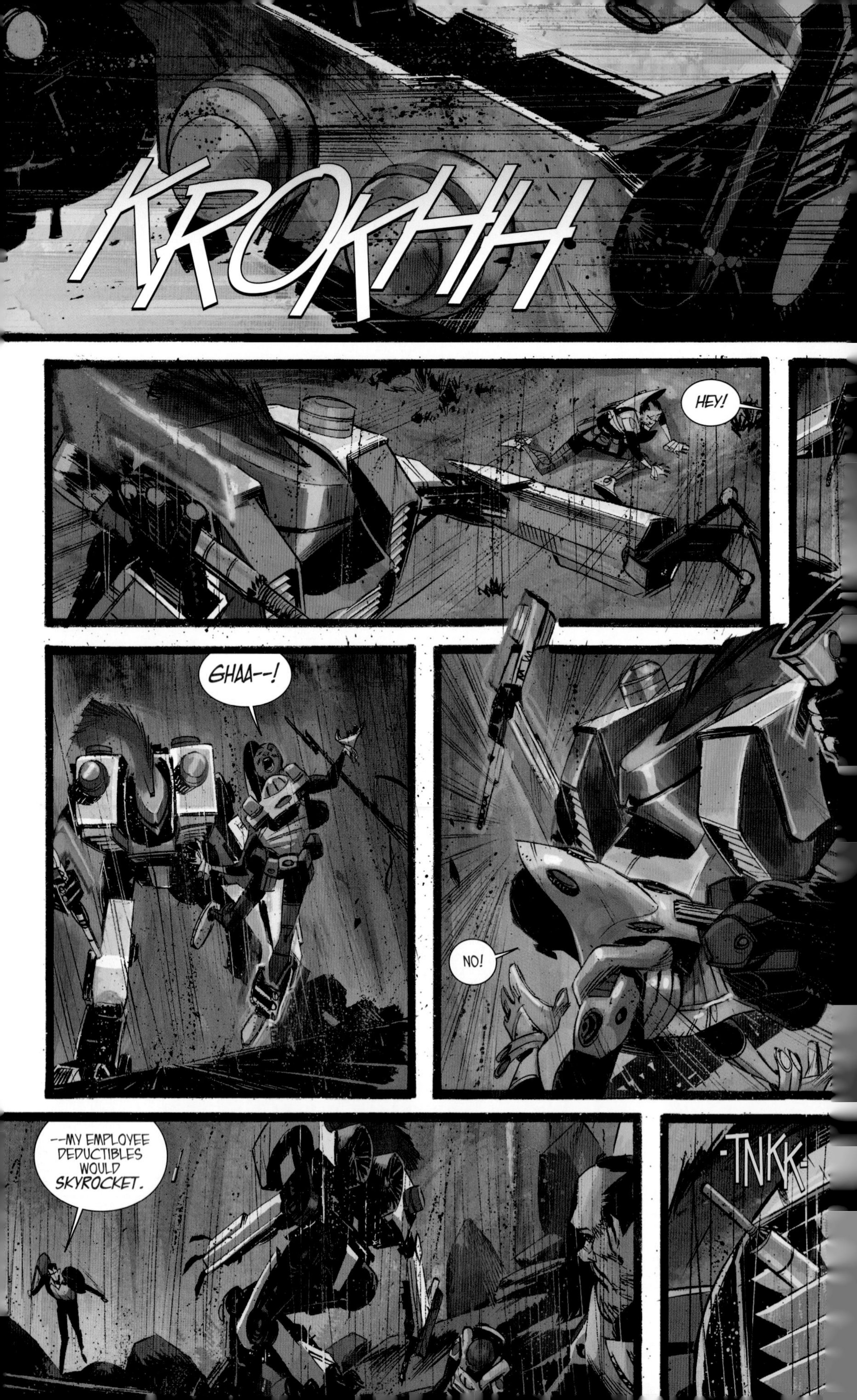
KROKHH
HEY!
GHAA--!
NO!
--MY EMPLOYEE DEDUCTIBLES WOULD SKYROCKET.
TNKK

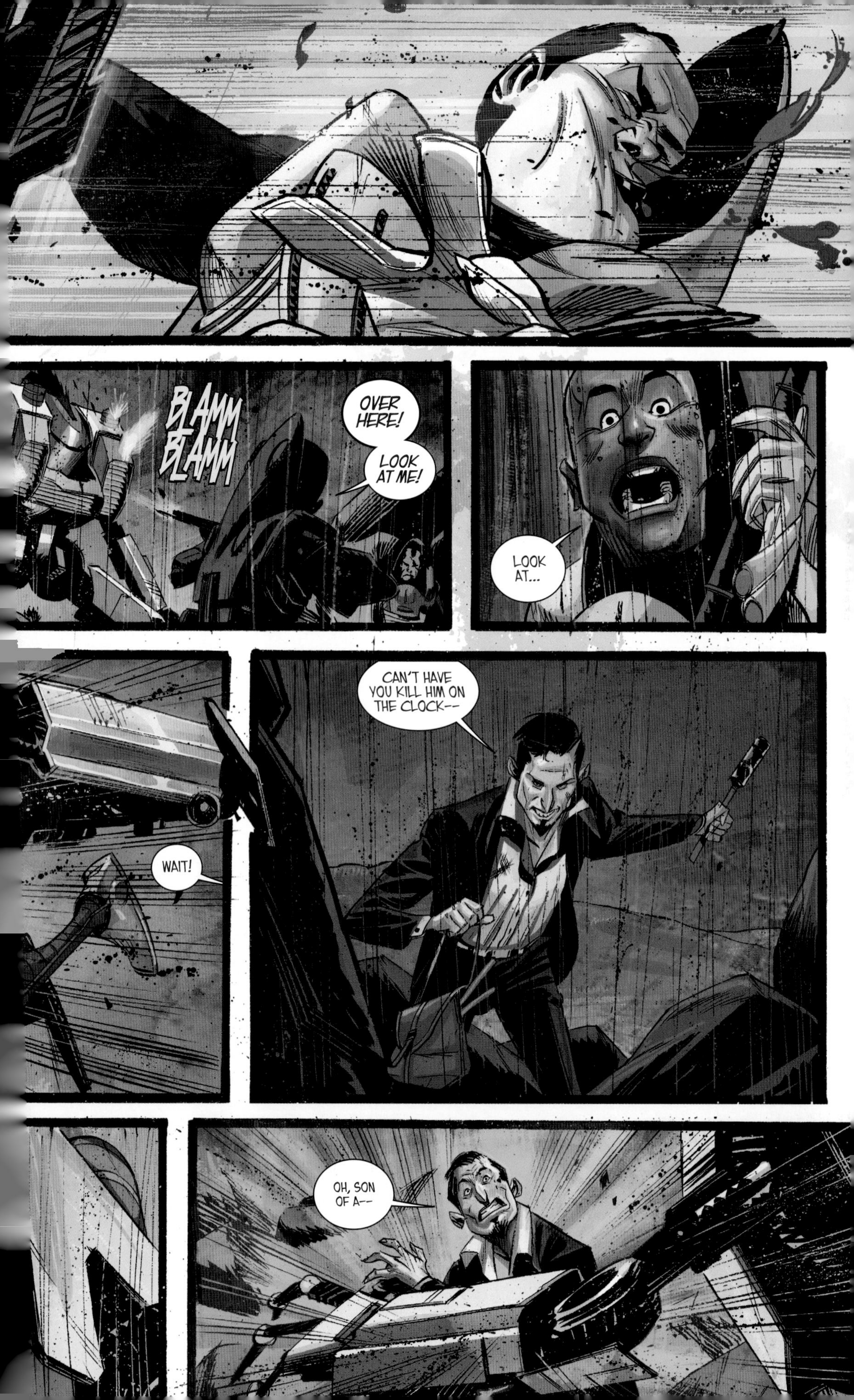
BLAMM
BLAMM
OVER HERE!
LOOK AT ME!
LOOK AT...
CAN'T HAVE YOU KILL HIM ON THE CLOCK--
WAIT!
OH, SON OF A--

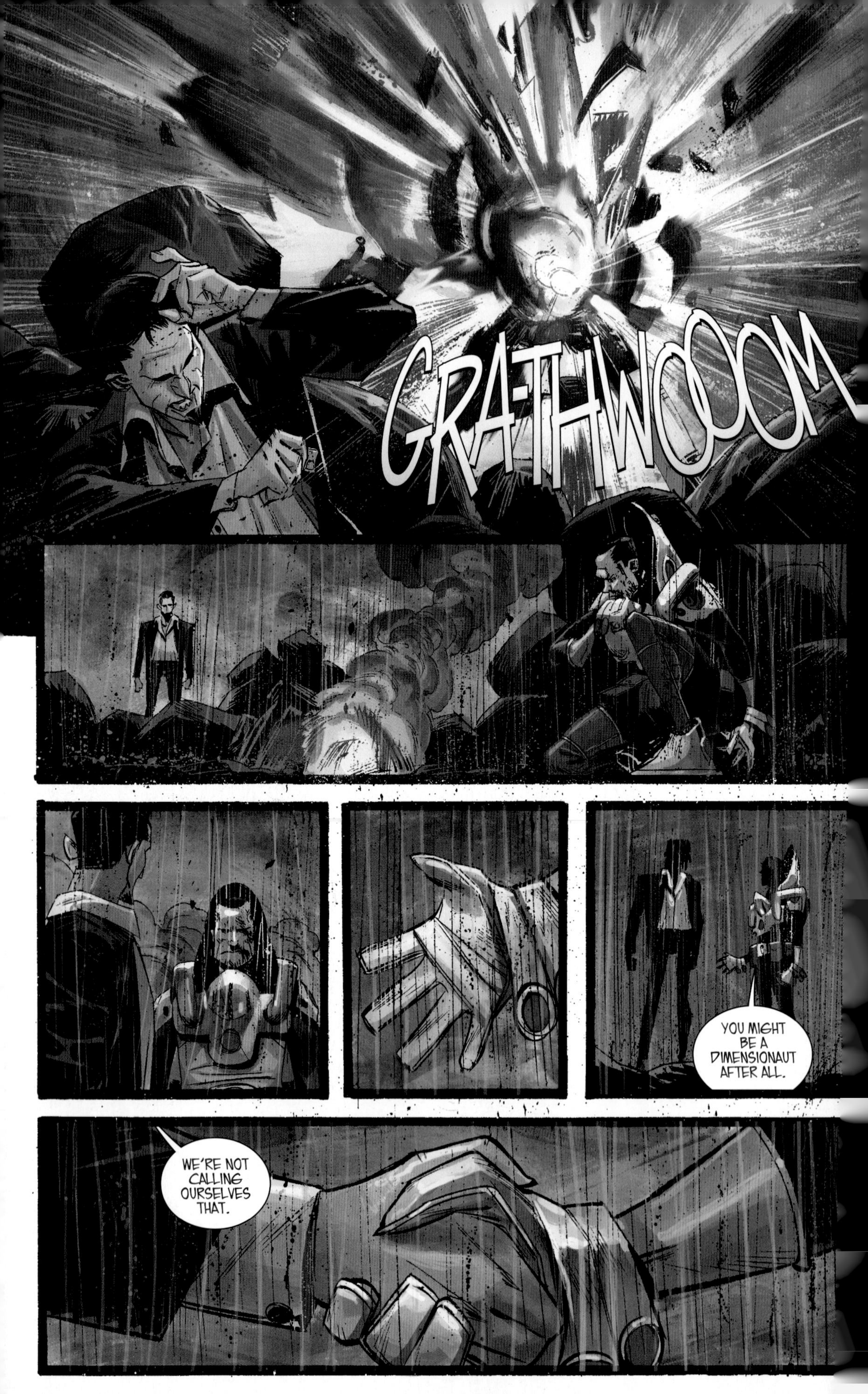
GRA-THWOOOM
YOU MIGHT BE A DIMENSIONAUT AFTER ALL.
WE'RE NOT CALLING OURSELVES THAT.

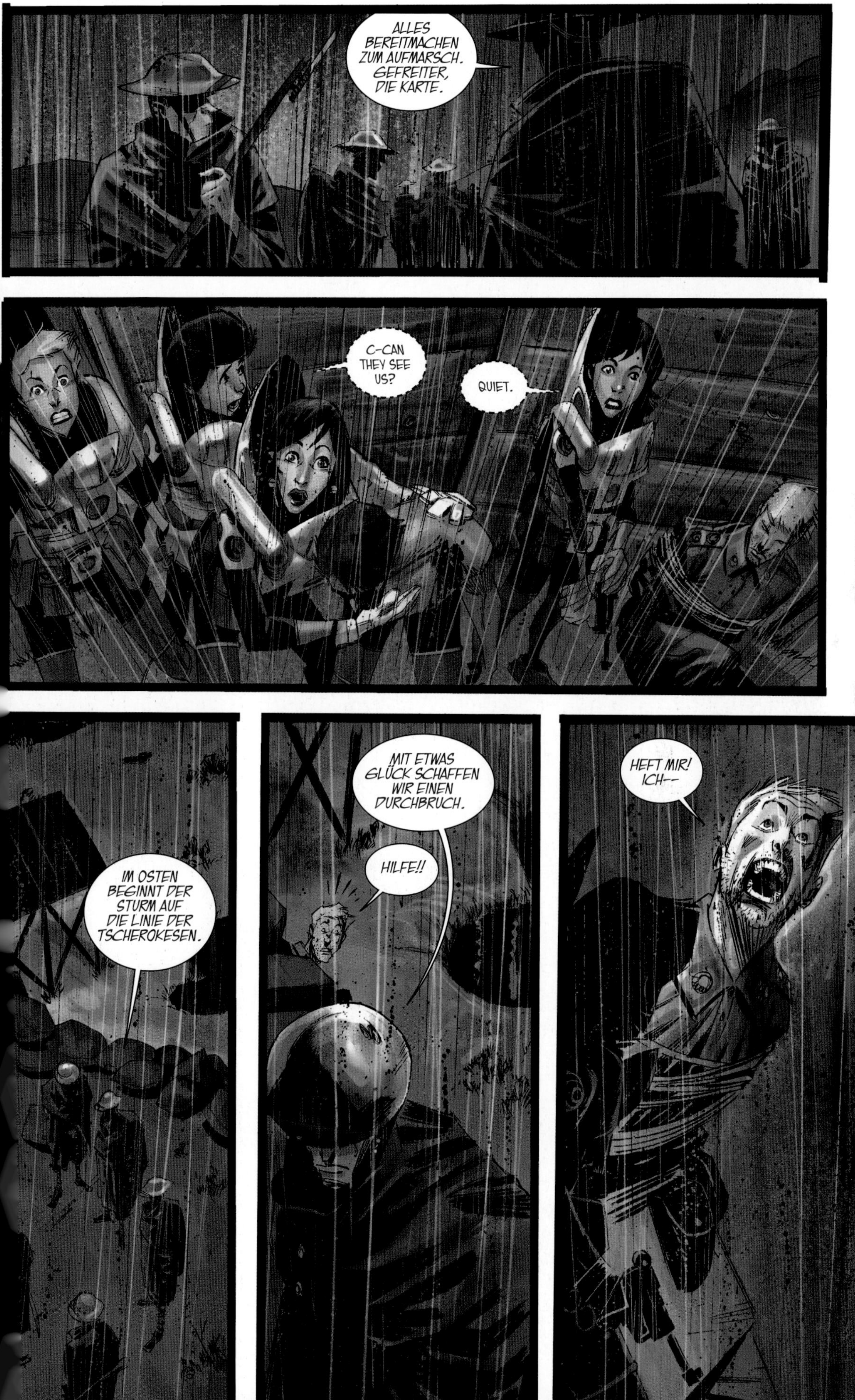
ALLES BEREITMACHEN ZUM AUFMARSCH. GEFREITER, DIE KARTE.
C-CAN THEY SEE US?
QUIET.
IM OSTEN BEGINNT DER STURM AUF DIE LINIE DER TSCHEROKESEN.
MIT ETWAS GLÜCK SCHAFFEN WIR EINEN DURCHBRUCH.
HILFE!!
HEFT MIR! ICH--

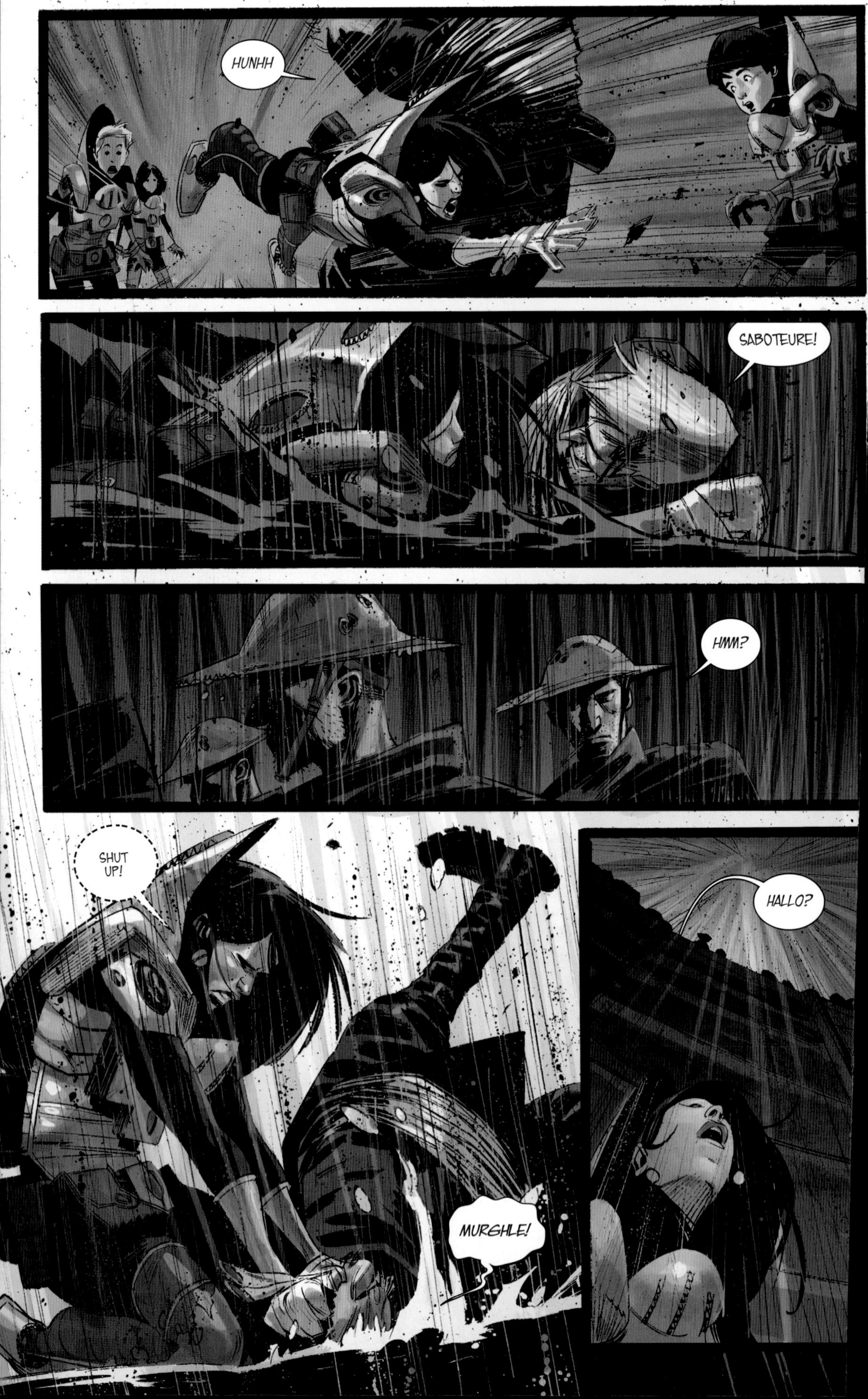
HUNHH
SABOTEURE!
HMM?
SHUT UP!
MURGHLE!
HALLO?

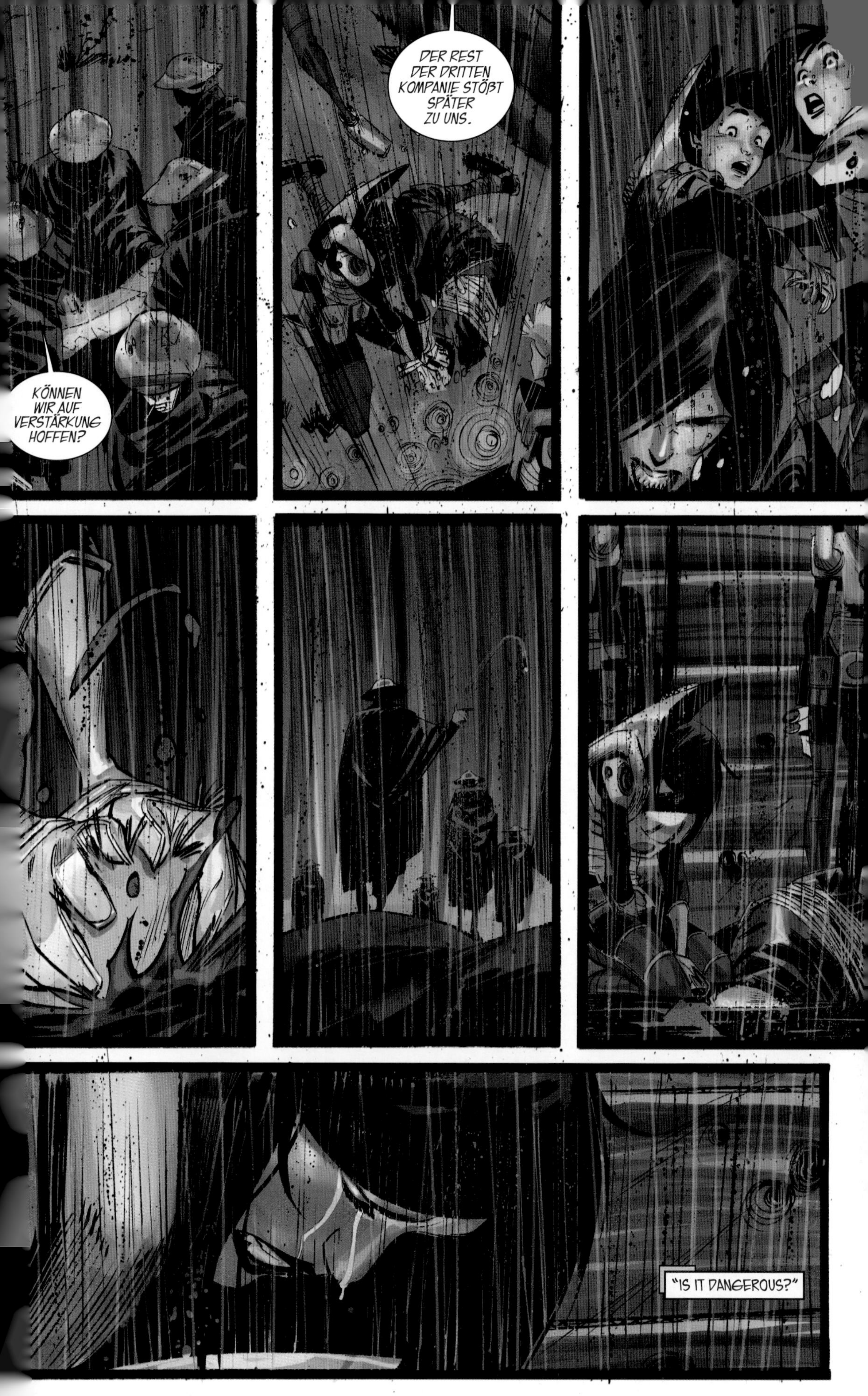
KÖNNEN WIR AUF VERSTÄRKUNG HOFFEN?
DER REST DER DRITTEN KOMPANIE STÖßT SPÄTER ZU UNS.
"IS IT DANGEROUS?"

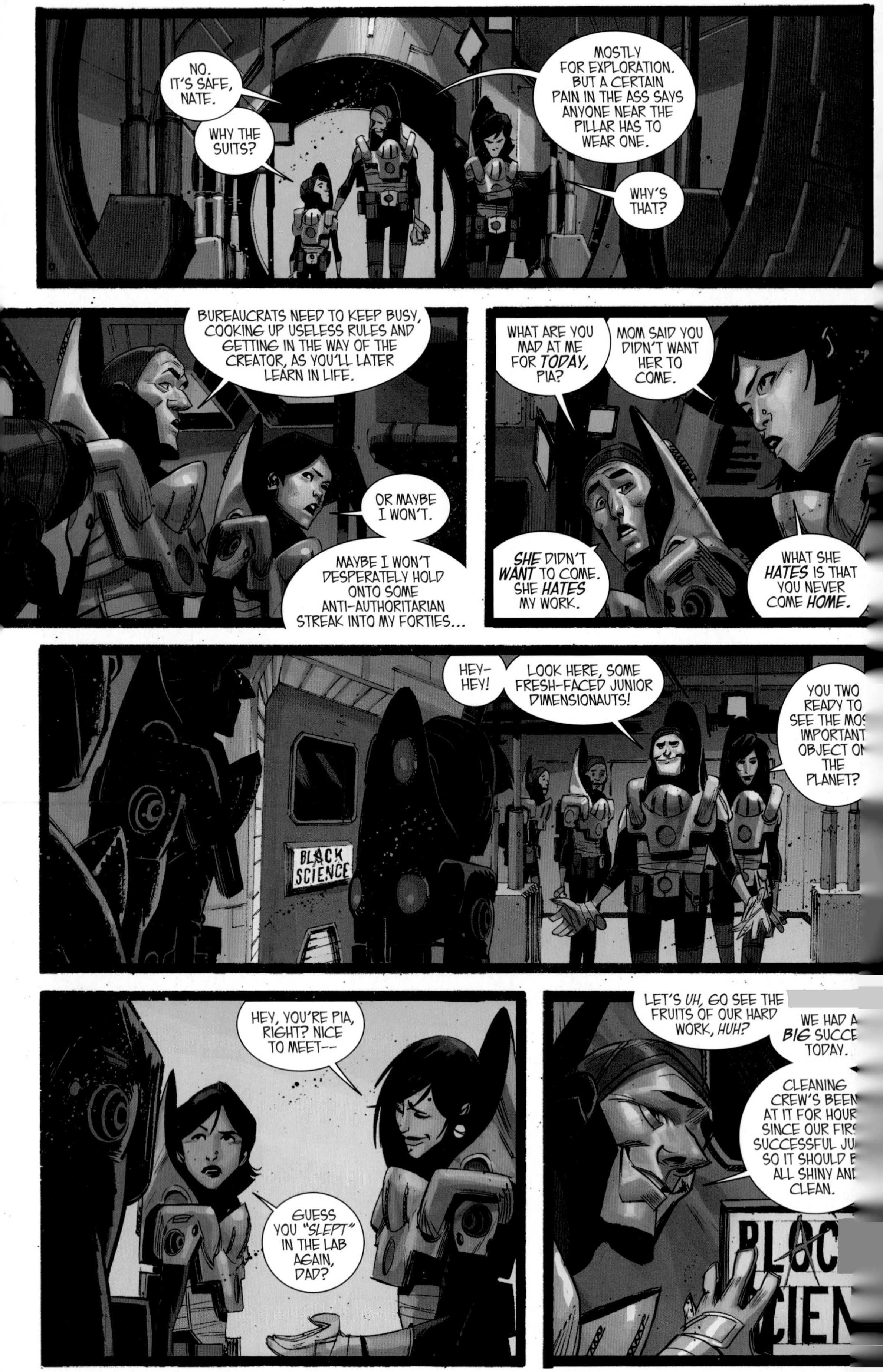
NO. IT'S SAFE, NATE.
WHY THE SUITS?
MOSTLY FOR EXPLORATION. BUT A CERTAIN PAIN IN THE ASS SAYS ANYONE NEAR THE PILLAR HAS TO WEAR ONE.
WHY'S THAT?
BUREAUCRATS NEED TO KEEP BUSY, COOKING UP USELESS RULES AND GETTING IN THE WAY OF THE CREATOR, AS YOU'LL LATER LEARN IN LIFE.
OR MAYBE I WON'T.
MAYBE I WON'T DESPERATELY HOLD ONTO SOME ANTI-AUTHORITARIAN STREAK INTO MY FORTIES...
WHAT ARE YOU MAD AT ME FOR *TODAY,* PIA?
MOM SAID YOU DIDN'T WANT HER TO COME.
SHE DIDN'T *WANT* TO COME. SHE *HATES* MY WORK.
WHAT SHE *HATES* IS THAT YOU NEVER COME *HOME.*
HEY-HEY!
LOOK HERE, SOME FRESH-FACED JUNIOR DIMENSIONAUTS!
YOU TWO READY TO SEE THE MOS IMPORTANT OBJECT O THE PLANET?
BLACK SCIENCE
HEY, YOU'RE PIA, RIGHT? NICE TO MEET--
GUESS YOU *"SLEPT"* IN THE LAB AGAIN, DAD?
LET'S *UH,* GO SEE THE FRUITS OF OUR HARD WORK, *HUH?*
WE HAD A *BIG* SUCCE TODAY.
CLEANING CREW'S BEEN AT IT FOR HOUR SINCE OUR FIR SUCCESSFUL JU SO IT SHOULD B ALL SHINY AND CLEAN.

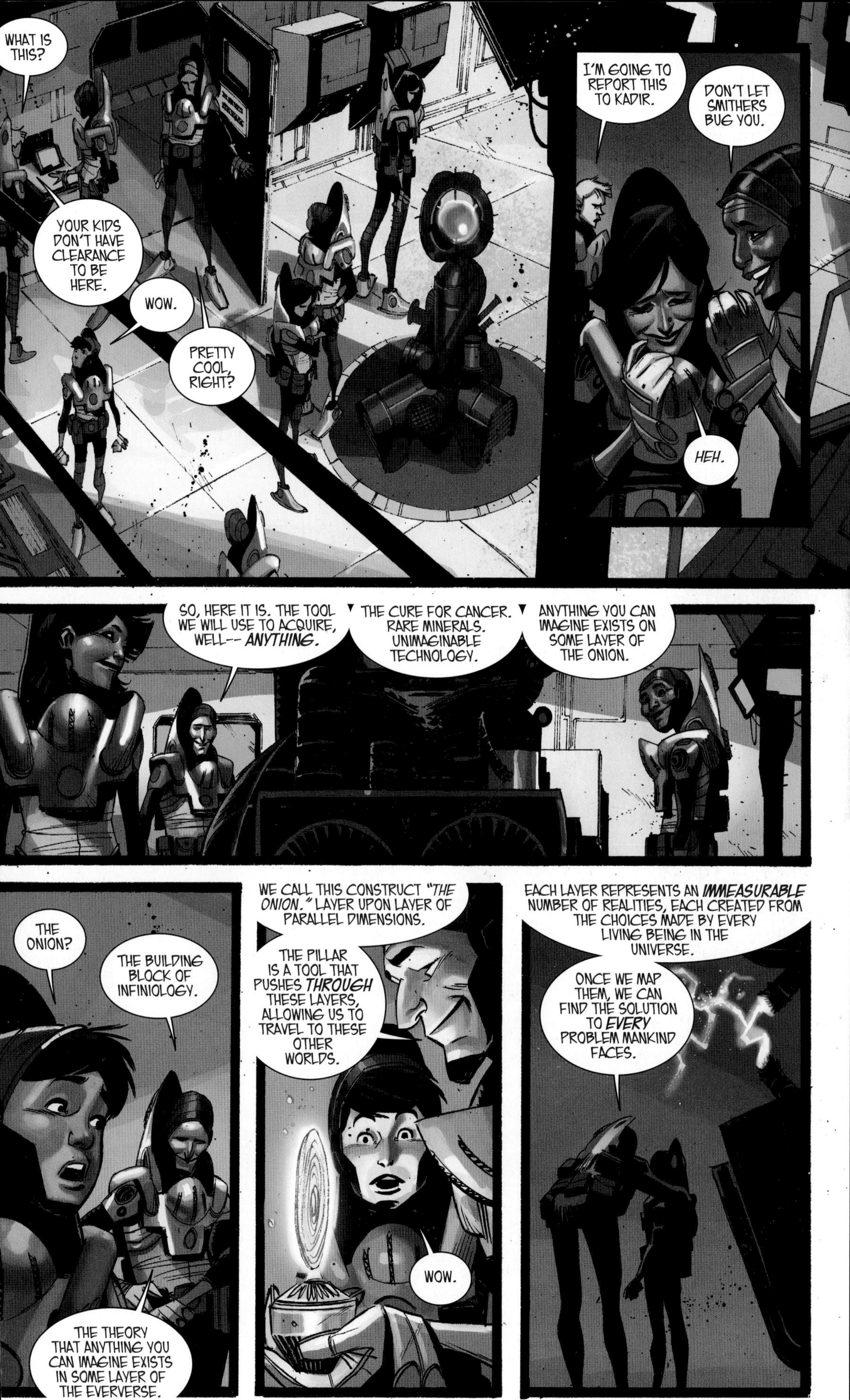
WHAT IS THIS?
YOUR KIDS DON'T HAVE CLEARANCE TO BE HERE.
WOW.
PRETTY COOL, RIGHT?
I'M GOING TO REPORT THIS TO KADIR.
DON'T LET SMITHERS BUG YOU.
HEH.
SO, HERE IT IS. THE TOOL WE WILL USE TO ACQUIRE, WELL-- *ANYTHING.*
THE CURE FOR CANCER. RARE MINERALS. UNIMAGINABLE TECHNOLOGY.
ANYTHING YOU CAN IMAGINE EXISTS ON SOME LAYER OF THE ONION.
THE ONION?
THE BUILDING BLOCK OF INFINIOLOGY.
THE THEORY THAT ANYTHING YOU CAN IMAGINE EXISTS IN SOME LAYER OF THE EVERVERSE.
WE CALL THIS CONSTRUCT *"THE ONION."* LAYER UPON LAYER OF PARALLEL DIMENSIONS.
THE PILLAR IS A TOOL THAT PUSHES *THROUGH* THESE LAYERS, ALLOWING US TO TRAVEL TO THESE OTHER WORLDS.
WOW.
EACH LAYER REPRESENTS AN *IMMEASURABLE* NUMBER OF REALITIES, EACH CREATED FROM THE CHOICES MADE BY EVERY LIVING BEING IN THE UNIVERSE.
ONCE WE MAP THEM, WE CAN FIND THE SOLUTION TO *EVERY* PROBLEM MANKIND FACES.

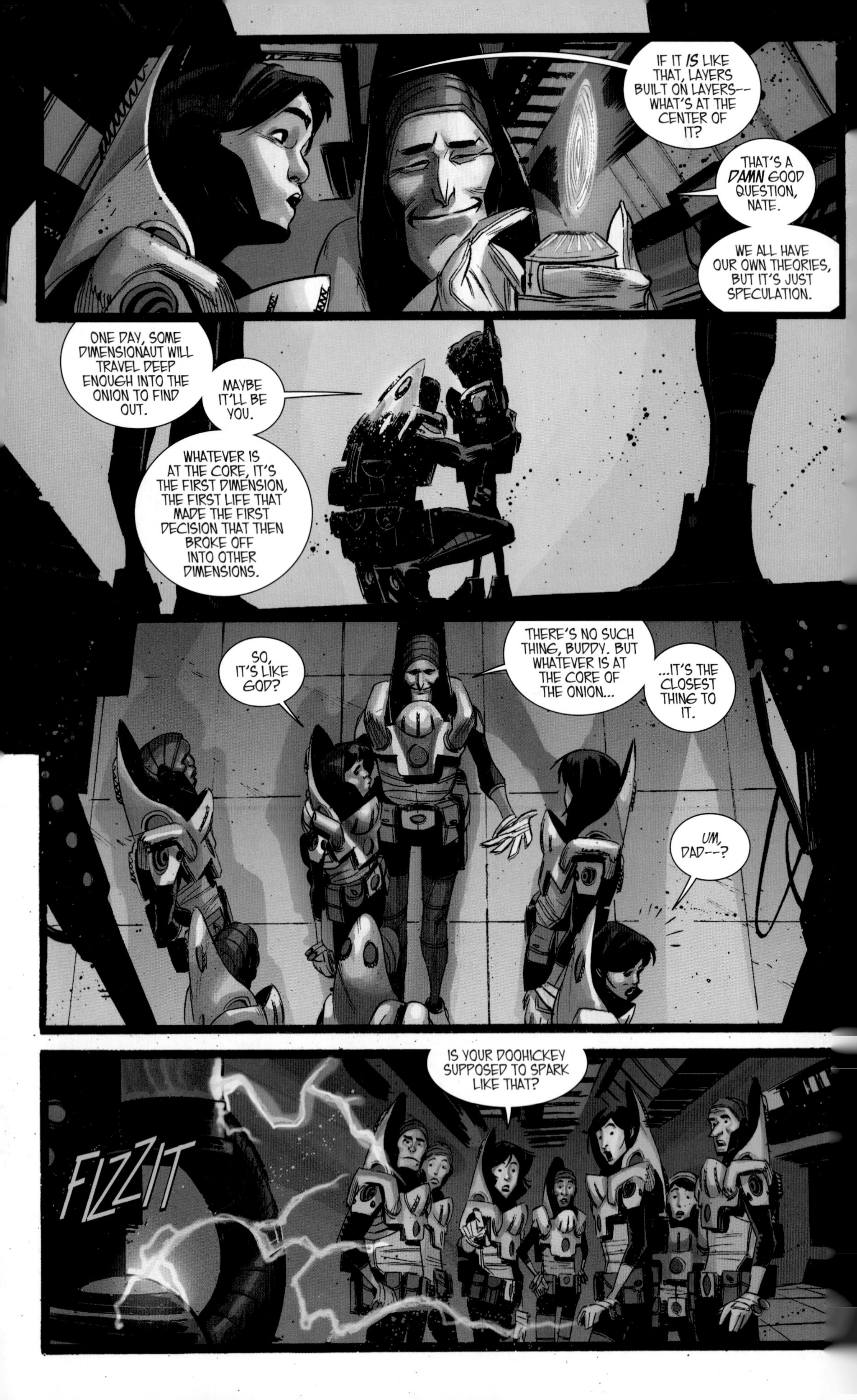
IF IT IS LIKE THAT, LAYERS BUILT ON LAYERS-- WHAT'S AT THE CENTER OF IT?
THAT'S A DAMN GOOD QUESTION, NATE.
WE ALL HAVE OUR OWN THEORIES, BUT IT'S JUST SPECULATION.
ONE DAY, SOME DIMENSIONAUT WILL TRAVEL DEEP ENOUGH INTO THE ONION TO FIND OUT.
MAYBE IT'LL BE YOU.
WHATEVER IS AT THE CORE, IT'S THE FIRST DIMENSION, THE FIRST LIFE THAT MADE THE FIRST DECISION THAT THEN BROKE OFF INTO OTHER DIMENSIONS.
SO, IT'S LIKE GOD?
THERE'S NO SUCH THING, BUDDY. BUT WHATEVER IS AT THE CORE OF THE ONION...
...IT'S THE CLOSEST THING TO IT.
UM, DAD--?
IS YOUR DOOHICKEY SUPPOSED TO SPARK LIKE THAT?
FIZZIT

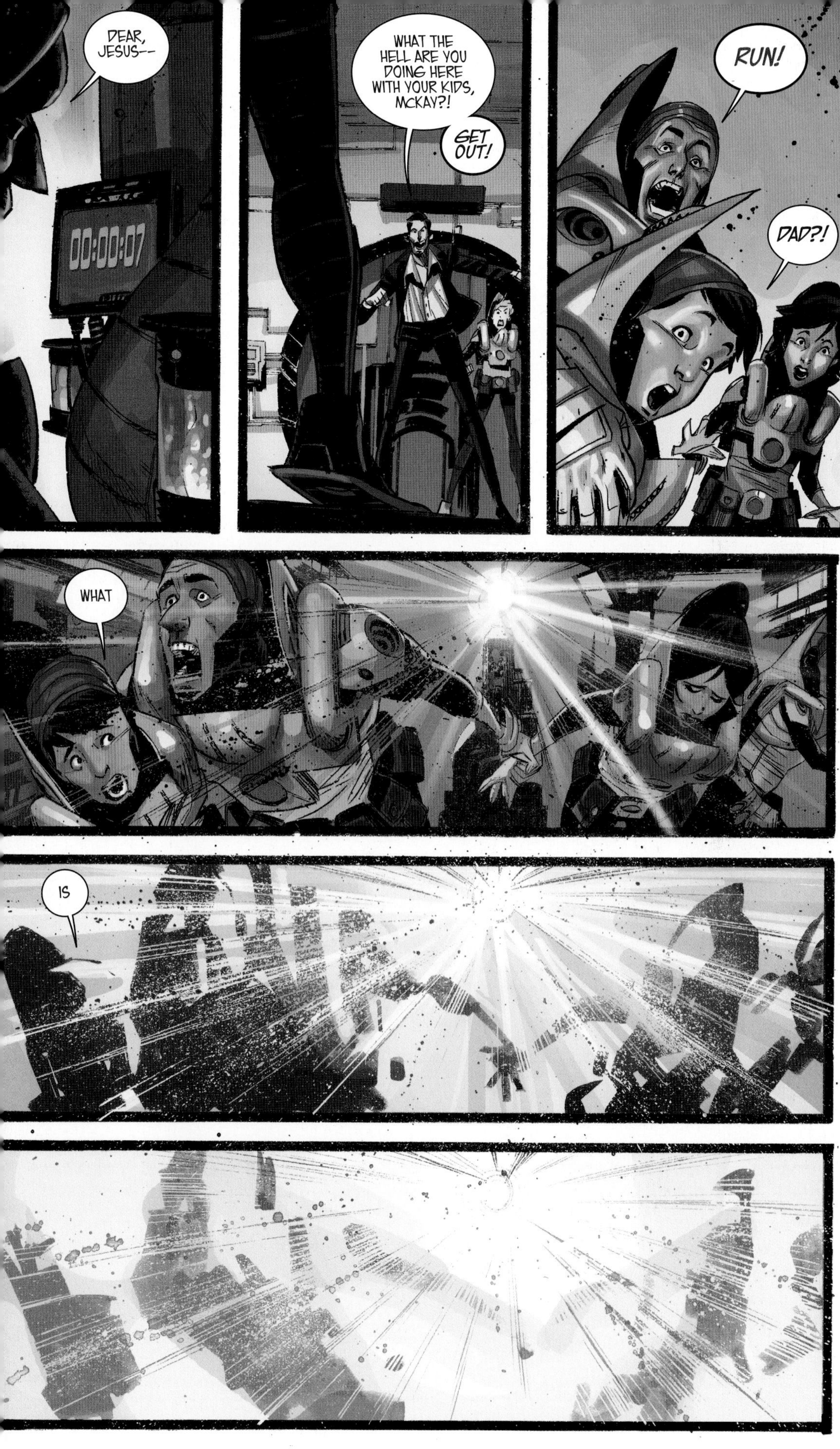
DEAR, JESUS--
WHAT THE HELL ARE YOU DOING HERE WITH YOUR KIDS, MCKAY?!
GET OUT!
RUN!
DAD?!
WHAT
IS

4

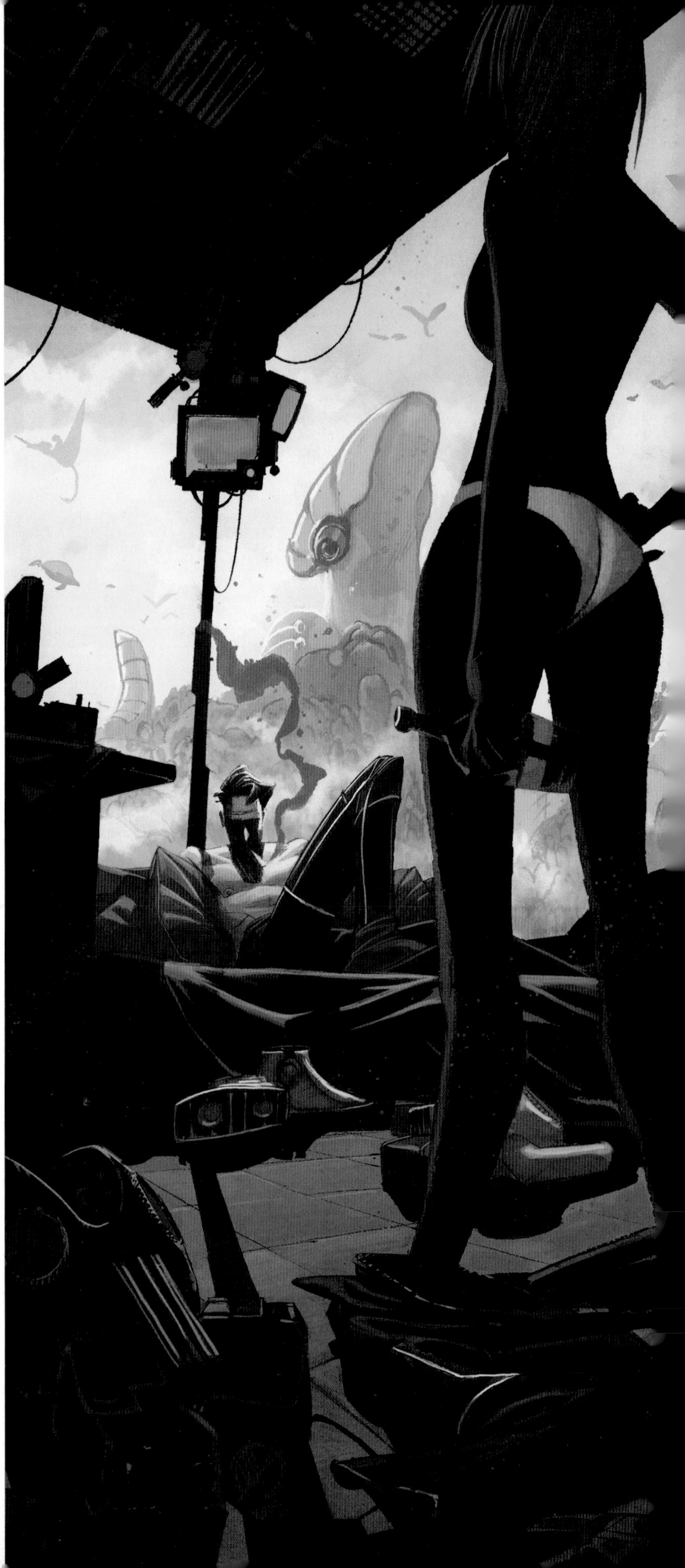

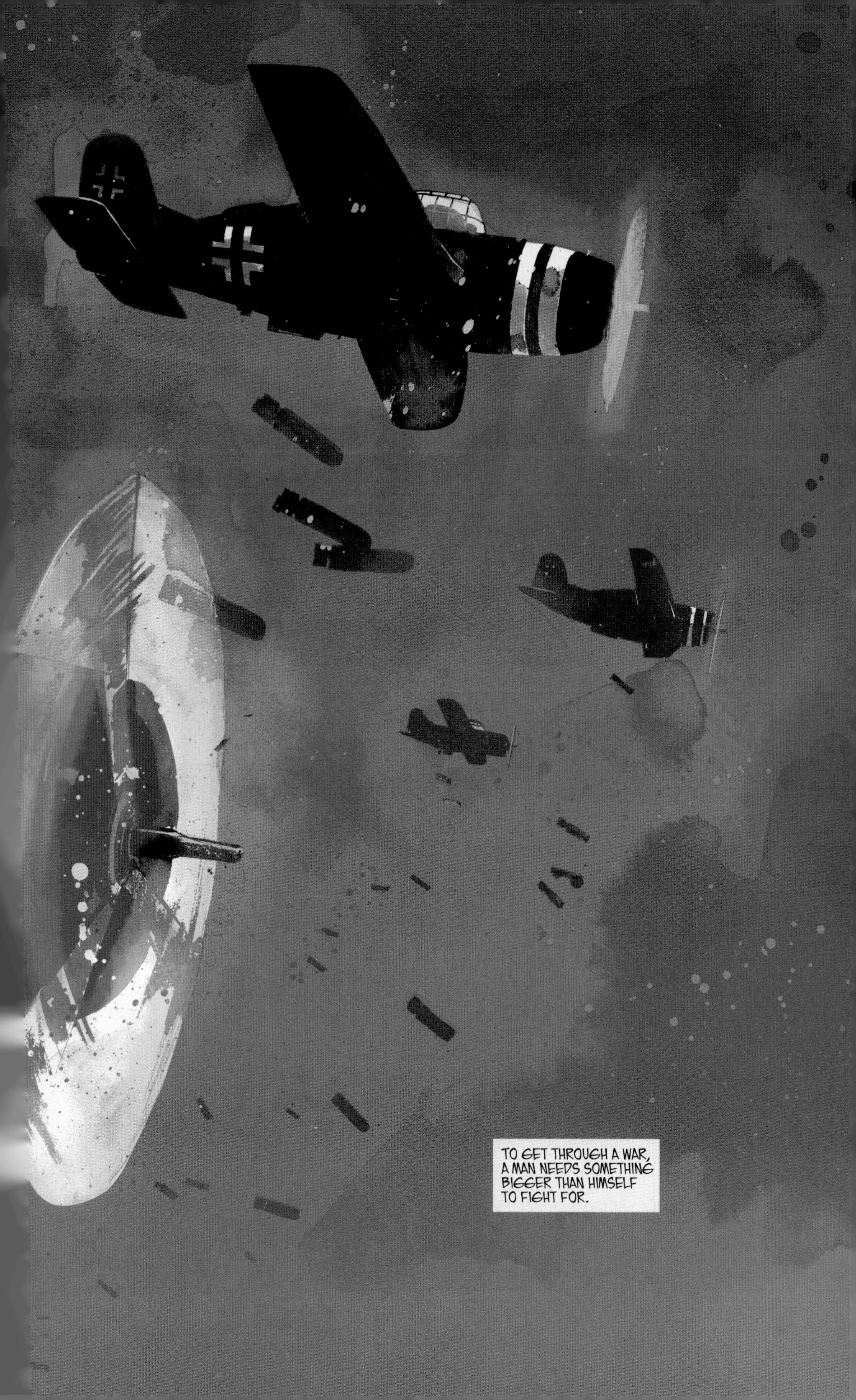
TO GET THROUGH A WAR, A MAN NEEDS SOMETHING BIGGER THAN HIMSELF TO FIGHT FOR.

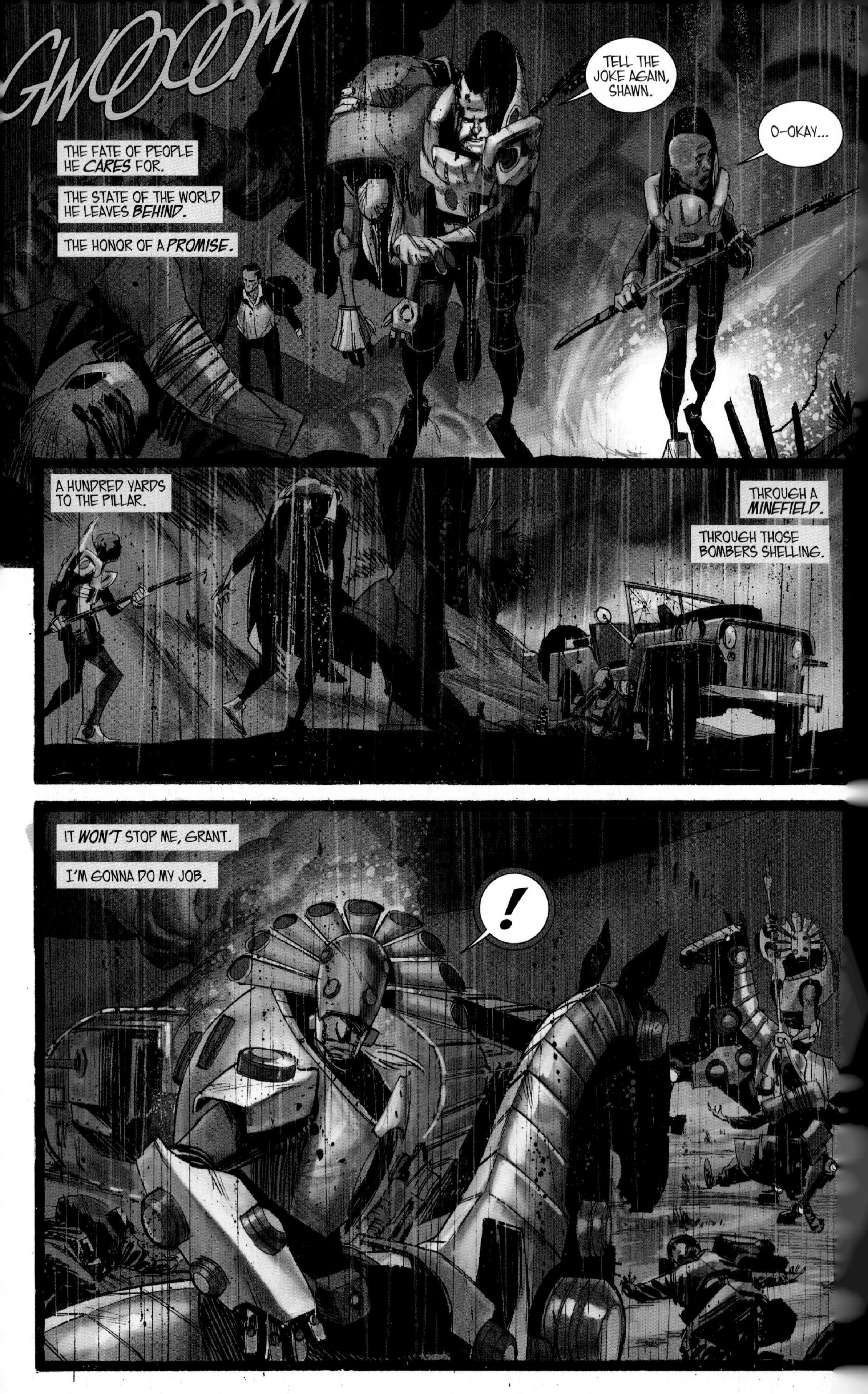
GWOOOM
TELL THE JOKE AGAIN, SHAWN.
O-OKAY...
THE FATE OF PEOPLE HE CARES FOR.
THE STATE OF THE WORLD HE LEAVES BEHIND.
THE HONOR OF A PROMISE.
A HUNDRED YARDS TO THE PILLAR.
THROUGH A MINEFIELD.
THROUGH THOSE BOMBERS SHELLING.
IT WON'T STOP ME, GRANT.
I'M GONNA DO MY JOB.
!

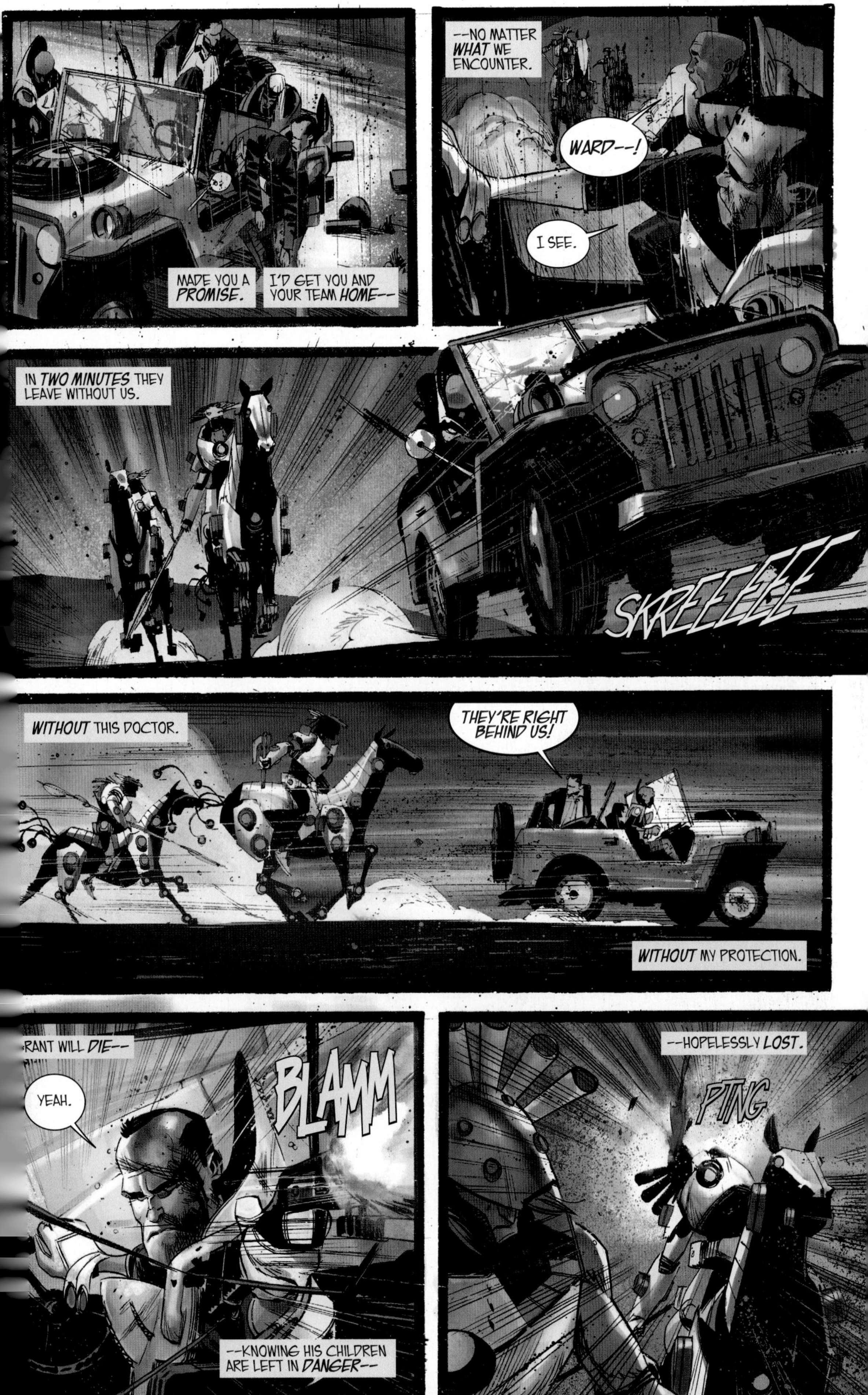
MADE YOU A PROMISE.
I'D GET YOU AND YOUR TEAM HOME--
--NO MATTER WHAT WE ENCOUNTER.
WARD--!
I SEE.
IN TWO MINUTES THEY LEAVE WITHOUT US.
SKREEEEEE
WITHOUT THIS DOCTOR.
THEY'RE RIGHT BEHIND US!
WITHOUT MY PROTECTION.
RANT WILL DIE--
YEAH.
BLAMM
--KNOWING HIS CHILDREN ARE LEFT IN DANGER--
--HOPELESSLY LOST.
PTING

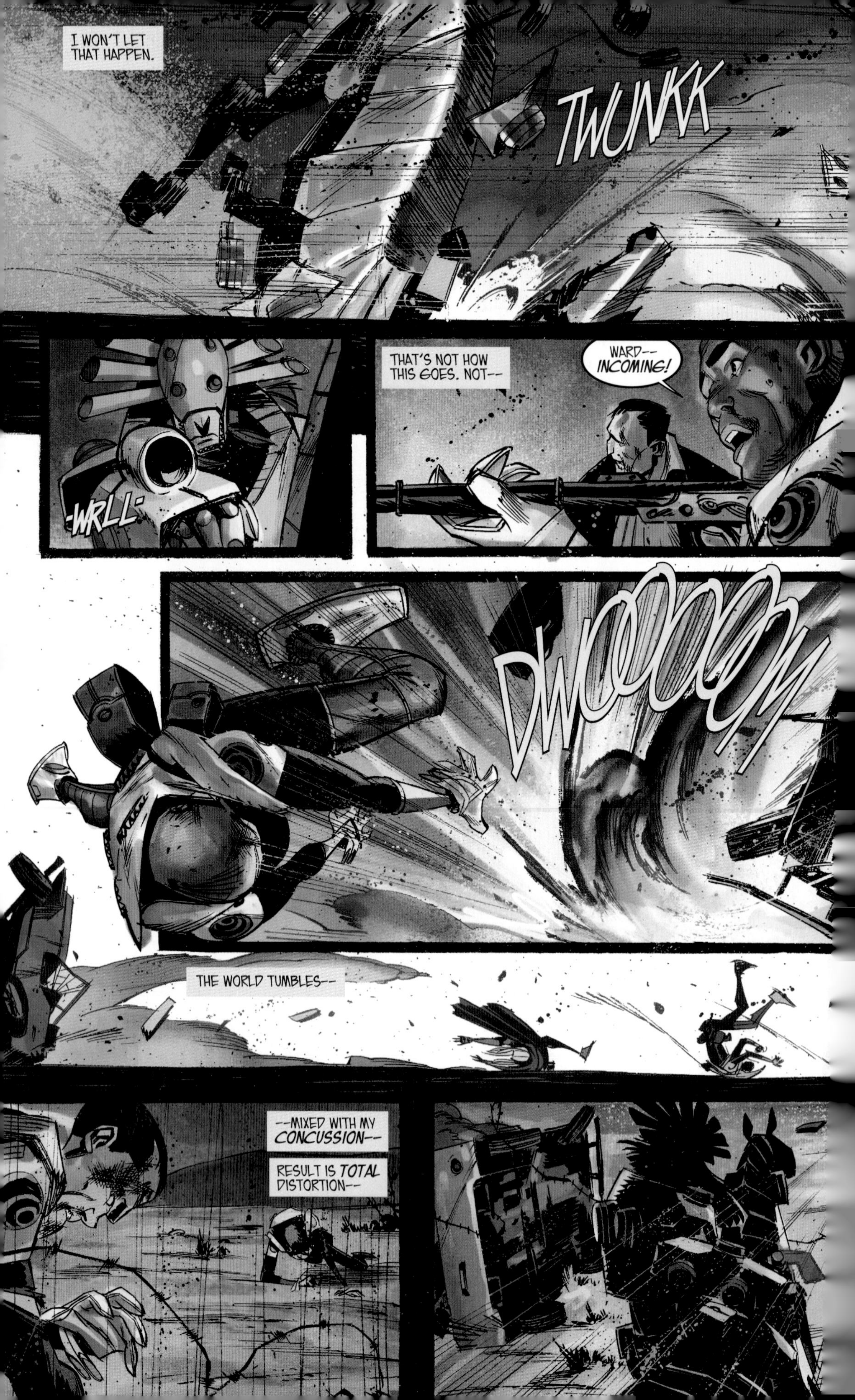
I WON'T LET THAT HAPPEN.
TWUNKK
-WRLL-
THAT'S NOT HOW THIS GOES. NOT--
WARD-- INCOMING!
DWOOOOOM
THE WORLD TUMBLES--
--MIXED WITH MY CONCUSSION--
RESULT IS TOTAL DISTORTION--

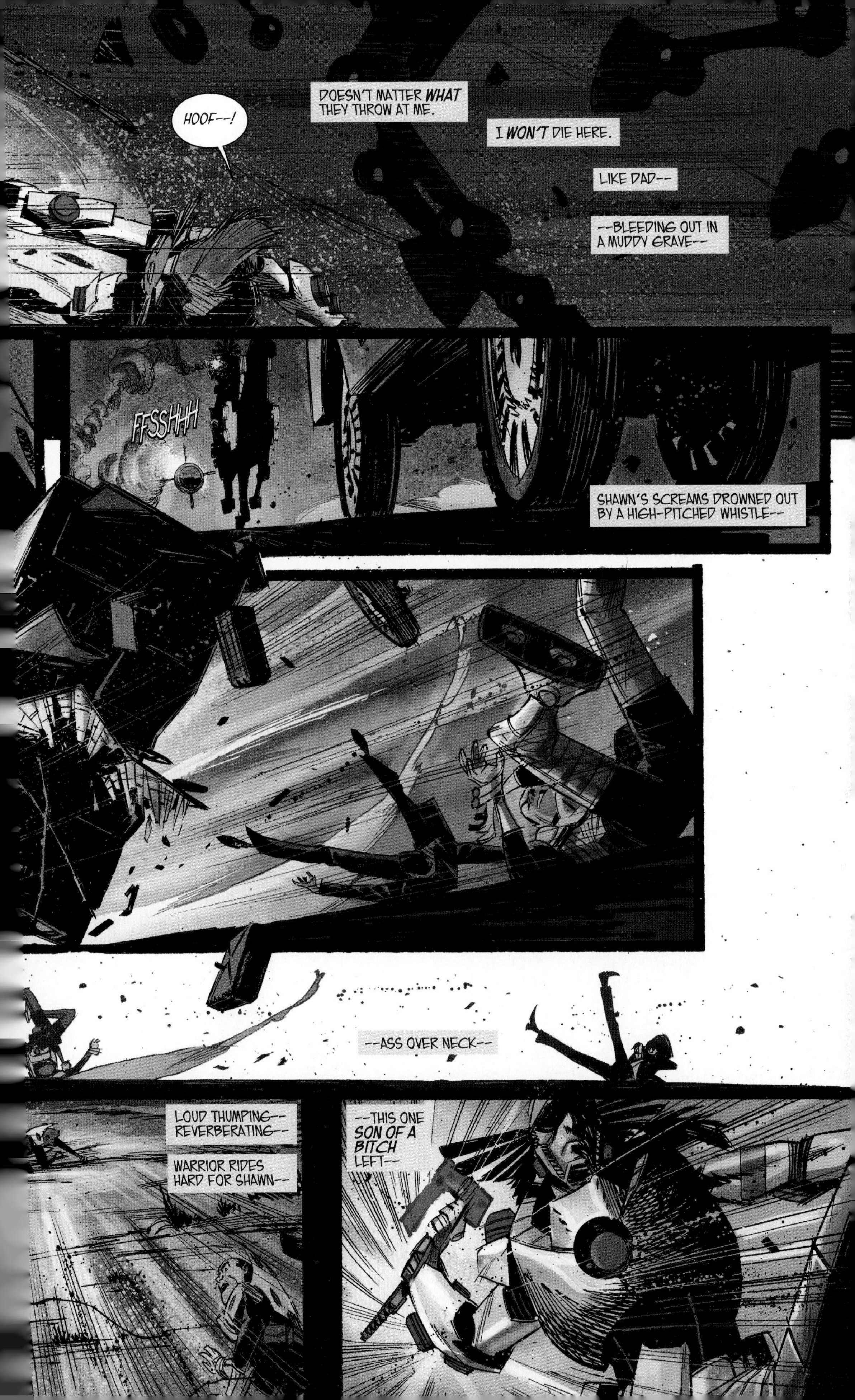
HOOF--!
DOESN'T MATTER WHAT THEY THROW AT ME.
I WON'T DIE HERE.
LIKE DAD--
--BLEEDING OUT IN A MUDDY GRAVE--
FFSSHHH
SHAWN'S SCREAMS DROWNED OUT BY A HIGH-PITCHED WHISTLE--
--ASS OVER NECK--
LOUD THUMPING--
REVERBERATING--
WARRIOR RIDES HARD FOR SHAWN--
--THIS ONE SON OF A BITCH LEFT--

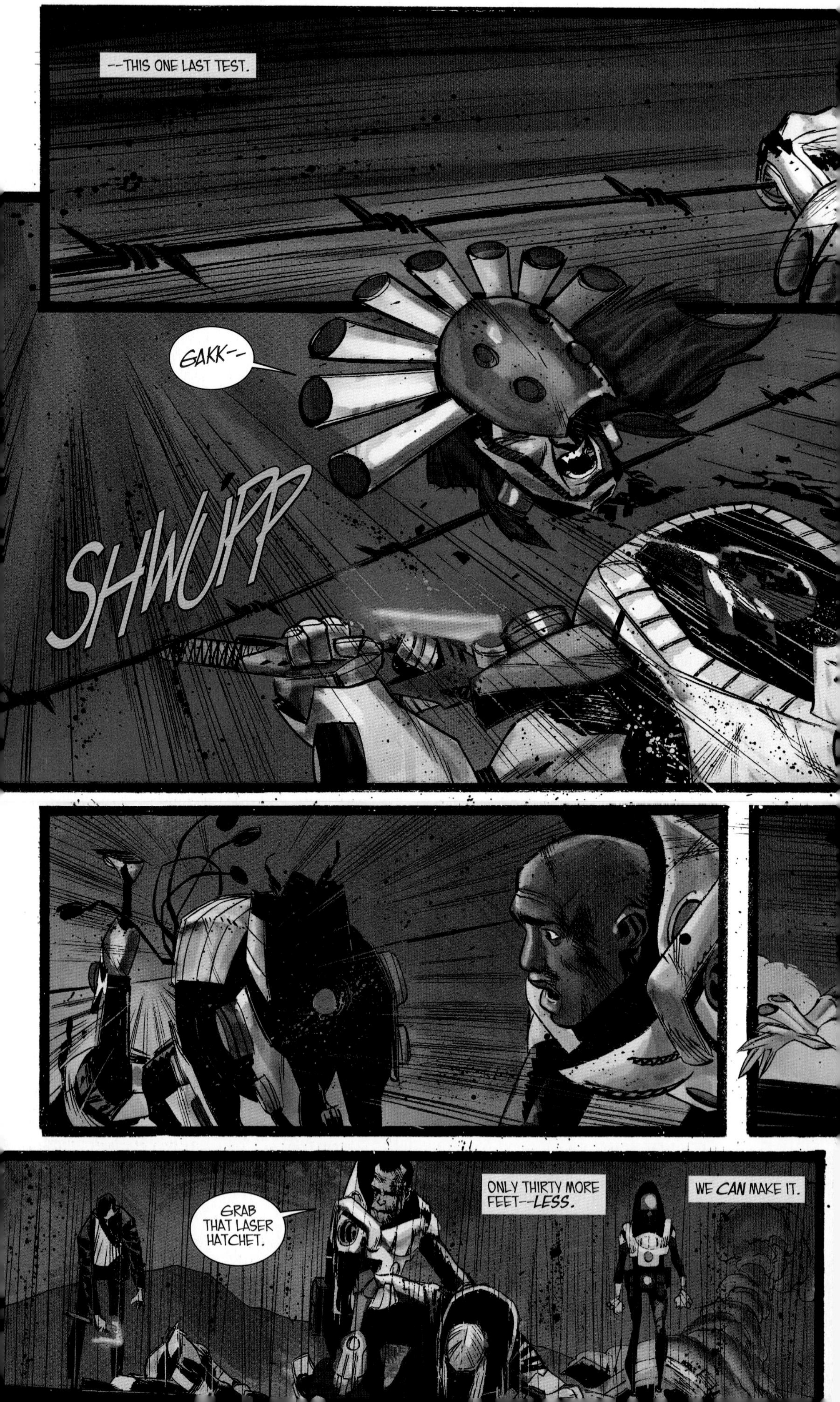
--THIS ONE LAST TEST.
GAKK--
SHWUPP
GRAB THAT LASER HATCHET.
ONLY THIRTY MORE FEET--LESS.
WE CAN MAKE IT.

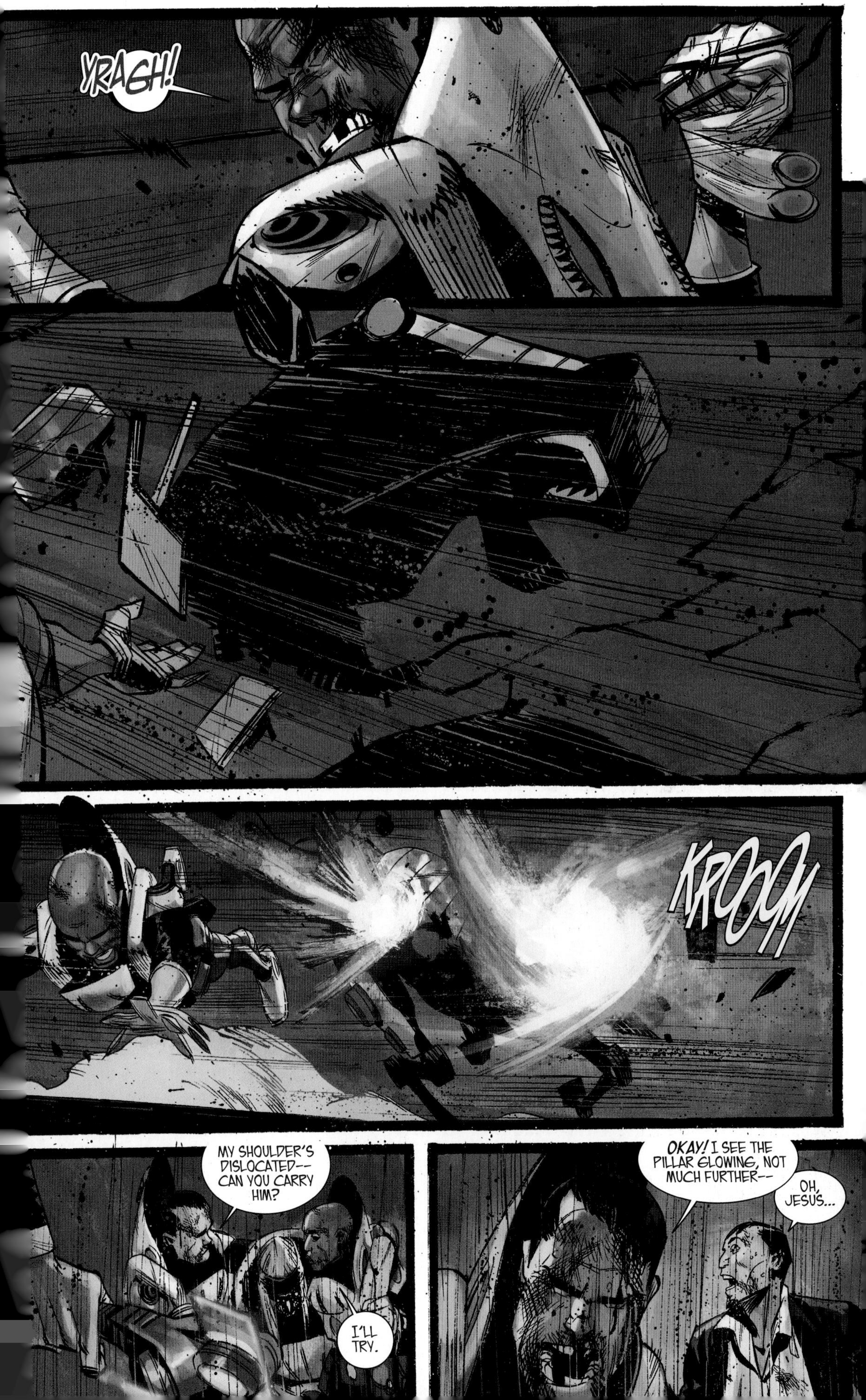
YRAGH!
KROOM
MY SHOULDER'S DISLOCATED-- CAN YOU CARRY HIM?
I'LL TRY.
OKAY! I SEE THE PILLAR GLOWING, NOT MUCH FURTHER--
OH, JESUS...

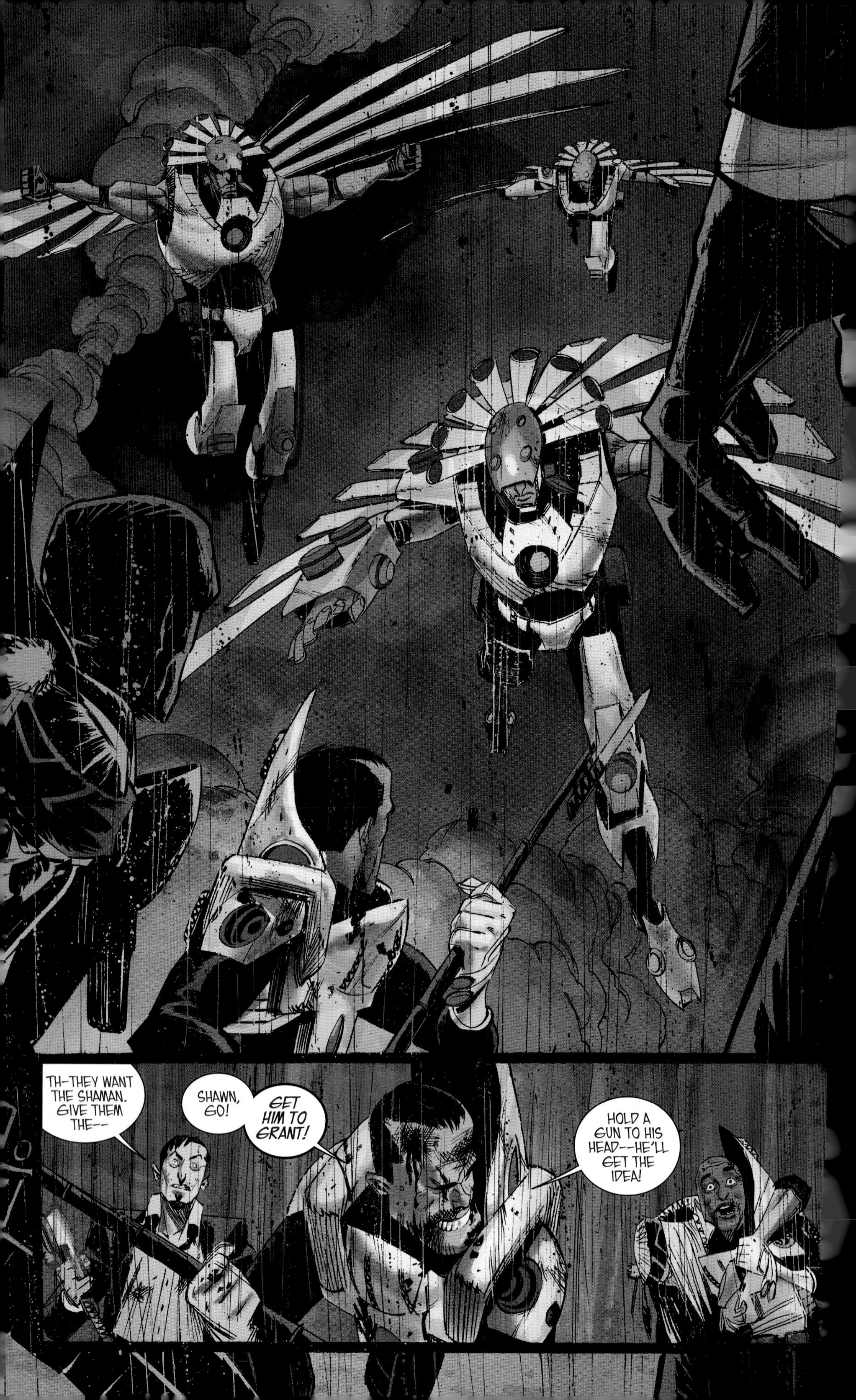
TH-THEY WANT THE SHAMAN. GIVE THEM THE--
SHAWN, GO!
GET HIM TO GRANT!
HOLD A GUN TO HIS HEAD--HE'LL GET THE IDEA!

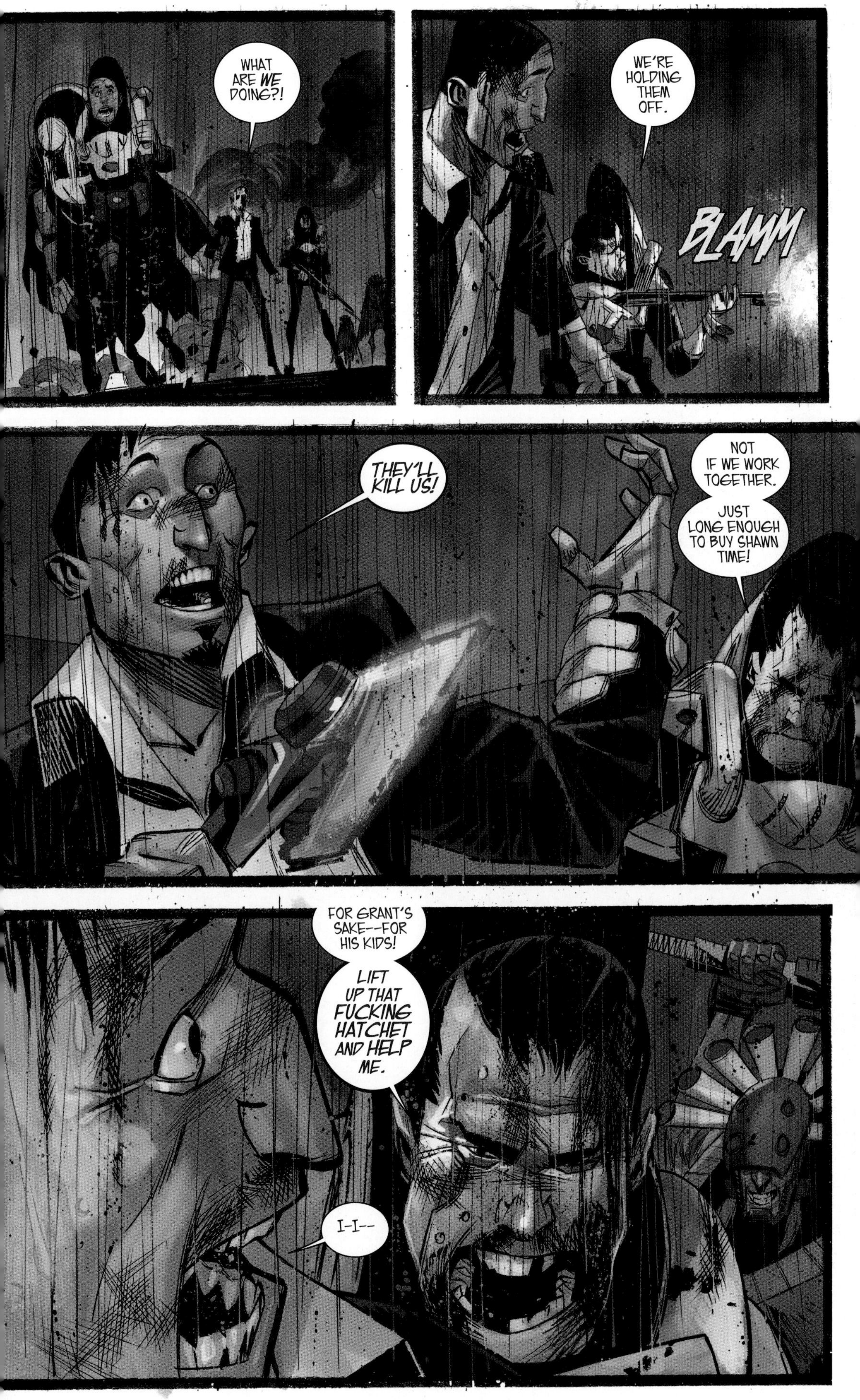
WHAT ARE WE DOING?!
WE'RE HOLDING THEM OFF.
BLAMM
THEY'LL KILL US!
NOT IF WE WORK TOGETHER.
JUST LONG ENOUGH TO BUY SHAWN TIME!
FOR GRANT'S SAKE--FOR HIS KIDS!
LIFT UP THAT FUCKING HATCHET AND HELP ME.
I-I--

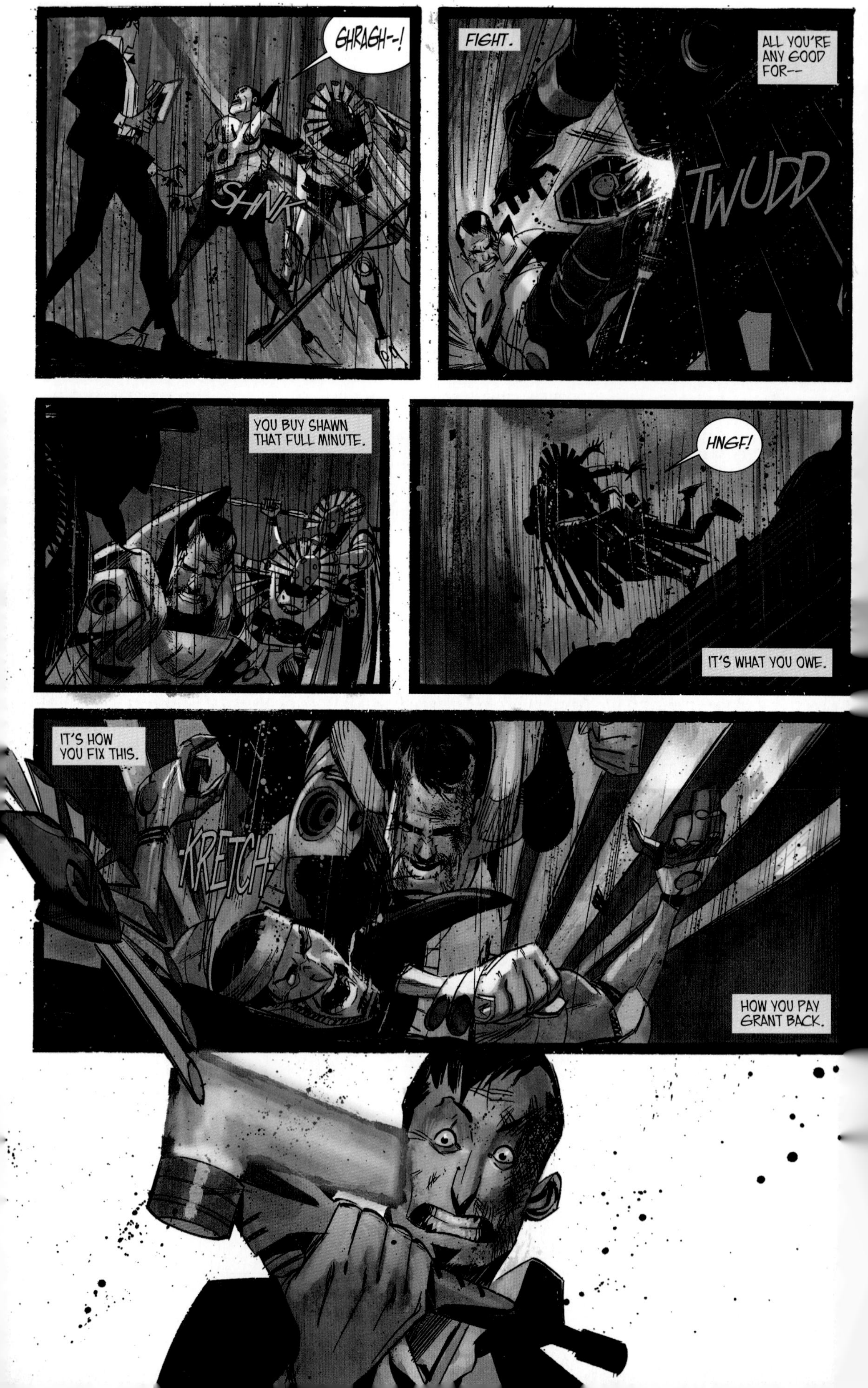
GHRAGH--!
SHNK
FIGHT.
ALL YOU'RE ANY GOOD FOR--
TWUDD
YOU BUY SHAWN THAT FULL MINUTE.
HNGF!
IT'S WHAT YOU OWE.
IT'S HOW YOU FIX THIS.
-KRETCH-
HOW YOU PAY GRANT BACK.

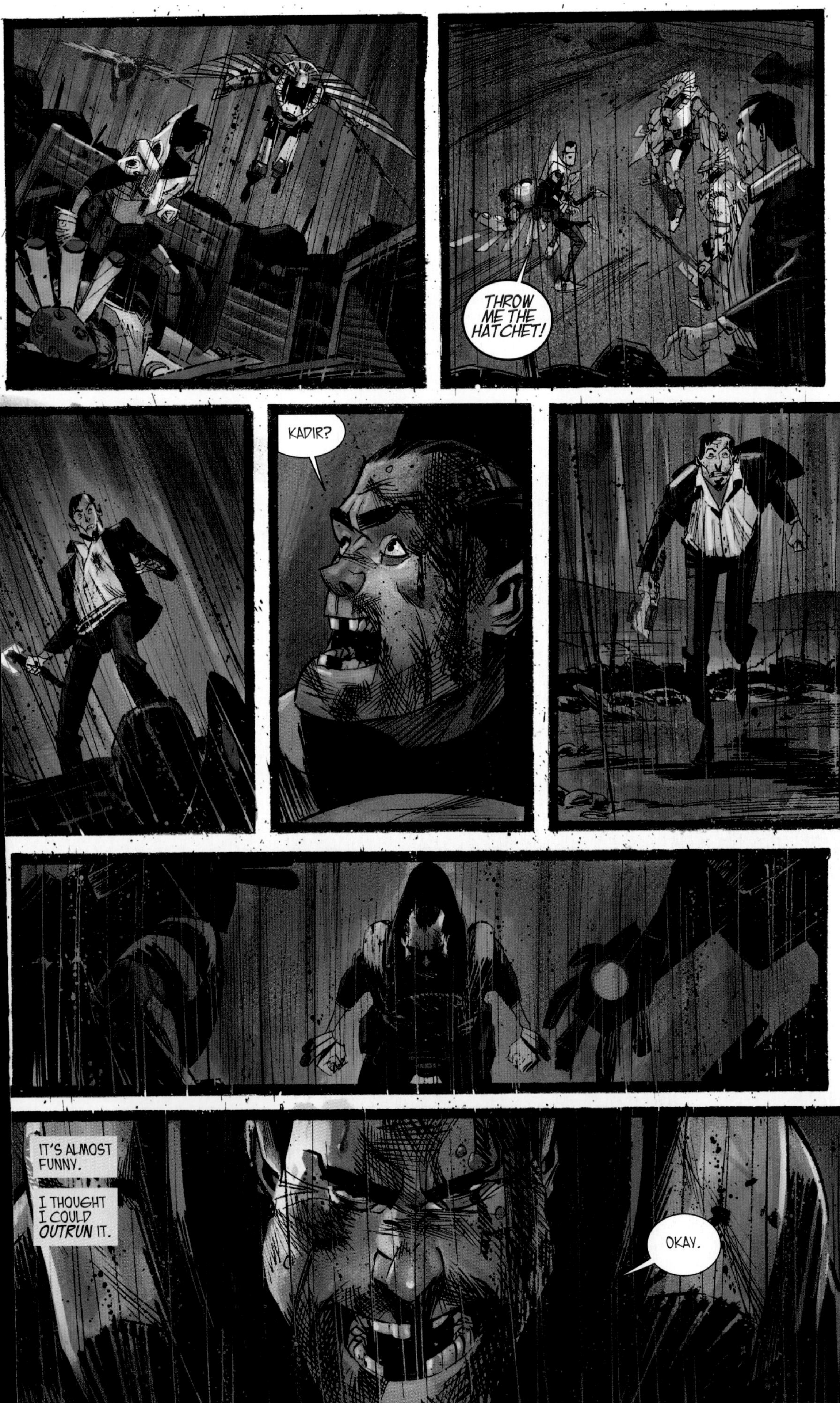
THROW ME THE HATCHET!
KADIR?
IT'S ALMOST FUNNY.
I THOUGHT I COULD *OUTRUN* IT.
OKAY.

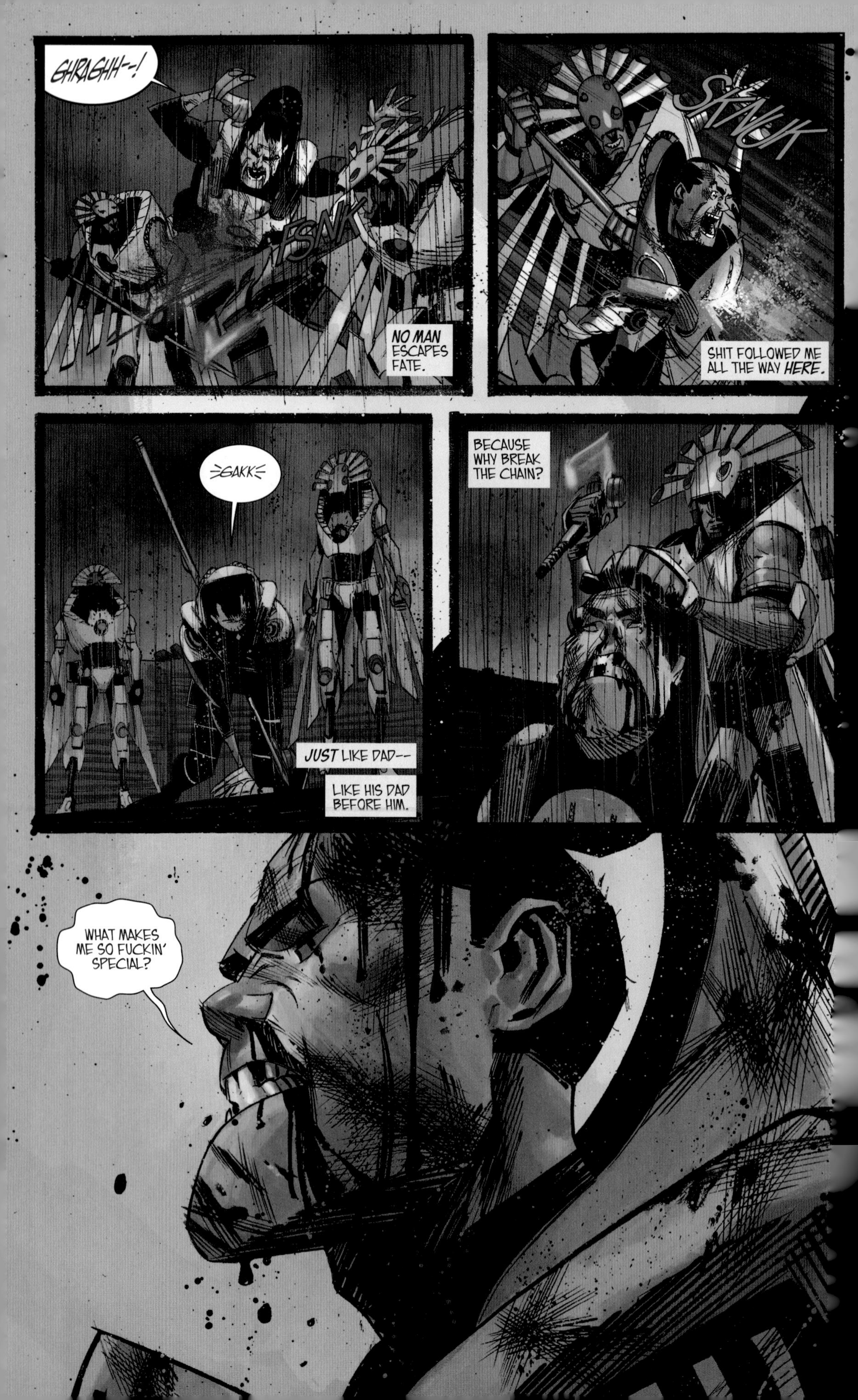
GHRAGHH--!
FSNK
NO MAN ESCAPES FATE.
SKNUK
SHIT FOLLOWED ME ALL THE WAY HERE.
GAKK
JUST LIKE DAD--
LIKE HIS DAD BEFORE HIM.
BECAUSE WHY BREAK THE CHAIN?
WHAT MAKES ME SO FUCKIN' SPECIAL?

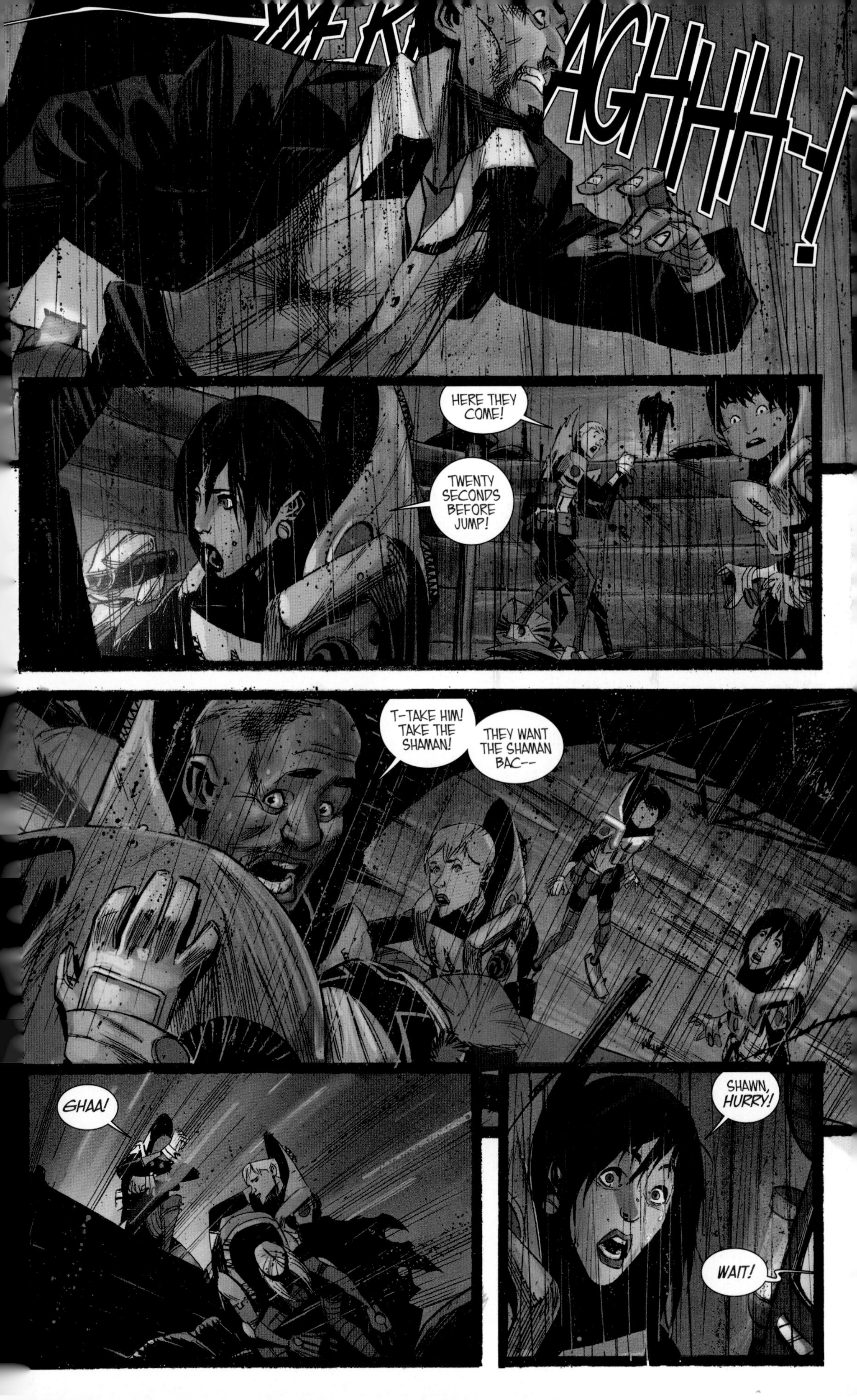
AGHHH-!
HERE THEY COME!
TWENTY SECONDS BEFORE JUMP!
T-TAKE HIM! TAKE THE SHAMAN!
THEY WANT THE SHAMAN BAC--
GHAA!
SHAWN, HURRY!
WAIT!

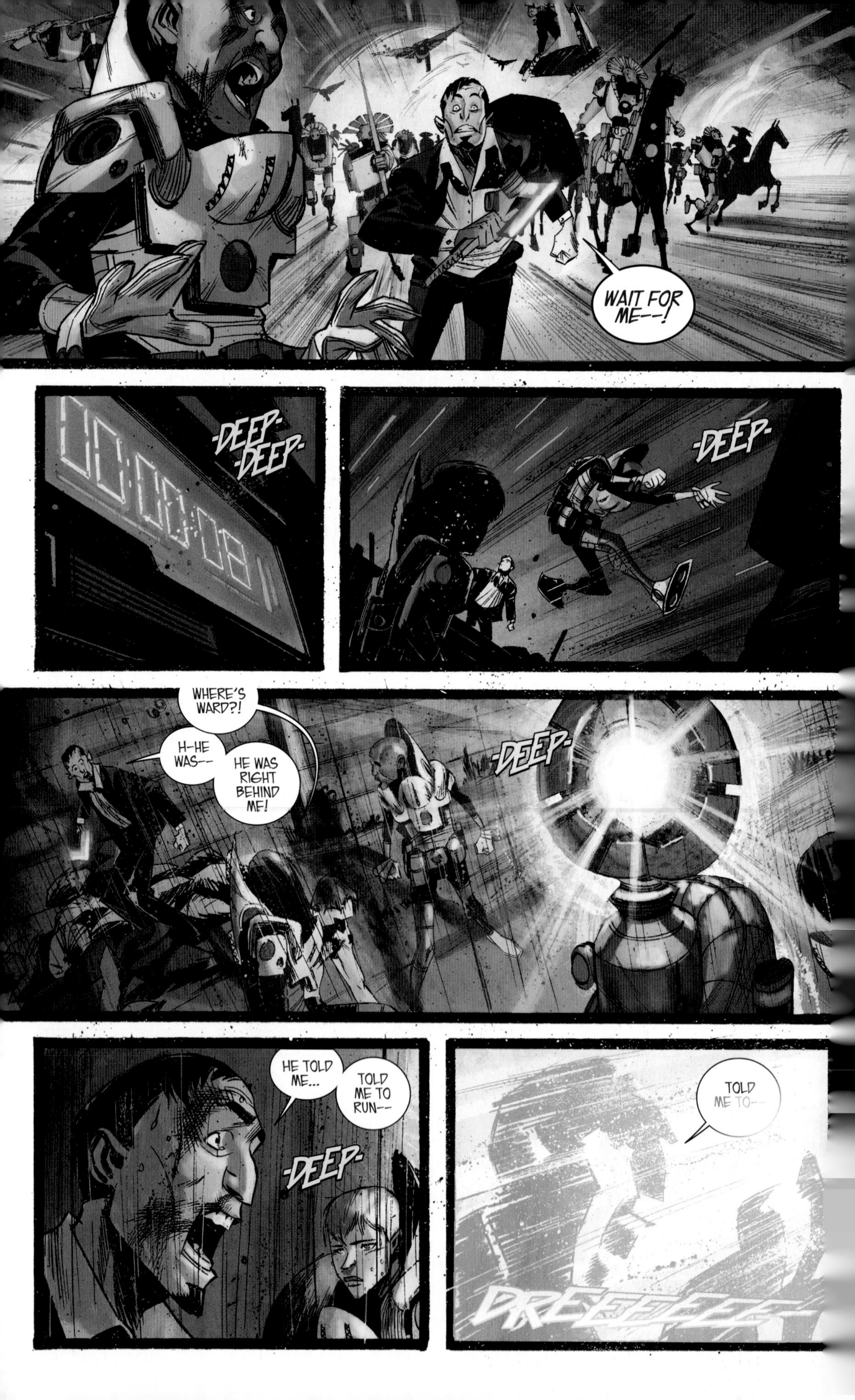
WAIT FOR ME--!
-DEEP-
-DEEP-
00:00:08
-DEEP-
WHERE'S WARD?!
H-HE WAS--
HE WAS RIGHT BEHIND ME!
-DEEP-
HE TOLD ME...
TOLD ME TO RUN--
-DEEP-
TOLD ME TO--
DREEEEEEE-

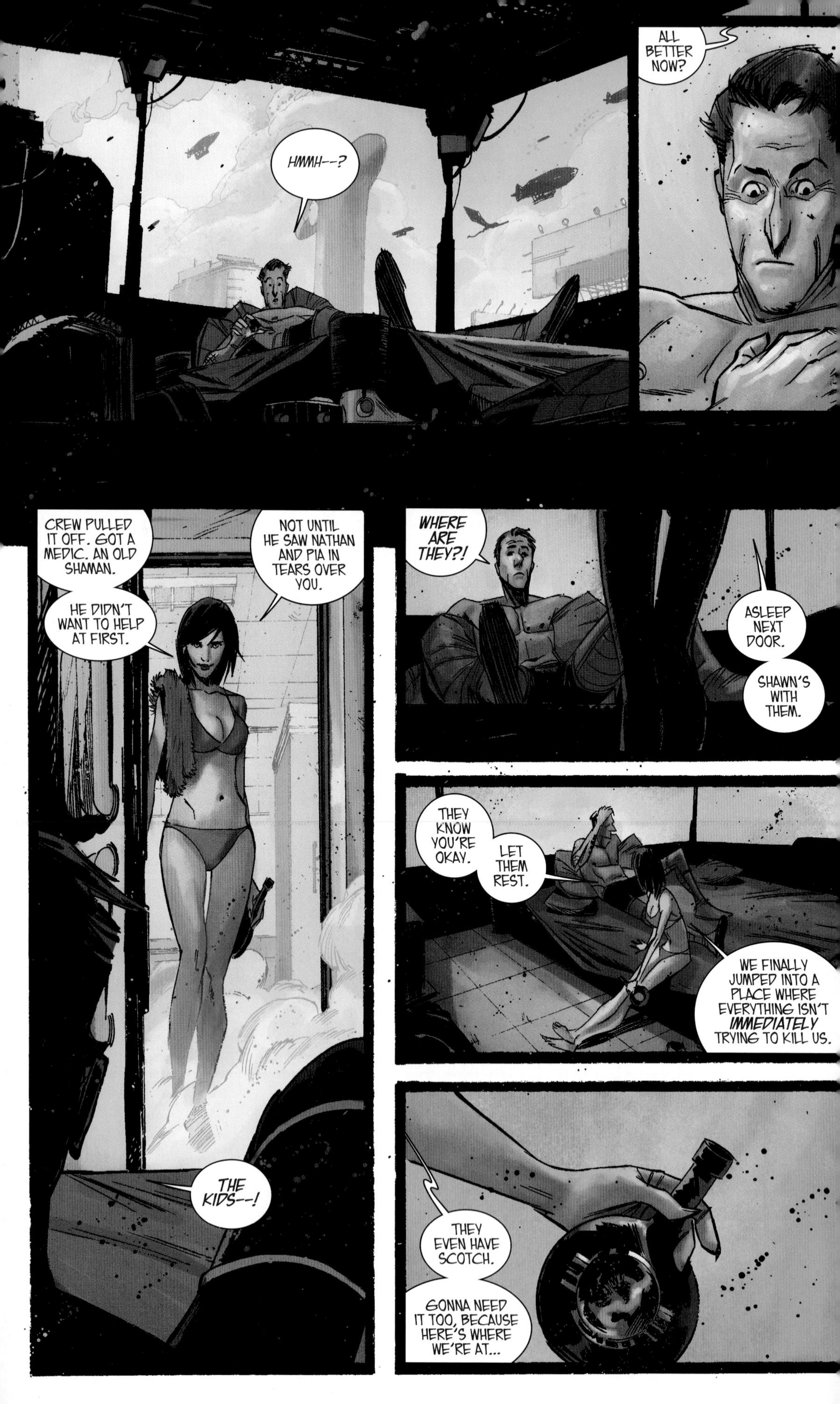
HMMH--?
ALL BETTER NOW?
CREW PULLED IT OFF. GOT A MEDIC. AN OLD SHAMAN.
HE DIDN'T WANT TO HELP AT FIRST.
NOT UNTIL HE SAW NATHAN AND PIA IN TEARS OVER YOU.
THE KIDS--!
WHERE ARE THEY?!
ASLEEP NEXT DOOR.
SHAWN'S WITH THEM.
THEY KNOW YOU'RE OKAY.
LET THEM REST.
WE FINALLY JUMPED INTO A PLACE WHERE EVERYTHING ISN'T IMMEDIATELY TRYING TO KILL US.
THEY EVEN HAVE SCOTCH.
GONNA NEED IT TOO, BECAUSE HERE'S WHERE WE'RE AT...

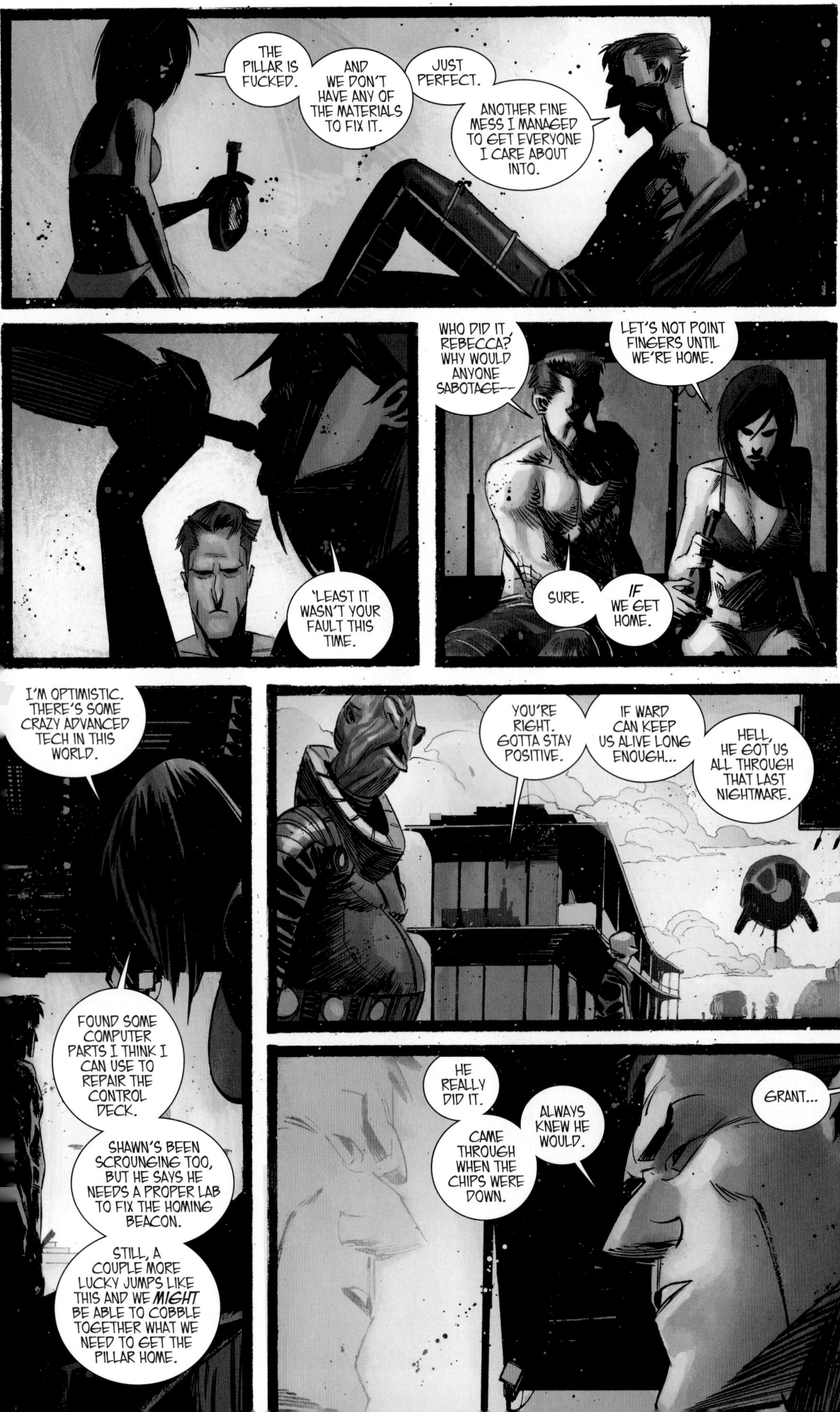
THE PILLAR IS FUCKED.
AND WE DON'T HAVE ANY OF THE MATERIALS TO FIX IT.
JUST PERFECT.
ANOTHER FINE MESS I MANAGED TO GET EVERYONE I CARE ABOUT INTO.
'LEAST IT WASN'T YOUR FAULT THIS TIME.
WHO DID IT, REBECCA? WHY WOULD ANYONE SABOTAGE--
LET'S NOT POINT FINGERS UNTIL WE'RE HOME.
SURE.
IF WE GET HOME.
I'M OPTIMISTIC. THERE'S SOME CRAZY ADVANCED TECH IN THIS WORLD.
FOUND SOME COMPUTER PARTS I THINK I CAN USE TO REPAIR THE CONTROL DECK.
SHAWN'S BEEN SCROUNGING TOO, BUT HE SAYS HE NEEDS A PROPER LAB TO FIX THE HOMING BEACON.
STILL, A COUPLE MORE LUCKY JUMPS LIKE THIS AND WE MIGHT BE ABLE TO COBBLE TOGETHER WHAT WE NEED TO GET THE PILLAR HOME.
YOU'RE RIGHT. GOTTA STAY POSITIVE.
IF WARD CAN KEEP US ALIVE LONG ENOUGH...
HELL, HE GOT US ALL THROUGH THAT LAST NIGHTMARE.
HE REALLY DID IT.
CAME THROUGH WHEN THE CHIPS WERE DOWN.
ALWAYS KNEW HE WOULD.
GRANT...

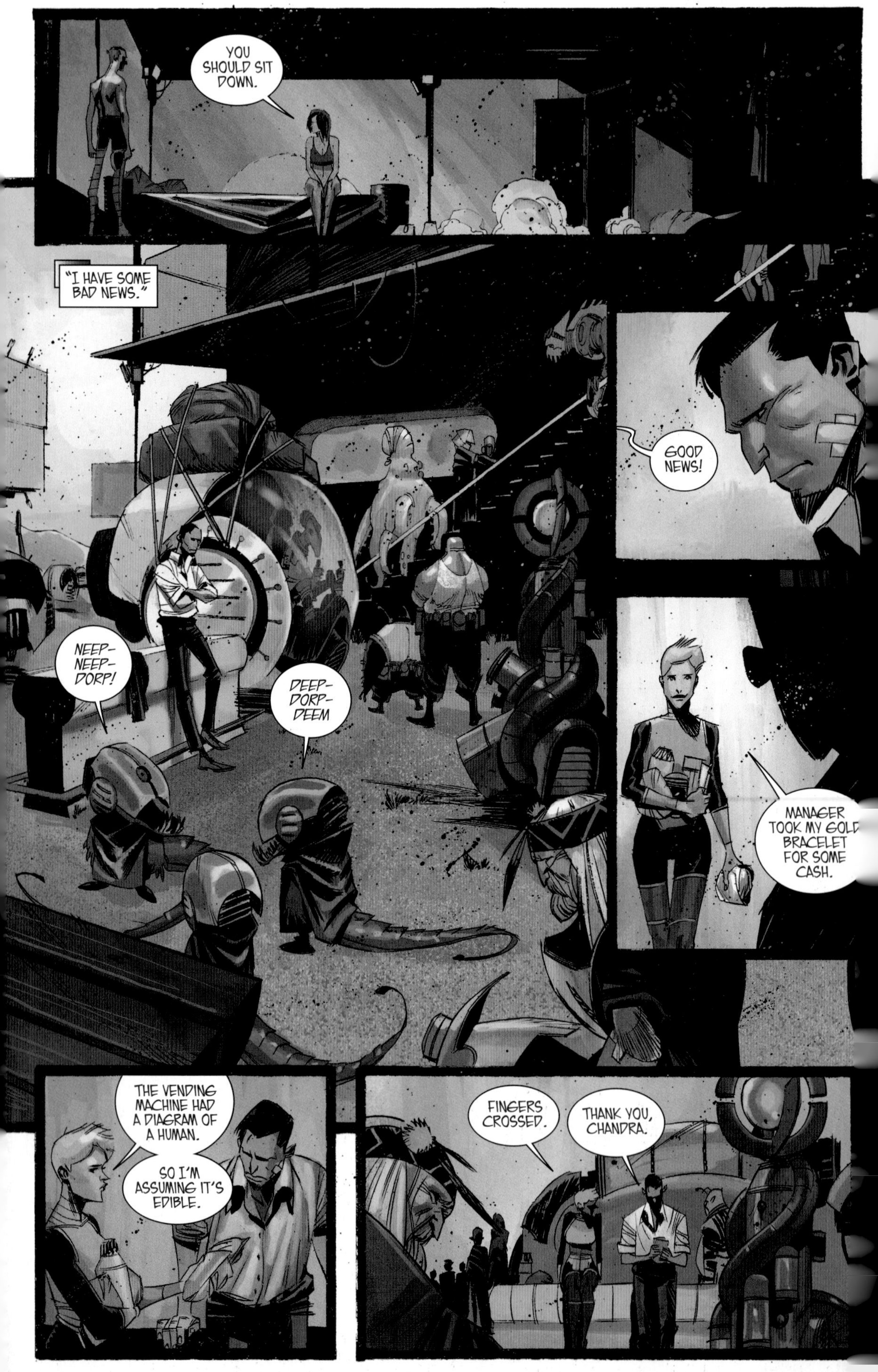
YOU SHOULD SIT DOWN.
"I HAVE SOME BAD NEWS."
GOOD NEWS!
NEEP-NEEP-DORP!
DEEP-DORP-DEEM
MANAGER TOOK MY GOLD BRACELET FOR SOME CASH.
THE VENDING MACHINE HAD A DIAGRAM OF A HUMAN.
SO I'M ASSUMING IT'S EDIBLE.
FINGERS CROSSED.
THANK YOU, CHANDRA.

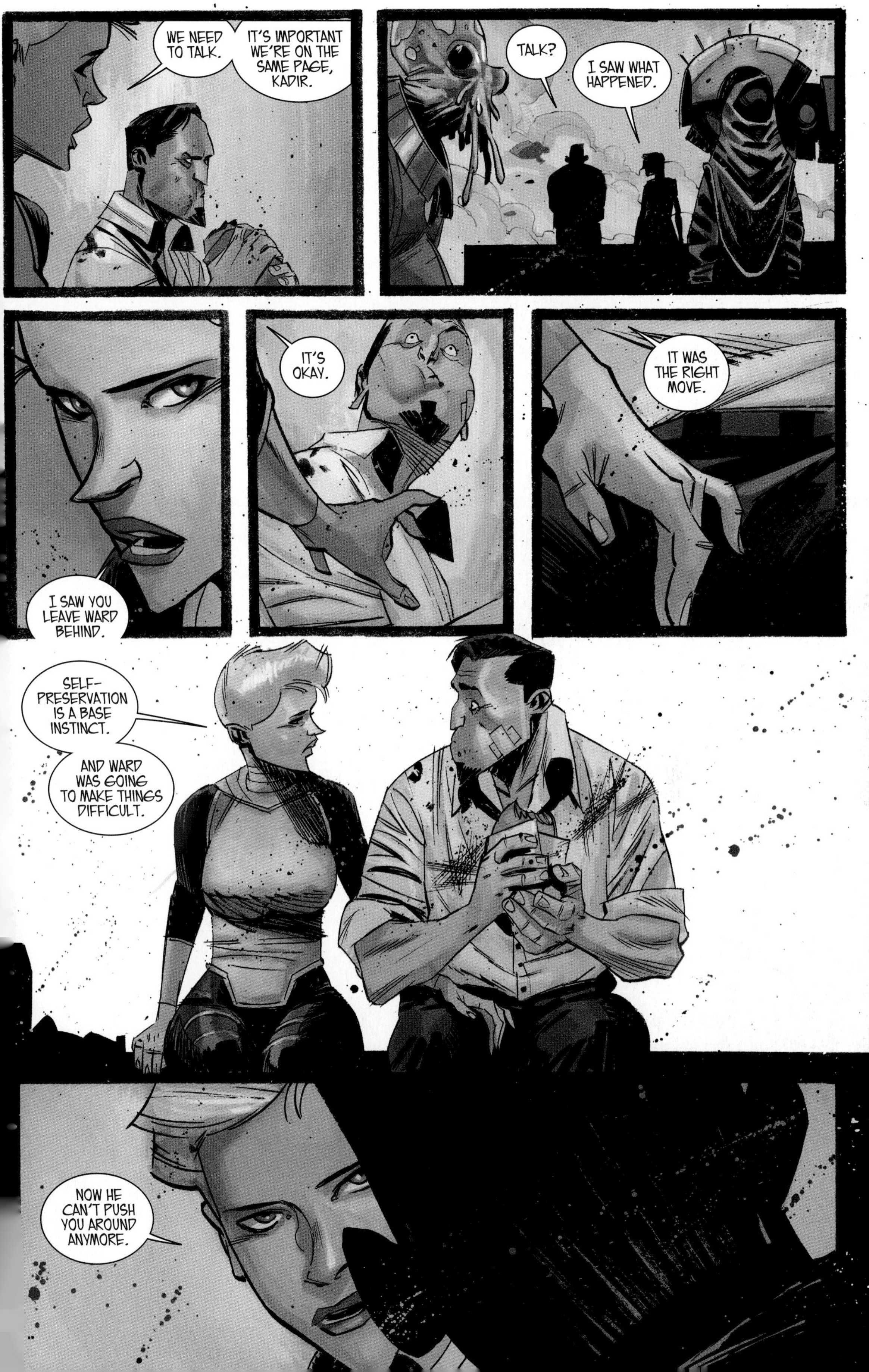
WE NEED TO TALK.
IT'S IMPORTANT WE'RE ON THE SAME PAGE, KADIR.
TALK?
I SAW WHAT HAPPENED.
I SAW YOU LEAVE WARD BEHIND.
IT'S OKAY.
IT WAS THE RIGHT MOVE.
SELF-PRESERVATION IS A BASE INSTINCT.
AND WARD WAS GOING TO MAKE THINGS DIFFICULT.
NOW HE CAN'T PUSH YOU AROUND ANYMORE.

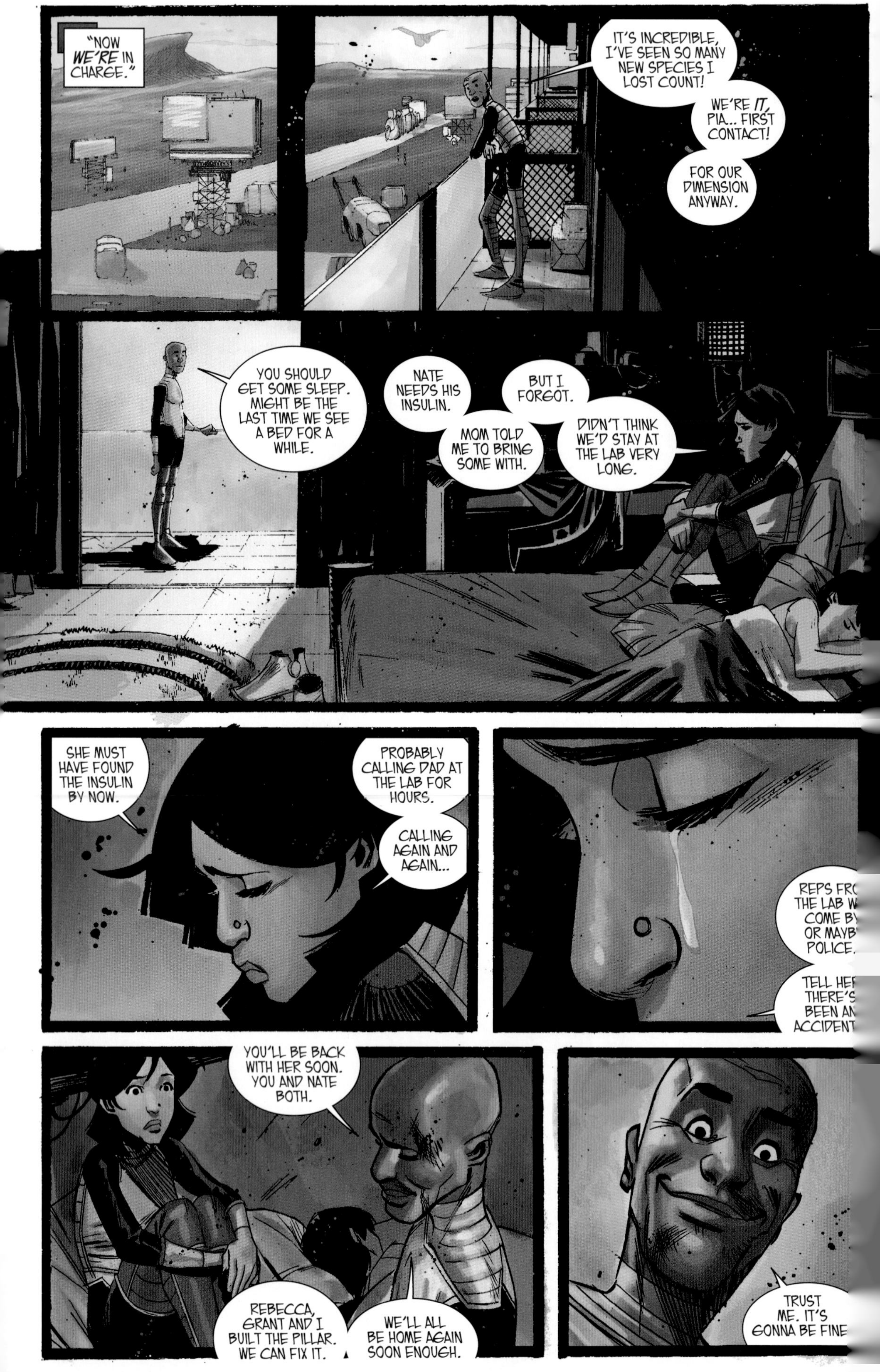
"NOW WE'RE IN CHARGE."
IT'S INCREDIBLE, I'VE SEEN SO MANY NEW SPECIES I LOST COUNT!
WE'RE IT, PIA... FIRST CONTACT!
FOR OUR DIMENSION ANYWAY.
YOU SHOULD GET SOME SLEEP. MIGHT BE THE LAST TIME WE SEE A BED FOR A WHILE.
NATE NEEDS HIS INSULIN.
MOM TOLD ME TO BRING SOME WITH.
BUT I FORGOT.
DIDN'T THINK WE'D STAY AT THE LAB VERY LONG.
SHE MUST HAVE FOUND THE INSULIN BY NOW.
PROBABLY CALLING DAD AT THE LAB FOR HOURS.
CALLING AGAIN AND AGAIN...
REPS FRO
THE LAB W
COME BY
OR MAYB
POLICE.
TELL HER
THERE'S
BEEN AN
ACCIDENT
YOU'LL BE BACK WITH HER SOON. YOU AND NATE BOTH.
REBECCA, GRANT AND I BUILT THE PILLAR. WE CAN FIX IT.
WE'LL ALL BE HOME AGAIN SOON ENOUGH.
TRUST ME. IT'S GONNA BE FINE

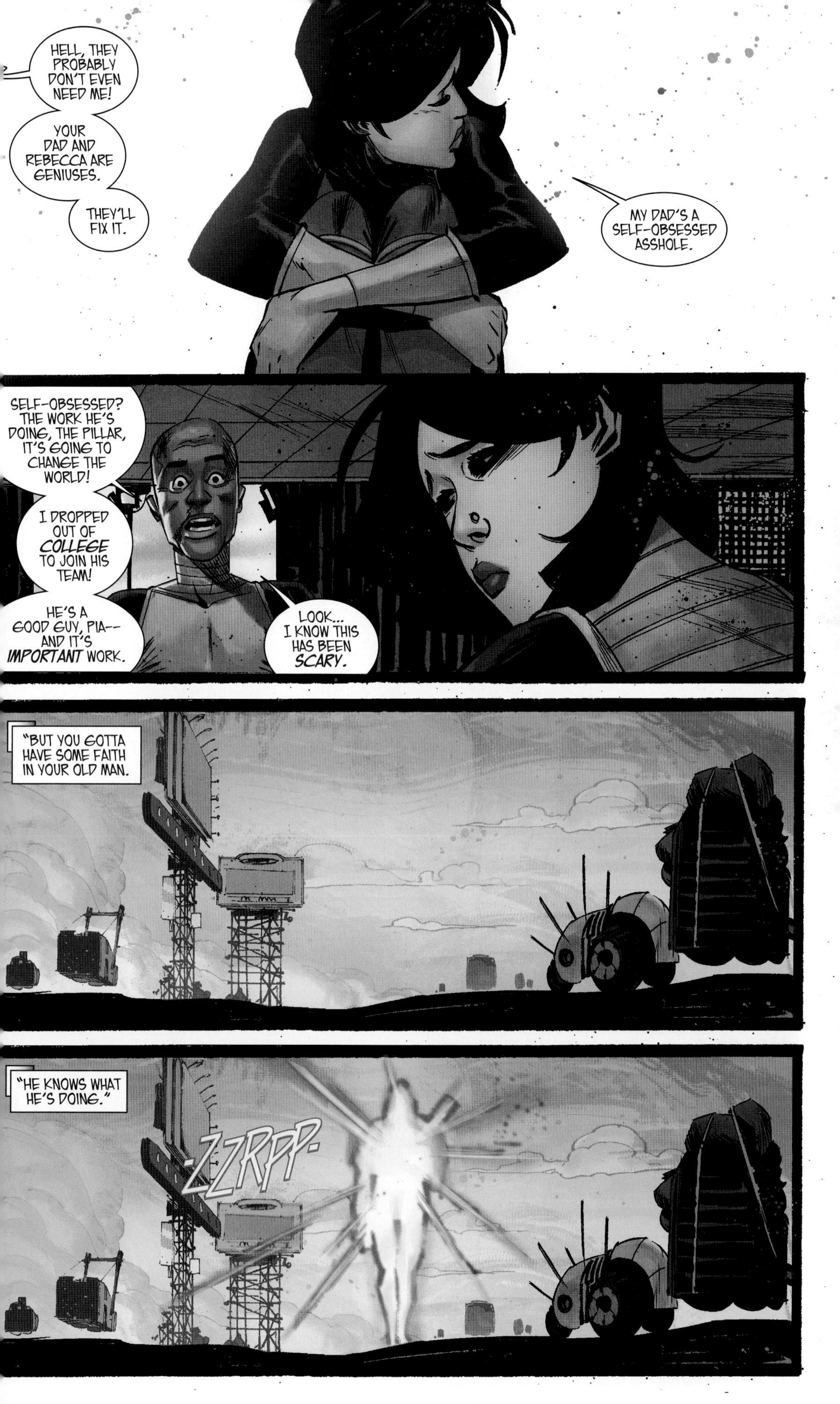
HELL, THEY PROBABLY DON'T EVEN NEED ME!
YOUR DAD AND REBECCA ARE GENIUSES.
THEY'LL FIX IT.
MY DAD'S A SELF-OBSESSED ASSHOLE.
SELF-OBSESSED? THE WORK HE'S DOING, THE PILLAR, IT'S GOING TO CHANGE THE WORLD!
I DROPPED OUT OF COLLEGE TO JOIN HIS TEAM!
HE'S A GOOD GUY, PIA-- AND IT'S IMPORTANT WORK.
LOOK... I KNOW THIS HAS BEEN SCARY.
"BUT YOU GOTTA HAVE SOME FAITH IN YOUR OLD MAN.
"HE KNOWS WHAT HE'S DOING."
-ZZRPP-

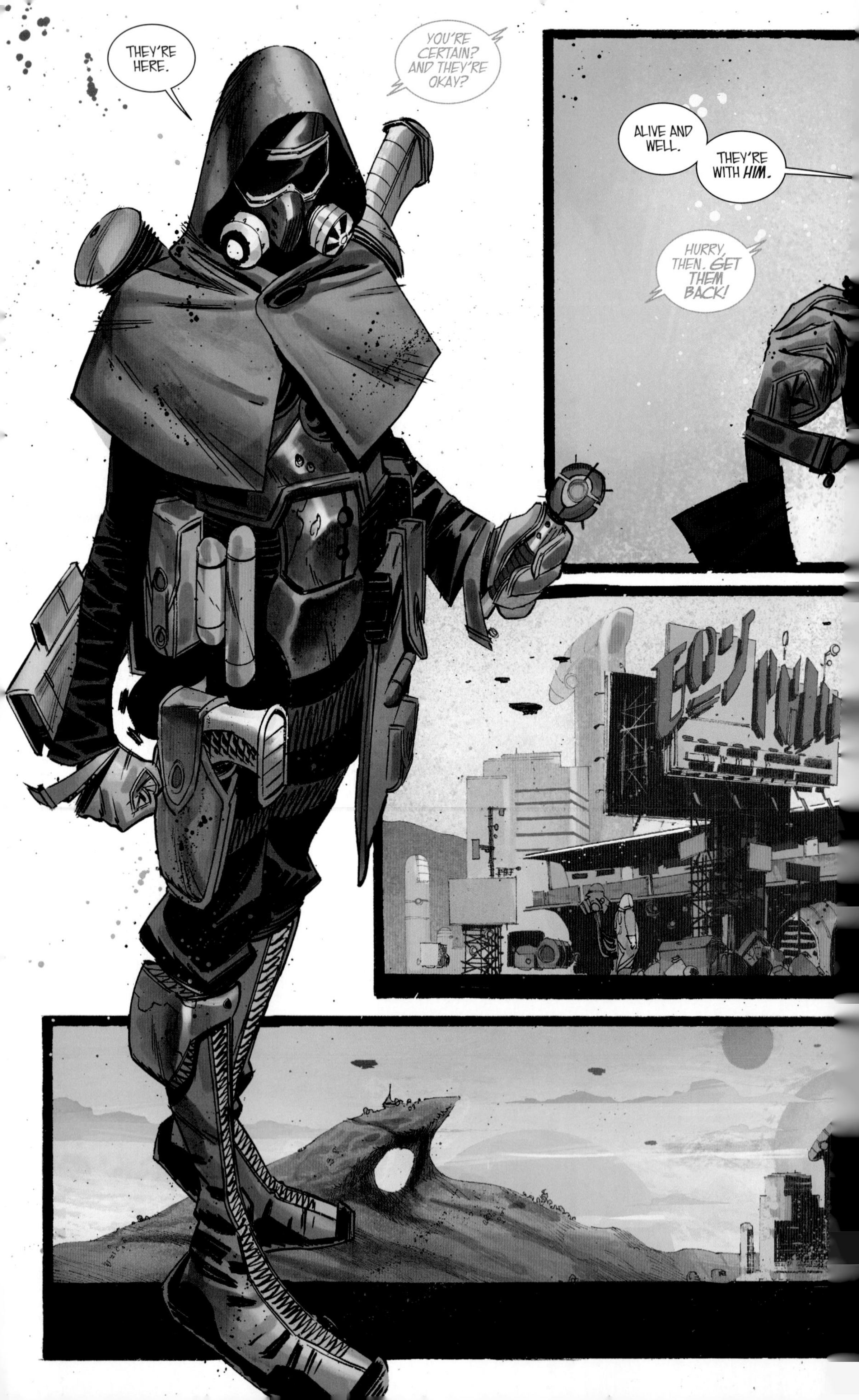
THEY'RE HERE.
YOU'RE CERTAIN? AND THEY'RE OKAY?
ALIVE AND WELL.
THEY'RE WITH HIM.
HURRY, THEN. GET THEM BACK!

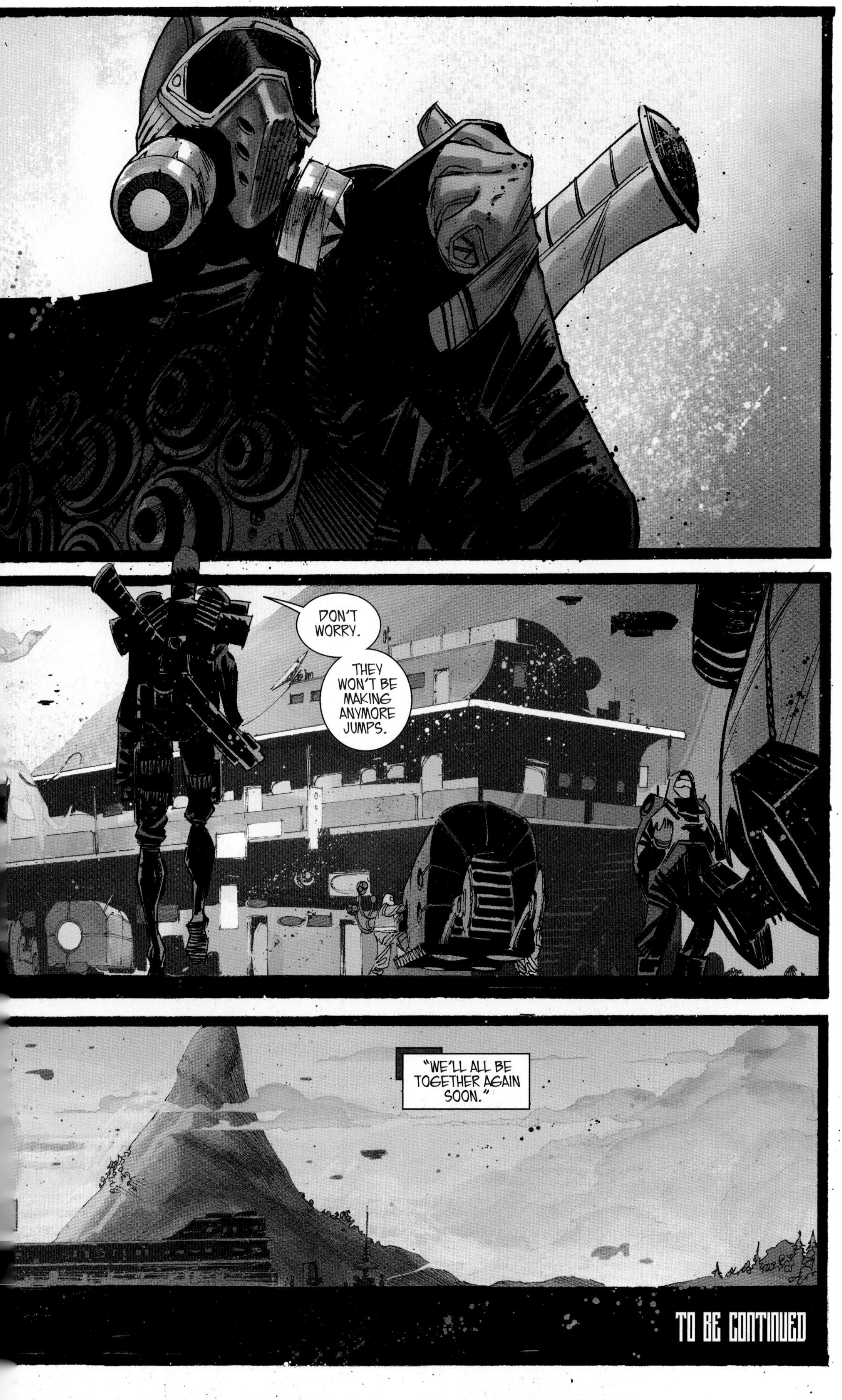
DON'T WORRY.
THEY WON'T BE MAKING ANYMORE JUMPS.
"WE'LL ALL BE TOGETHER AGAIN SOON."
TO BE CONTINUED

5

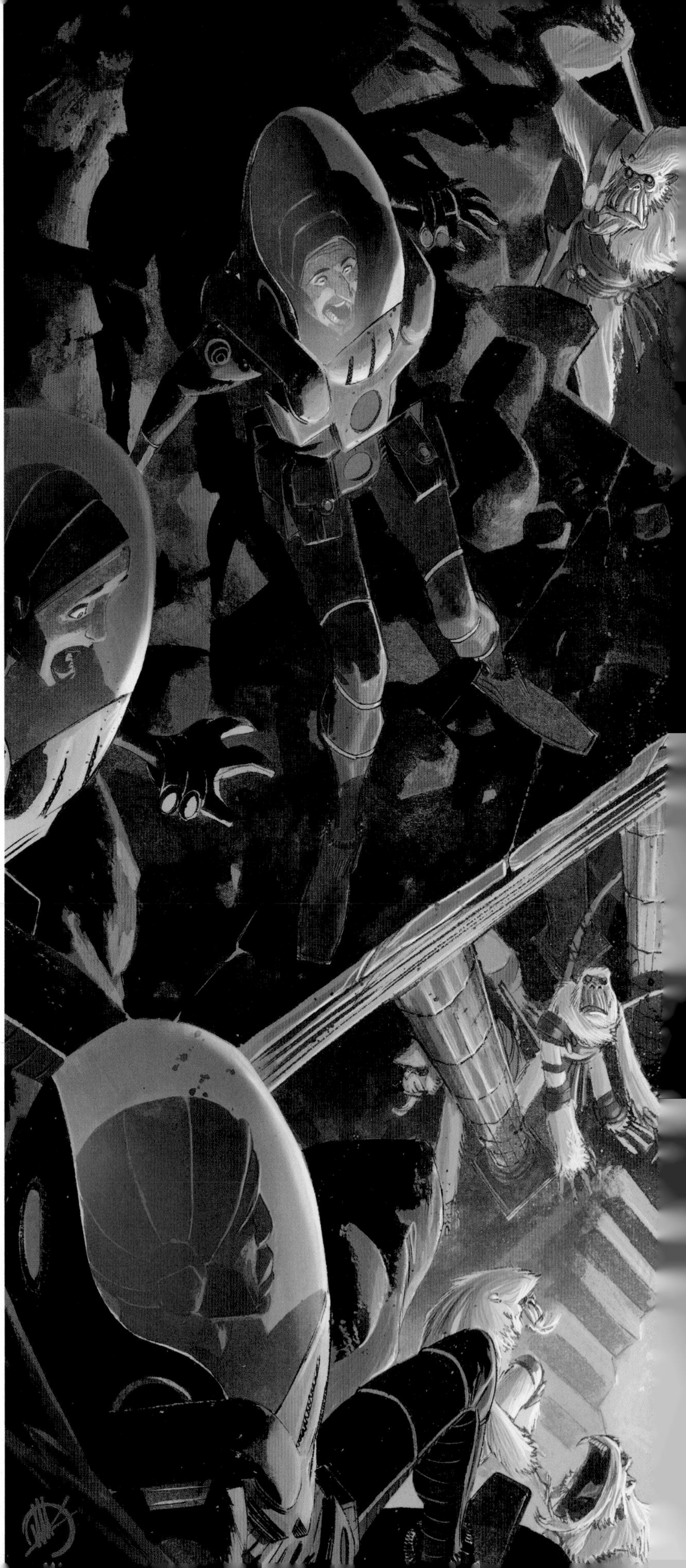

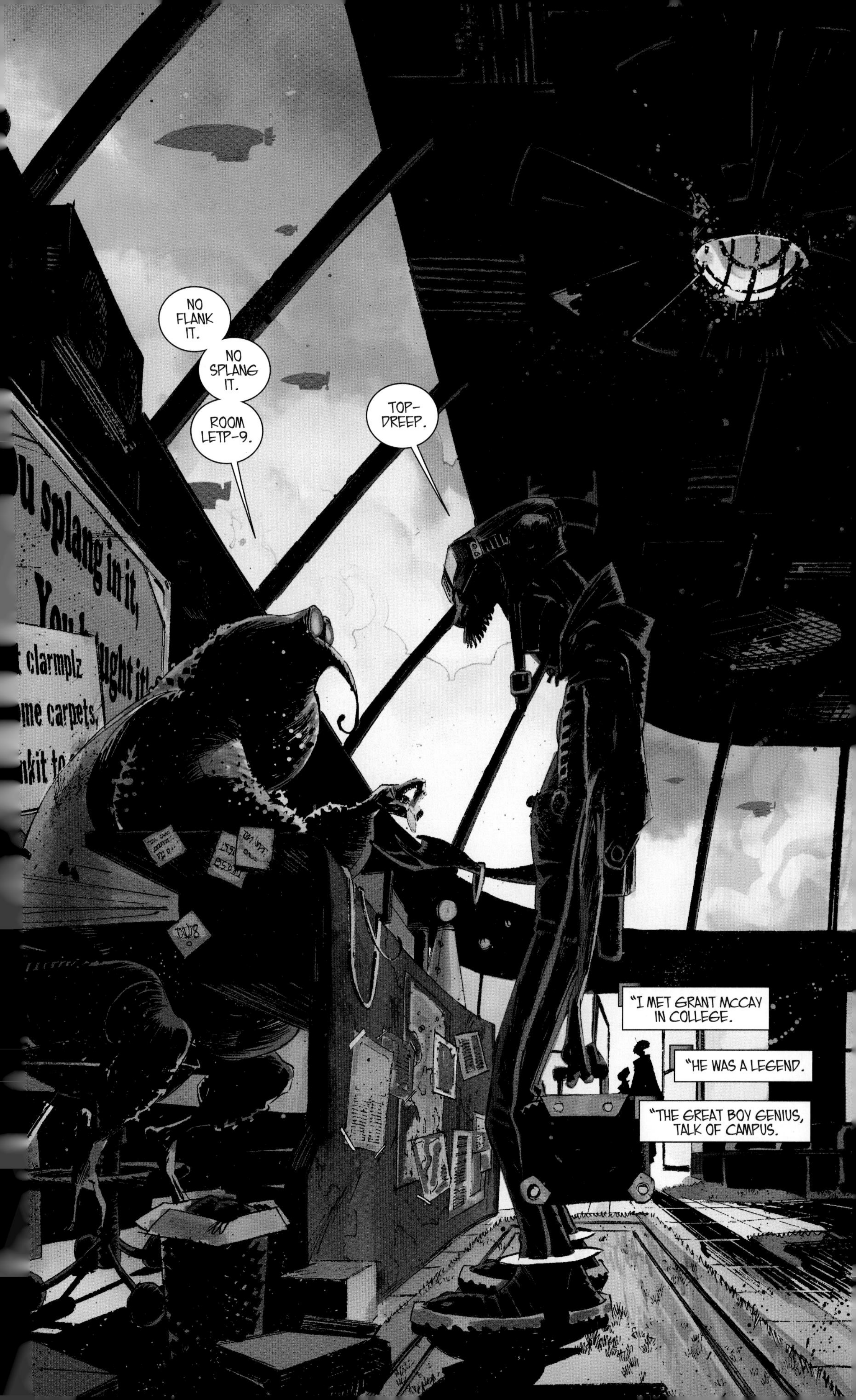
NO FLANK IT.
NO SPLANG IT.
ROOM LETP-9.
TOP-DREEP.
splang in it,
clarmplz
"I MET GRANT McCAY IN COLLEGE.
"HE WAS A LEGEND.
"THE GREAT BOY GENIUS, TALK OF CAMPUS.

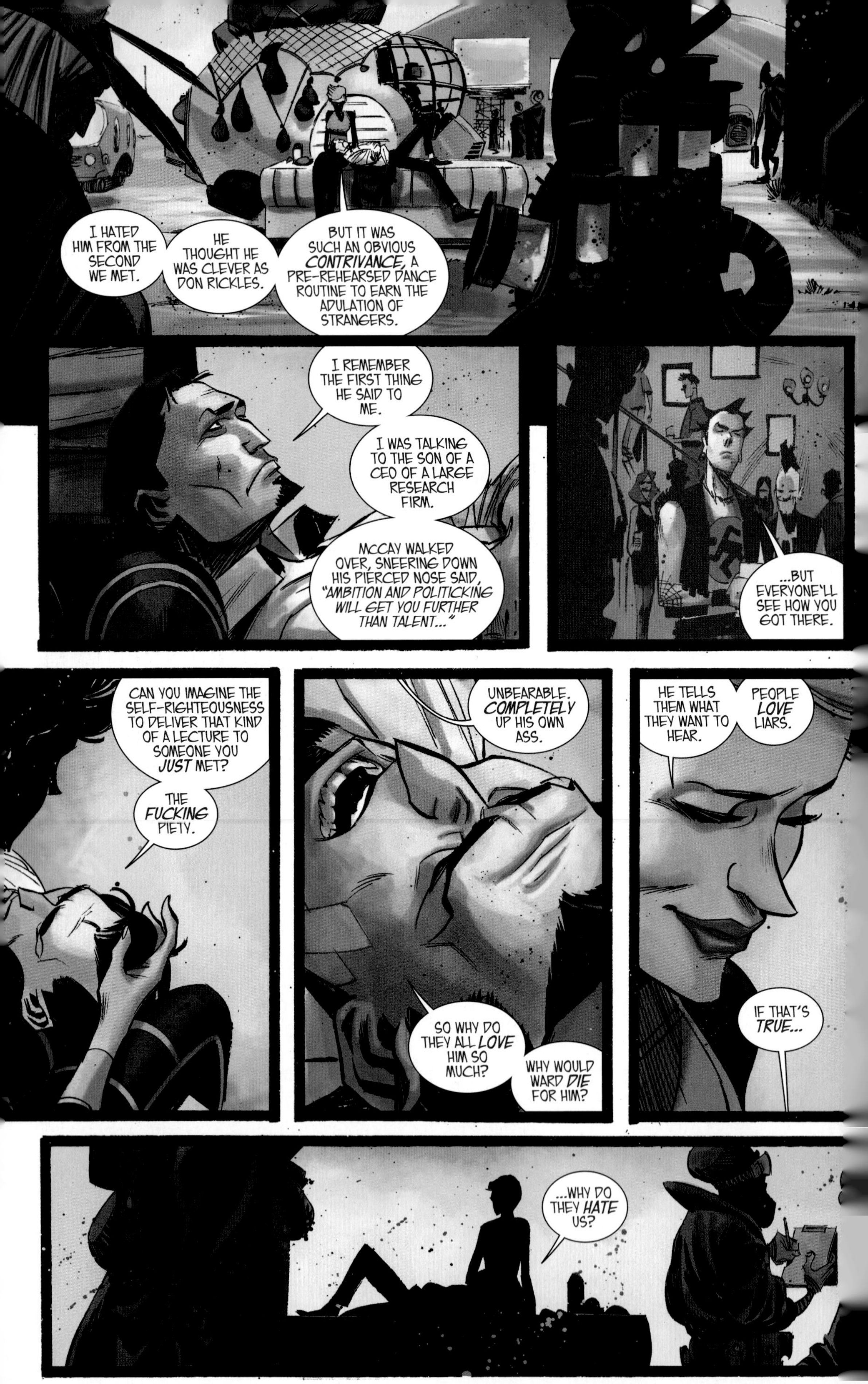
I HATED HIM FROM THE SECOND WE MET.
HE THOUGHT HE WAS CLEVER AS DON RICKLES.
BUT IT WAS SUCH AN OBVIOUS CONTRIVANCE, A PRE-REHEARSED DANCE ROUTINE TO EARN THE ADULATION OF STRANGERS.
I REMEMBER THE FIRST THING HE SAID TO ME.
I WAS TALKING TO THE SON OF A CEO OF A LARGE RESEARCH FIRM.
MCCAY WALKED OVER, SNEERING DOWN HIS PIERCED NOSE SAID, "AMBITION AND POLITICKING WILL GET YOU FURTHER THAN TALENT..."
...BUT EVERYONE'LL SEE HOW YOU GOT THERE.
CAN YOU IMAGINE THE SELF-RIGHTEOUSNESS TO DELIVER THAT KIND OF A LECTURE TO SOMEONE YOU JUST MET?
THE FUCKING PIETY.
UNBEARABLE. COMPLETELY UP HIS OWN ASS.
SO WHY DO THEY ALL LOVE HIM SO MUCH?
WHY WOULD WARD DIE FOR HIM?
HE TELLS THEM WHAT THEY WANT TO HEAR.
PEOPLE LOVE LIARS.
IF THAT'S TRUE...
...WHY DO THEY HATE US?

PIA?

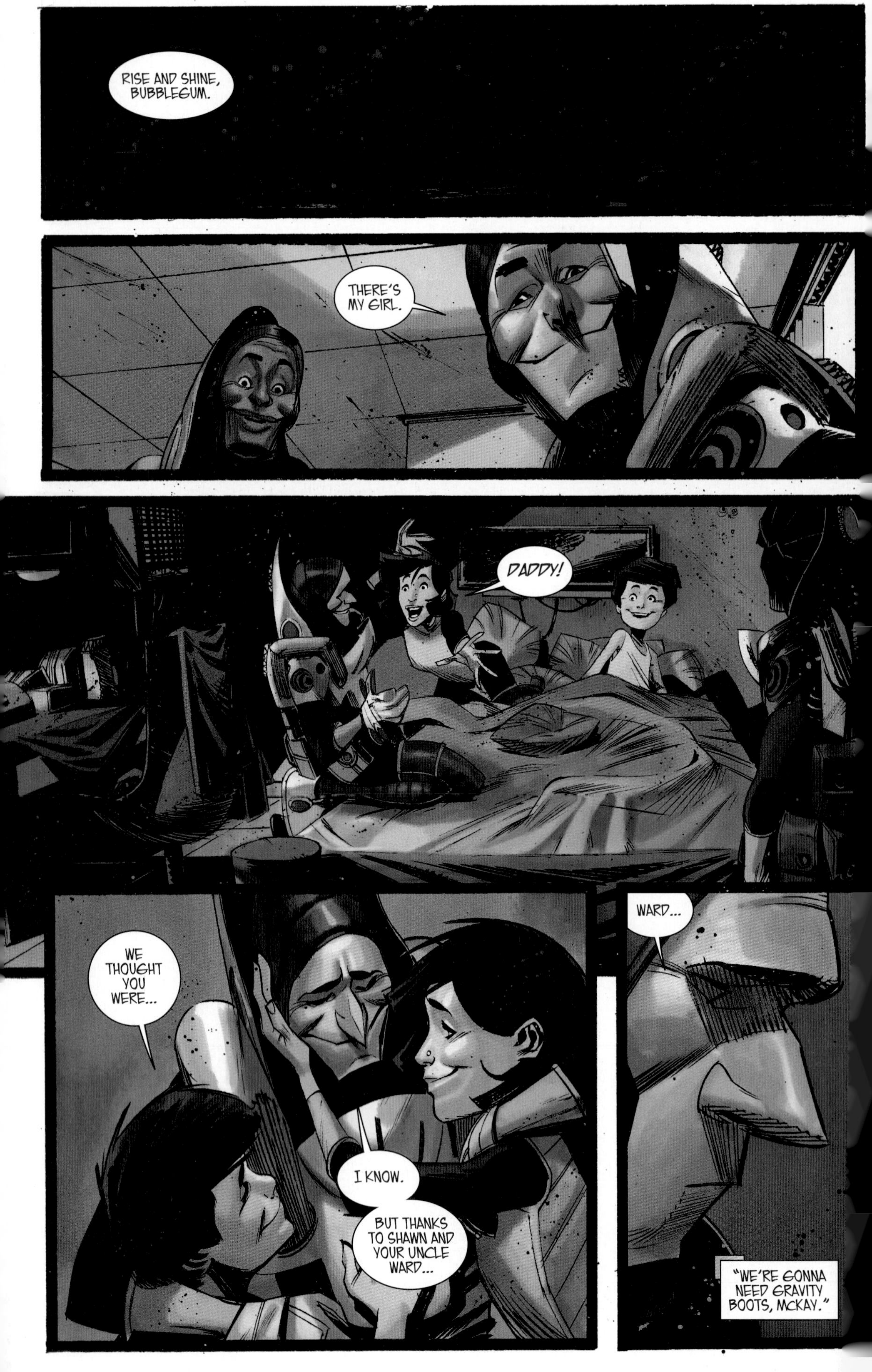

RISE AND SHINE, BUBBLEGUM.
THERE'S MY GIRL.
DADDY!
WE THOUGHT YOU WERE...
I KNOW.
BUT THANKS TO SHAWN AND YOUR UNCLE WARD...
WARD...
"WE'RE GONNA NEED GRAVITY BOOTS, MCKAY."

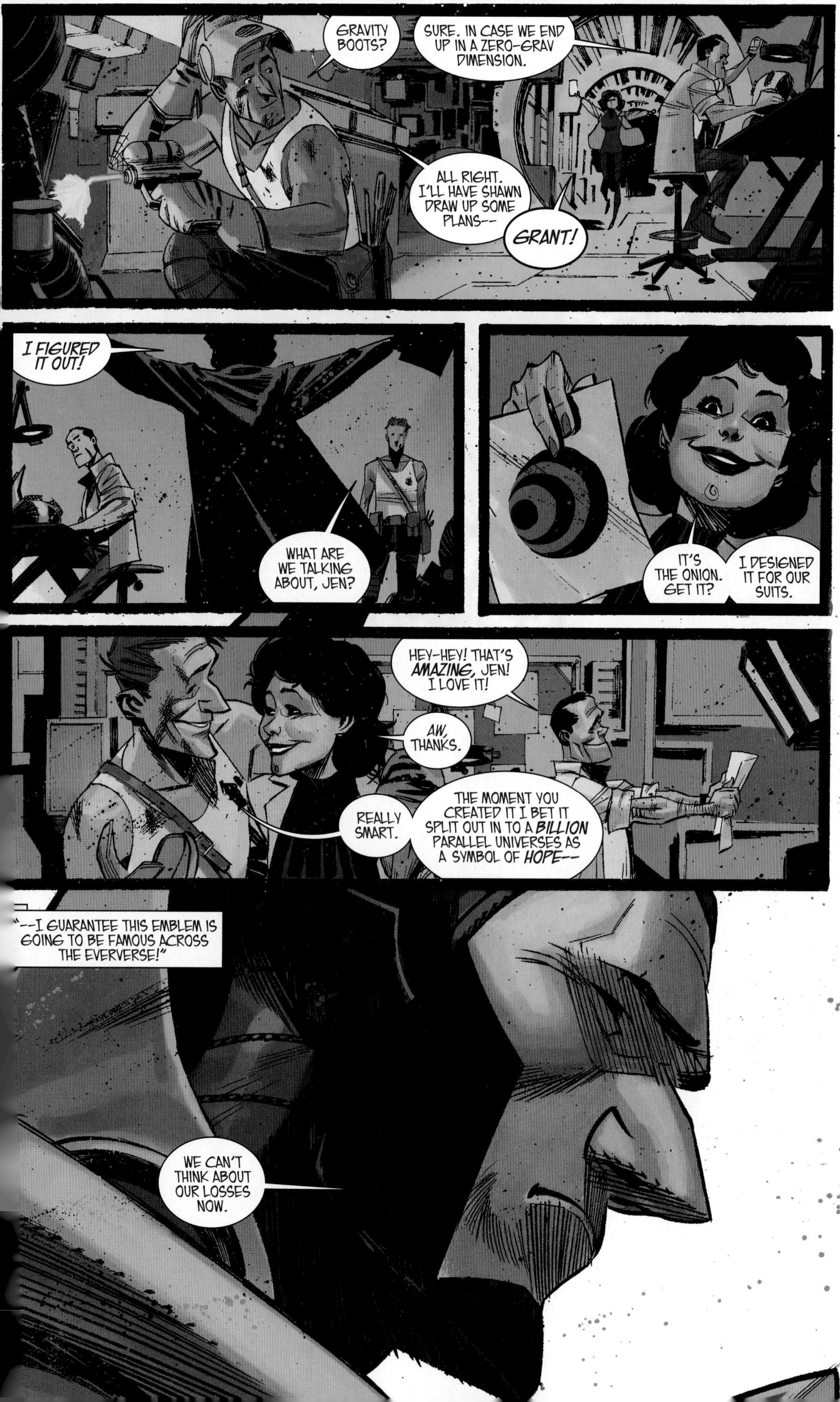
GRAVITY BOOTS?
SURE. IN CASE WE END UP IN A ZERO-GRAV DIMENSION.
ALL RIGHT. I'LL HAVE SHAWN DRAW UP SOME PLANS--
GRANT!
I FIGURED IT OUT!
WHAT ARE WE TALKING ABOUT, JEN?
IT'S THE ONION. GET IT?
I DESIGNED IT FOR OUR SUITS.
HEY-HEY! THAT'S AMAZING, JEN! I LOVE IT!
AW, THANKS.
REALLY SMART.
THE MOMENT YOU CREATED IT I BET IT SPLIT OUT IN TO A BILLION PARALLEL UNIVERSES AS A SYMBOL OF HOPE--
"--I GUARANTEE THIS EMBLEM IS GOING TO BE FAMOUS ACROSS THE EVERVERSE!"
WE CAN'T THINK ABOUT OUR LOSSES NOW.

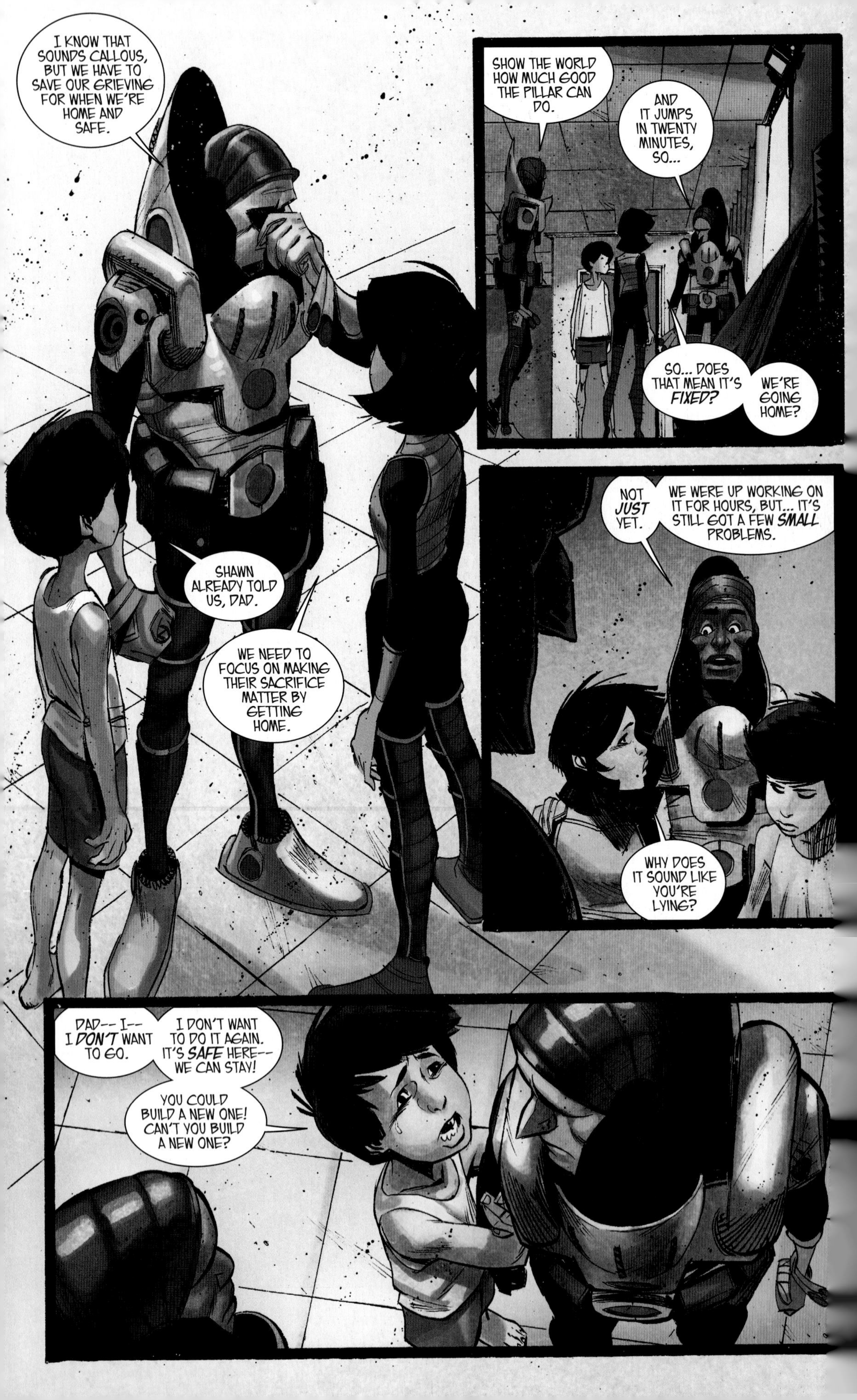
I KNOW THAT SOUNDS CALLOUS, BUT WE HAVE TO SAVE OUR GRIEVING FOR WHEN WE'RE HOME AND SAFE.
SHAWN ALREADY TOLD US, DAD.
WE NEED TO FOCUS ON MAKING THEIR SACRIFICE MATTER BY GETTING HOME.
SHOW THE WORLD HOW MUCH GOOD THE PILLAR CAN DO.
AND IT JUMPS IN TWENTY MINUTES, SO...
SO... DOES THAT MEAN IT'S FIXED?
WE'RE GOING HOME?
NOT JUST YET.
WE WERE UP WORKING ON IT FOR HOURS, BUT... IT'S STILL GOT A FEW SMALL PROBLEMS.
WHY DOES IT SOUND LIKE YOU'RE LYING?
DAD-- I-- I DON'T WANT TO GO.
I DON'T WANT TO DO IT AGAIN. IT'S SAFE HERE-- WE CAN STAY!
YOU COULD BUILD A NEW ONE! CAN'T YOU BUILD A NEW ONE?

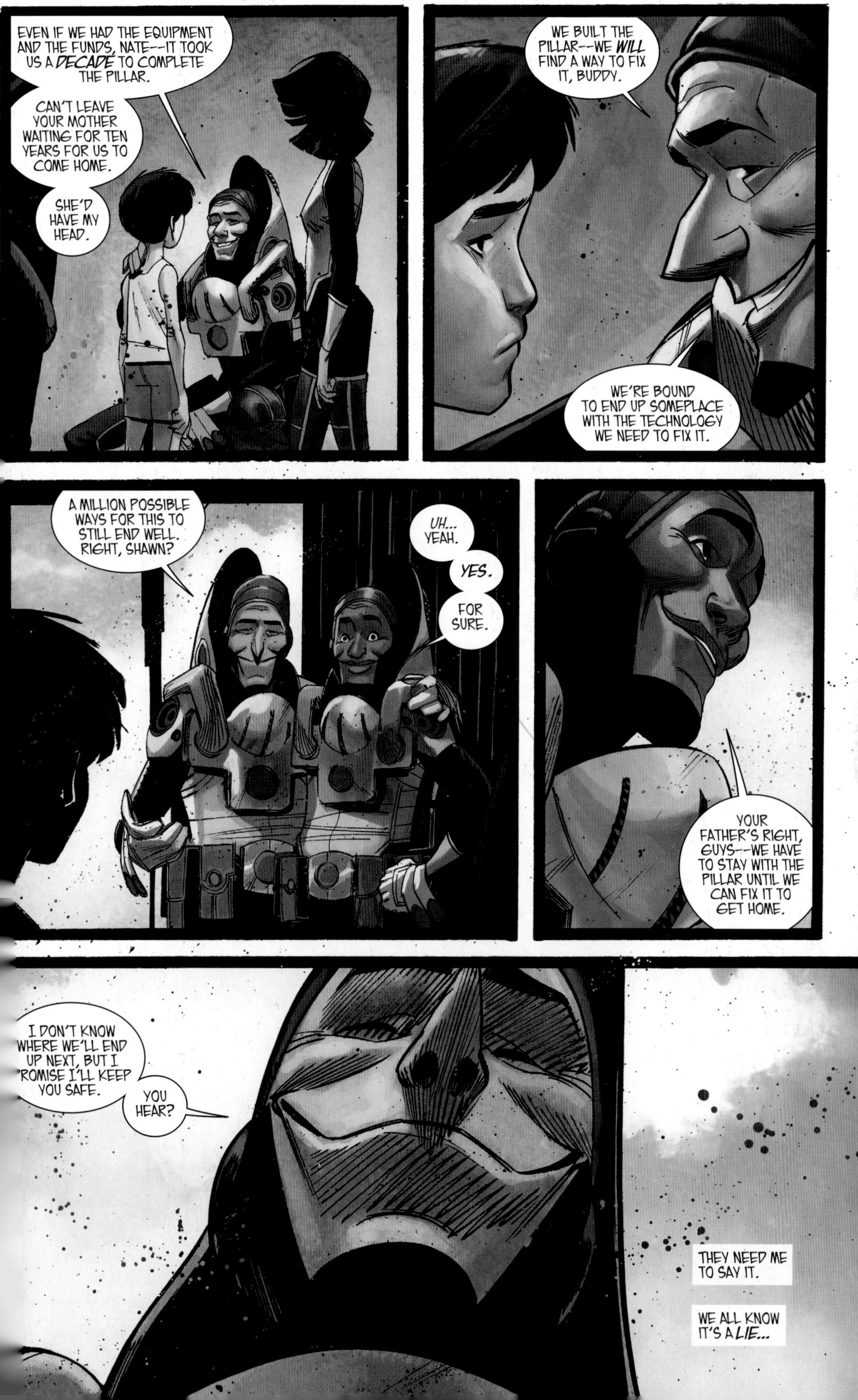
EVEN IF WE HAD THE EQUIPMENT AND THE FUNDS, NATE--IT TOOK US A DECADE TO COMPLETE THE PILLAR.
CAN'T LEAVE YOUR MOTHER WAITING FOR TEN YEARS FOR US TO COME HOME.
SHE'D HAVE MY HEAD.
WE BUILT THE PILLAR--WE WILL FIND A WAY TO FIX IT, BUDDY.
WE'RE BOUND TO END UP SOMEPLACE WITH THE TECHNOLOGY WE NEED TO FIX IT.
A MILLION POSSIBLE WAYS FOR THIS TO STILL END WELL. RIGHT, SHAWN?
UH... YEAH.
YES.
FOR SURE.
YOUR FATHER'S RIGHT, GUYS--WE HAVE TO STAY WITH THE PILLAR UNTIL WE CAN FIX IT TO GET HOME.
I DON'T KNOW WHERE WE'LL END UP NEXT, BUT I PROMISE I'LL KEEP YOU SAFE.
YOU HEAR?
THEY NEED ME TO SAY IT.
WE ALL KNOW IT'S A LIE...

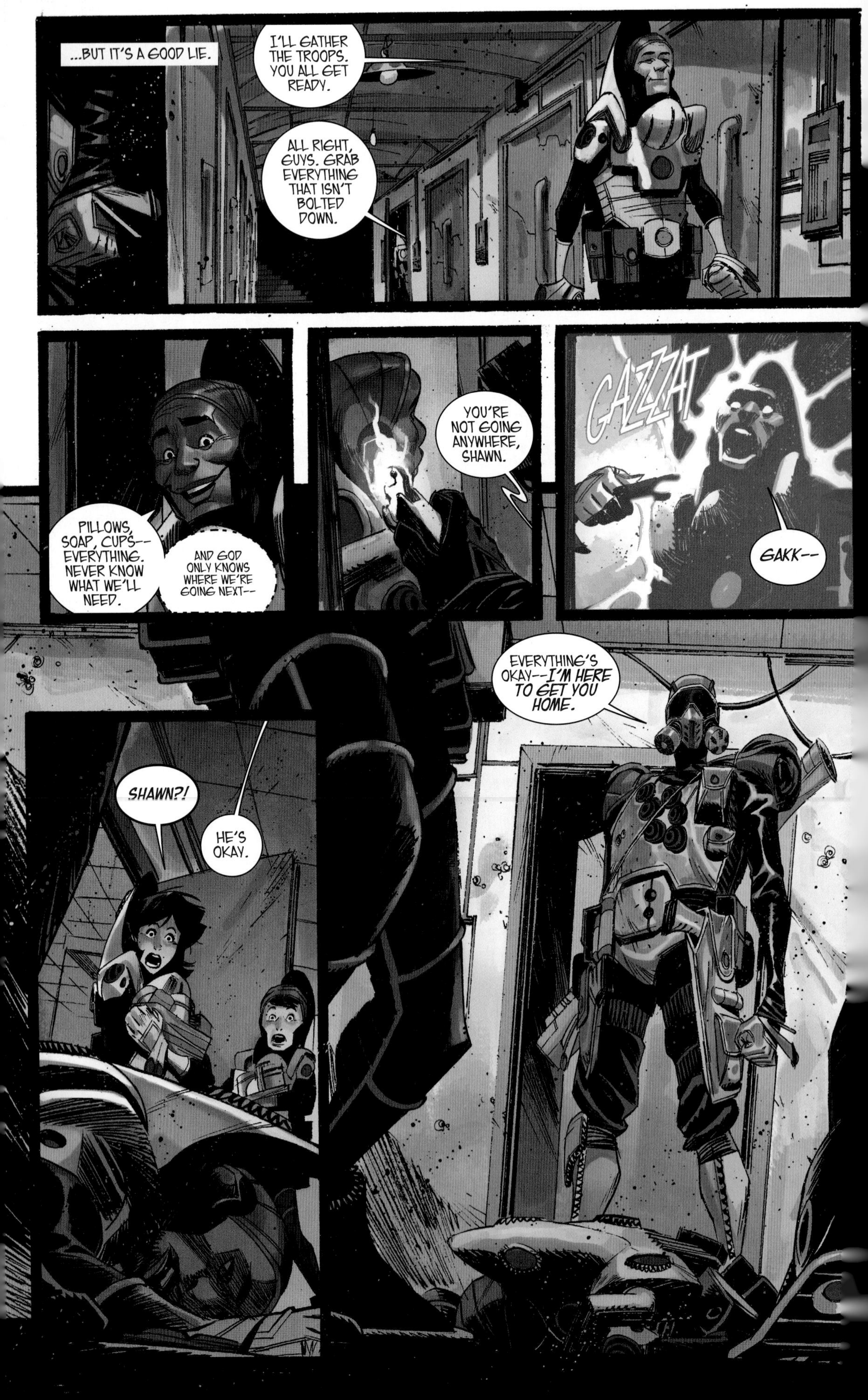
...BUT IT'S A GOOD LIE.
I'LL GATHER THE TROOPS. YOU ALL GET READY.
ALL RIGHT, GUYS. GRAB EVERYTHING THAT ISN'T BOLTED DOWN.
PILLOWS, SOAP, CUPS-- EVERYTHING. NEVER KNOW WHAT WE'LL NEED.
AND GOD ONLY KNOWS WHERE WE'RE GOING NEXT--
YOU'RE NOT GOING ANYWHERE, SHAWN.
GAZZZAT
GAKK--
EVERYTHING'S OKAY--I'M HERE TO GET YOU HOME.
SHAWN?!
HE'S OKAY.

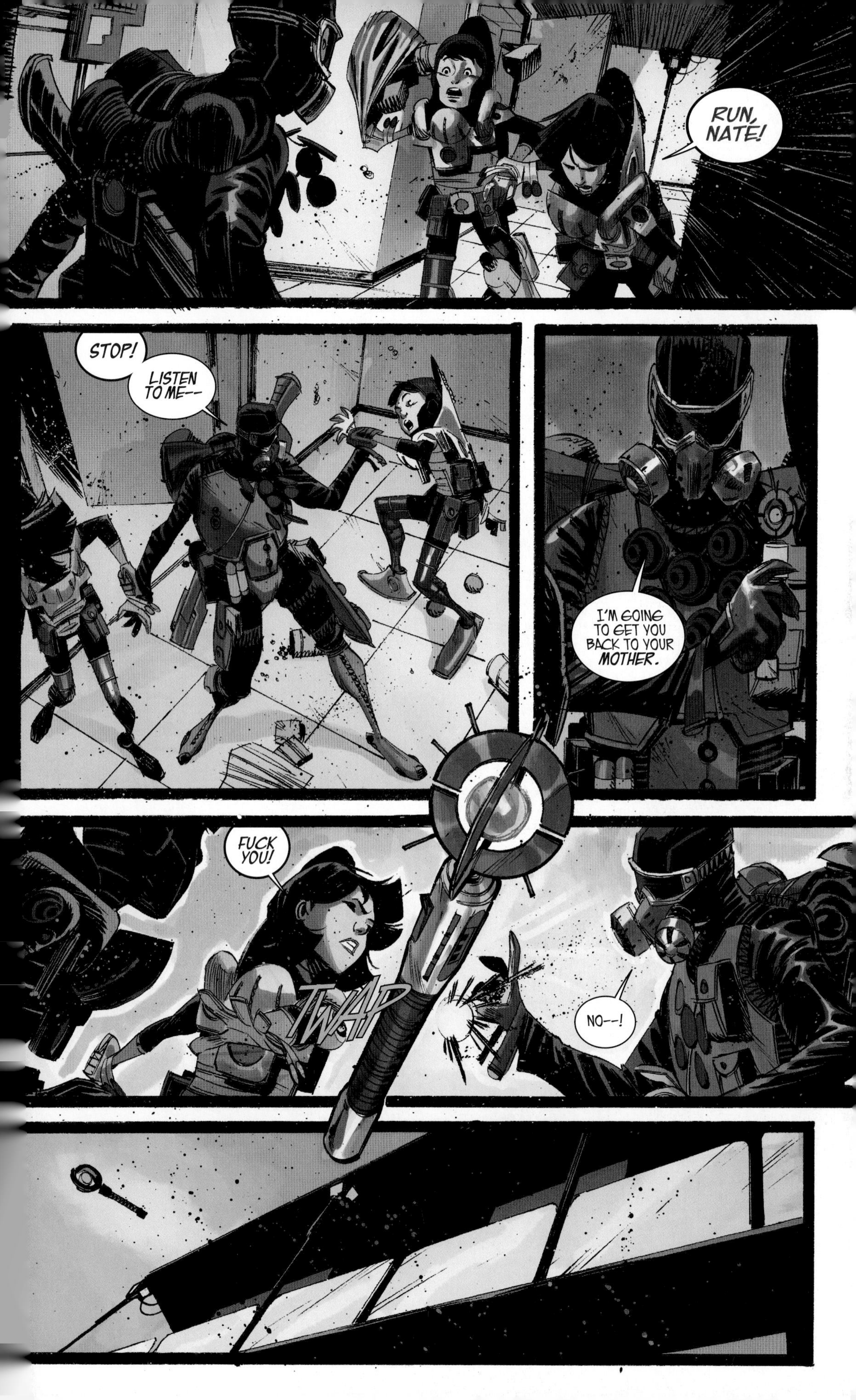
RUN, NATE!
STOP!
LISTEN TO ME--
I'M GOING TO GET YOU BACK TO YOUR MOTHER.
FUCK YOU!
TWAP
NO--!

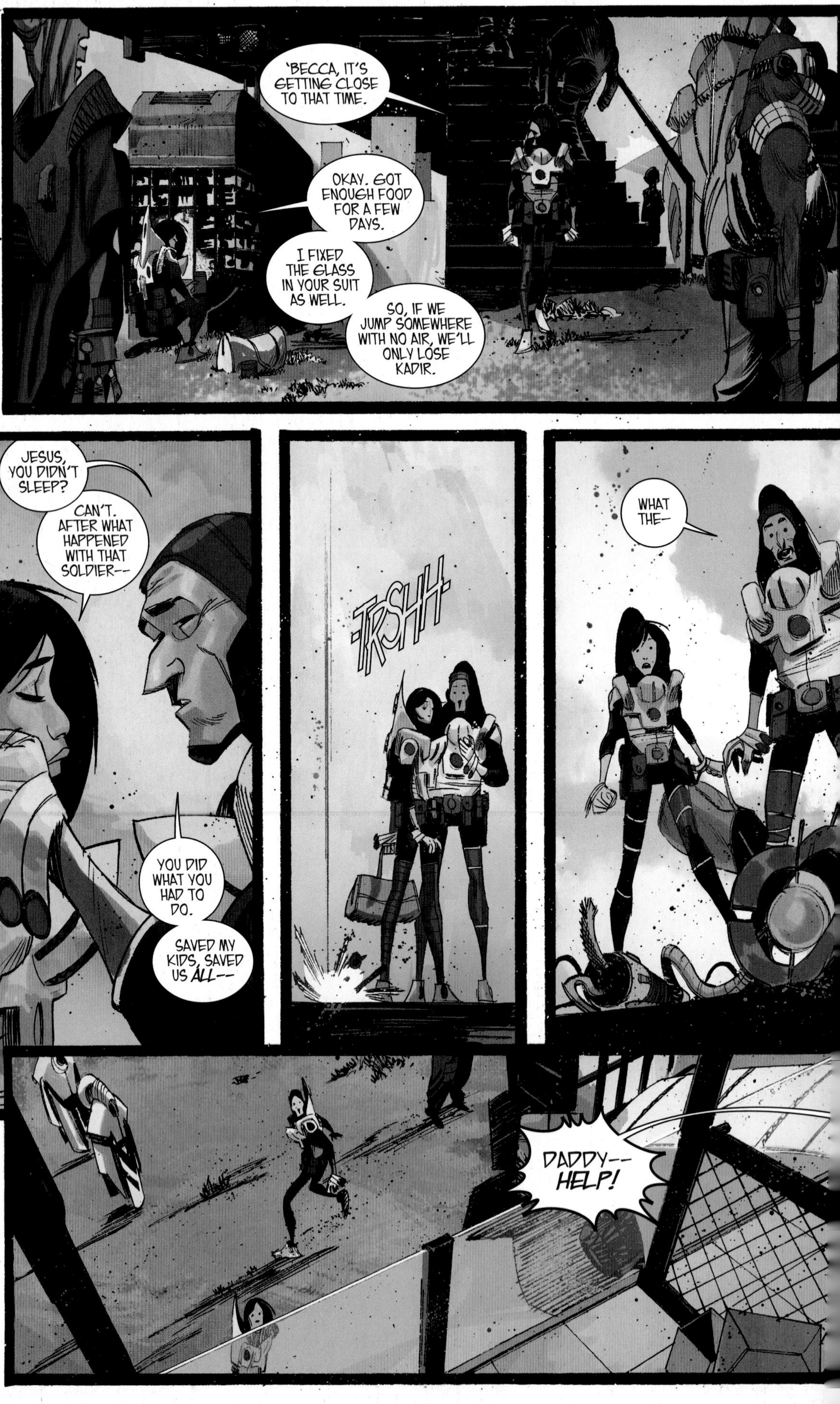
'BECCA, IT'S GETTING CLOSE TO THAT TIME.
OKAY. GOT ENOUGH FOOD FOR A FEW DAYS.
I FIXED THE GLASS IN YOUR SUIT AS WELL.
SO, IF WE JUMP SOMEWHERE WITH NO AIR, WE'LL ONLY LOSE KADIR.
JESUS, YOU DIDN'T SLEEP?
CAN'T. AFTER WHAT HAPPENED WITH THAT SOLDIER--
YOU DID WHAT YOU HAD TO DO.
SAVED MY KIDS, SAVED US *ALL*--
TRSHH
WHAT THE--
DADDY-- *HELP!*

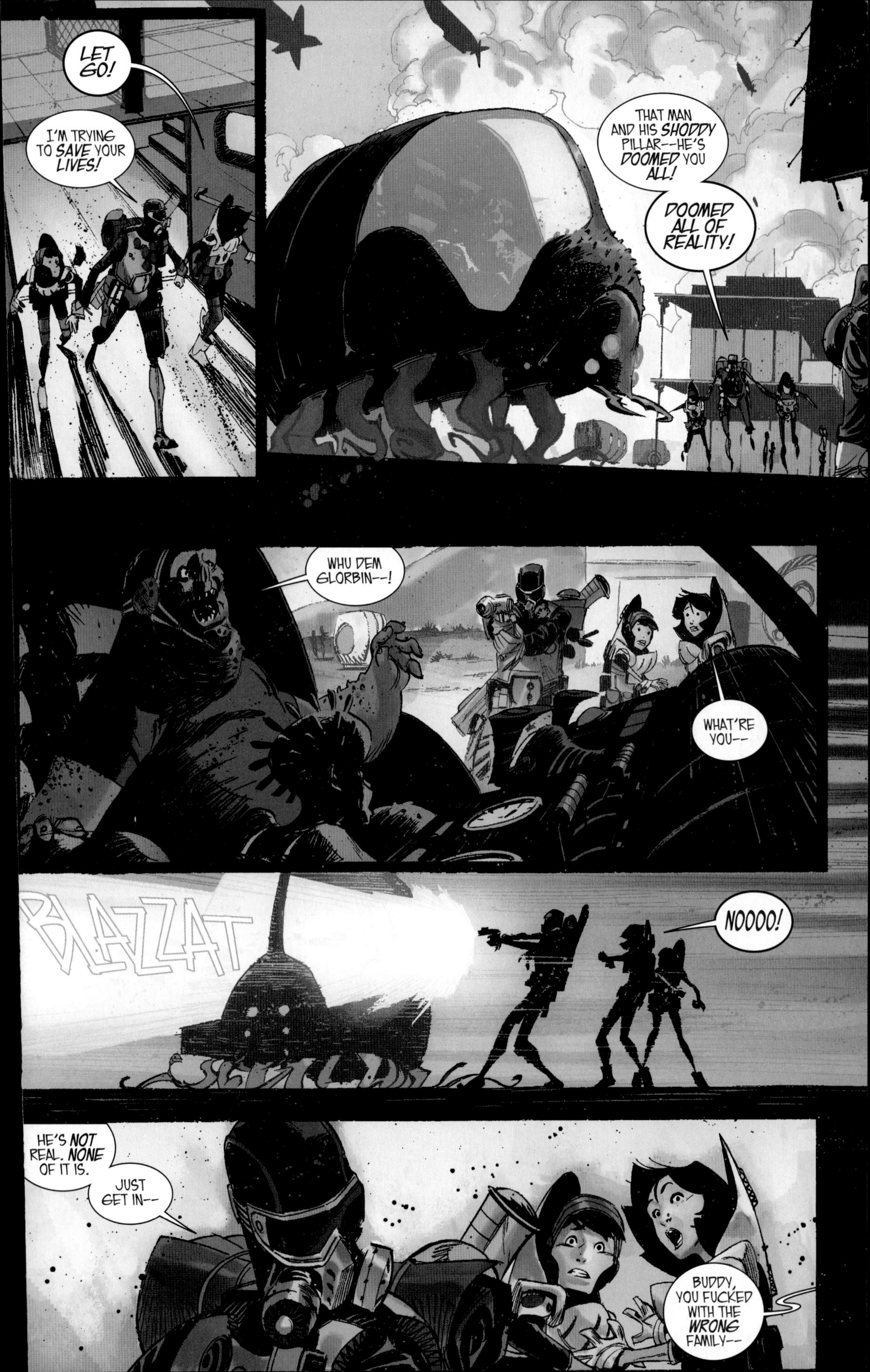
LET GO!
I'M TRYING TO SAVE YOUR LIVES!
THAT MAN AND HIS SHODDY PILLAR--HE'S DOOMED YOU ALL!
DOOMED ALL OF REALITY!
WHU DEM GLORBIN--!
WHAT'RE YOU--
BLAZZAT
NOOOO!
HE'S NOT REAL. NONE OF IT IS.
JUST GET IN--
BUDDY, YOU FUCKED WITH THE WRONG FAMILY--

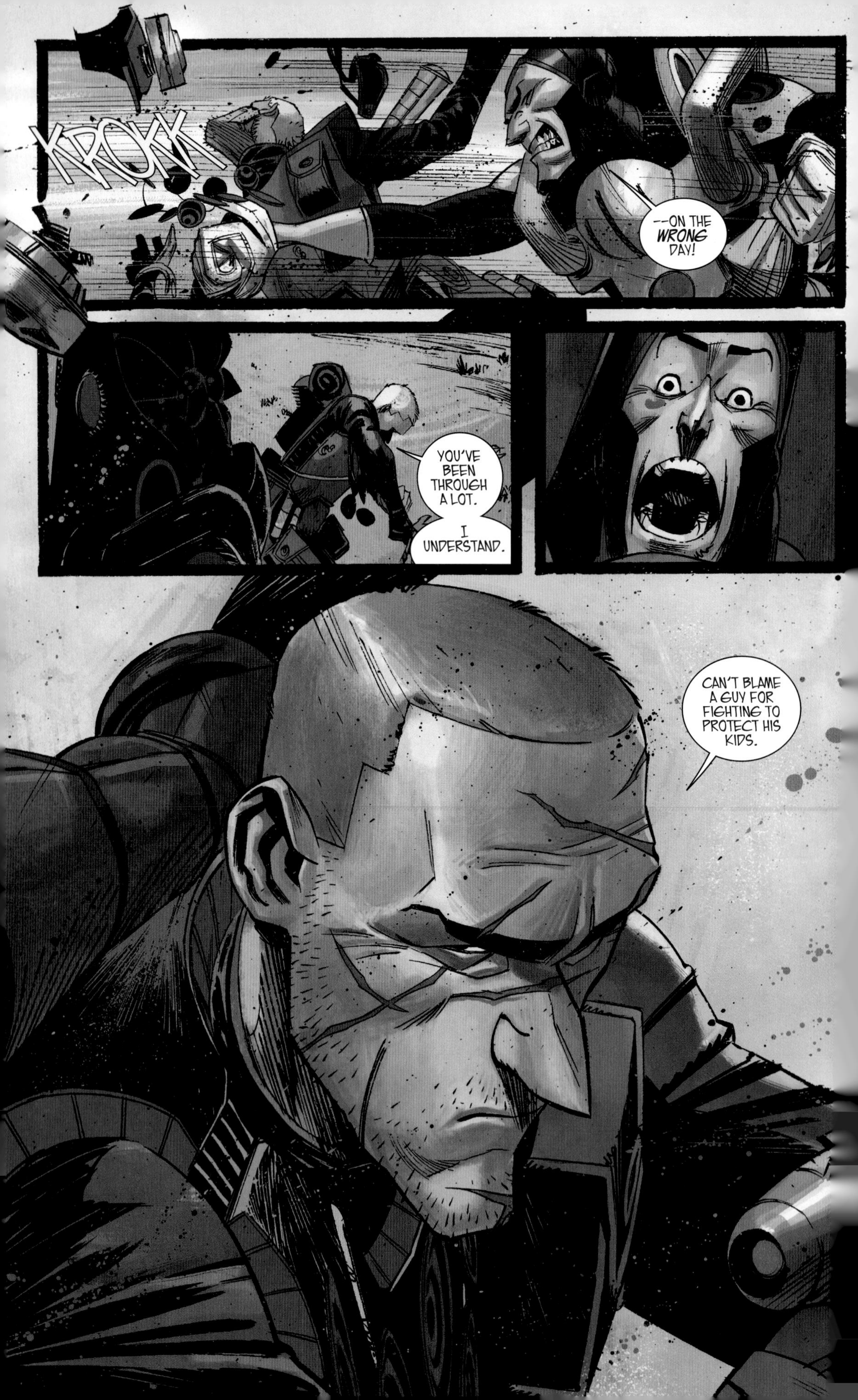
KROKK
--ON THE WRONG DAY!
YOU'VE BEEN THROUGH A LOT.
I UNDERSTAND.
CAN'T BLAME A GUY FOR FIGHTING TO PROTECT HIS KIDS.

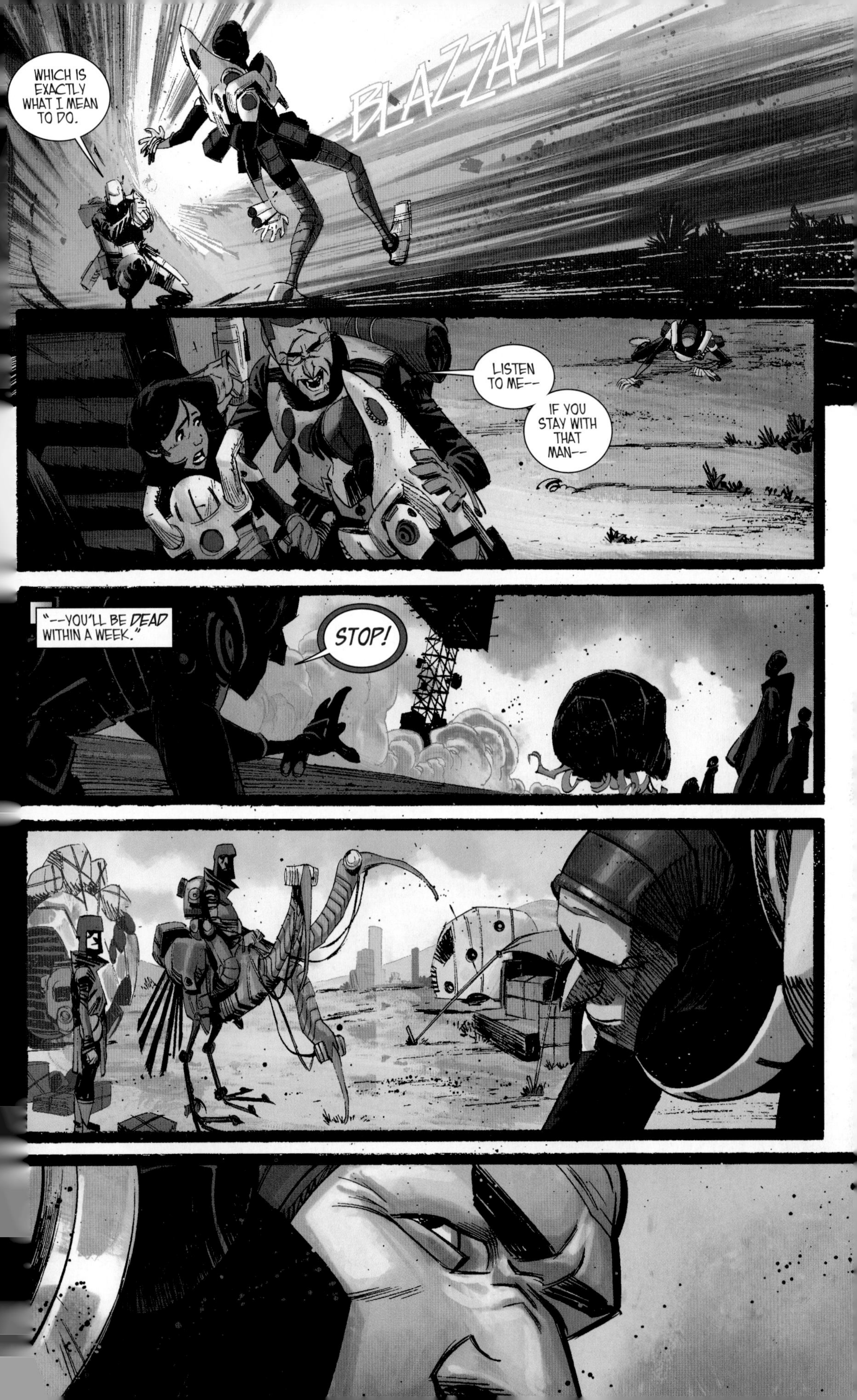
WHICH IS EXACTLY WHAT I MEAN TO DO.
BLAZZAAT
LISTEN TO ME--
IF YOU STAY WITH THAT MAN--
"--YOU'LL BE DEAD WITHIN A WEEK."
STOP!

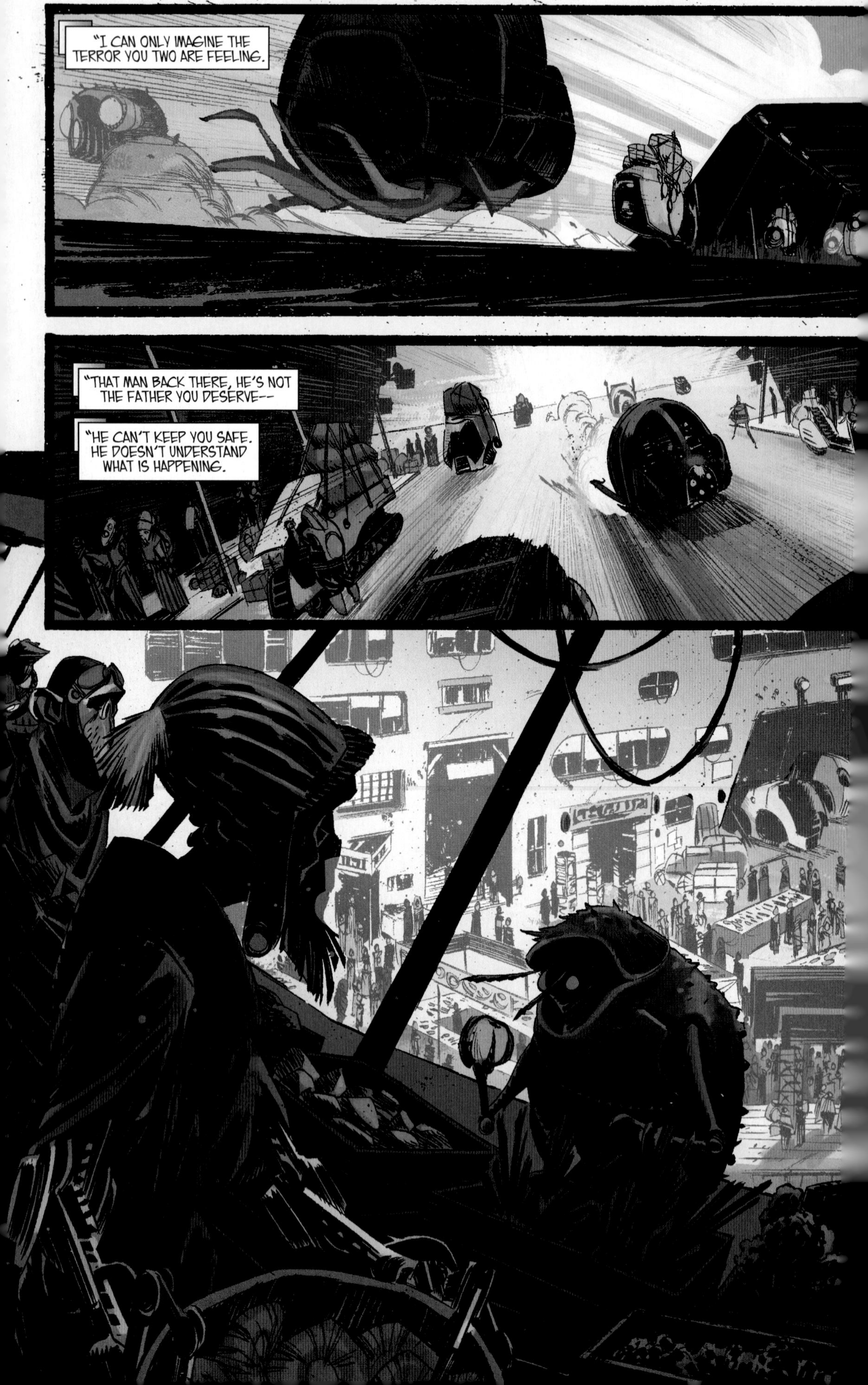
"I CAN ONLY IMAGINE THE TERROR YOU TWO ARE FEELING.
"THAT MAN BACK THERE, HE'S NOT THE FATHER YOU DESERVE--
"HE CAN'T KEEP YOU SAFE. HE DOESN'T UNDERSTAND WHAT IS HAPPENING.

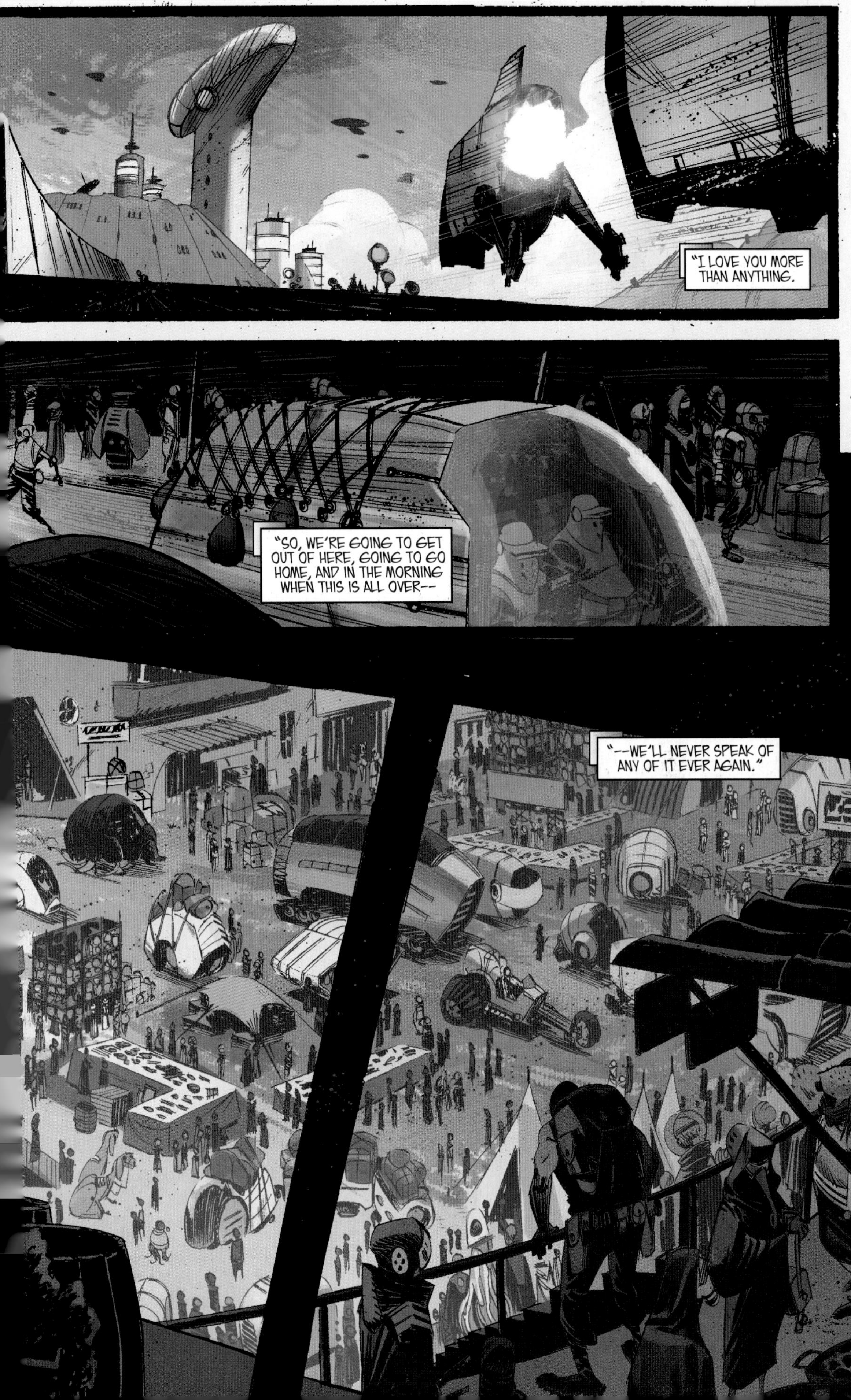
"I LOVE YOU MORE THAN ANYTHING.
"SO, WE'RE GOING TO GET OUT OF HERE, GOING TO GO HOME, AND IN THE MORNING WHEN THIS IS ALL OVER--
"--WE'LL NEVER SPEAK OF ANY OF IT EVER AGAIN."

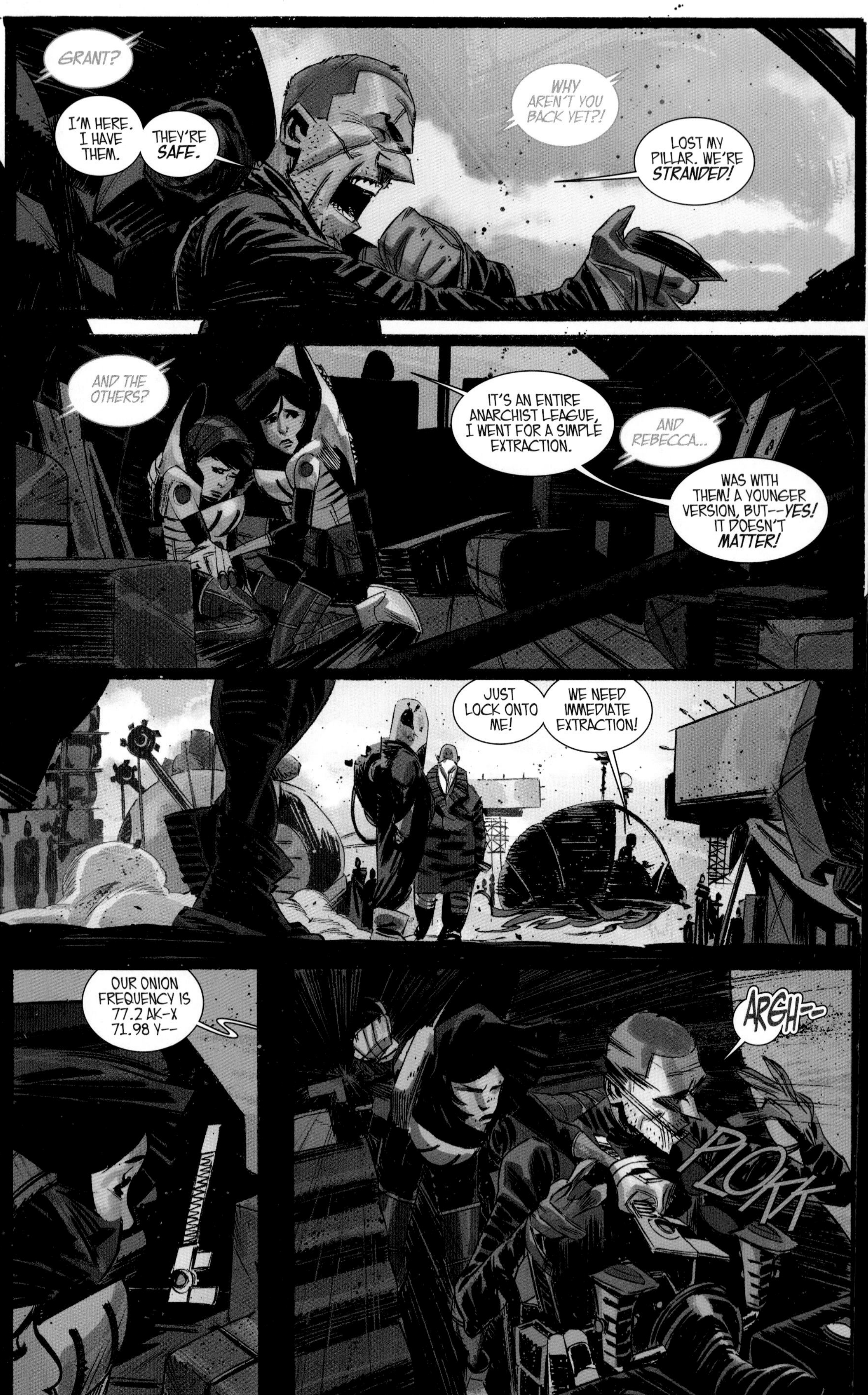
GRANT?
I'M HERE. I HAVE THEM.
THEY'RE SAFE.
WHY AREN'T YOU BACK YET?!
LOST MY PILLAR. WE'RE STRANDED!
AND THE OTHERS?
IT'S AN ENTIRE ANARCHIST LEAGUE, I WENT FOR A SIMPLE EXTRACTION.
AND REBECCA...
WAS WITH THEM! A YOUNGER VERSION, BUT--YES! IT DOESN'T MATTER!
JUST LOCK ONTO ME!
WE NEED IMMEDIATE EXTRACTION!
OUR ONION FREQUENCY IS 77.2 AK-X 71.98 Y--
ARGH--
PLOKK

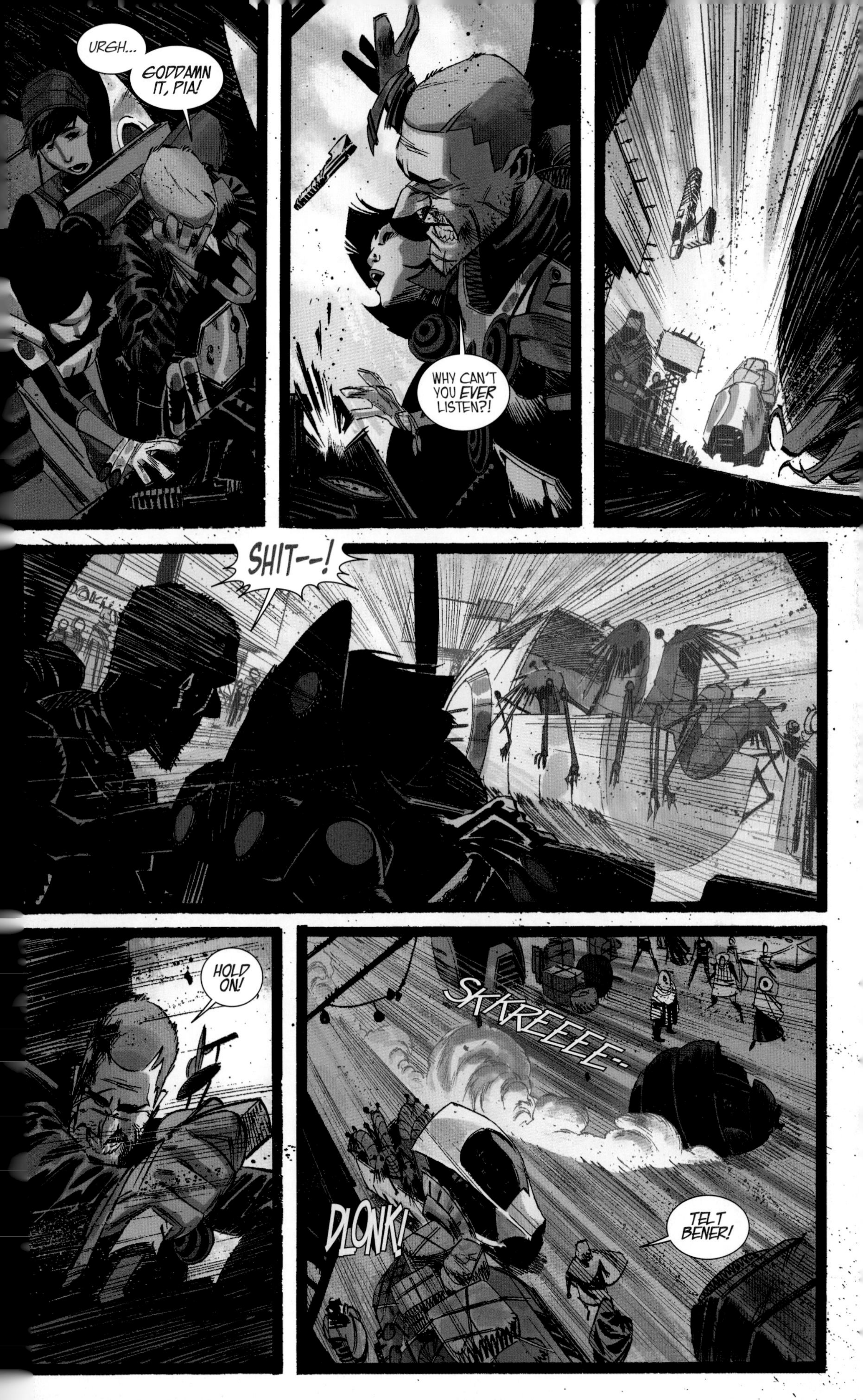
URGH...
GODDAMN IT, PIA!
WHY CAN'T YOU EVER LISTEN?!
SHIT--!
HOLD ON!
SKKREEEEE--
DLONK!
TELT BENER!

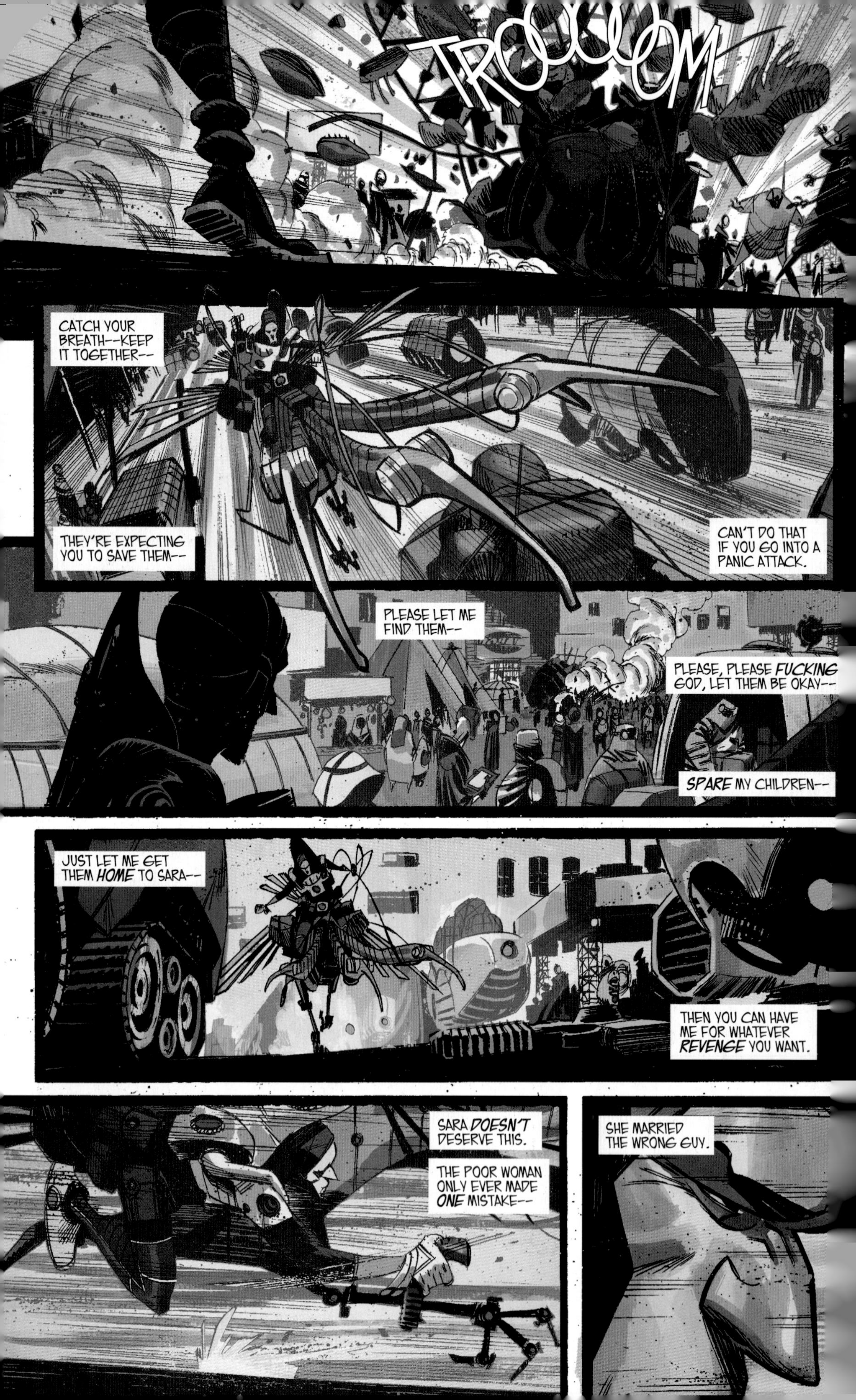
TROOOOOM
CATCH YOUR BREATH--KEEP IT TOGETHER--
THEY'RE EXPECTING YOU TO SAVE THEM--
CAN'T DO THAT IF YOU GO INTO A PANIC ATTACK.
PLEASE LET ME FIND THEM--
PLEASE, PLEASE FUCKING GOD, LET THEM BE OKAY--
SPARE MY CHILDREN--
JUST LET ME GET THEM HOME TO SARA--
THEN YOU CAN HAVE ME FOR WHATEVER REVENGE YOU WANT.
SARA DOESN'T DESERVE THIS.
THE POOR WOMAN ONLY EVER MADE ONE MISTAKE--
SHE MARRIED THE WRONG GUY.

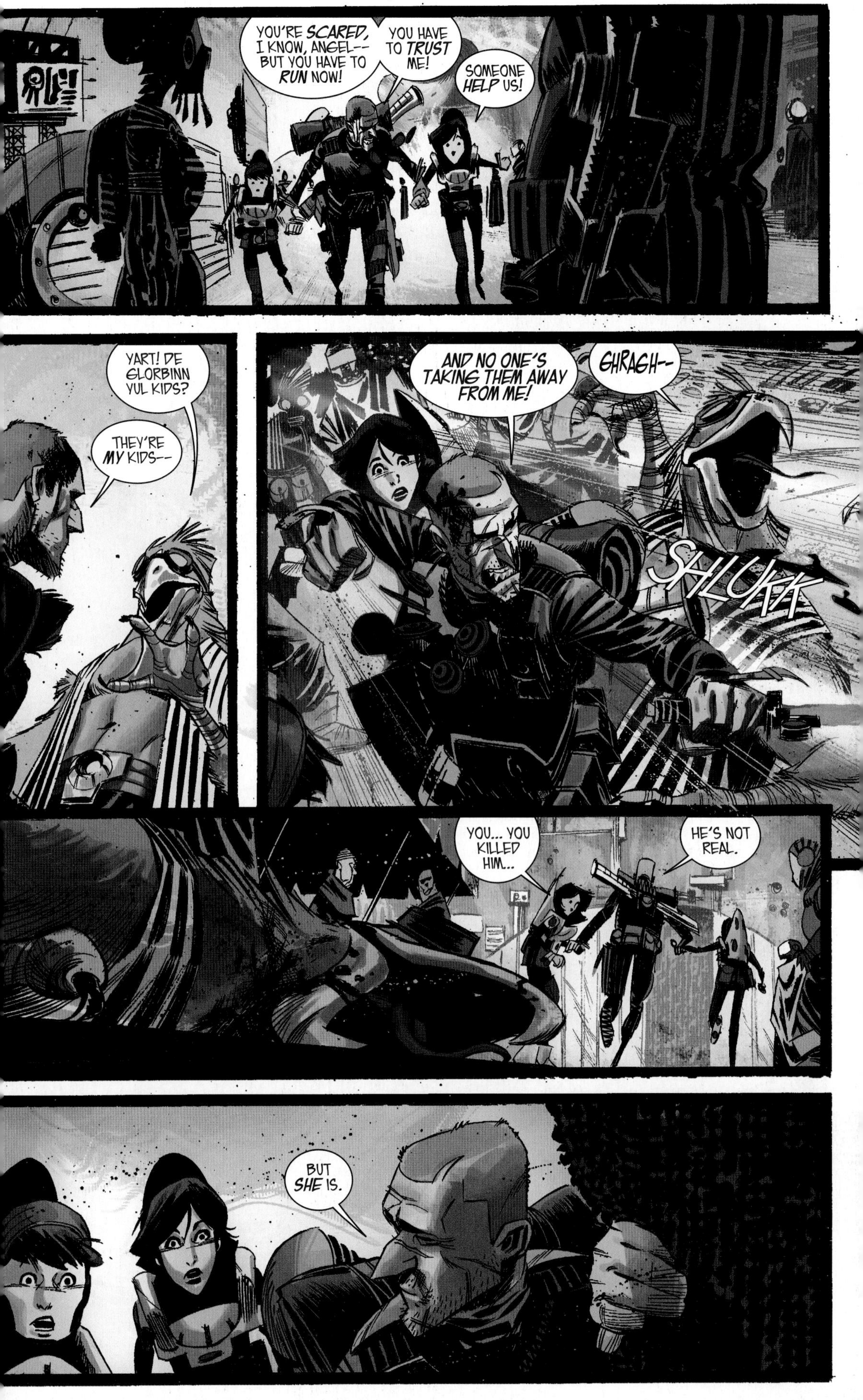
YOU'RE SCARED, I KNOW, ANGEL-- BUT YOU HAVE TO RUN NOW!
YOU HAVE TO TRUST ME!
SOMEONE HELP US!
YART! DE GLORBINN YUL KIDS?
THEY'RE MY KIDS--
AND NO ONE'S TAKING THEM AWAY FROM ME!
GHRAGH--
SHLUKK
YOU... YOU KILLED HIM...
HE'S NOT REAL.
BUT SHE IS.

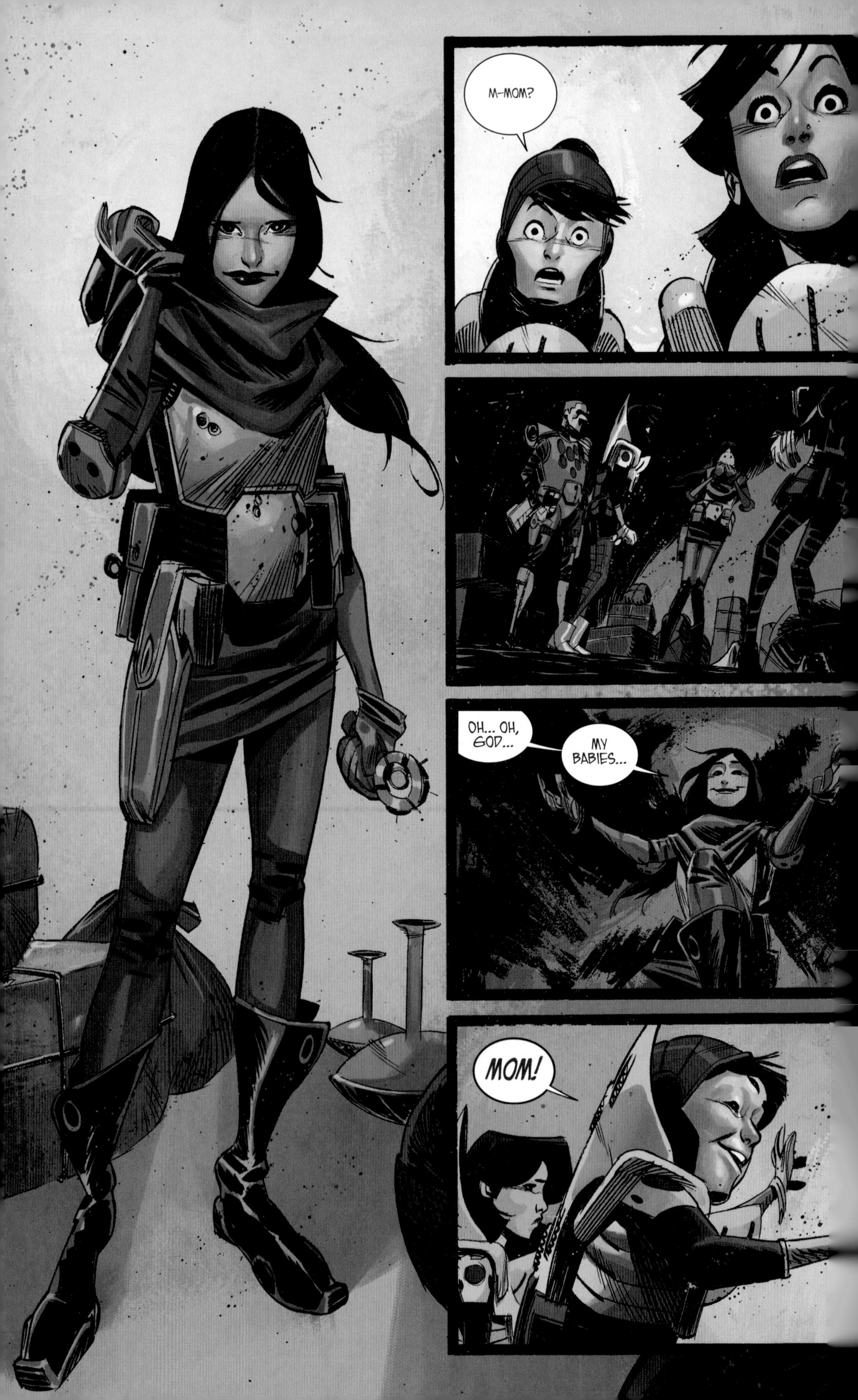
M-MOM?
OH... OH, GOD...
MY BABIES...
MOM!

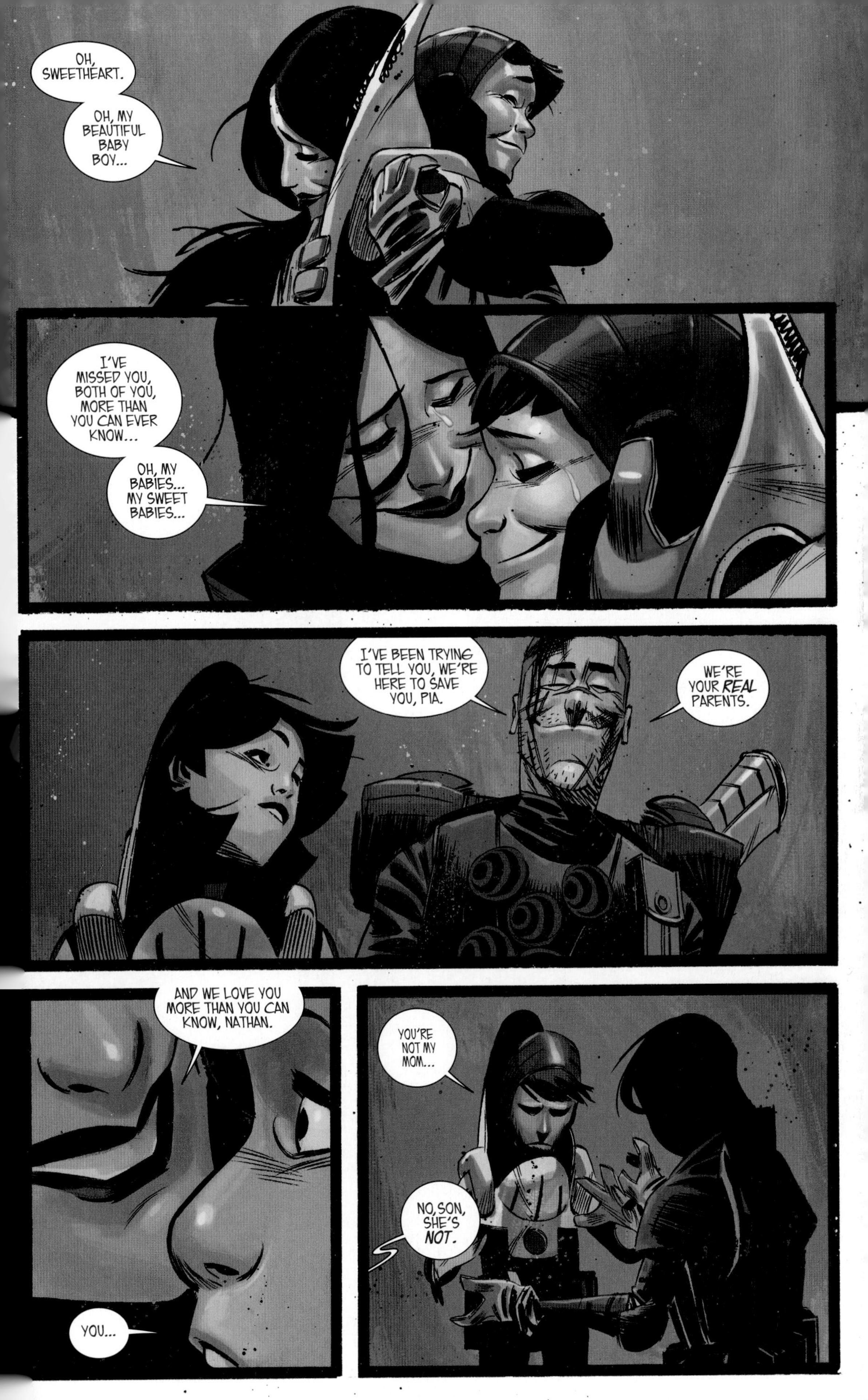

OH, SWEETHEART.
OH, MY BEAUTIFUL BABY BOY...
I'VE MISSED YOU, BOTH OF YOU, MORE THAN YOU CAN EVER KNOW...
OH, MY BABIES... MY SWEET BABIES...
I'VE BEEN TRYING TO TELL YOU, WE'RE HERE TO SAVE YOU, PIA.
WE'RE YOUR REAL PARENTS.
AND WE LOVE YOU MORE THAN YOU CAN KNOW, NATHAN.
YOU...
YOU'RE NOT MY MOM...
NO, SON, SHE'S NOT.

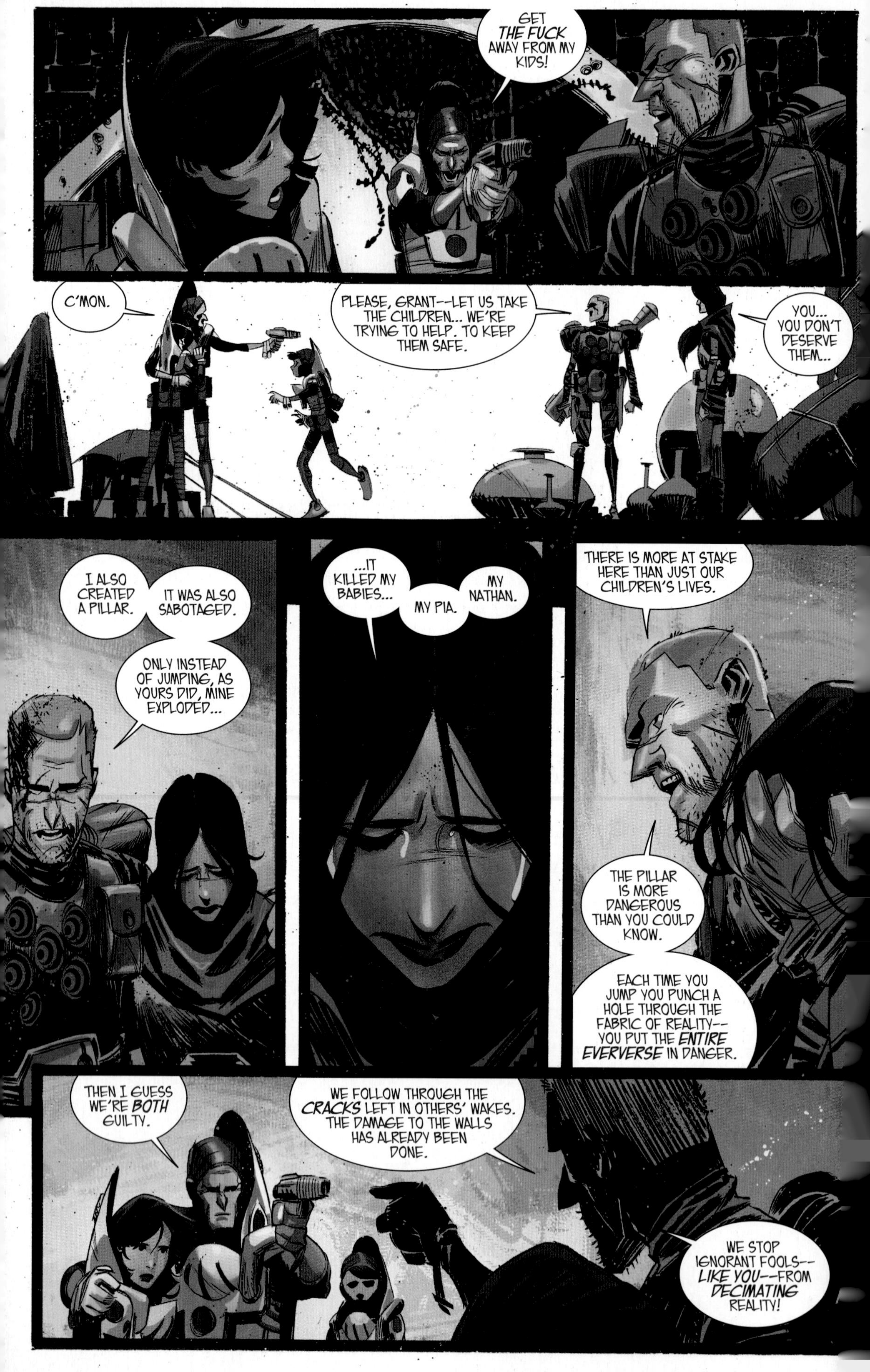
GET THE FUCK AWAY FROM MY KIDS!
C'MON.
PLEASE, GRANT--LET US TAKE THE CHILDREN... WE'RE TRYING TO HELP. TO KEEP THEM SAFE.
YOU... YOU DON'T DESERVE THEM...
I ALSO CREATED A PILLAR.
IT WAS ALSO SABOTAGED.
ONLY INSTEAD OF JUMPING, AS YOURS DID, MINE EXPLODED...
...IT KILLED MY BABIES...
MY PIA.
MY NATHAN.
THERE IS MORE AT STAKE HERE THAN JUST OUR CHILDREN'S LIVES.
THE PILLAR IS MORE DANGEROUS THAN YOU COULD KNOW.
EACH TIME YOU JUMP YOU PUNCH A HOLE THROUGH THE FABRIC OF REALITY--YOU PUT THE ENTIRE EVERVERSE IN DANGER.
THEN I GUESS WE'RE BOTH GUILTY.
WE FOLLOW THROUGH THE CRACKS LEFT IN OTHERS' WAKES. THE DAMAGE TO THE WALLS HAS ALREADY BEEN DONE.
WE STOP IGNORANT FOOLS--LIKE YOU--FROM DECIMATING REALITY!

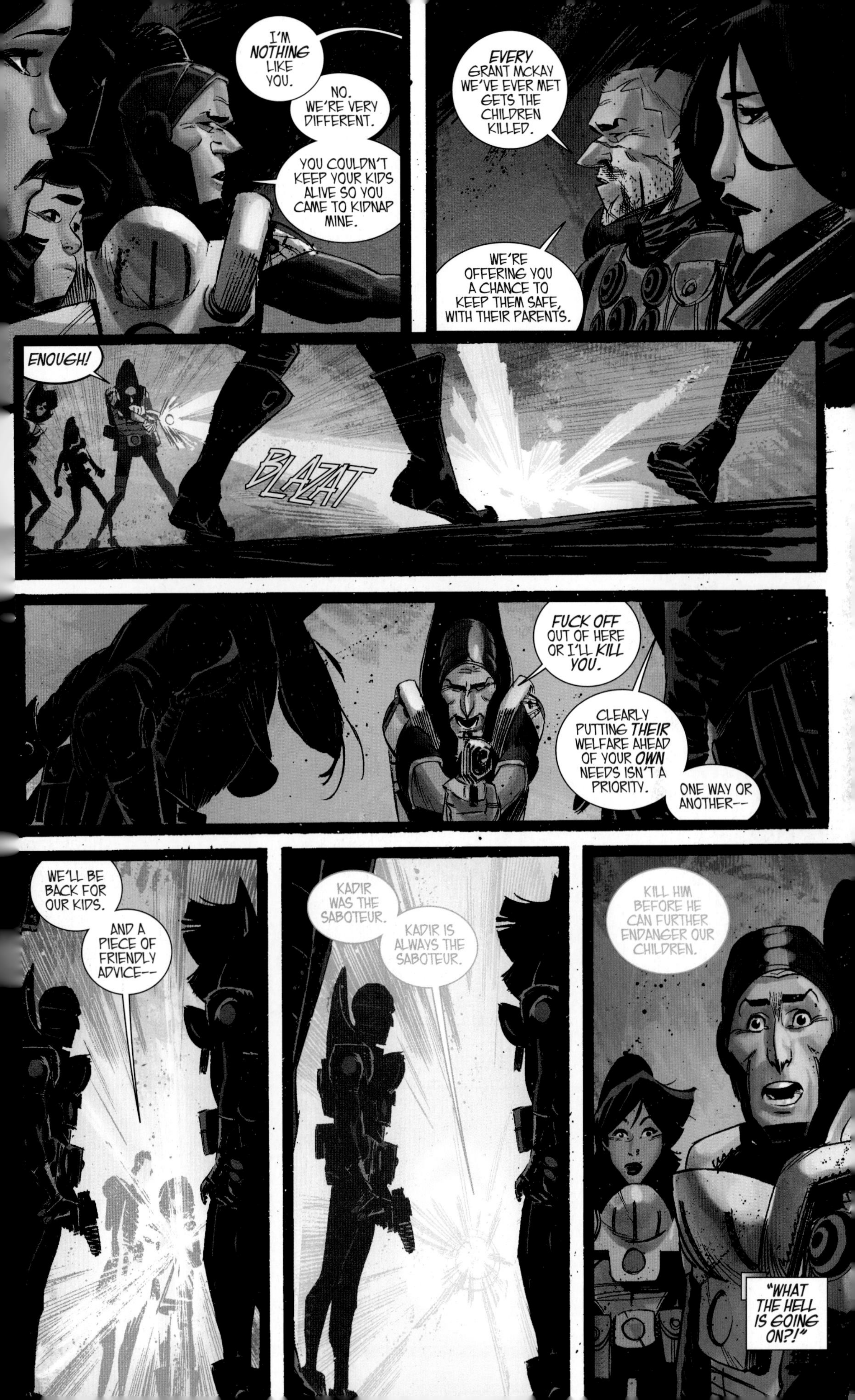
I'M NOTHING LIKE YOU.
NO. WE'RE VERY DIFFERENT.
YOU COULDN'T KEEP YOUR KIDS ALIVE SO YOU CAME TO KIDNAP MINE.
EVERY GRANT MCKAY WE'VE EVER MET GETS THE CHILDREN KILLED.
WE'RE OFFERING YOU A CHANCE TO KEEP THEM SAFE, WITH THEIR PARENTS.
ENOUGH!
BLAZAT
FUCK OFF OUT OF HERE OR I'LL KILL YOU.
CLEARLY PUTTING THEIR WELFARE AHEAD OF YOUR OWN NEEDS ISN'T A PRIORITY.
ONE WAY OR ANOTHER--
WE'LL BE BACK FOR OUR KIDS.
AND A PIECE OF FRIENDLY ADVICE--
KADIR WAS THE SABOTEUR.
KADIR IS ALWAYS THE SABOTEUR.
KILL HIM BEFORE HE CAN FURTHER ENDANGER OUR CHILDREN.
"WHAT THE HELL IS GOING ON?!"

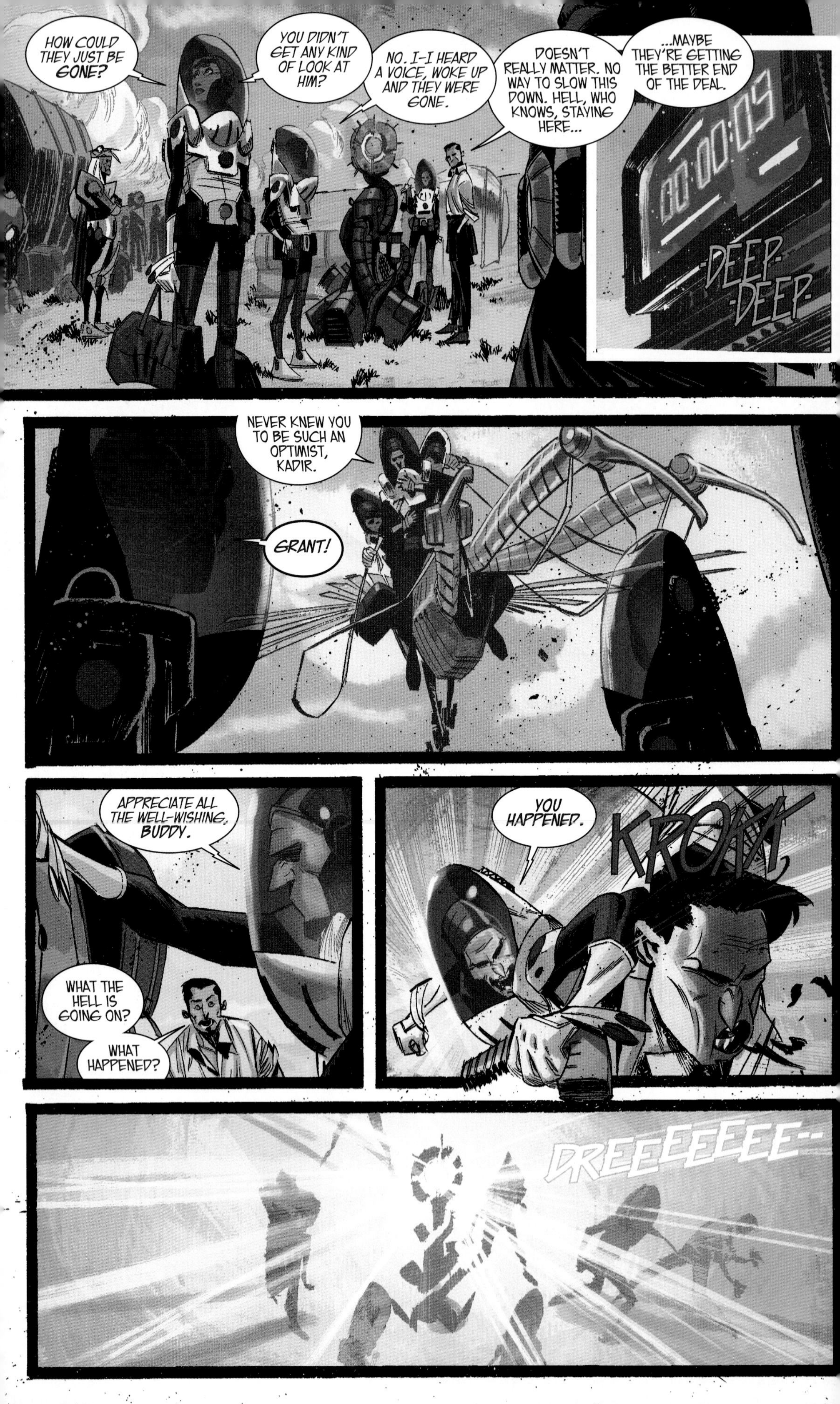
HOW COULD THEY JUST BE GONE?
YOU DIDN'T GET ANY KIND OF LOOK AT HIM?
NO. I-I HEARD A VOICE, WOKE UP AND THEY WERE GONE.
DOESN'T REALLY MATTER. NO WAY TO SLOW THIS DOWN. HELL, WHO KNOWS, STAYING HERE...
...MAYBE THEY'RE GETTING THE BETTER END OF THE DEAL.
00:00:09
-DEEP-
-DEEP-
NEVER KNEW YOU TO BE SUCH AN OPTIMIST, KADIR.
GRANT!
APPRECIATE ALL THE WELL-WISHING, BUDDY.
WHAT THE HELL IS GOING ON?
WHAT HAPPENED?
YOU HAPPENED.
KROKK
DREEEEEEE--

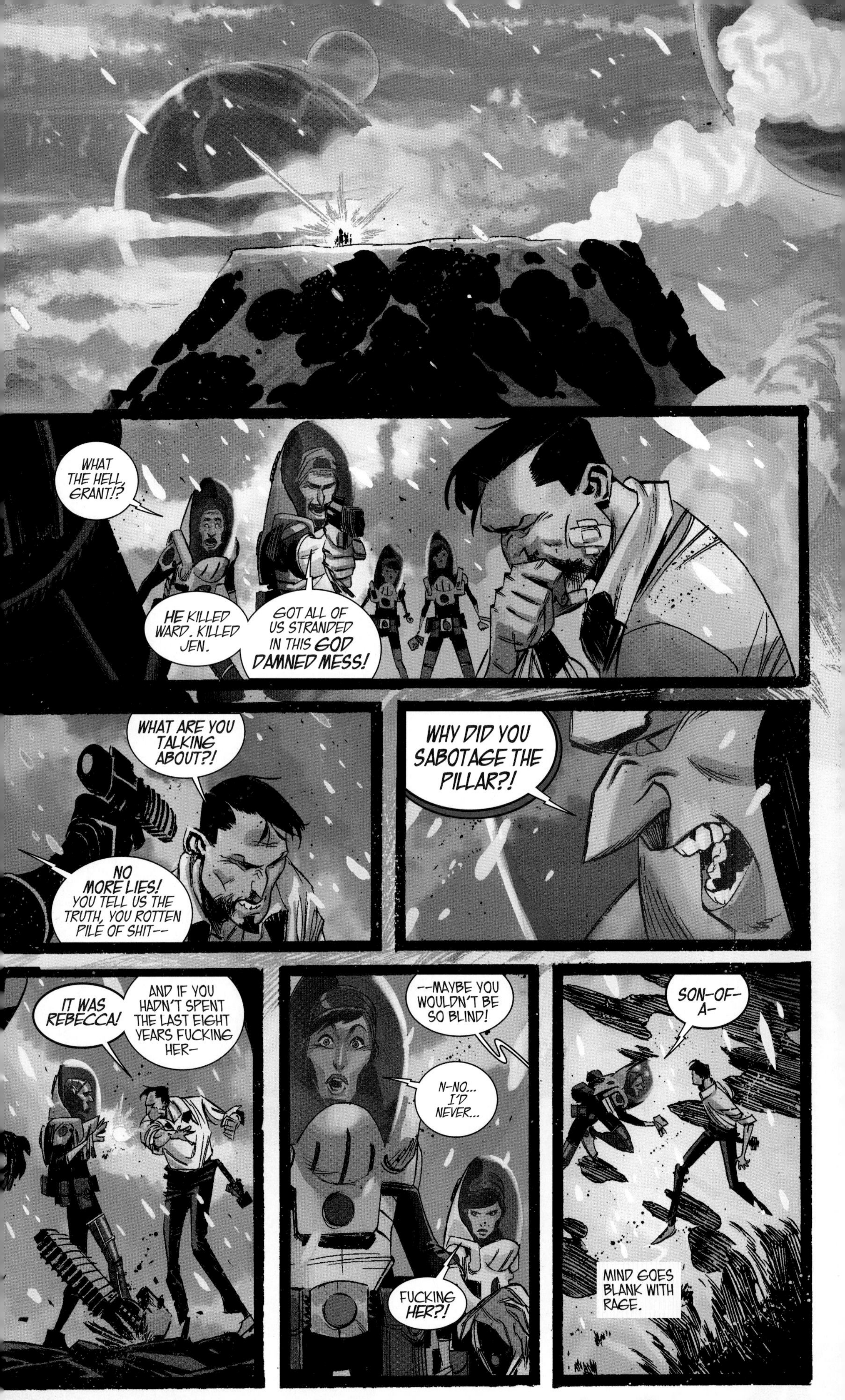
WHAT THE HELL, GRANT!?
HE KILLED WARD. KILLED JEN.
GOT ALL OF US STRANDED IN THIS GOD DAMNED MESS!
WHAT ARE YOU TALKING ABOUT?!
NO MORE LIES! YOU TELL US THE TRUTH, YOU ROTTEN PILE OF SHIT--
WHY DID YOU SABOTAGE THE PILLAR?!
IT WAS REBECCA!
AND IF YOU HADN'T SPENT THE LAST EIGHT YEARS FUCKING HER-
--MAYBE YOU WOULDN'T BE SO BLIND!
N-NO... I'D NEVER...
FUCKING HER?!
SON-OF-A-
MIND GOES BLANK WITH RAGE.

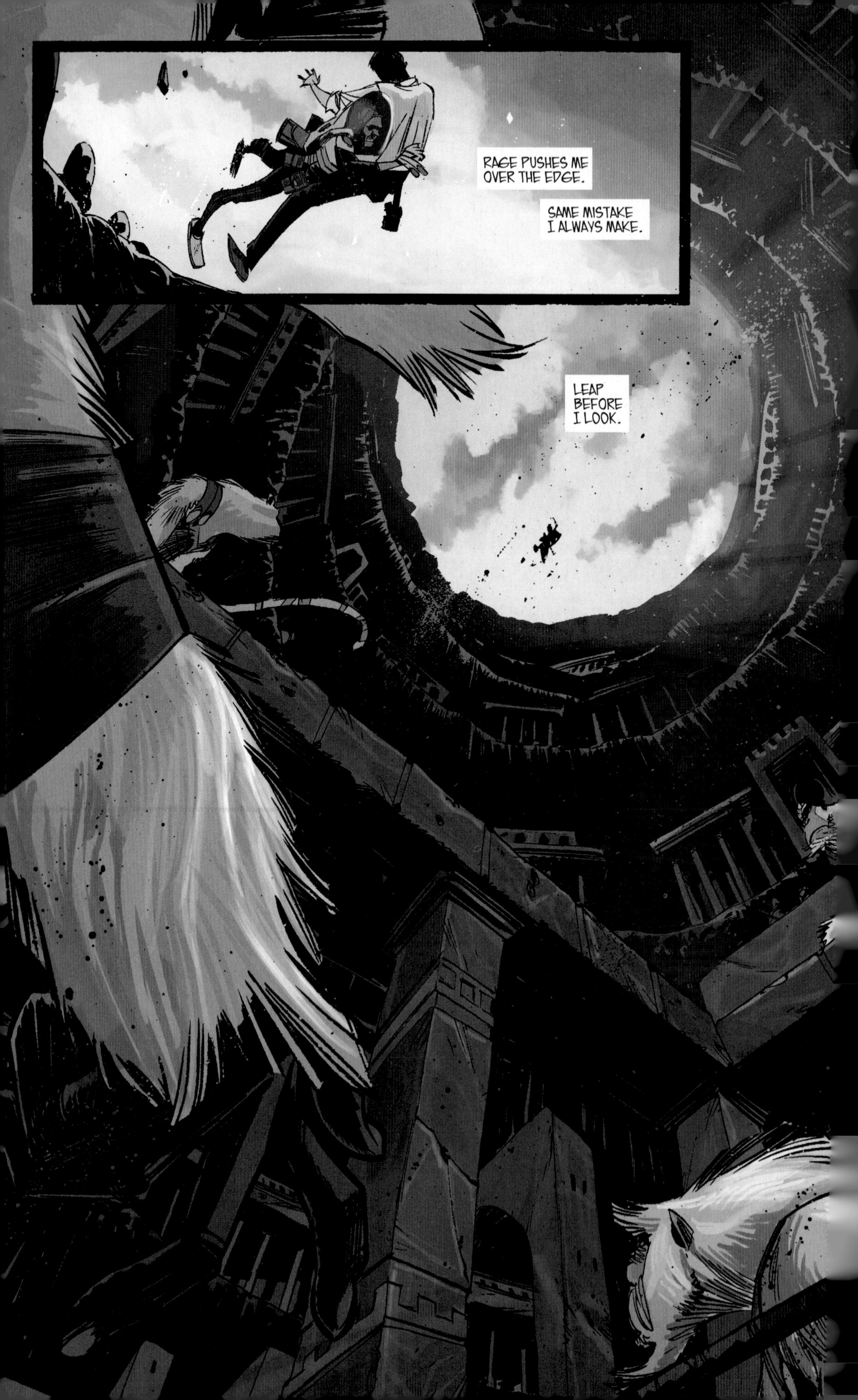
RAGE PUSHES ME OVER THE EDGE.
SAME MISTAKE I ALWAYS MAKE.
LEAP BEFORE I LOOK.

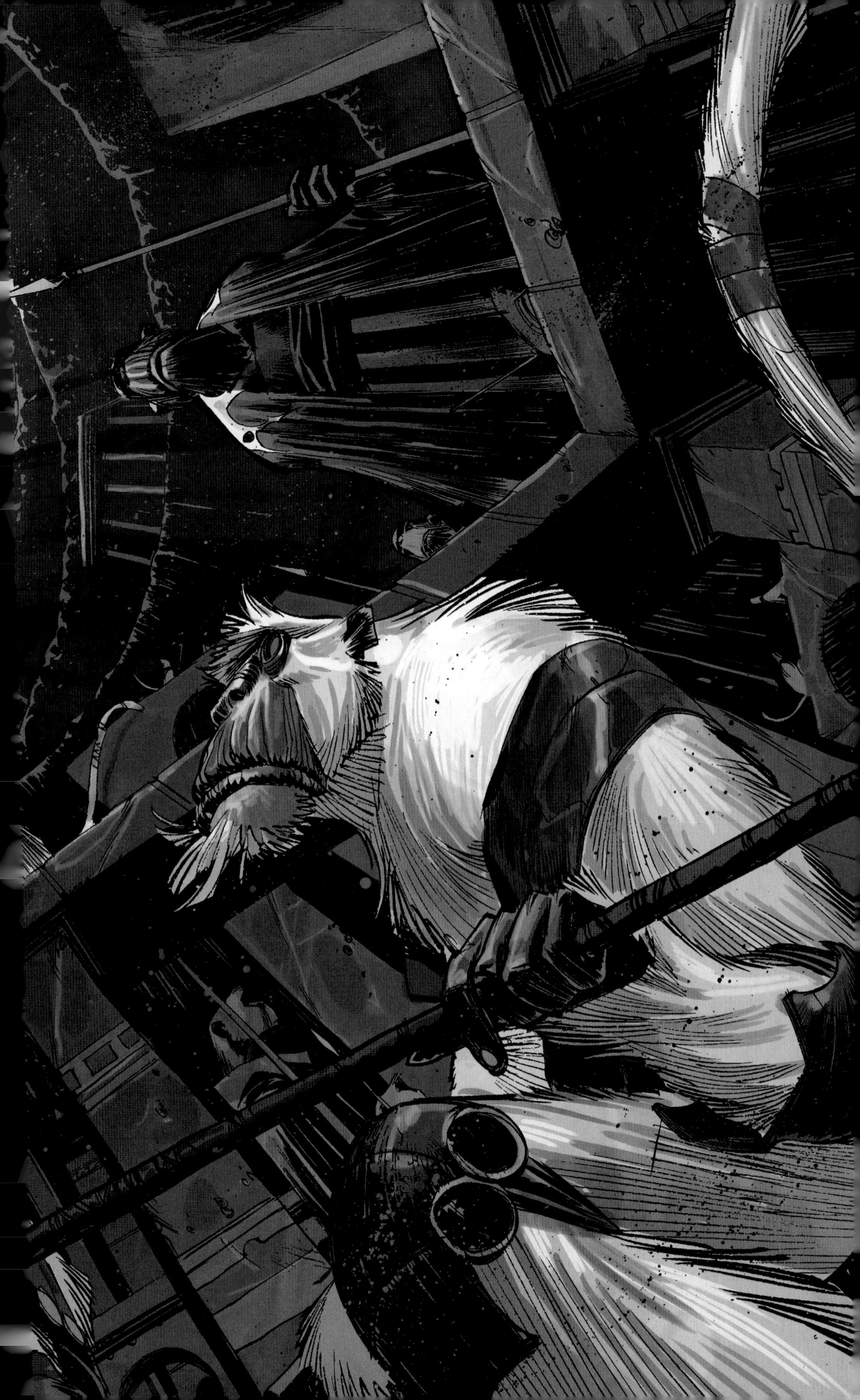

6

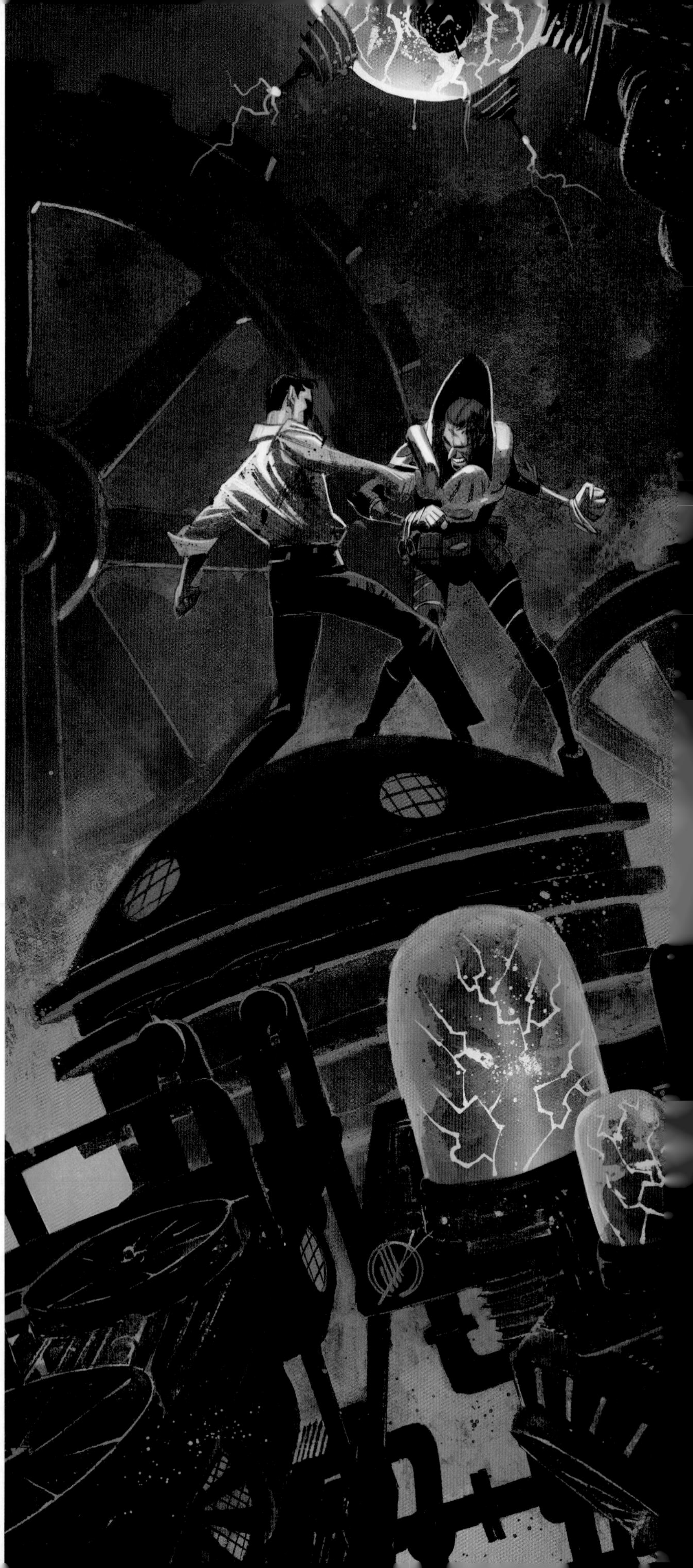

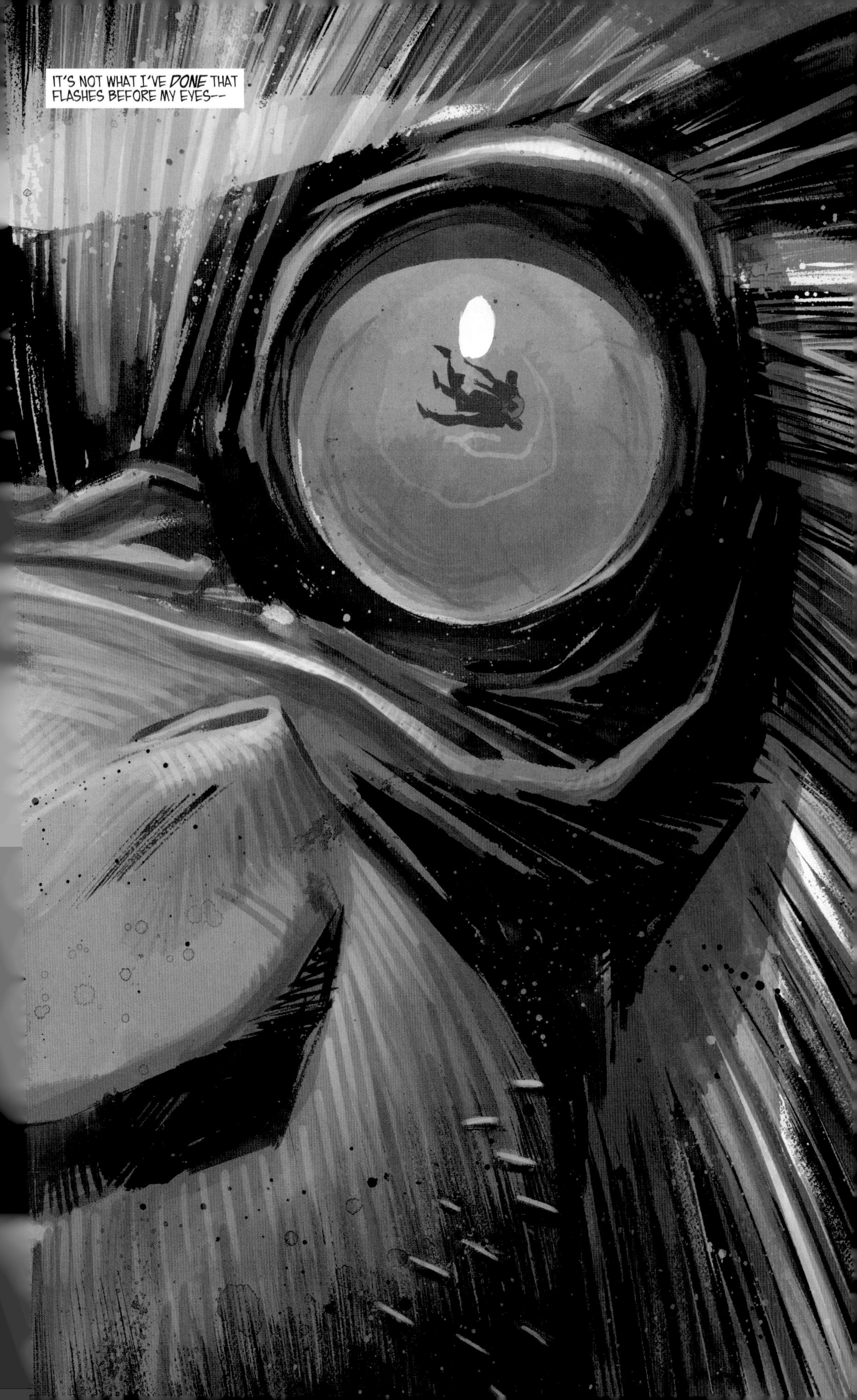
IT'S NOT WHAT I'VE DONE THAT FLASHES BEFORE MY EYES--

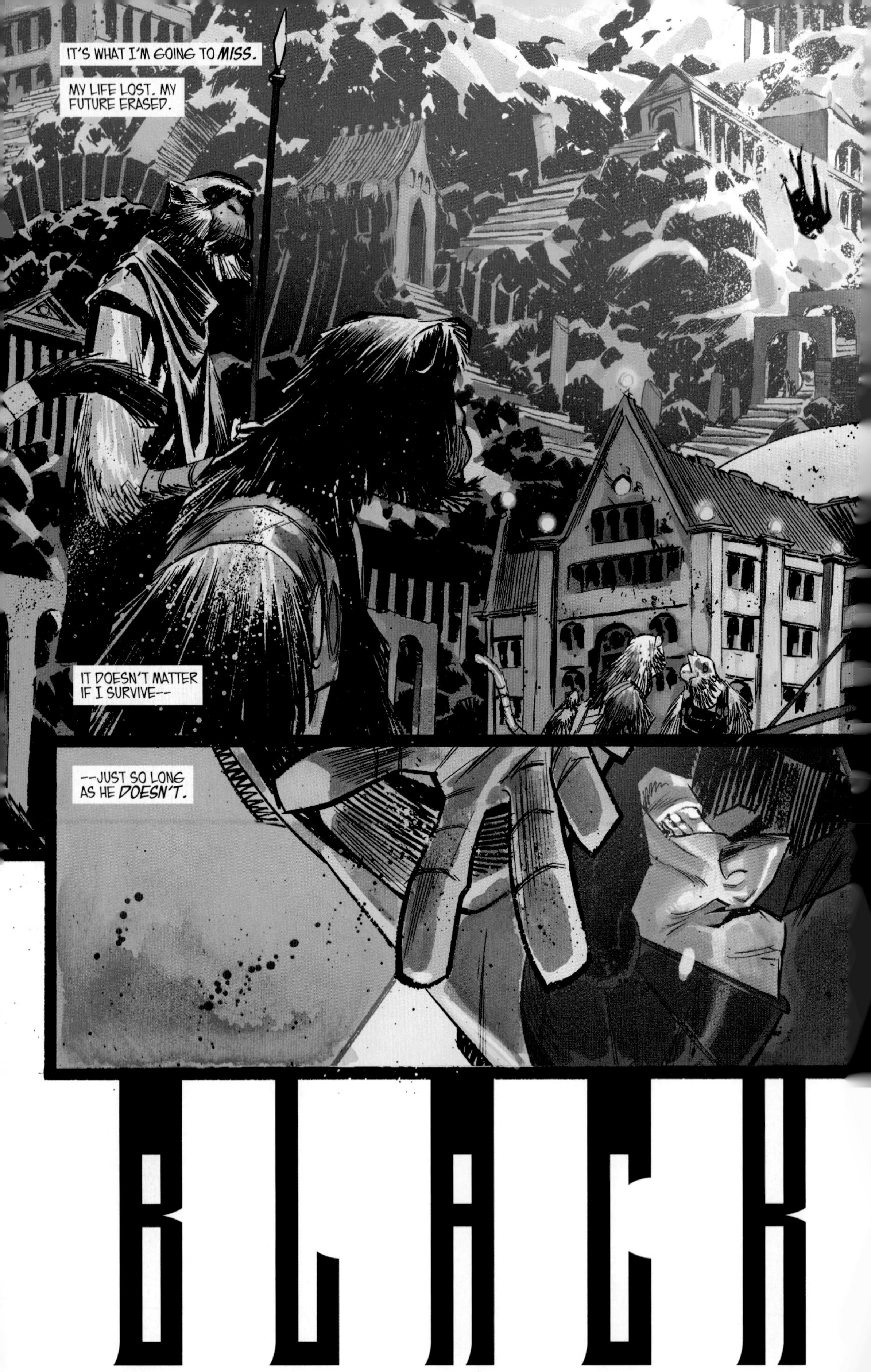
IT'S WHAT I'M GOING TO MISS.
MY LIFE LOST. MY FUTURE ERASED.
IT DOESN'T MATTER IF I SURVIVE--
--JUST SO LONG AS HE DOESN'T.

BLACK

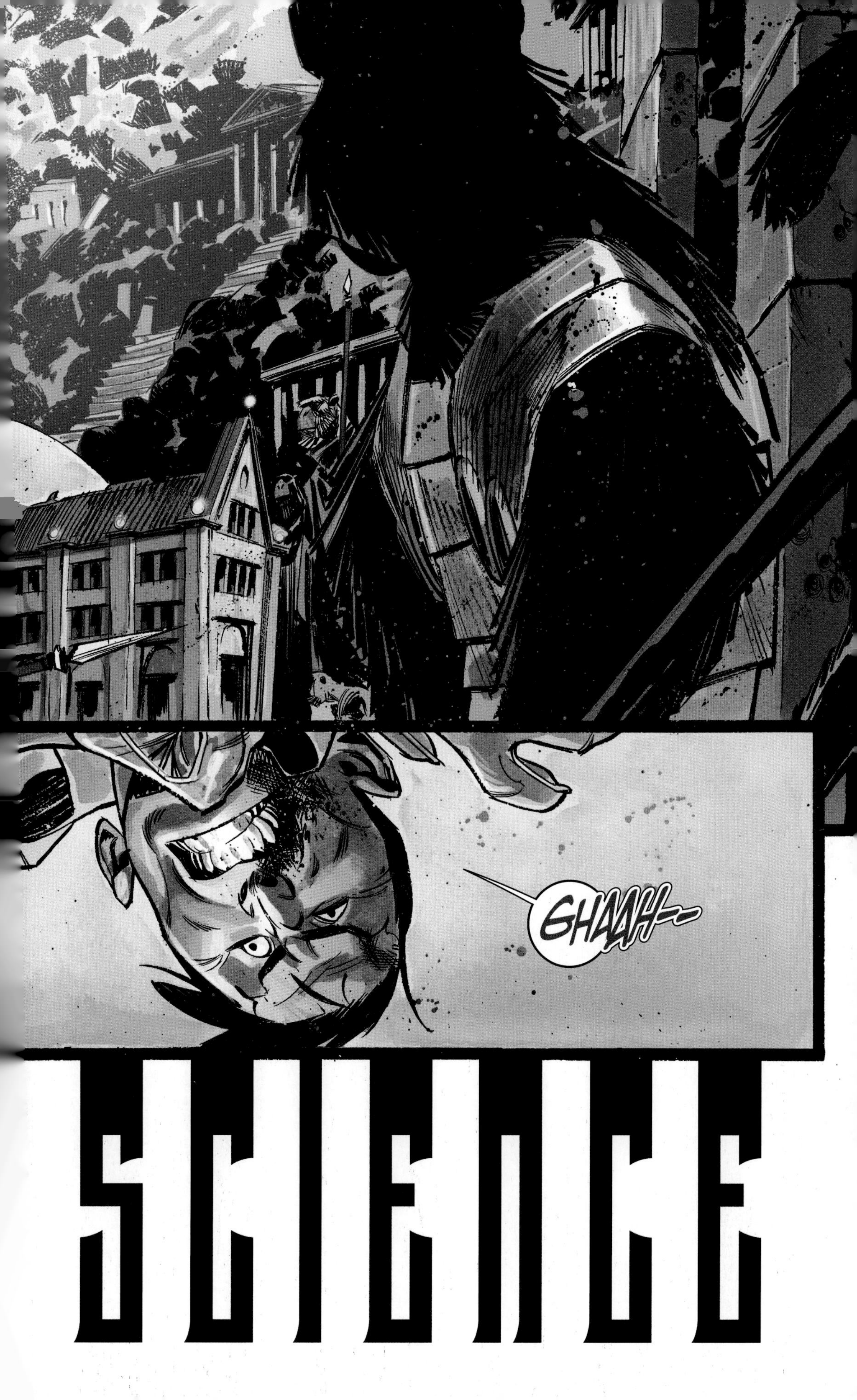
GHAAH--
SCIENCE

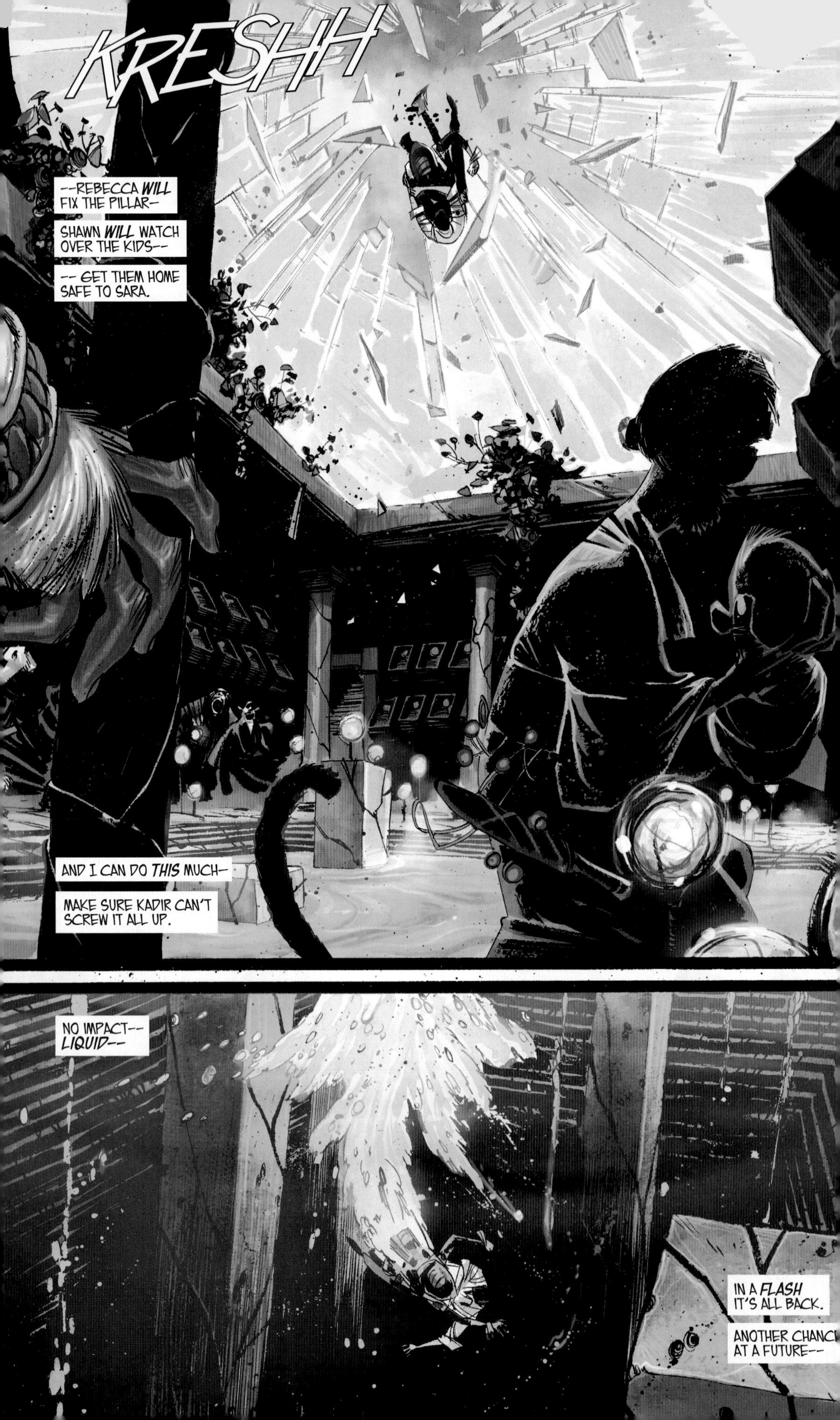
KRESHH
--REBECCA WILL FIX THE PILLAR--
SHAWN WILL WATCH OVER THE KIDS--
-- GET THEM HOME SAFE TO SARA.
AND I CAN DO THIS MUCH--
MAKE SURE KADIR CAN'T SCREW IT ALL UP.
NO IMPACT-- LIQUID--
IN A FLASH IT'S ALL BACK.
ANOTHER CHANC AT A FUTURE--

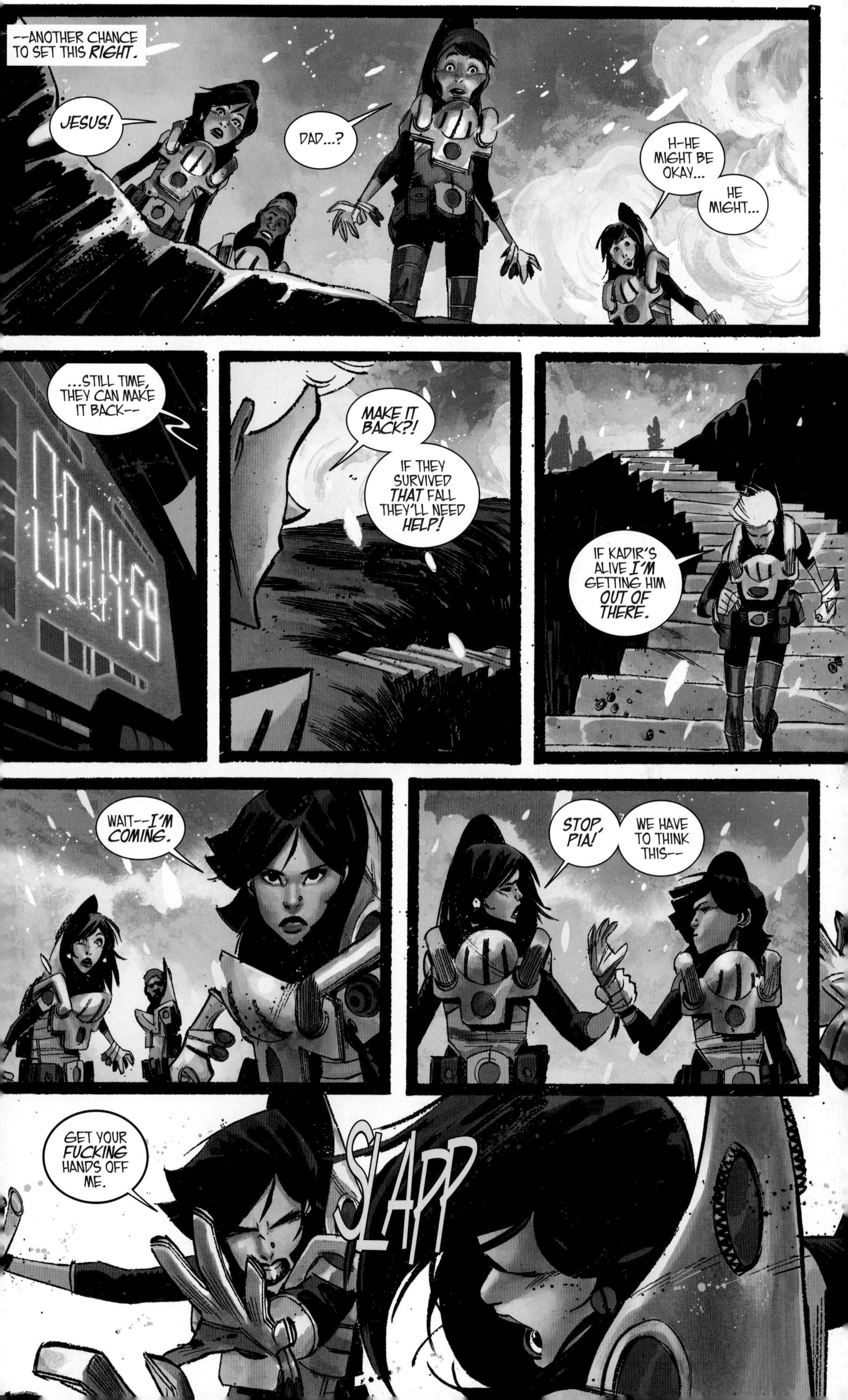
--ANOTHER CHANCE TO SET THIS RIGHT.
JESUS!
DAD...?
H-HE MIGHT BE OKAY...
HE MIGHT...
...STILL TIME, THEY CAN MAKE IT BACK--
MAKE IT BACK?!
IF THEY SURVIVED THAT FALL THEY'LL NEED HELP!
IF KADIR'S ALIVE I'M GETTING HIM OUT OF THERE.
WAIT--I'M COMING.
STOP, PIA!
WE HAVE TO THINK THIS--
GET YOUR FUCKING HANDS OFF ME.
SLAPP

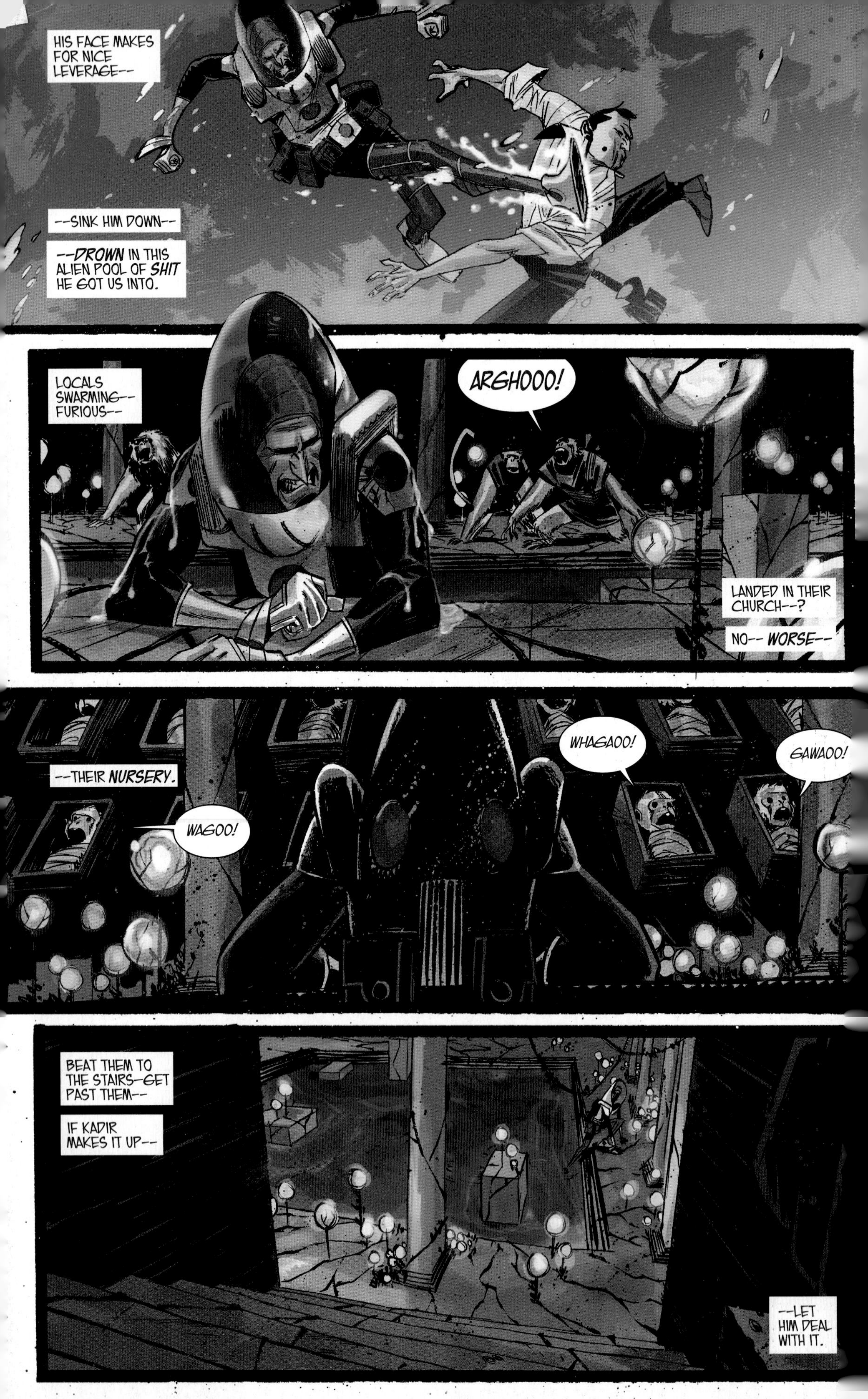
HIS FACE MAKES FOR NICE LEVERAGE--
--SINK HIM DOWN--
--DROWN IN THIS ALIEN POOL OF SHIT HE GOT US INTO.
LOCALS SWARMING-- FURIOUS--
ARGHOOO!
LANDED IN THEIR CHURCH--?
NO-- WORSE--
--THEIR NURSERY.
WHAGAOO!
GAWAOO!
WAGOO!
BEAT THEM TO THE STAIRS--GET PAST THEM--
IF KADIR MAKES IT UP--
--LET HIM DEAL WITH IT.

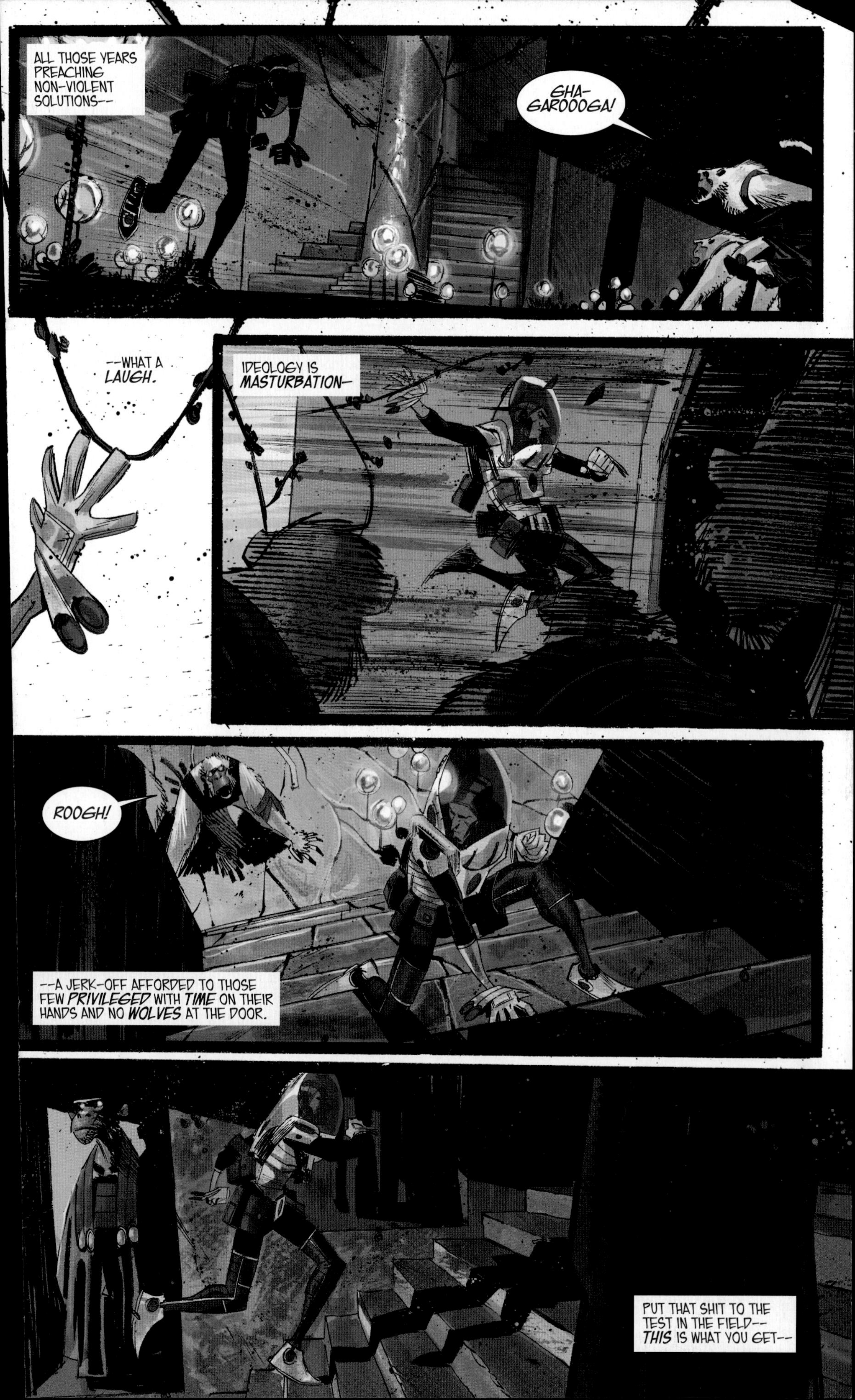
ALL THOSE YEARS PREACHING NON-VIOLENT SOLUTIONS--
GHA-GAROOOGA!
--WHAT A LAUGH.
IDEOLOGY IS MASTURBATION--
ROOGH!
--A JERK-OFF AFFORDED TO THOSE FEW PRIVILEGED WITH TIME ON THEIR HANDS AND NO WOLVES AT THE DOOR.
PUT THAT SHIT TO THE TEST IN THE FIELD--
THIS IS WHAT YOU GET--

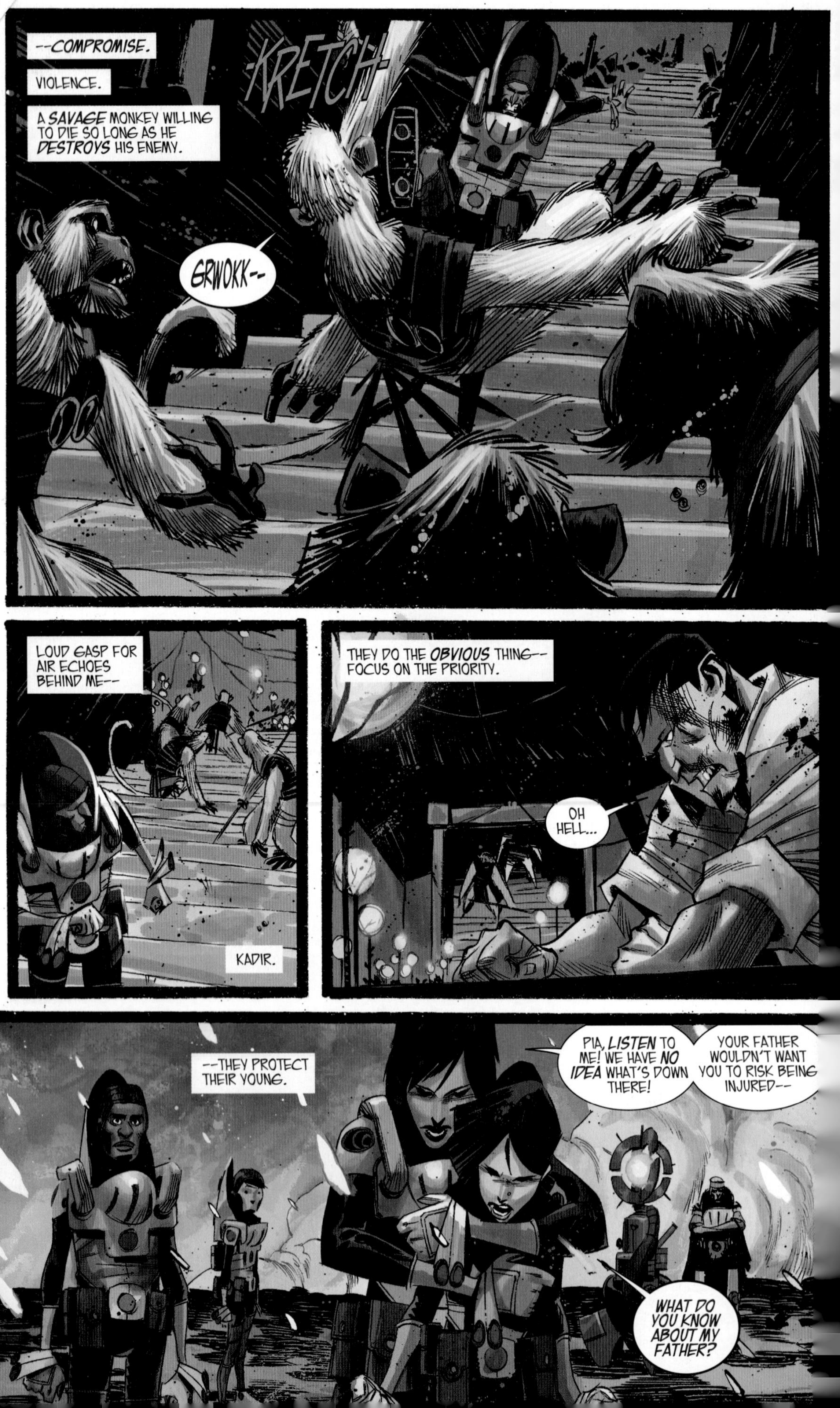
--COMPROMISE.
VIOLENCE.
A SAVAGE MONKEY WILLING TO DIE SO LONG AS HE DESTROYS HIS ENEMY.
-KRETCH-
GRWOKK--
LOUD GASP FOR AIR ECHOES BEHIND ME--
KADIR.
THEY DO THE OBVIOUS THING--FOCUS ON THE PRIORITY.
OH HELL...
--THEY PROTECT THEIR YOUNG.
PIA, LISTEN TO ME! WE HAVE NO IDEA WHAT'S DOWN THERE!
YOUR FATHER WOULDN'T WANT YOU TO RISK BEING INJURED--
WHAT DO YOU KNOW ABOUT MY FATHER?

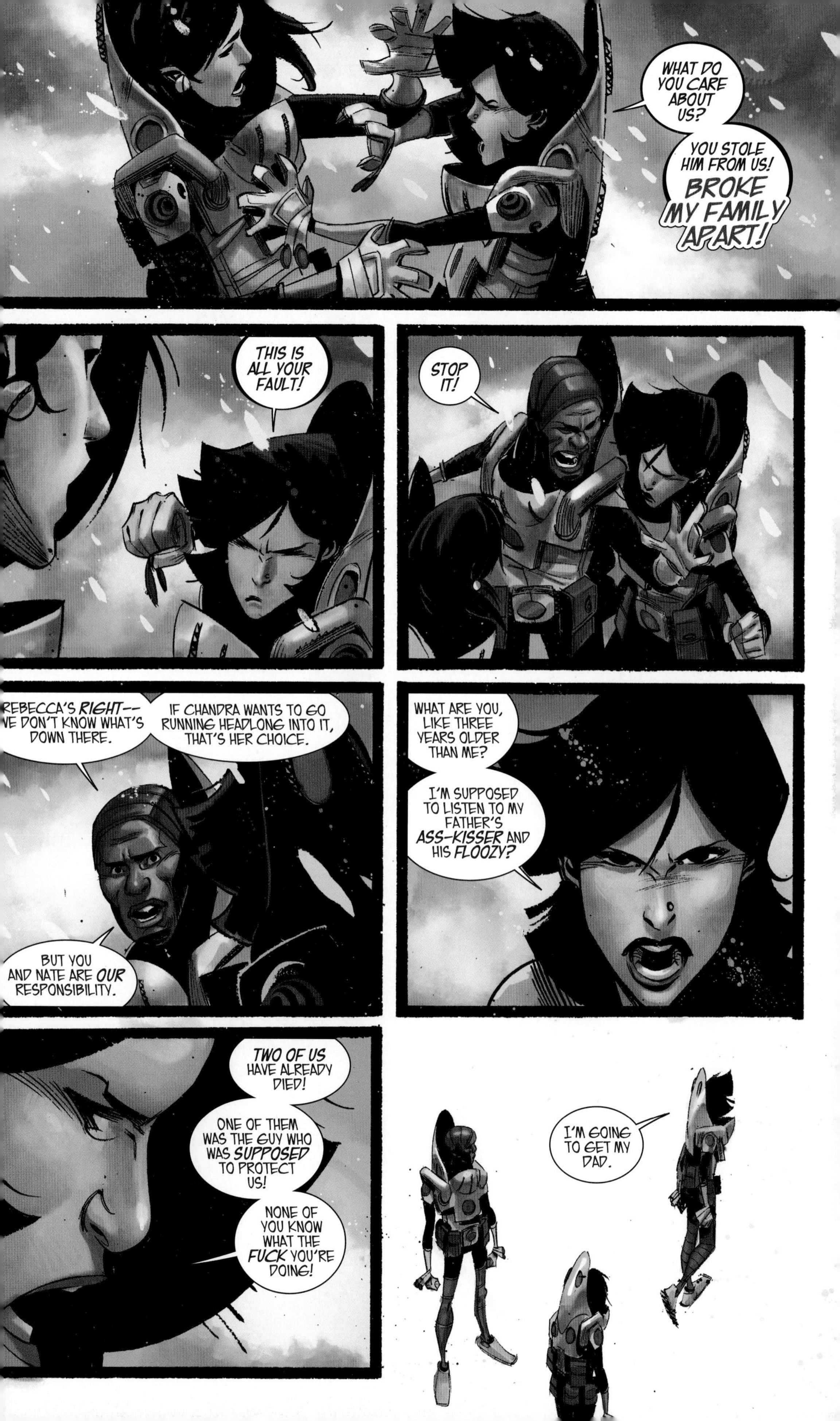
WHAT DO YOU CARE ABOUT US?
YOU STOLE HIM FROM US! BROKE MY FAMILY APART!
THIS IS ALL YOUR FAULT!
STOP IT!
REBECCA'S RIGHT-- WE DON'T KNOW WHAT'S DOWN THERE.
IF CHANDRA WANTS TO GO RUNNING HEADLONG INTO IT, THAT'S HER CHOICE.
BUT YOU AND NATE ARE OUR RESPONSIBILITY.
WHAT ARE YOU, LIKE THREE YEARS OLDER THAN ME?
I'M SUPPOSED TO LISTEN TO MY FATHER'S ASS-KISSER AND HIS FLOOZY?
TWO OF US HAVE ALREADY DIED!
ONE OF THEM WAS THE GUY WHO WAS SUPPOSED TO PROTECT US!
NONE OF YOU KNOW WHAT THE FUCK YOU'RE DOING!
I'M GOING TO GET MY DAD.

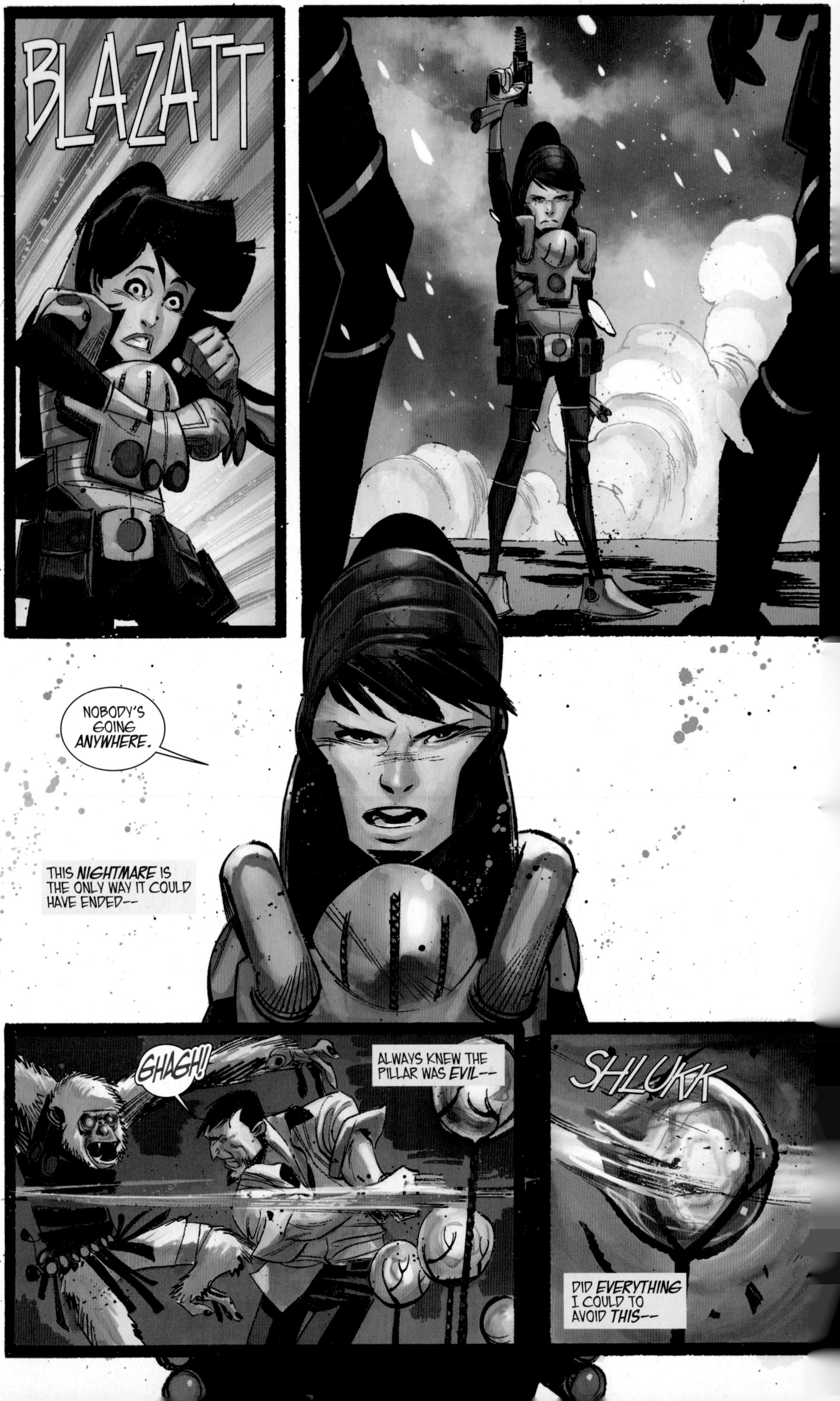

BLAZATT
NOBODY'S GOING ANYWHERE.
THIS NIGHTMARE IS THE ONLY WAY IT COULD HAVE ENDED--
GHAGH!
ALWAYS KNEW THE PILLAR WAS EVIL--
SHLUKK
DID EVERYTHING I COULD TO AVOID THIS--

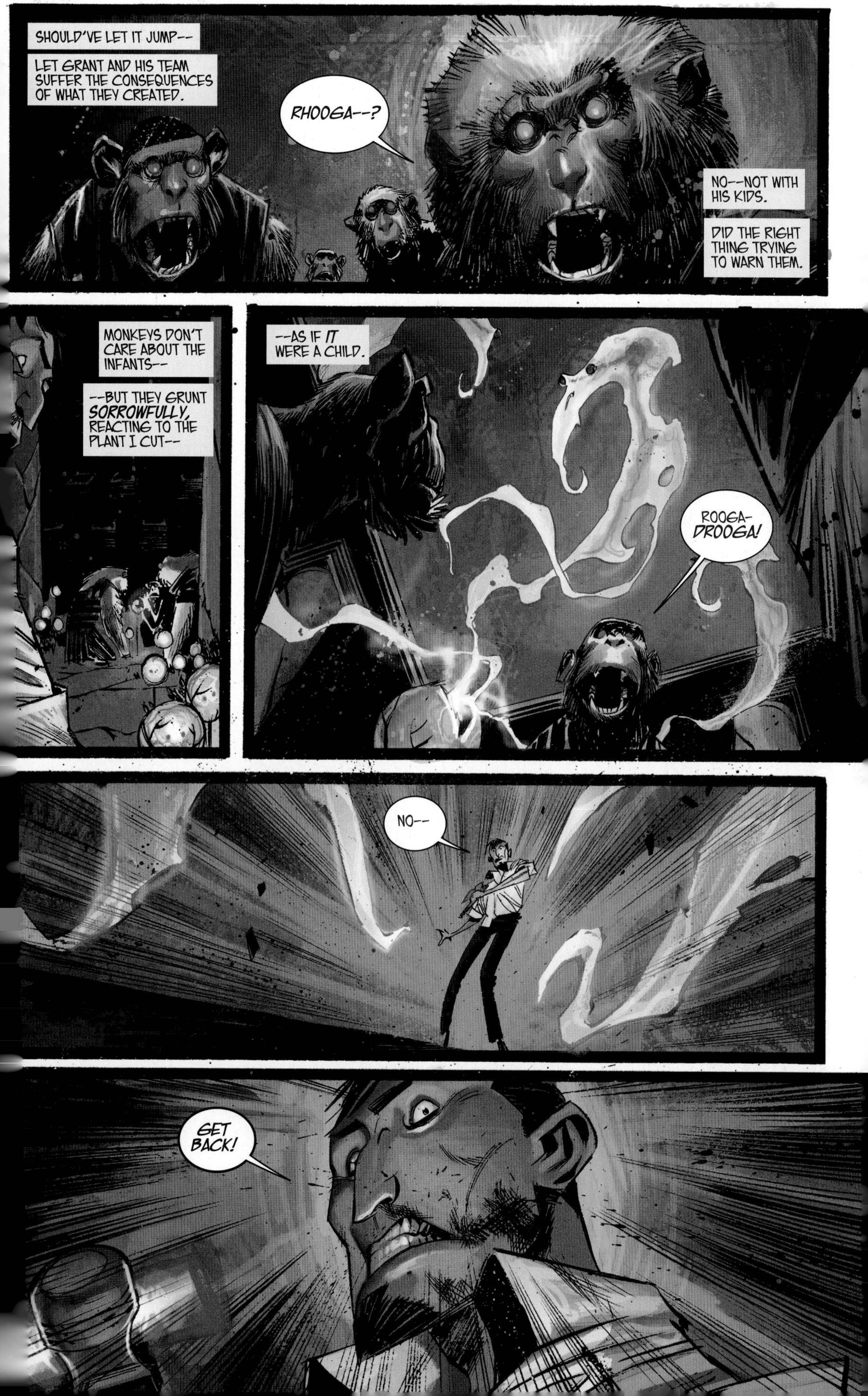
SHOULD'VE LET IT JUMP--
LET GRANT AND HIS TEAM SUFFER THE CONSEQUENCES OF WHAT THEY CREATED.
RHOOGA--?
NO--NOT WITH HIS KIDS.
DID THE RIGHT THING TRYING TO WARN THEM.
MONKEYS DON'T CARE ABOUT THE INFANTS--
--BUT THEY GRUNT SORROWFULLY, REACTING TO THE PLANT I CUT--
--AS IF IT WERE A CHILD.
ROOGA-DROOGA!
NO--
GET BACK!

KREEEEEE

GET THE HELL BACK!

GHOSTS.

NO--ALWAYS A SCIENTIFIC EXPLANATION--

HATCHET BURNS IT--

SOMEWHAT PHYSICAL--

SENTIENT GAS LIFE.

MONKEYS ARE JUST HOSTS--

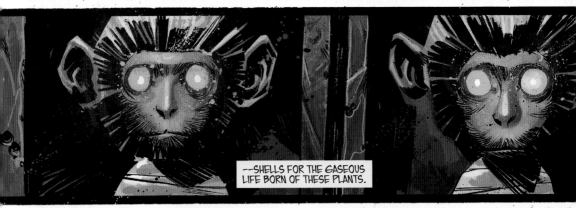

--SHELLS FOR THE GASEOUS LIFE BORN OF THESE PLANTS.

RUN--GET OUT OF THERE BEFORE THEY REMEMBER ME--

NOT MY FAULT-- DID THE RIGHT THING.

ALWAYS KNEW-- EVEN IN THEORETICAL STAGES:

WE WERE NEVER MEANT TO BREACH THESE WALLS.

DOOR TO EVERY VARIETY OF *VIRUS*, EVERY ASSORTMENT OF *PREDATOR*, EVERY POTENTIAL *WEAPON*—

INTERDIMENSIONAL TRAVEL CAN ONLY END IN *CATASTROPHE*.

CHAOS POINTS IN ALL DIRECTIONS.

ORDER POINTS IN ONLY *ONE*—

SKROOOM

—LIFE'S FRAGILE *LIMITATIONS* DEMAND THE LAWS OF *ORDER* BE OBEYED--

OOF—

--NOT ONLY FOR THE PROTECTION OF *OUR* WORLD--

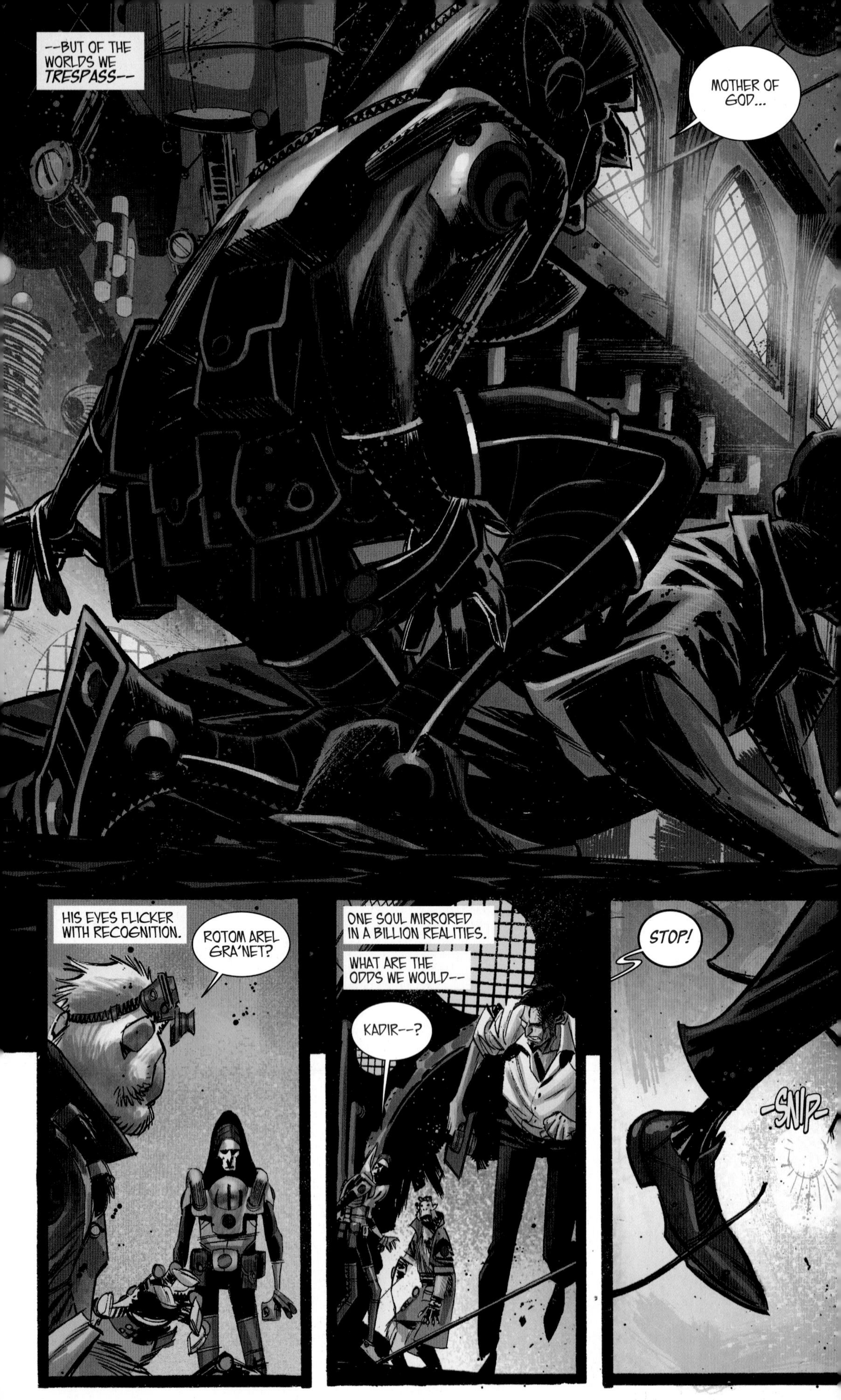
--BUT OF THE WORLDS WE TRESPASS--
MOTHER OF GOD...
HIS EYES FLICKER WITH RECOGNITION.
ROTOM AREL GRA'NET?
ONE SOUL MIRRORED IN A BILLION REALITIES.
WHAT ARE THE ODDS WE WOULD--
KADIR--?
STOP!
-SNIP-

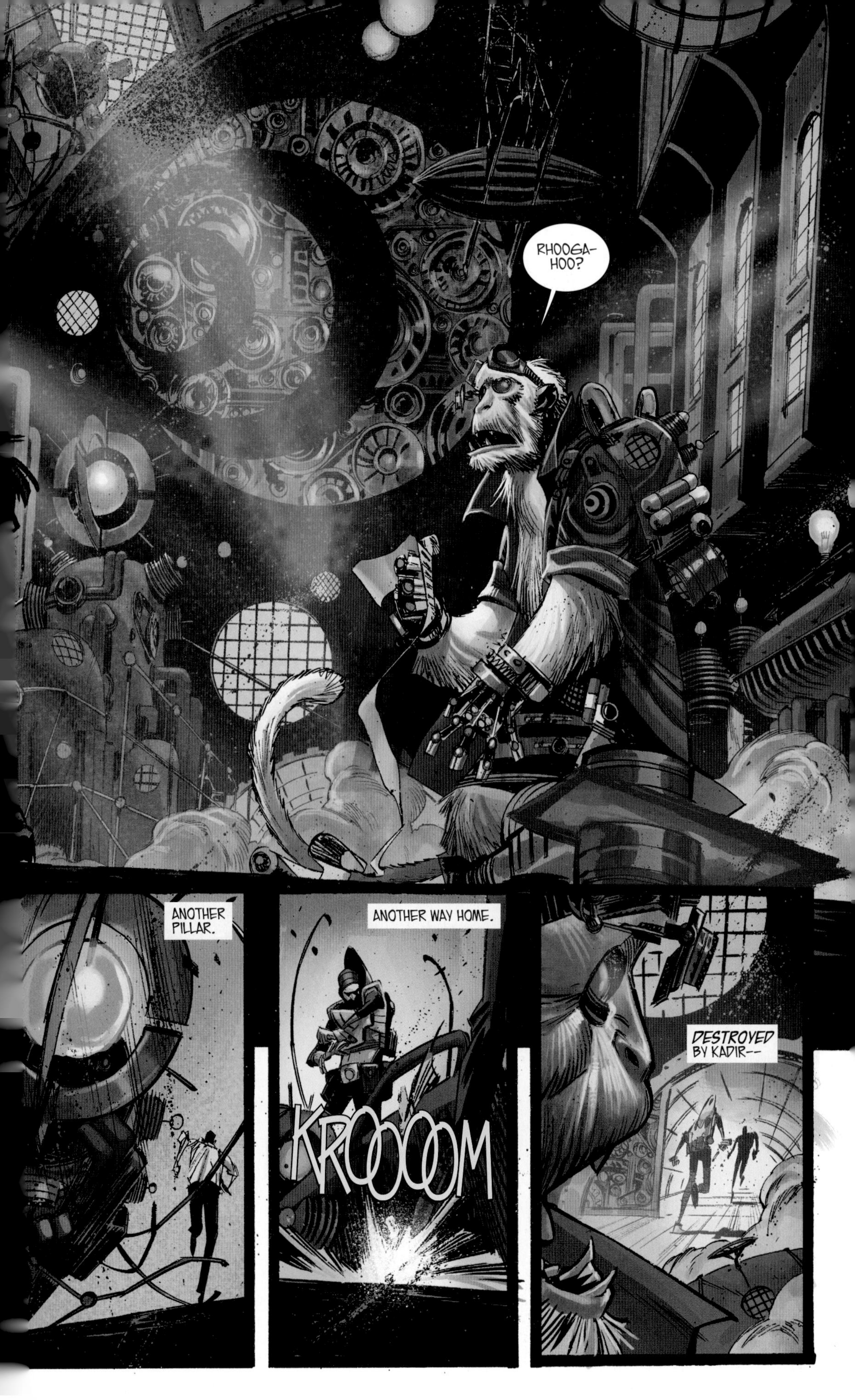
RHOOGA-HOO?
ANOTHER PILLAR.
ANOTHER WAY HOME.
KROOOOM
DESTROYED BY KADIR--

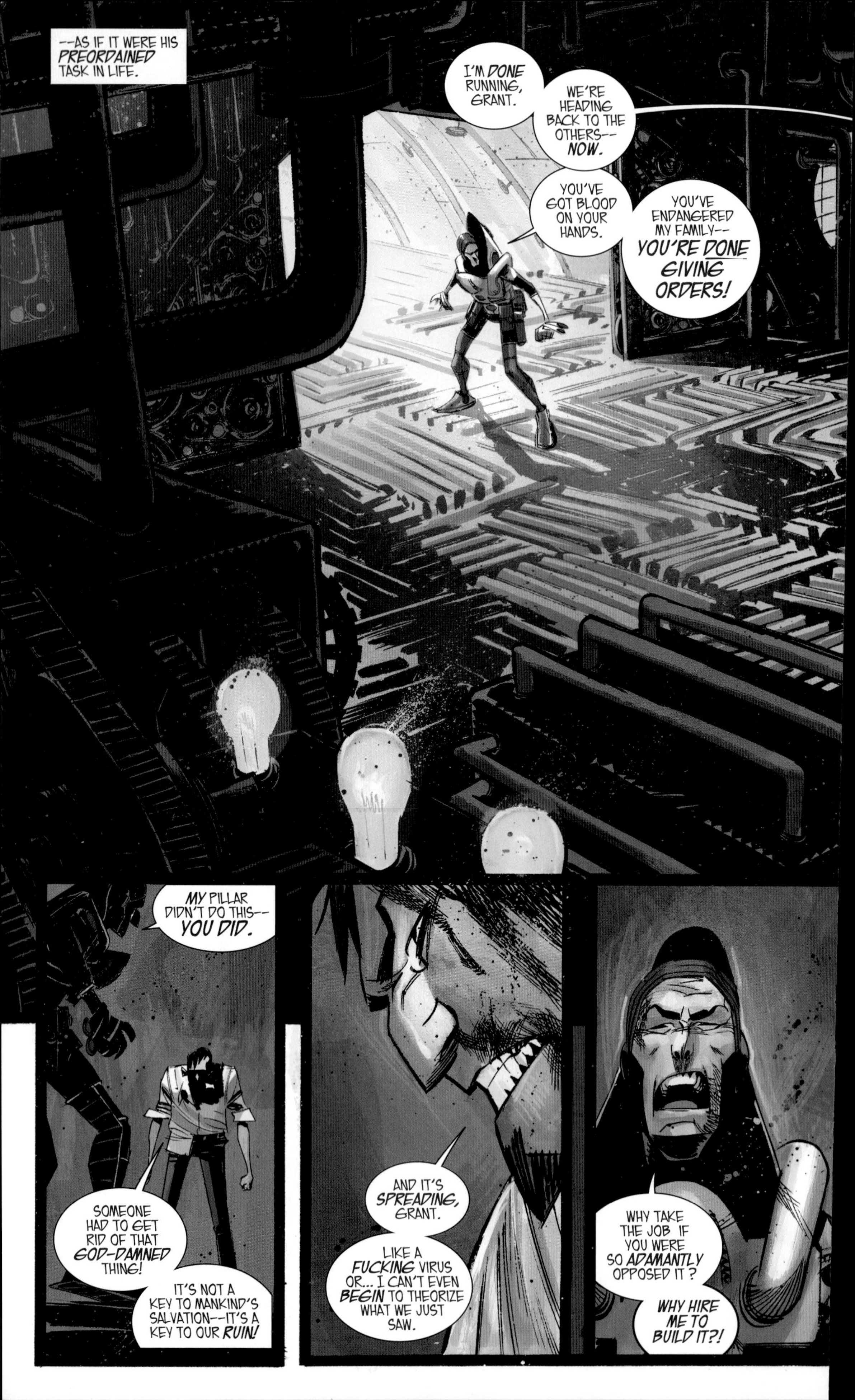
--AS IF IT WERE HIS PREORDAINED TASK IN LIFE.
I'M DONE RUNNING, GRANT.
WE'RE HEADING BACK TO THE OTHERS--NOW.
YOU'VE GOT BLOOD ON YOUR HANDS.
YOU'VE ENDANGERED MY FAMILY--YOU'RE DONE GIVING ORDERS!
MY PILLAR DIDN'T DO THIS--YOU DID.
SOMEONE HAD TO GET RID OF THAT GOD-DAMNED THING!
IT'S NOT A KEY TO MANKIND'S SALVATION--IT'S A KEY TO OUR RUIN!
AND IT'S SPREADING, GRANT.
LIKE A FUCKING VIRUS OR... I CAN'T EVEN BEGIN TO THEORIZE WHAT WE JUST SAW.
WHY TAKE THE JOB IF YOU WERE SO ADAMANTLY OPPOSED IT?
WHY HIRE ME TO BUILD IT?!

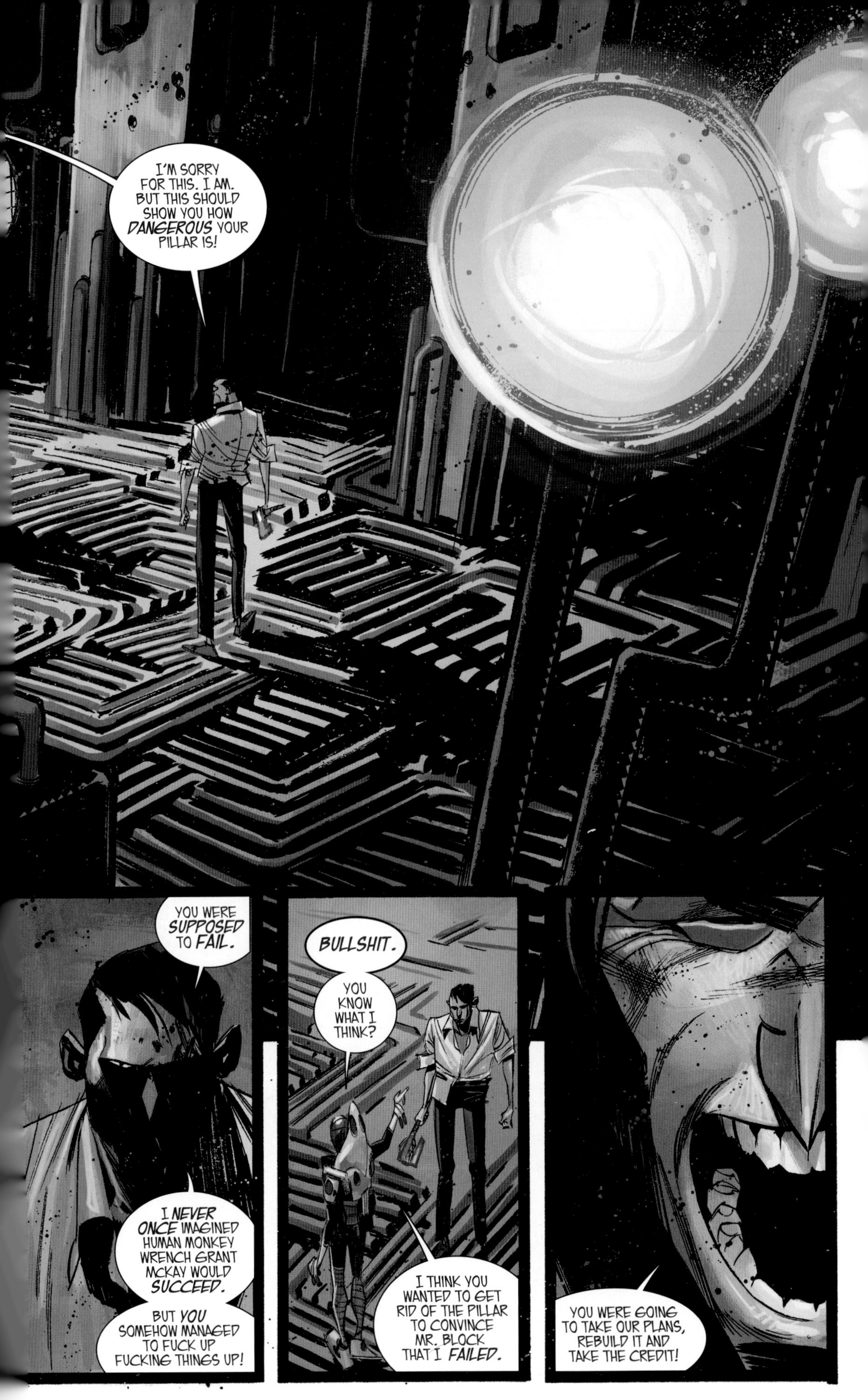
I'M SORRY FOR THIS. I AM. BUT THIS SHOULD SHOW YOU HOW DANGEROUS YOUR PILLAR IS!
YOU WERE SUPPOSED TO FAIL.
I NEVER ONCE IMAGINED HUMAN MONKEY WRENCH GRANT MCKAY WOULD SUCCEED.
BUT YOU SOMEHOW MANAGED TO FUCK UP FUCKING THINGS UP!
BULLSHIT.
YOU KNOW WHAT I THINK?
I THINK YOU WANTED TO GET RID OF THE PILLAR TO CONVINCE MR. BLOCK THAT I FAILED.
YOU WERE GOING TO TAKE OUR PLANS, REBUILD IT AND TAKE THE CREDIT!

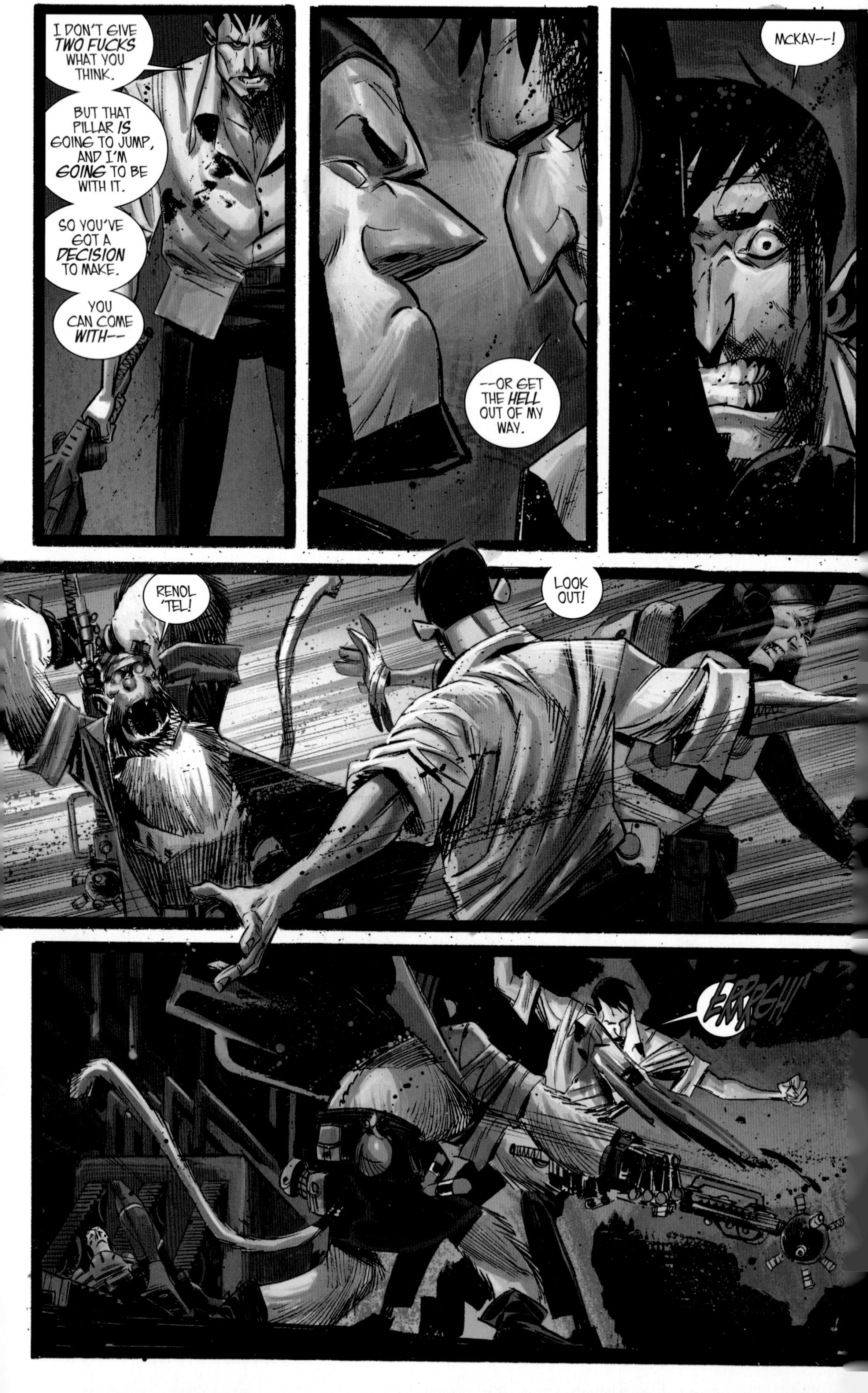
I DON'T GIVE TWO FUCKS WHAT YOU THINK.
BUT THAT PILLAR IS GOING TO JUMP, AND I'M GOING TO BE WITH IT.
SO YOU'VE GOT A DECISION TO MAKE.
YOU CAN COME WITH--
--OR GET THE HELL OUT OF MY WAY.
MCKAY--!
RENOL 'TEL!
LOOK OUT!
ERRRGH!

KRECHH

NO--

DWOOOOM

YHERAGHHH

RUR?!

GHA--
ARRAAGHGHH!

SHLAK

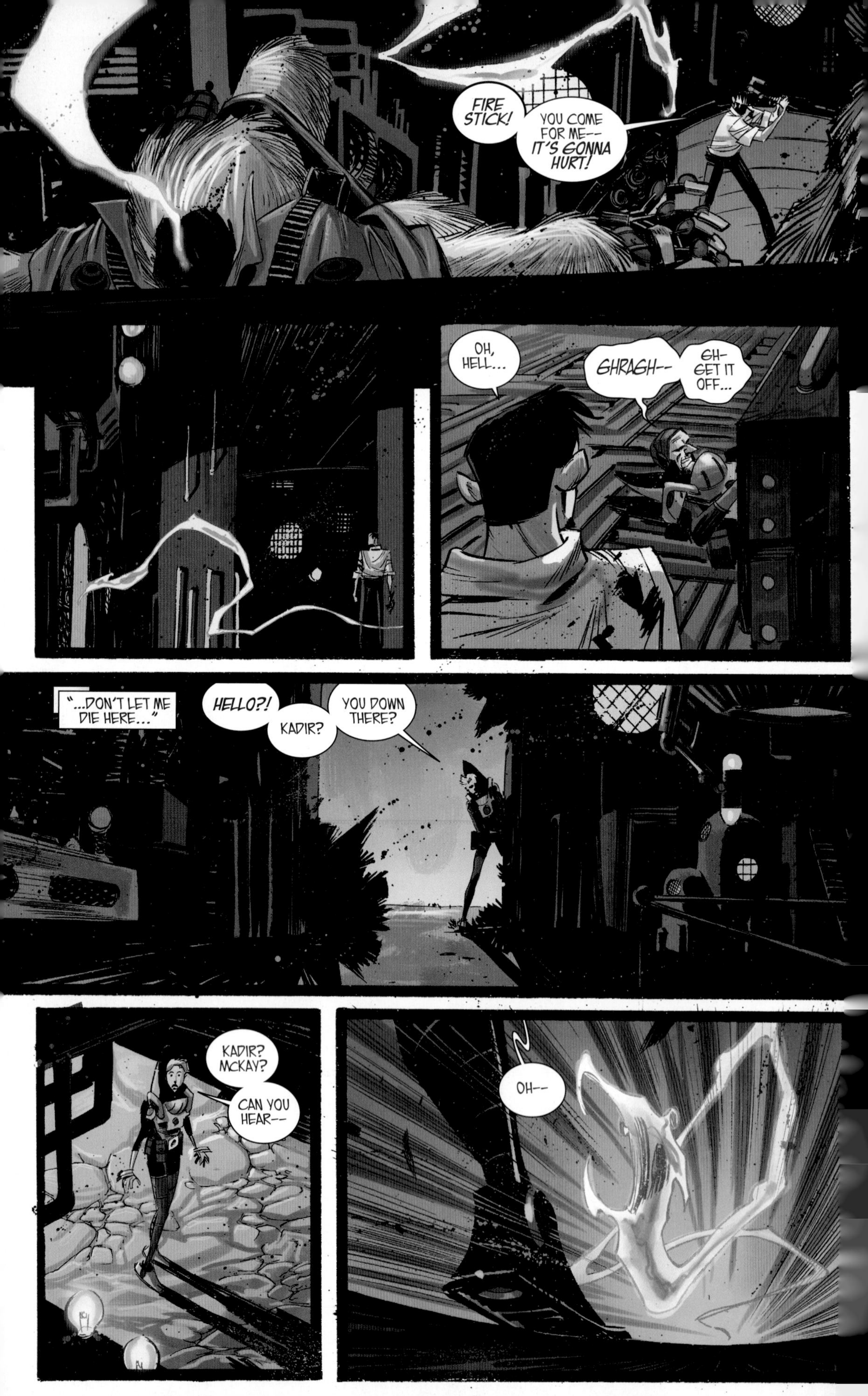
FIRE STICK!
YOU COME FOR ME-- IT'S GONNA HURT!
OH, HELL...
GHRAGH--
GH- GET IT OFF...
"...DON'T LET ME DIE HERE..."
HELLO?!
KADIR?
YOU DOWN THERE?
KADIR? MCKAY?
CAN YOU HEAR--
OH--

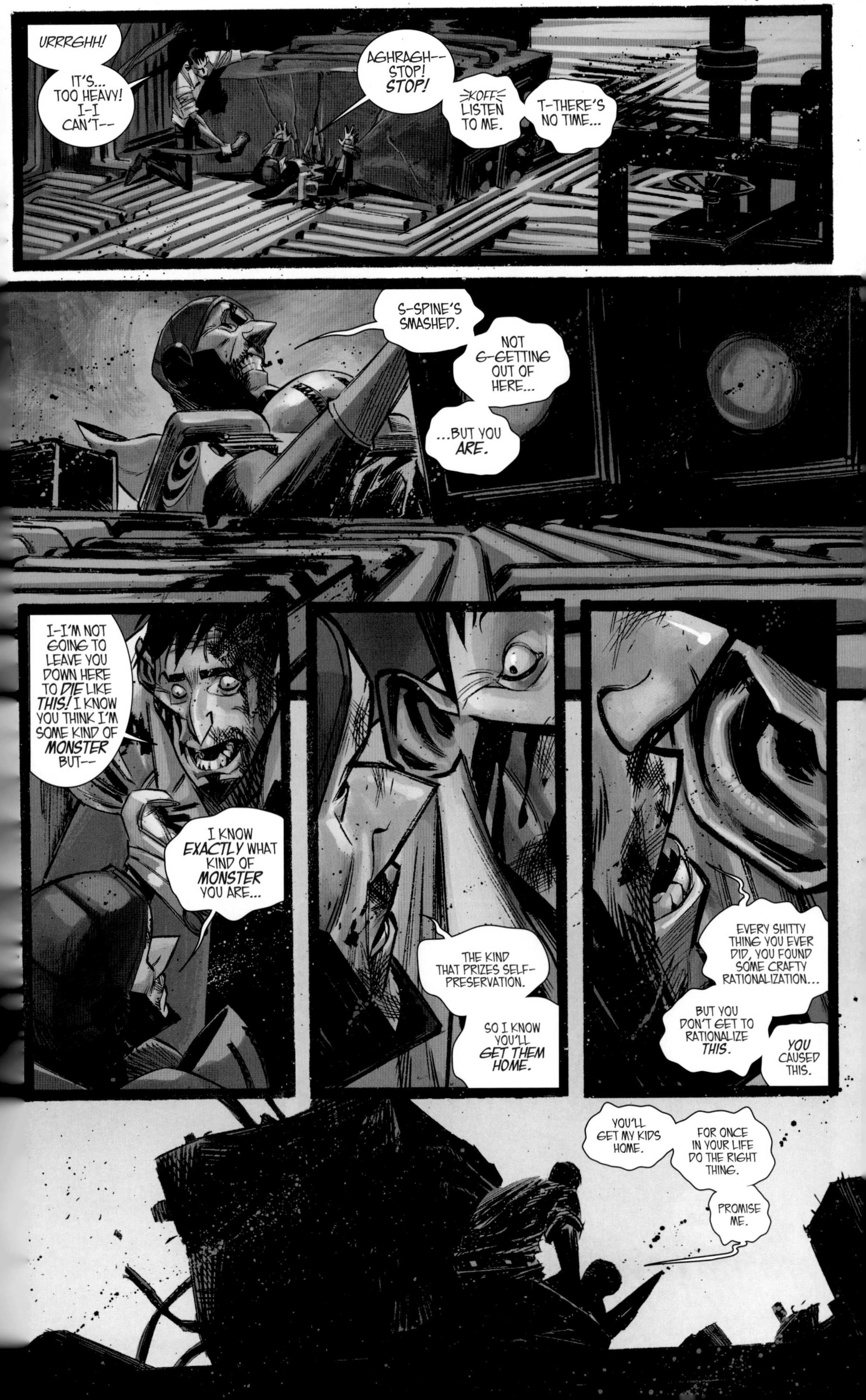
URRRGHH!
IT'S... TOO HEAVY! I-I CAN'T--
AGHRAGH-- STOP! STOP!
KOFF LISTEN TO ME.
T-THERE'S NO TIME...
S-SPINE'S SMASHED.
NOT G-GETTING OUT OF HERE...
...BUT YOU ARE.
I-I'M NOT GOING TO LEAVE YOU DOWN HERE TO DIE LIKE THIS! I KNOW YOU THINK I'M SOME KIND OF MONSTER BUT--
I KNOW EXACTLY WHAT KIND OF MONSTER YOU ARE...
THE KIND THAT PRIZES SELF-PRESERVATION.
SO I KNOW YOU'LL GET THEM HOME.
EVERY SHITTY THING YOU EVER DID, YOU FOUND SOME CRAFTY RATIONALIZATION...
BUT YOU DON'T GET TO RATIONALIZE THIS.
YOU CAUSED THIS.
YOU'LL GET MY KIDS HOME.
FOR ONCE IN YOUR LIFE DO THE RIGHT THING.
PROMISE ME.

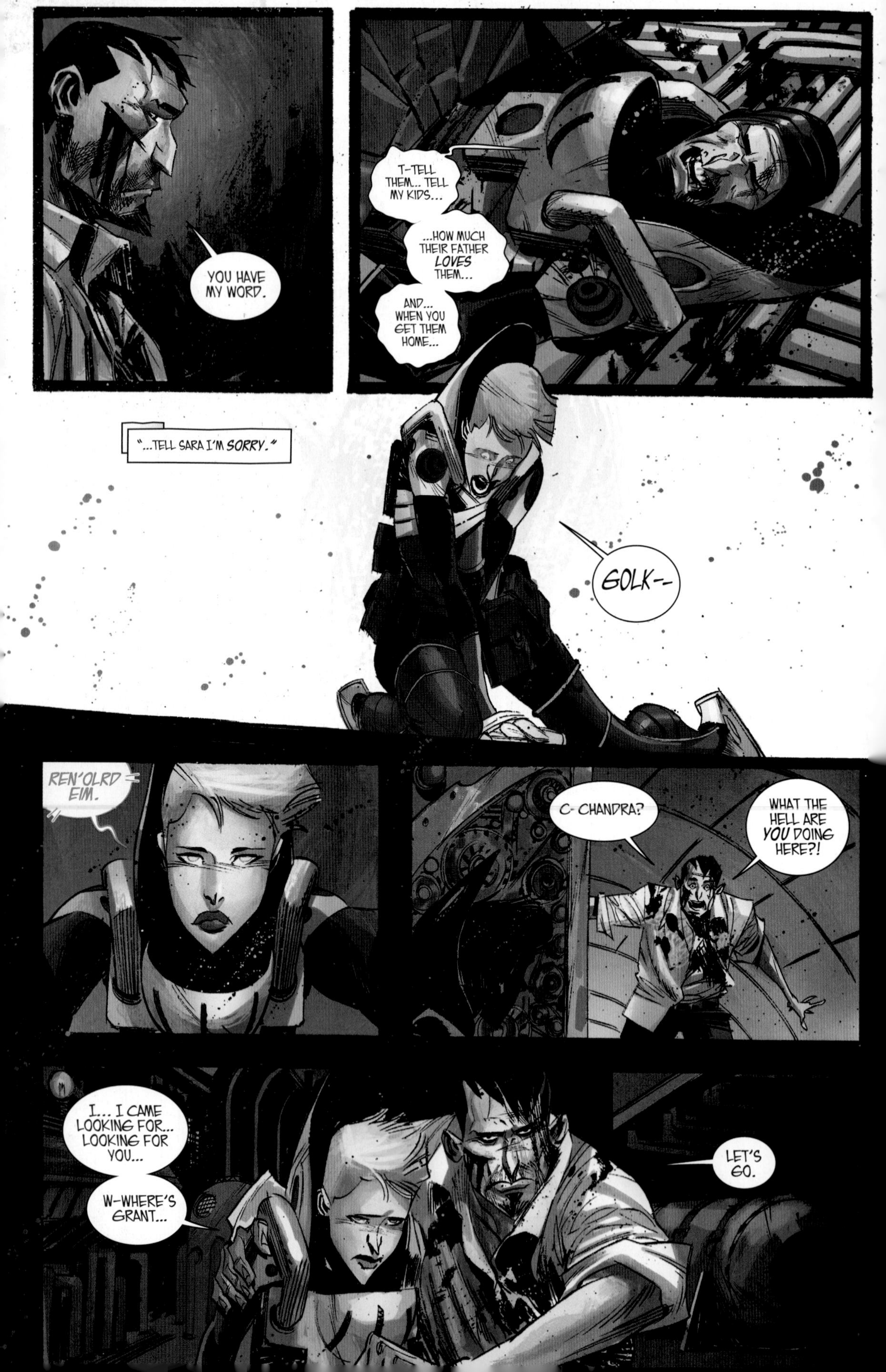
YOU HAVE MY WORD.
T-TELL THEM... TELL MY KIDS...
...HOW MUCH THEIR FATHER LOVES THEM...
AND... WHEN YOU GET THEM HOME...
"...TELL SARA I'M SORRY."
GOLK--
REN'OLRD EIM.
C-CHANDRA?
WHAT THE HELL ARE YOU DOING HERE?!
I... I CAME LOOKING FOR... LOOKING FOR YOU...
W-WHERE'S GRANT...
LET'S GO.

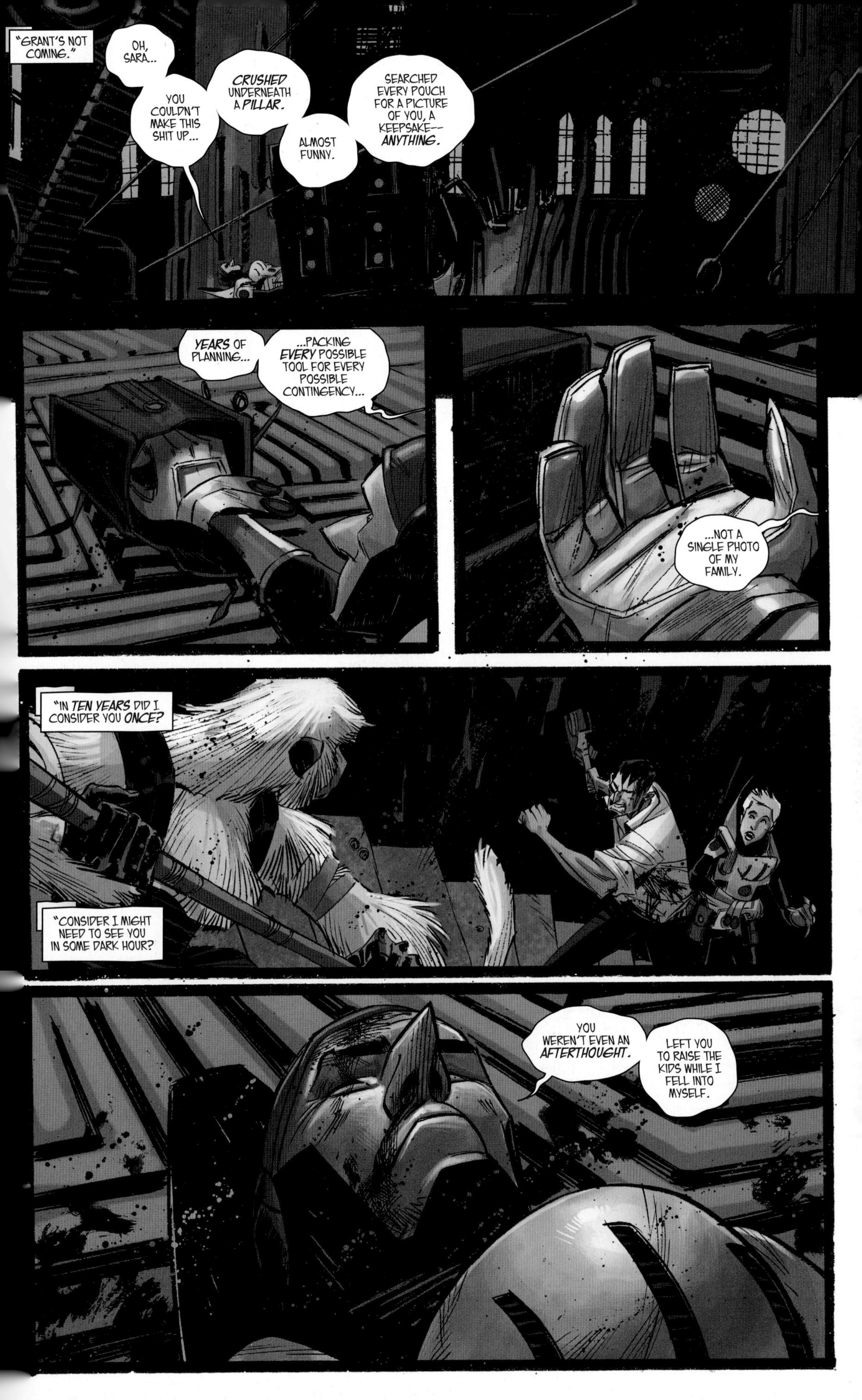

"GRANT'S NOT COMING."
OH, SARA...
YOU COULDN'T MAKE THIS SHIT UP...
CRUSHED UNDERNEATH A PILLAR.
ALMOST FUNNY.
SEARCHED EVERY POUCH FOR A PICTURE OF YOU, A KEEPSAKE-- ANYTHING.
YEARS OF PLANNING...
...PACKING EVERY POSSIBLE TOOL FOR EVERY POSSIBLE CONTINGENCY...
...NOT A SINGLE PHOTO OF MY FAMILY.
"IN TEN YEARS DID I CONSIDER YOU ONCE?
"CONSIDER I MIGHT NEED TO SEE YOU IN SOME DARK HOUR?
YOU WEREN'T EVEN AN AFTERTHOUGHT.
LEFT YOU TO RAISE THE KIDS WHILE I FELL INTO MYSELF.

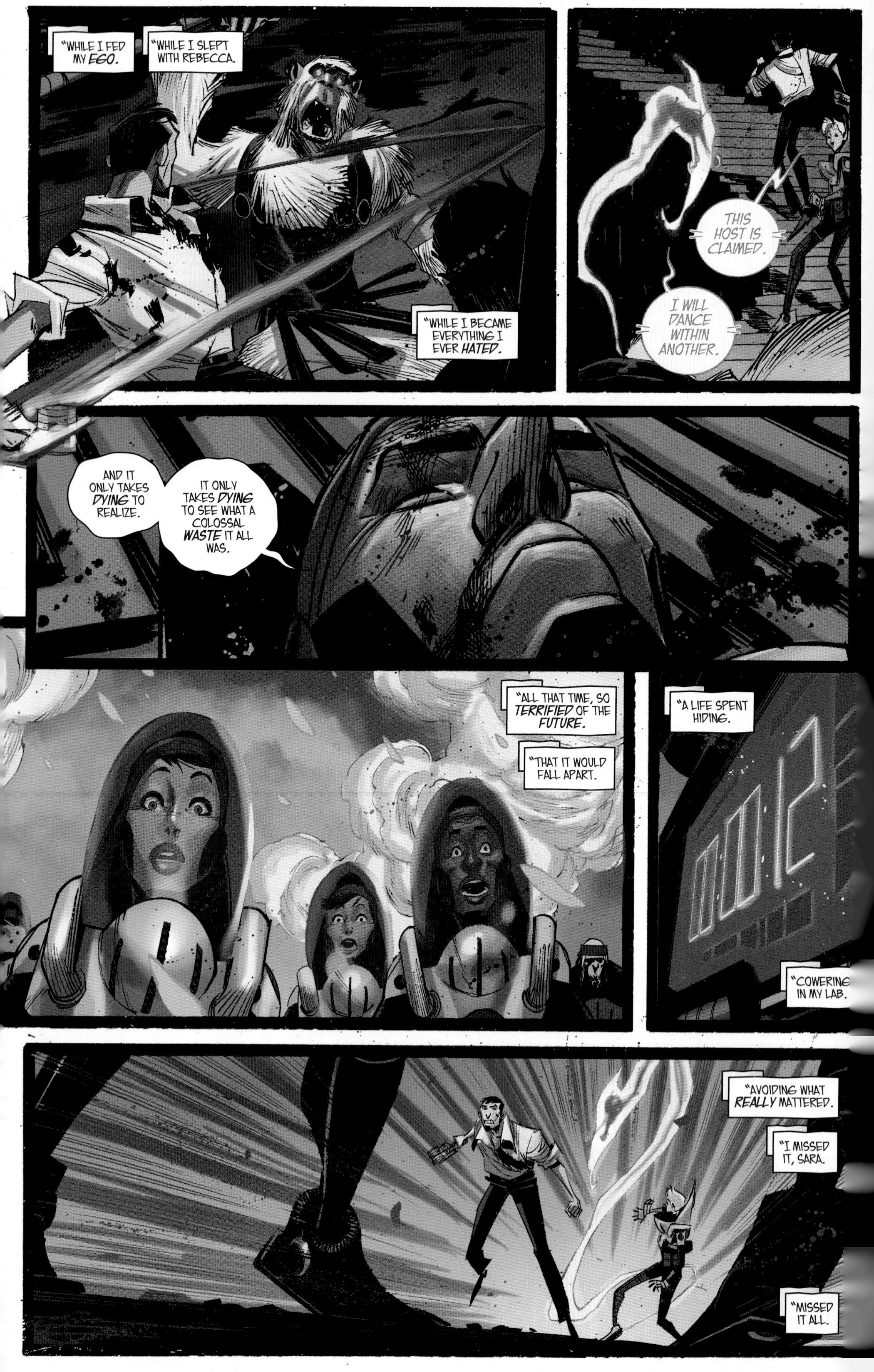

"WHILE I FED MY EGO.
"WHILE I SLEPT WITH REBECCA.
"WHILE I BECAME EVERYTHING I EVER HATED.
THIS HOST IS CLAIMED.
I WILL DANCE WITHIN ANOTHER.
AND IT ONLY TAKES DYING TO REALIZE.
IT ONLY TAKES DYING TO SEE WHAT A COLOSSAL WASTE IT ALL WAS.
"ALL THAT TIME, SO TERRIFIED OF THE FUTURE.
"THAT IT WOULD FALL APART.
"A LIFE SPENT HIDING.
00:00:12
"COWERING IN MY LAB.
"AVOIDING WHAT REALLY MATTERED.
"I MISSED IT, SARA.
"MISSED IT ALL.

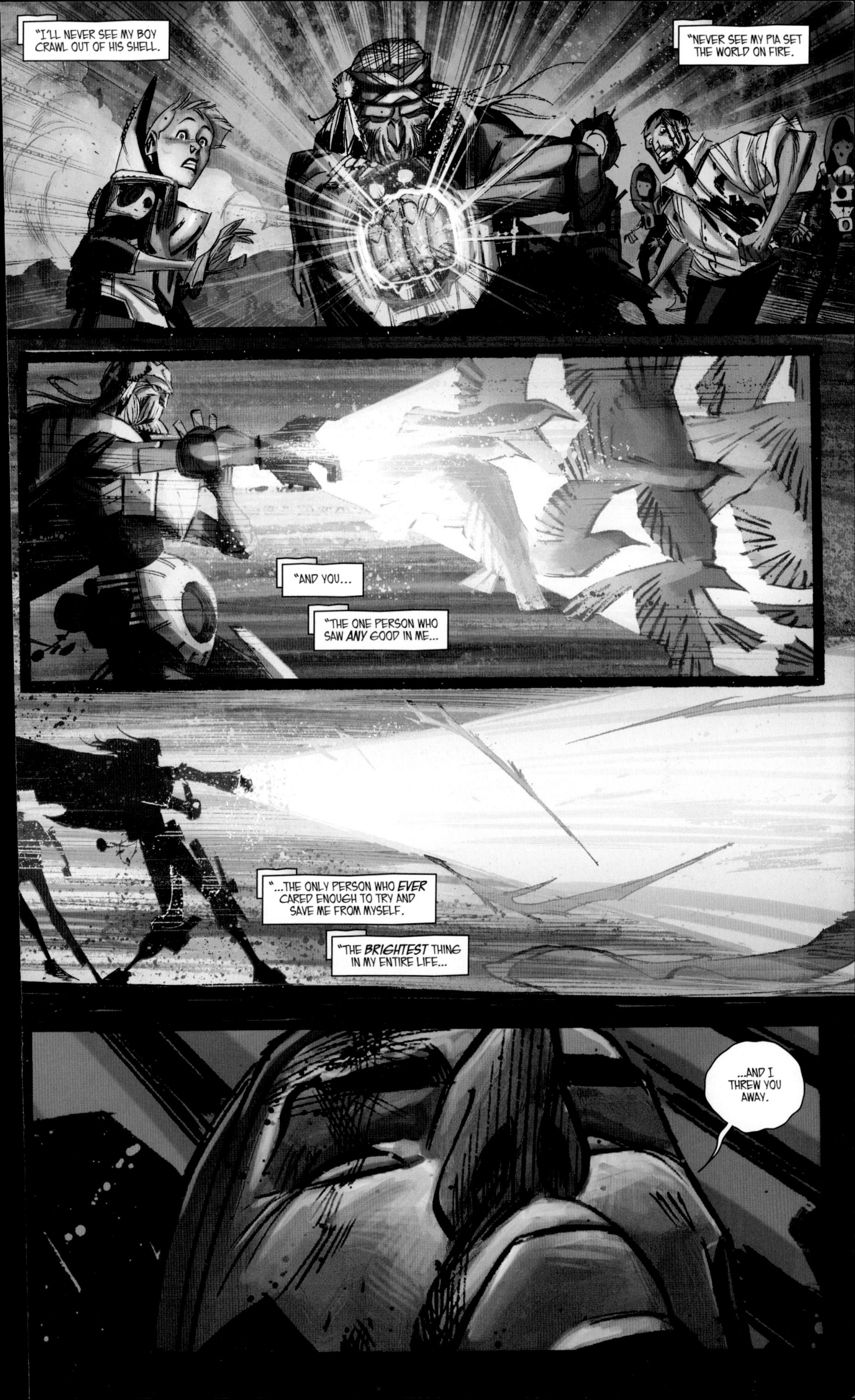
"I'LL NEVER SEE MY BOY CRAWL OUT OF HIS SHELL.
"NEVER SEE MY PIA SET THE WORLD ON FIRE.
"AND YOU...
"THE ONE PERSON WHO SAW *ANY* GOOD IN ME...
"...THE ONLY PERSON WHO *EVER* CARED ENOUGH TO TRY AND SAVE ME FROM MYSELF.
"THE *BRIGHTEST* THING IN MY ENTIRE LIFE...
...AND I THREW YOU AWAY.

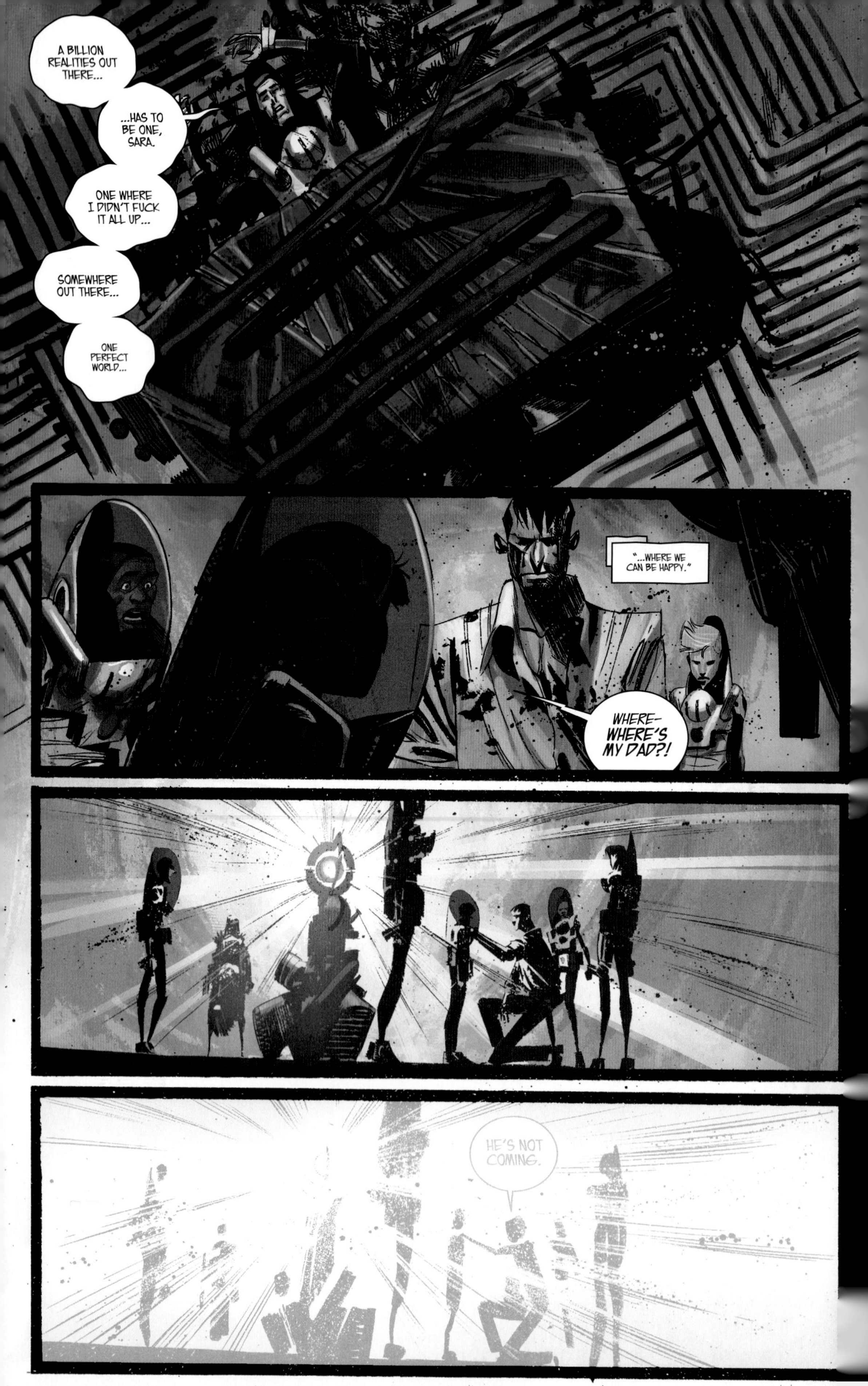
A BILLION REALITIES OUT THERE...
...HAS TO BE ONE, SARA.
ONE WHERE I DIDN'T FUCK IT ALL UP...
SOMEWHERE OUT THERE...
ONE PERFECT WORLD...
"...WHERE WE CAN BE HAPPY."
WHERE-WHERE'S MY DAD?!
HE'S NOT COMING.

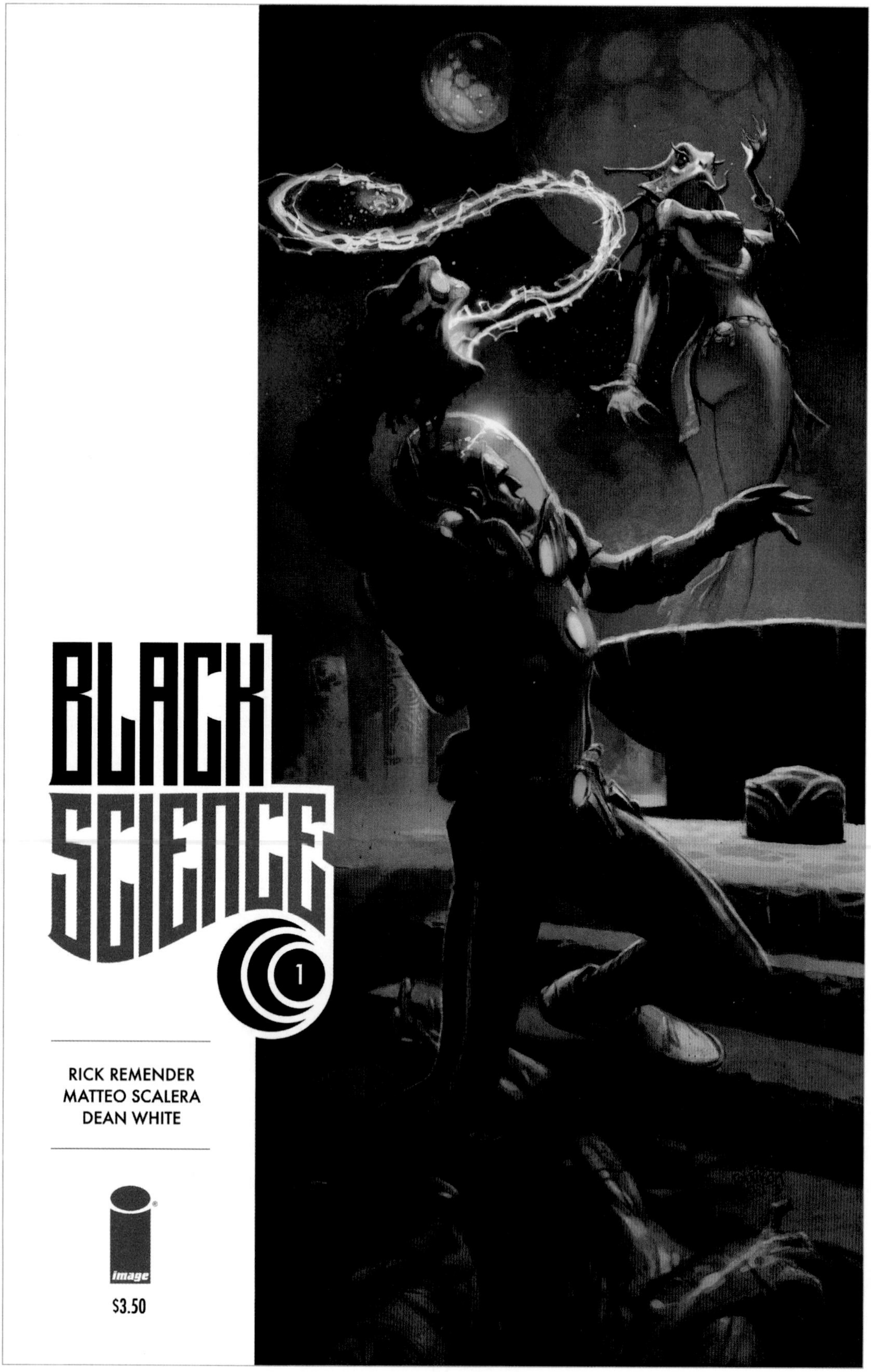
BLACK SCIENCE
1
RICK REMENDER
MATTEO SCALERA
DEAN WHITE
image
$3.50

#1 VARIANT BY ANDREW ROBINSON

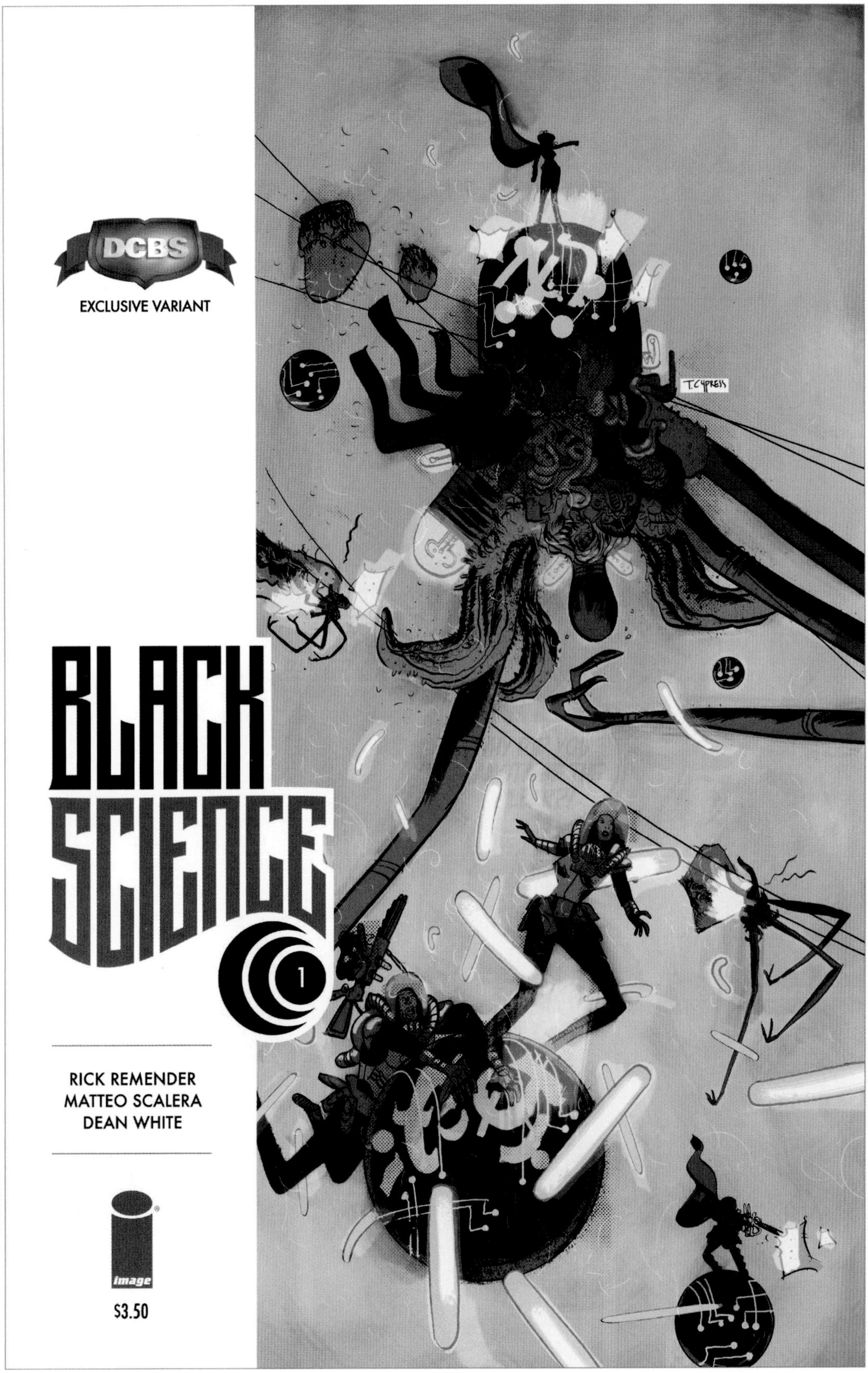
DCBS
EXCLUSIVE VARIANT
BLACK SCIENCE
1
RICK REMENDER
MATTEO SCALERA
DEAN WHITE
image
$3.50
T.CYPRESS

#1 DCBS VARIANT BY TOBY CYPRESS

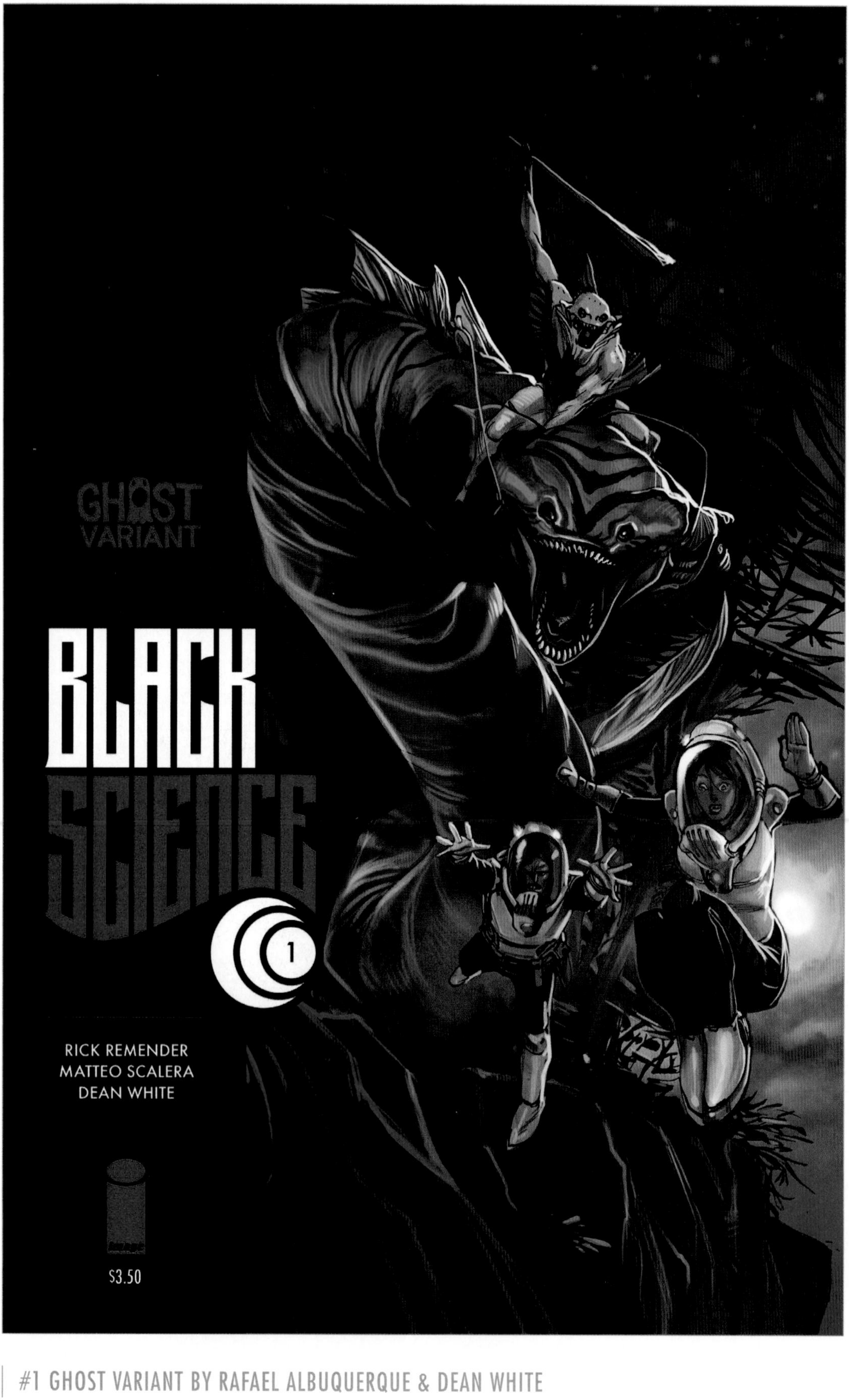
GHOST
VARIANT
BLACK
SCIENCE
1
RICK REMENDER
MATTEO SCALERA
DEAN WHITE
$3.50

#1 GHOST VARIANT BY RAFAEL ALBUQUERQUE & DEAN WHITE

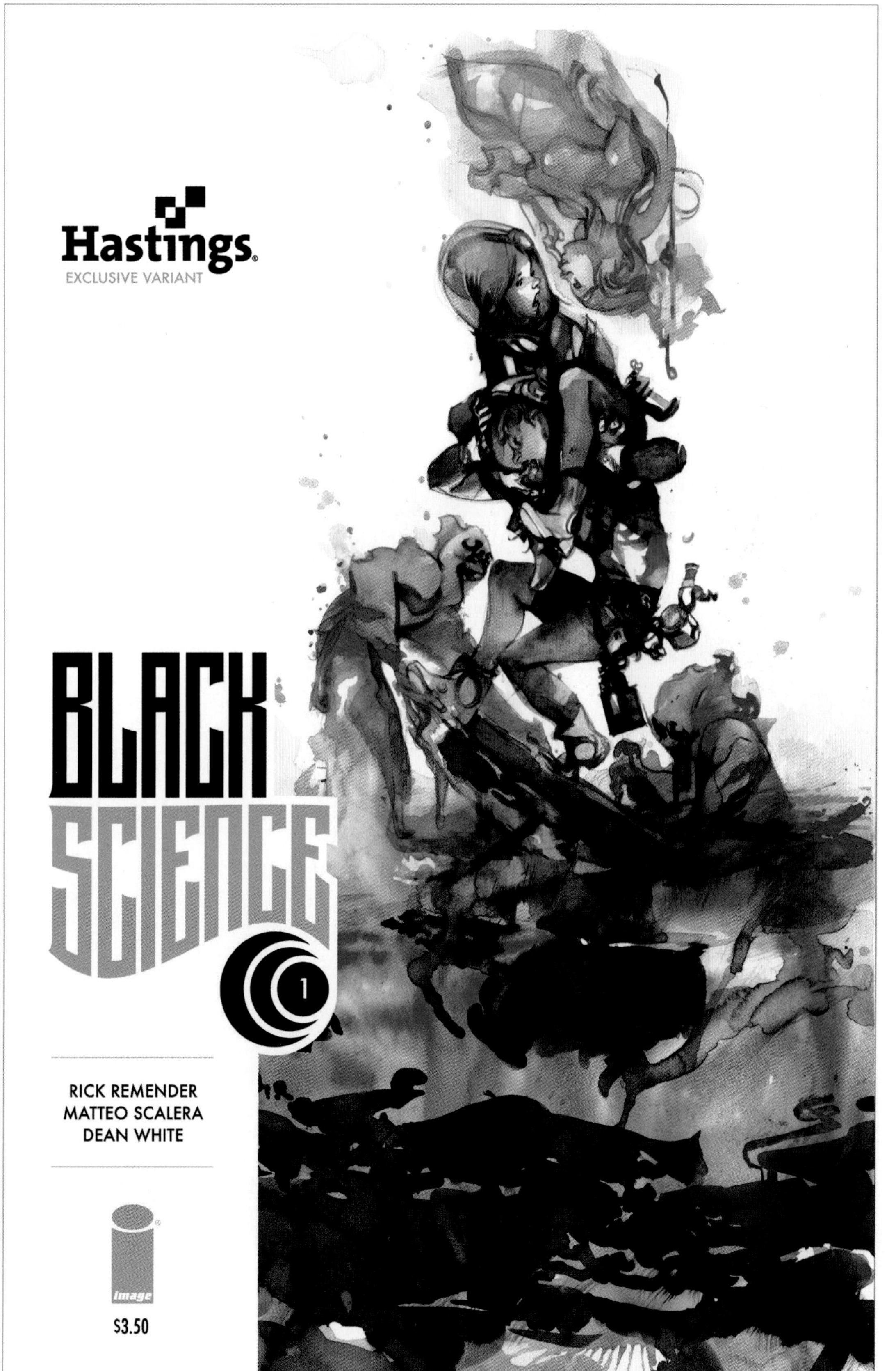
Hastings
EXCLUSIVE VARIANT
BLACK SCIENCE
1
RICK REMENDER
MATTEO SCALERA
DEAN WHITE
image
$3.50

#1 HASTINGS VARIANT BY GREG TOCCHINI

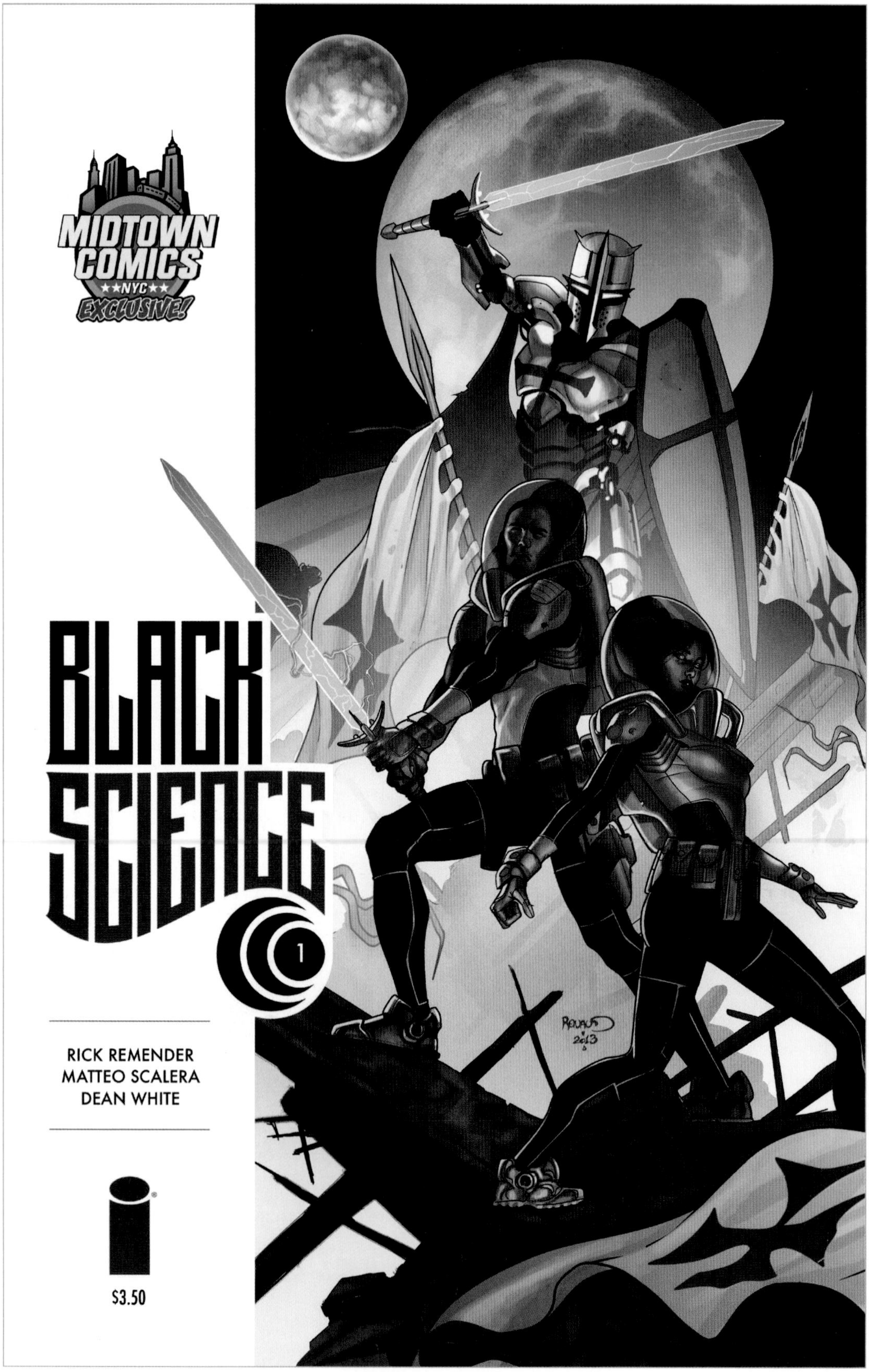
MIDTOWN COMICS
NYC
EXCLUSIVE!
BLACK SCIENCE
1
RICK REMENDER
MATTEO SCALERA
DEAN WHITE
$3.50

#1 MIDTOWN COMICS VARIANT BY PAUL RENAUD

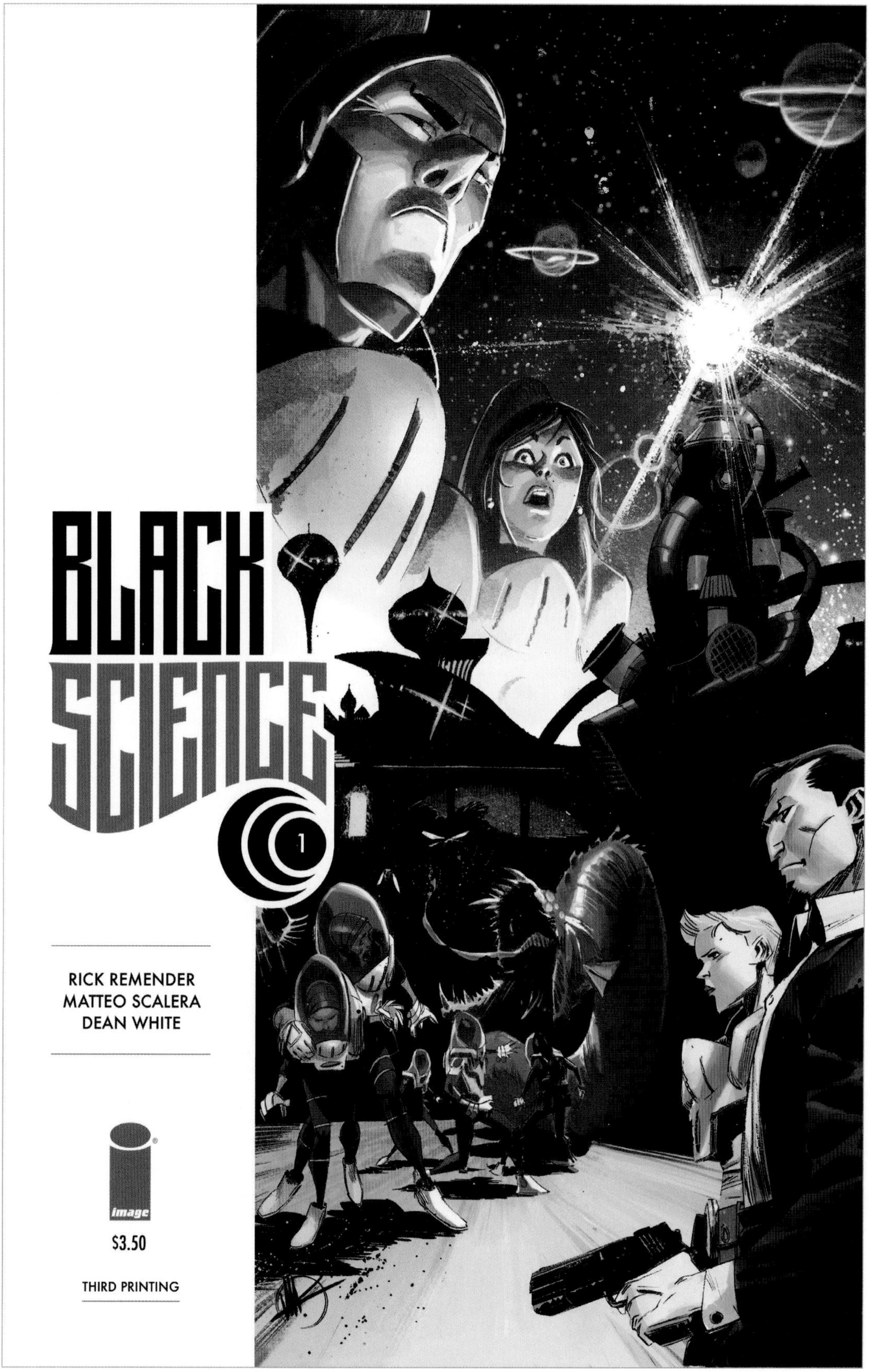
BLACK SCIENCE
1
RICK REMENDER
MATTEO SCALERA
DEAN WHITE
image
$3.50
THIRD PRINTING

#1 3RD PRINTING VARIANT BY MATTEO SCALERA & DEAN WHITE

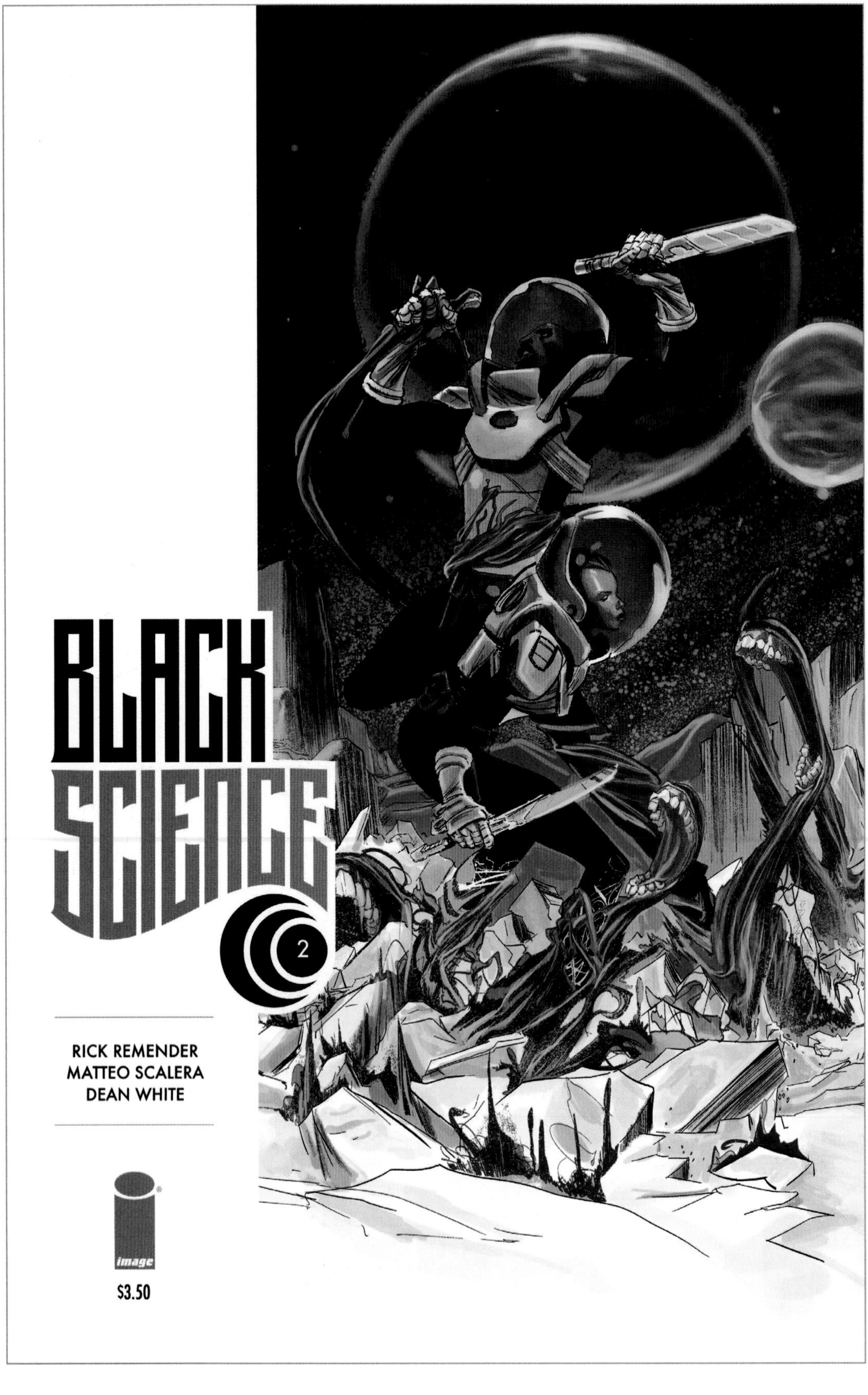
BLACK SCIENCE
2
RICK REMENDER
MATTEO SCALERA
DEAN WHITE
image
$3.50

#2 VARIANT BY ROBBI RODRIGUEZ & DEAN WHITE

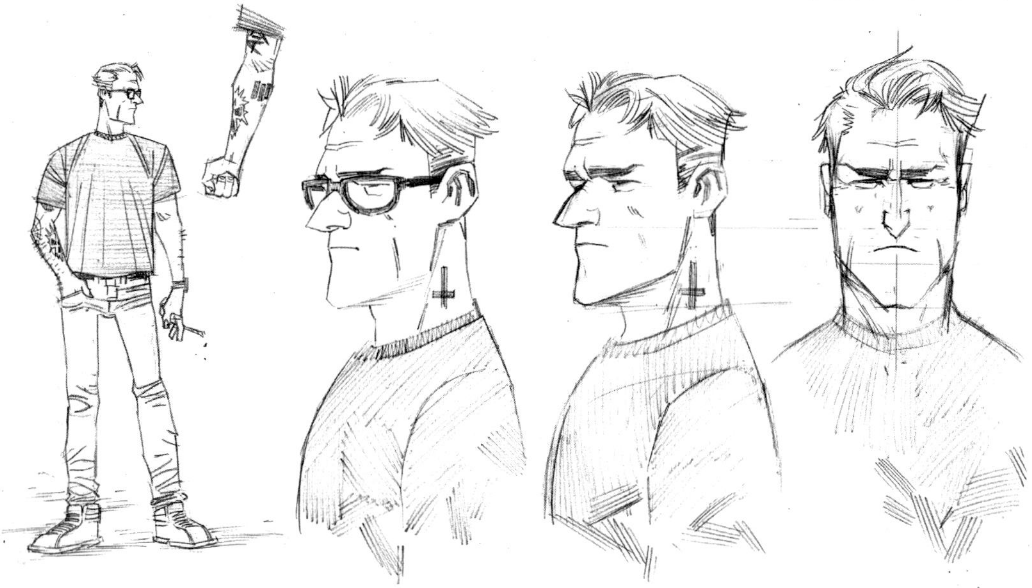

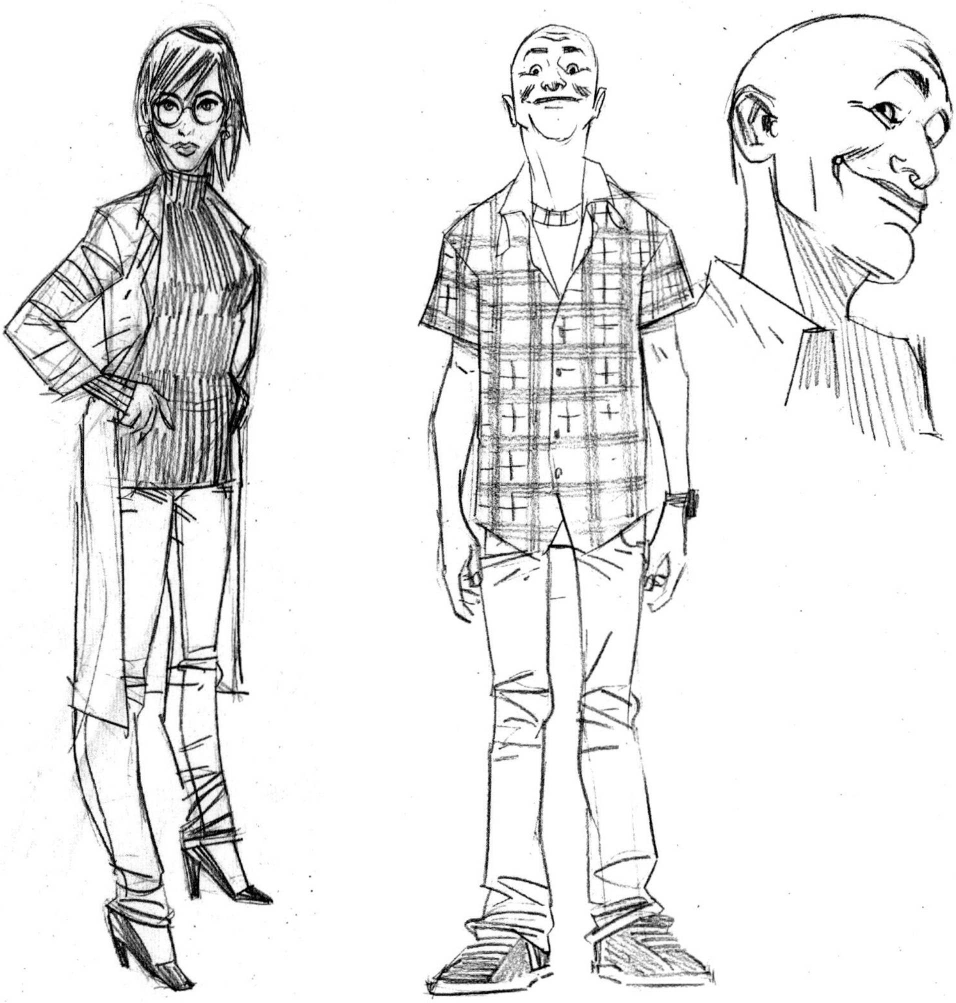

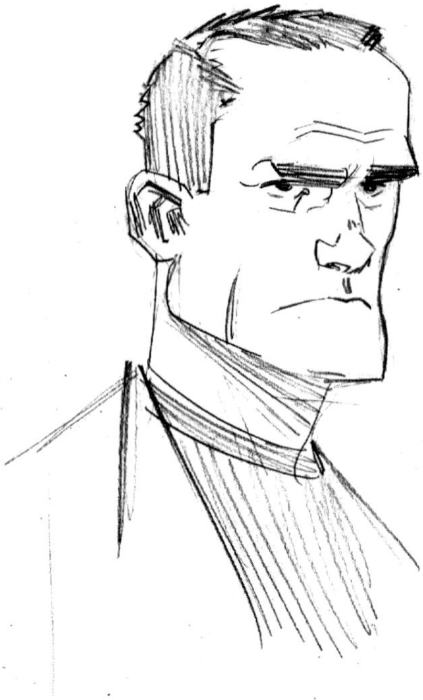

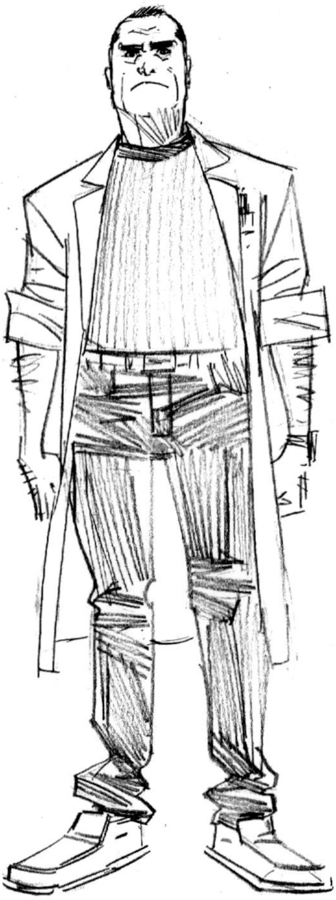

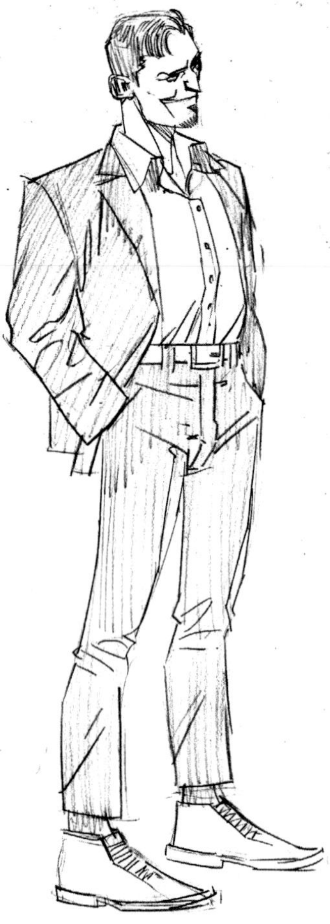

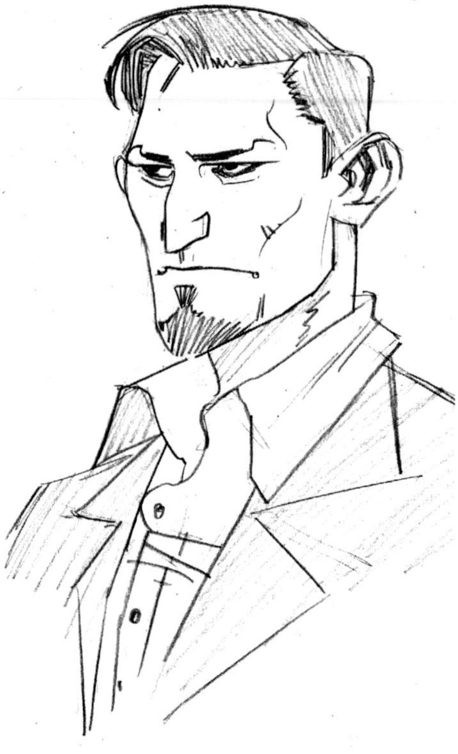

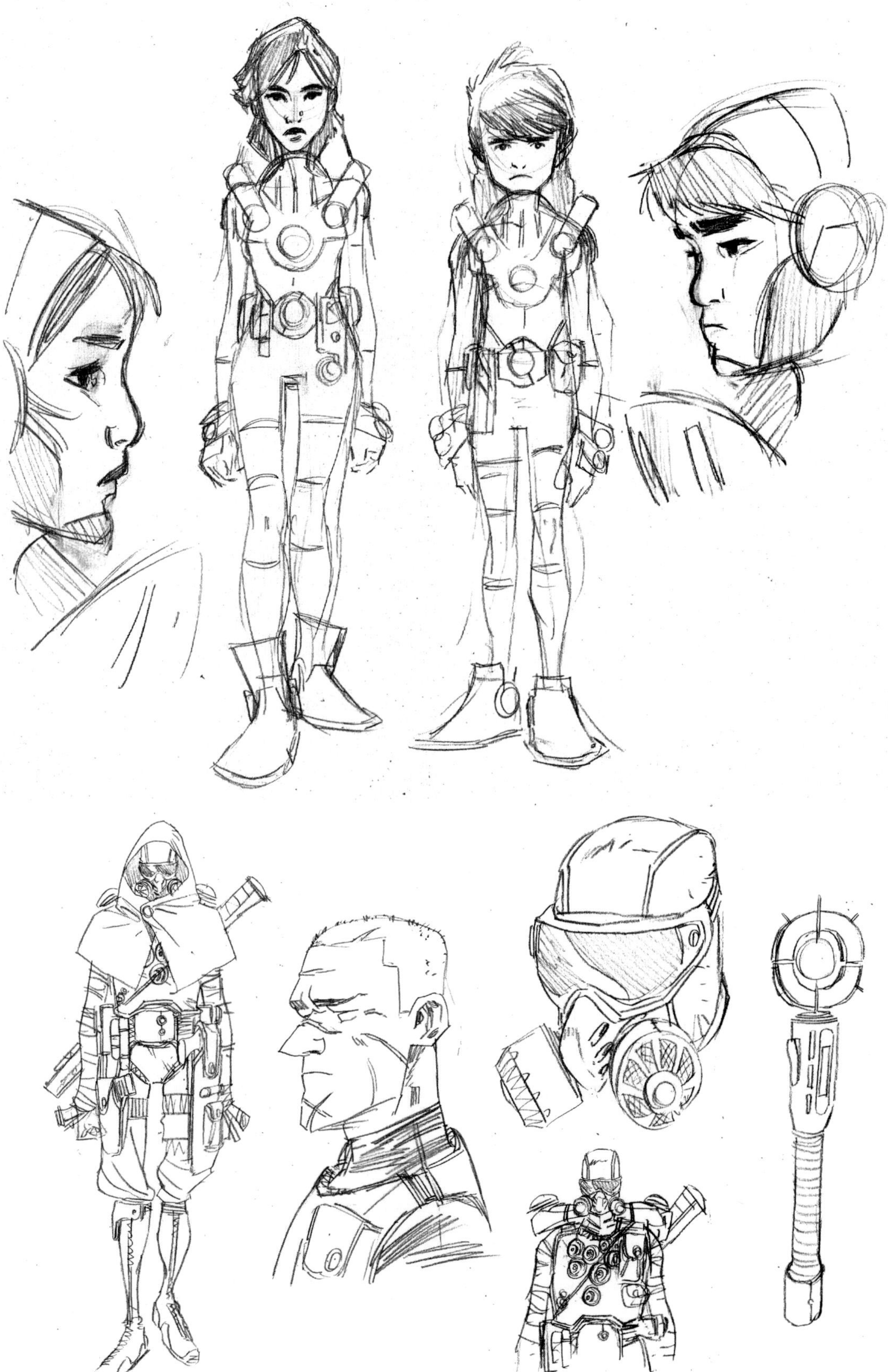

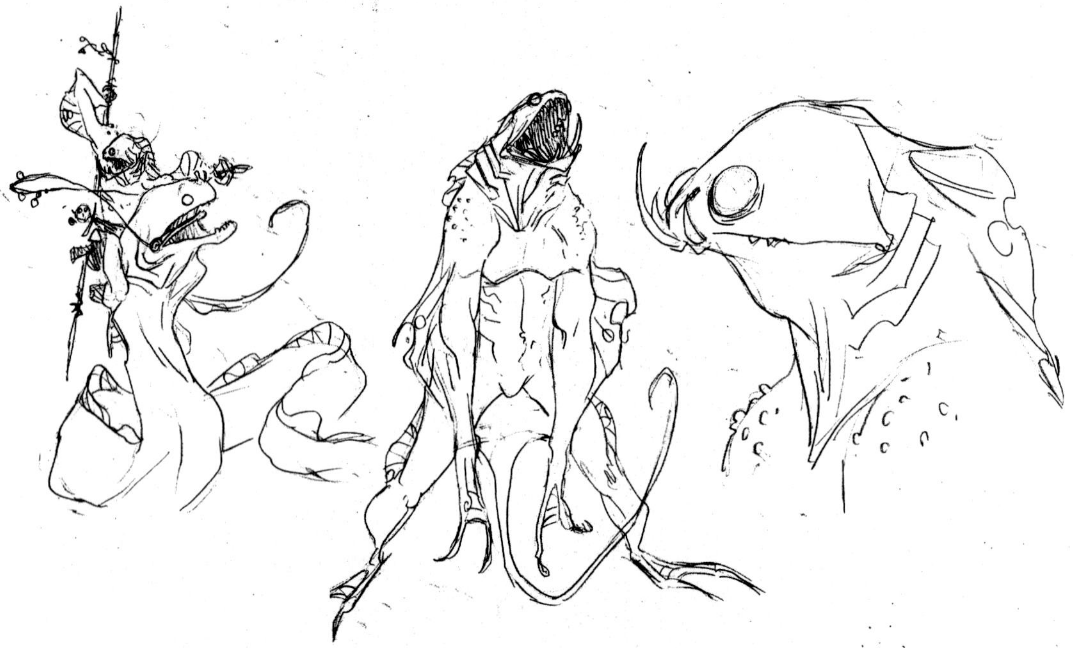

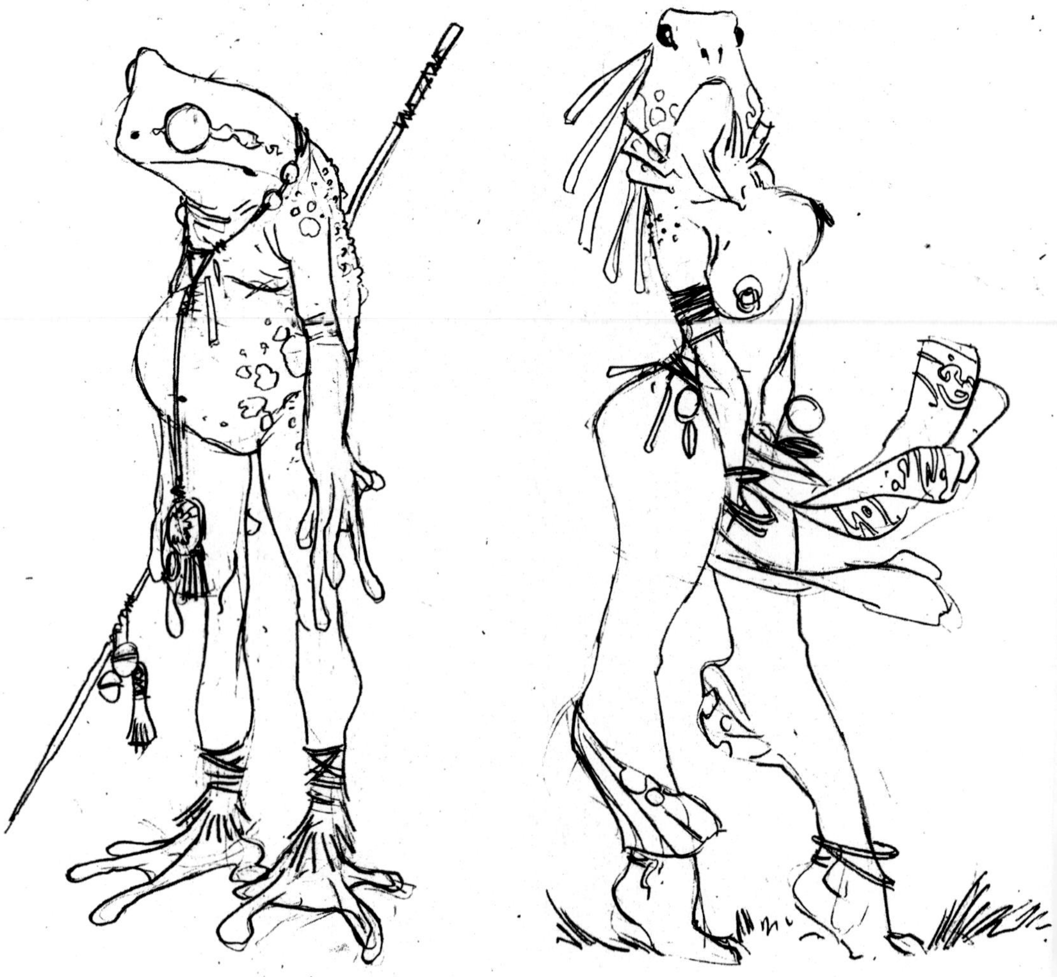

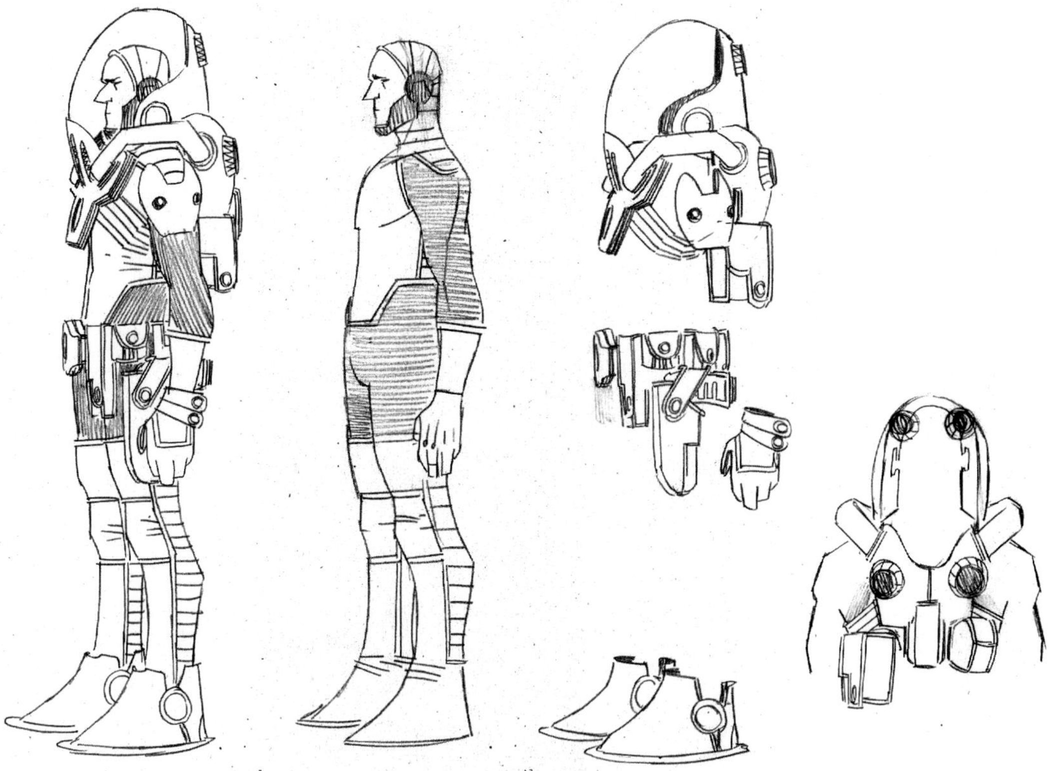

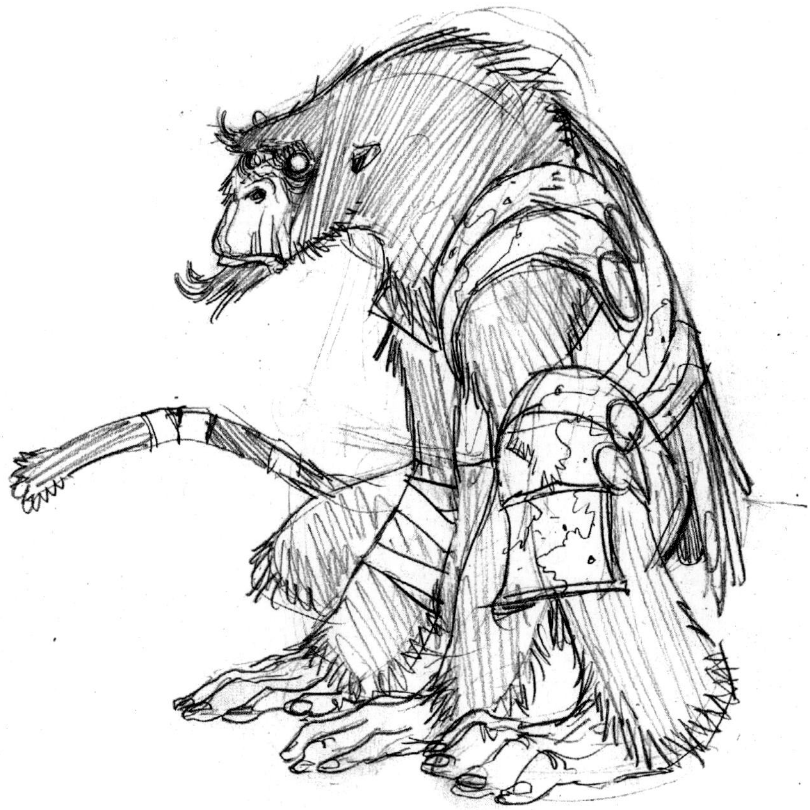

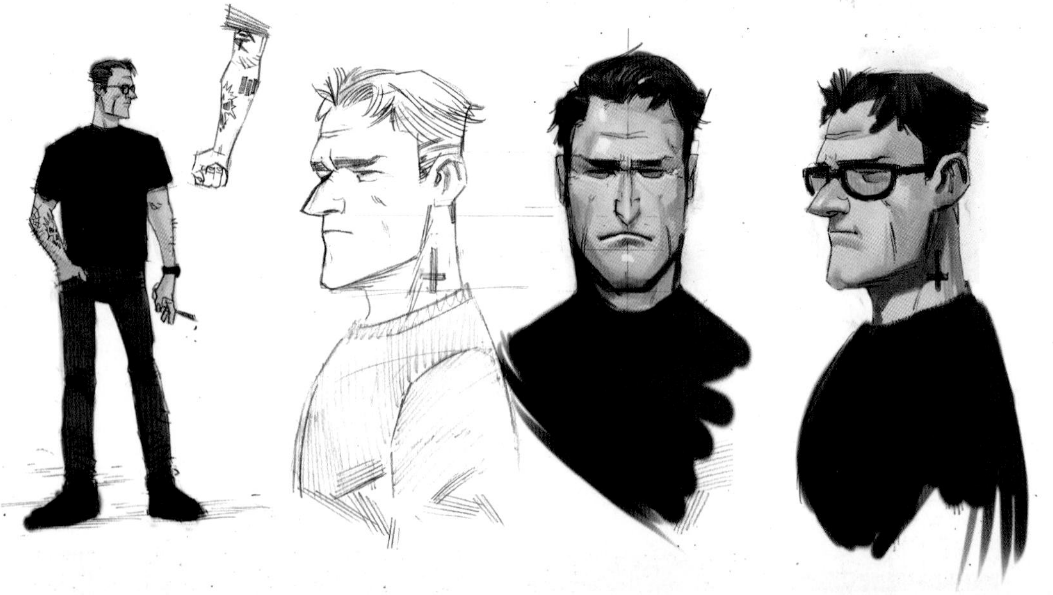

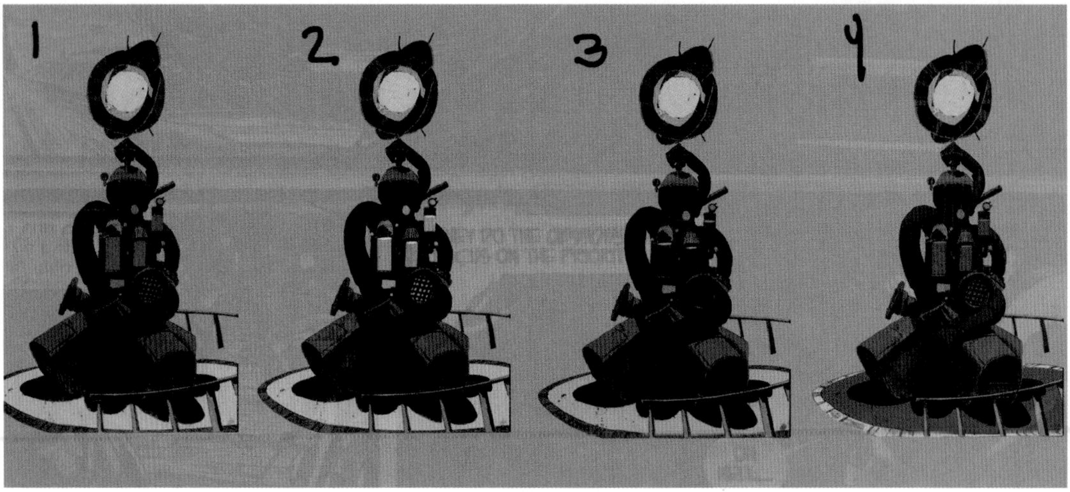
1
2
3
4

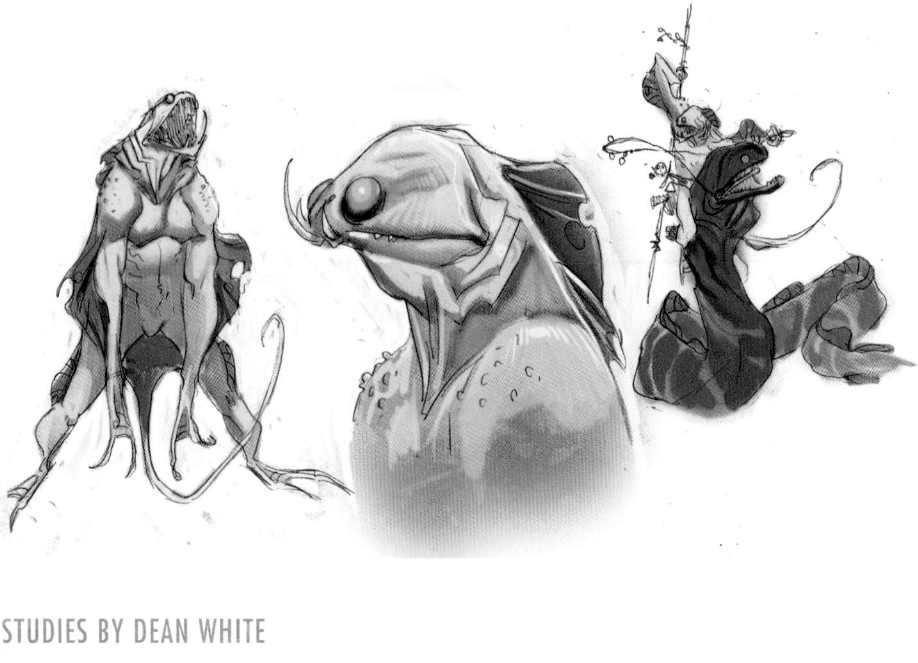

COLOR STUDIES BY DEAN WHITE